WARFARE IN HISTORY

The Norman Campaigns in the Balkans, 1081–1108

T0385521

WARFARE IN HISTORY

ISSN 1358–779X

Series editors
Matthew Bennett, Royal Military Academy, Sandhurst, UK
Anne Curry, University of Southampton, UK
Stephen Morillo, Wabash College, Crawfordsville, USA

This series aims to provide a wide-ranging and scholarly approach to military history, offering both individual studies of topics or wars, and volumes giving a selection of contemporary and later accounts of particular battles; its scope ranges from the early medieval to the early modern period.

New proposals for the series are welcomed; they should be sent to the publisher at the address below.

Boydell and Brewer Limited, PO Box 9, Woodbridge, Suffolk, IP12 3DF

Previously published titles in this series are listed at the back of this volume

The Norman Campaigns
in the Balkans, 1081–1108

Georgios Theotokis

THE BOYDELL PRESS

© Georgios Theotokis 2014

All Rights Reserved. Except as permitted under current legislation
no part of this work may be photocopied, stored in a retrieval system,
published, performed in public, adapted, broadcast,
transmitted, recorded or reproduced in any form or by any means,
without the prior permission of the copyright owner

The right of Georgios Theotokis to be identified as
the author of this work has been asserted in accordance with
sections 77 and 78 of the Copyright, Designs and Patents Act 1988

First published 2014
The Boydell Press, Woodbridge
Paperback edition 2016

ISBN 978 1 84383 921 7 hardback
ISBN 978 1 78327 139 9 paperback

The Boydell Press is an imprint of Boydell & Brewer Ltd
PO Box 9, Woodbridge, Suffolk IP12 3DF, UK
and of Boydell & Brewer Inc.
668 Mt Hope Avenue, Rochester, NY 14620–2731, USA
website: www.boydellandbrewer.com

A CIP catalogue record for this book is available
from the British Library

The publisher has no responsibility for the continued existence or accuracy of
URLs for external or third-party internet websites referred to in this book,
and does not guarantee that any content on such websites is,
or will remain, accurate or appropriate

This publication is printed on acid-free paper

Typeset by Word and Page, Chester

Contents

Acknowledgements

This book is the outcome of laborious research and study that have dominated the best part of the last five years. These years have been, without any doubt, the most tiring and stressful of my life, and I recall the words of my mentor, who said to me once, full of kind honesty, that 'academic research is not good for the soul'. But while writing these lines and looking back to what I have achieved thus far, I can only say that all of this was worth it! Being a part of the British – or shall I say, Scottish – educational system has taught me a great deal, both as a researcher and a person.

I owe my mentors, Matthew Strickland and Marilyn Dunn, a great debt of gratitude for their helpful guidance, their smiles and encouragement. I sincerely hope I will not let them down! I would like to thank the academic and administrative staff of the Department of History of the University of Glasgow and the Scottish Centre for War Studies, the staff of the Glasgow University Library and the Medieval Institute of the University of Notre Dame, for providing me with an ideal working environment. Special thanks are owed to Matthew Bennett and Caroline Palmer for encouraging this young researcher to publish his work. Also, I am grateful to Ioannis and Serdar for the very relaxing "wine-nights", which I hope I did not ruin with my complaints about work.

Finally, this work is dedicated wholeheartedly to my parents for their endless encouragement and support throughout my career.

Abbreviations

Alexiad	*Annae Comnenae Alexiadis libri XV*, ed. L. Schopenus, CSHB, 2 vols. (Bonn, 1839–78).
Amatus	*L'Ystoire de li Normant et la Chronique de Robert Viscart par Aimé, moine du Mont-Cassin*, ed. M. Champollion-Figeac (Paris, 1835).
Anonymus Barensis, *Chronicon*	
	Anonymus Barensis, *Chronicon*, RIS, vol. 151.
Attaleiates	Michaelis Attaliotae, *Historia*, ed. I. Bekker, E. Weber, CSHB 47 (Bonn, 1853).
Bryennius	Bryennius, Nicephorus, *Commentarii*, CSHB, vol. 25, ed. A. Meineke and E. Weber (Bonn, 1835).
Cecaumenus	Cecaumenos, *Strategikon*, ed. B. Wassiliewsky and V. Jernstedt (Amsterdam, 1965).
CSHB	Corpus Scriptorum Historiae Byzantinae (Bonn, 1828–97).
De Ceremoniis	Constantinus Porphyrogenitus, *De Ceremoniis Aulae Byzantinae*, ed. I. Reiski and E. Weber, CSHB 5 and 6 (Bonn, 1829–30).
Gesta	William of Apulia (Guillaume de Pouille), *La Geste de Robert Guiscard*, ed. and trans. M. Mathieu (Palermo, 1961).
Hill and Hill	Raymond d'Aguilers, *Historia Francorum qui ceperunt Iherusalem*, trans. J. H. and L. Hill (Philadelphia, 1968).
Leo VI, *Taktika*	*The Taktika of Leo VI*, trans. and commentary G. T. Dennis (Washington, DC, 2010).
Lupus Protospatharius, *Chronicon*	
	Lupus Protospatharius, *Chronicon Rerum in Regno Neapolitano Gestarum*, MGH, SS, LX.
Malaterra	Goffredus Malaterra, *De Rebus Gestis Rogerii Calabriae et Siciliae Comitis et Roberti Guiscardi Ducis Fratris Eius*, RIS, vol. 6.

MGH, SS	Monumenta Germaniae Historica inde ab anno Christi quingentesimo usque ad annum millesimum et quingentesimum. Scriptores, ed. G. H. Pertz (Hannover, 1826-).
On Skirmishing	*The Anonymous Byzantine Treatise On Skirmishing by the Emperor Lord Nicephoros*, in *Three Byzantine Military Treatises*, trans. G. T. Dennis (Washington, DC, 2008).
On Strategy	*The Anonymous Byzantine Treatise On Strategy*, in *Three Byzantine Military Treatises*.
On Tactics	*The Anonymous Book on Tactics*, in *Three Byzantine Military Treatises*.
Orderic Vitalis	*The Ecclesiastical History of Orderic Vitalis*, ed. M. Chibnall, 6 vols. (Oxford, 1969–80).
Praecepta Militaria	*Presentation and Composition on Warfare of the Emperor Nicephoros*, in *Sowing the Dragon's Teeth: Byzantine Warfare in the Tenth Century*, ed. and trans. E. McGeer (Washington, DC, 1995).
Psellus	Michael Psellus, *Fourteen Byzantine Rulers*, trans. E. R. A. Sewter (London, 1966).
RIS	Rerum Italicarum scriptores: raccolta degli storici Italiani dal cinquecento al millecinquecento, ed. L. A. Muratori (Città di Castello, 1900–).
Romuald of Salerno, *Chronicon*	Romualdus Salernitatis, *Chronicon*, RIS, VII.
Sewter	Anna Comnena, *The Alexiad*, trans. E. R. A. Sewter (London, 2003).
Scylitzes	Ioannes Skylitzes and Georgius Cedrenus, *Synopsis Historiarum*, ed. I. Bekker, CSHB XXXIV and XXXV (Bonn, 1838–9).
Vegetius, *Epitome*	Vegetius, *Epitome of Military Science*, trans. N. P. Milner (Liverpool, 2001).
Zonaras, *Annales*	Ioannis Zonaras, *Annales*, ed. I. Bekker, CSHB (Bonn, 1841–97), XLI, XLII.1 and XLII.2.

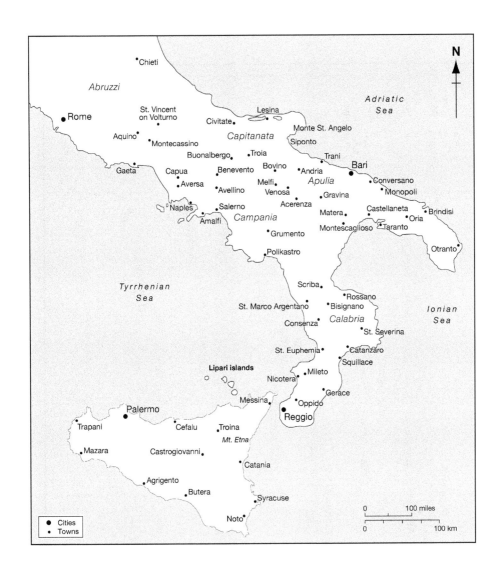

Map I. Southern Italy and Sicily

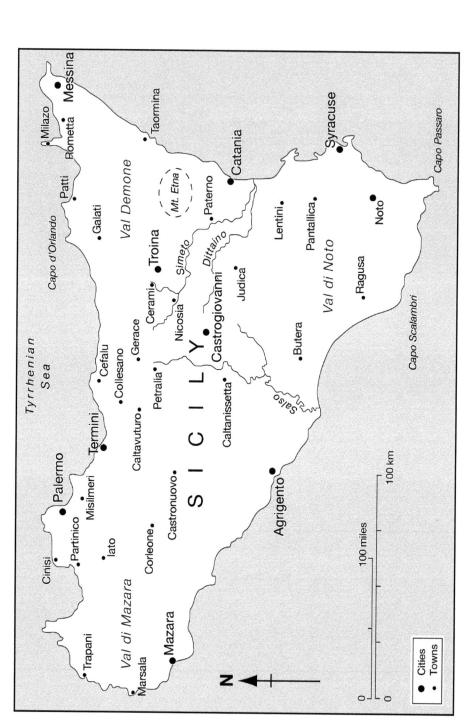

Map II. The island of Sicily

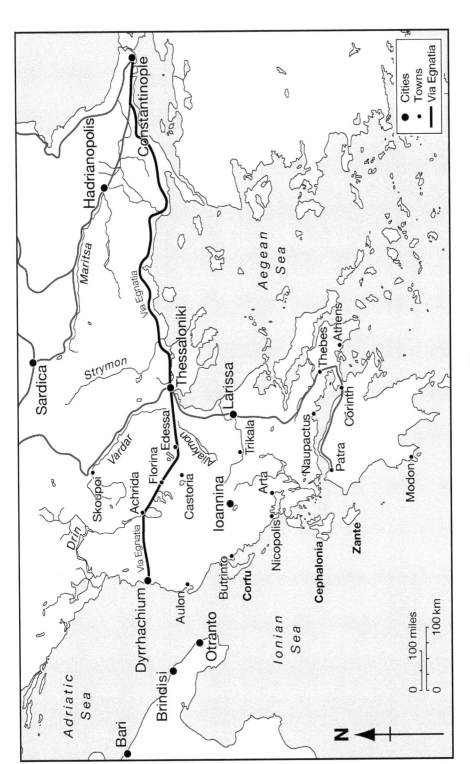

Map III. The southern Balkan peninsula

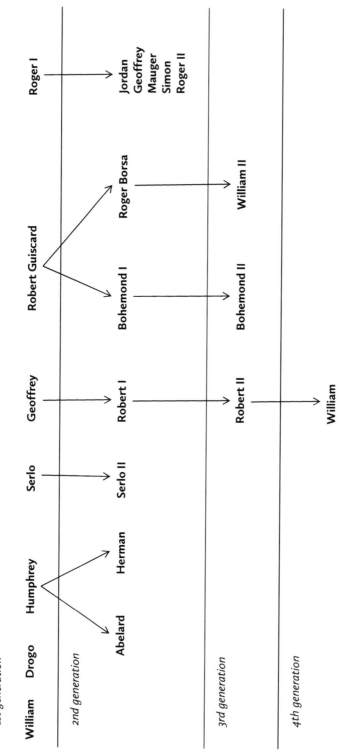

The Norman dukes

To my beloved parents

Introduction

Here lies the Guiscard, the terror of the world.
From the City, the king of the Italians and Germans he hurled.
Neither Parthians, Arabs, nor the army of Macedon could Alexius free,
Only flight: for Venice could prevail neither flight nor the sea.[1]

One of the most fascinating episodes of European history is the story of the small band of Norman pilgrims who, in the year 1000 (according to one account), took part in the siege of the Italian city of Salerno against the marauding Arabs of the Tyrrhenian Sea, who were demanding an annual payment from the inhabitants of the city. Ironically, they liked what they found there and they decided to tell their comrades back home about the land of Apulia; a 'land flowing with milk and honey and so many good things'.[2] They returned in the following decades to find employment in the armies of all political entities in the region, along with ample opportunities to quench their thirst for money, land and – according to the so-called Norman myth propagated by contemporary Norman chroniclers – fame, as warriors of great martial valour in the fields of battle. Setting aside the romanticised story of 'soldiers of fortune', what could be said of the actual geo-political significance of their establishment in the Mediterranean?

The Norman expansion in eleventh-century Europe was a movement of enormous historical importance, which saw men and women from the duchy of Normandy settling in England, Apulia, Calabria, Sicily and the principality of Antioch. The Norman establishment in the south is particularly interesting, because it represents the story of a few hundred mercenaries who managed to subdue local Lombard princes, drive out Byzantine and Muslim rulers who had ruled the areas for centuries, establish a principality in the Middle East during the turbulent period of the crusades and begin the process of unifying a political entity that would later develop into the kingdom of Sicily. Indeed, it was the Norman conquest that transformed a peripheral region of the Mediterranean and a frontier area between the Byzantine East, the Muslim South and the Latin West into a dominant political structure that encompassed the entire

---

[1] The epitaph on Robert Guiscard's tomb at the abbey of Venosa, recorded by William of Malmesbury, *Gesta Regum Anglorum*, ed. and trans. R. A. B. Mynors (Oxford, 1998), I, pp. 484–5.
[2] Amatus, I.16.

southern Italian peninsula and the island of Sicily, and which was to endure for some seven centuries, until 1816.

By the middle of the thirteenth century the region had witnessed an ethnographical, cultural and religious transformation prompted by the immigration of Latin Christians into Calabria, Apulia and Sicily, which fundamentally changed southern Italy and Sicily into a Latin kingdom. It would be no exaggeration to claim that none of this would have taken place without the Norman conquest. Yet this process of transformation was slower than modern scholars have perhaps recognised. In fact, in the first decades of the eleventh century one cannot speak of a Norman conquest of Italian territories per se, but rather a gradual, unstable and uncertain process of infiltration by mercenaries, who acted as auxiliary units to the armies of Lombard rebels, Muslim emirs, Byzantine catepans and German emperors.

There are three key dates for the Norman expansion in the south. In the year 1041, twelve Norman captains, so called by William of Apulia, and their followers established themselves in one of the most strategic towns in mainland Apulia, an event with major long-term consequences for the status quo in the region. This strategic move was preceded by the investment of a certain Rainulf, a man who would become the greatest of all the lords of Campania and a member of the local Lombard aristocracy, as an imperial vassal in the fortified town of Aversa by the German emperor Conrad II in May 1038. Throughout this period, from their establishment at Melfi (1041/2) to the battle at Civitate (1053), the Norman counts of Melfi systematically conquered large areas of Apulia from the Byzantines. Although the latter regained control of key coastal cities like Bari and Otranto and tried to win over the local Lombard communities by giving out tax exemptions, by 1047 almost all of northern and western Apulia belonged to the Normans.

The greatest opportunity for the Byzantines and the papacy to stop this systematic erosion of their territories presented itself in 1053 with one of the most crucial confrontations in medieval Italian history. Leo IX's coalition army was defeated at Civitate. Apart from the obvious political consequences this had on all the political powers of southern Italy, it also opened the way to the Normans for further conquests in all directions. Calabria and large parts of mainland Apulia had been conquered by the end of the decade, and in 1061 Robert Guiscard and his brother invaded Sicily in a major amphibious operation with unparalleled consequences for the future military operations of the Normans in Sicily and the Adriatic. Nevertheless, what sealed the fate of the Normans in Italy and proved to the world that these people from the north of the Alps had come to stay was the conquest in 1071 of the city of Bari, the capital of Byzantine Lombardy and the last bastion of Byzantine authority in the region.

In 1081, Robert Guiscard was free to launch his most ambitious military operation to date, the invasion of Illyria, and challenge the authority of God's representative on Earth, the Byzantine emperor. Four years later, on the sandy and beautiful beaches of the Ionian island of Cephalonia, named after him as Fiskardo, the duke was struck by a violent fever – probably malaria – and died on 17 July, putting an end to one of the most pressing periods of external aggression the Byzantine Empire had faced for centuries. By 1085, Robert Guiscard was one of the most powerful and famous warlords in Christendom, controlling a pope, and having humiliated one emperor and defeated – and nearly killed – another in battle. Popes and emperors alike courted his support and alliance, while his armies could threaten the heirs to Charlemagne and Constantine.³ It was not for another twenty years that the duke's ambitious son Bohemond would launch another expedition in the Balkans, this time masking his campaign as a crusade, which would see the same protagonists confronting each other again in the same place but with an entirely different outcome.

The first contacts between Normans and Byzantines can be traced to the second decade of the eleventh century and the battle at Cannae (1018). The Normans participated in this battle as an elite cavalry unit in a rebel Lombard army that faced the locally raised militia units of the Byzantine *strategos* (general). In the period before the battle of Civitate, the Normans were mere auxiliary units (bands of elite mercenaries hired by the highest bidder), numbering just a few hundred. According to the sources of the period, which point out the presence of elite imperial units from the mainland (such as the Varangian Guard), the Normans faced the Byzantine army three times in 1041, when the rebel Lombard-Norman army repeatedly routed the catepan's armies in northern Apulia. It was a band of these units – a few-hundred-strong according to the sources – that had taken part in Byzantium's expedition to Sicily in order to expel the Kalbite Muslims in 1038, an undertaking which dragged on for three years until the general in command, the notorious George Maniaces, rebelled and pronounced himself emperor before embarking on his invasion of the Balkans.

Contacts between the Normans and the Byzantines in the middle of the century were not confined to Italy. The 1040s were the decade that saw the arrival in large numbers of the first Frankish mercenaries in the Byzantine capital, in 1047. These were all primarily cavalry units, fighting in their usual Frankish manner of mounting a frontal cavalry charge against the enemy, a battle tactic that had been well known in France for several decades as well as in Byzantium, according to the writings of Leo VI in his *Taktika*. Their main operational role, judging by the evidence provided by the chroniclers, was the manning of key towns and fortresses in strategic border areas in both the Balkans and Asia Minor. Famous officers included Hervé, Robert Crispin and Roussel of Bailleul, all of them being active mostly in north-eastern Asia Minor between the 1050s and the 1080s, campaigning either with or without units of the imperial army. In addition, the German regiment of the Nemitzi was present at Manzikert (Malazgirt) (1071), while Anglo-Saxon mercenaries gradually replaced the Scandinavian element in the Varangian Guard in the 1080s to 1090s.

The Byzantine army was an institution that constantly evolved throughout its history and was a worthy successor to the vast mechanism set up by the Romans. What

³ G. A. Loud, *The Age of Robert Guiscard: Southern Italy and the Norman Conquest* (London, 2000), p. 4.

is indeed truly remarkable, however, is the degree of adaptability that characterised the army as an institution, along with the open-minded attitude of its officers and the tactics they applied in the battlefield. Certain military manuals like Maurice's *Strategikon*, Leo VI's *Taktika*, the *Praecepta Militaria* of Nicephorus Phocas, the *Taktika* of Nicephorus Uranus and the *Strategikon* of Cecaumenus offer us a thorough insight into the way the Byzantine officers thought and how they faced their enemies in each operational theatre. From the eighth century they had set up two distinct but mutually supportive mechanisms, the thematic armies which were clearly defensive in their role and whose main objective was to intercept and harass any invading army, and the *tagmata*, which were clearly professional units trained to deliver the final blow to the enemy in pitched battle. Fundamental changes in the structure and organisation of the Byzantine army, however, took place in the decades preceding the disaster at Manzikert in 1071. The old thematic and tagmatic units, composed of indigenous troops that had formed the backbone of the army's structure for centuries, were largely replaced by mercenaries, large bodies of paid troops of any ethnic background employed for long-term military service, like the Varangian Guard (largely consisting of Anglo-Saxons after 1081), the German Nemitzi and several Frankish regiments.

These fundamental changes in the structure and organisation of the Byzantine army, which had already taken shape by the year Alexius Comnenus rose to the throne, along with the economic and political collapse after decades of civil conflicts and barbarian invasions both in the Balkans (Pechenegs) and in Asia Minor (Seljuk Turks), had completely paralysed the imperial army. Such was the state of disarray that one finds the following comment by the princess Anna Comnena on the army her father was gathering against the Seljuk and Norman threats in the spring of 1081: 'Turkish infiltration had scattered the eastern armies in all directions and the Turks were in almost complete control of all the districts between the Black Sea and the Hellespont, the Syrian and Aegean waters'.[4] The basic argument, however, is that the army that Alexius deployed against the Normans in 1108 was different in both structure and composition from that which Romanus IV Diogenes had gathered for his Turkish campaigns that culminated in Manzikert or from the rabble that was beaten at Dyrrhachium (modern Durrës) ten years later.

This book aims to bring to the forefront a rather neglected aspect of the military history of this period in the Mediterranean: the comparative study of two different military cultures and the way in which each reacted and adapted to the strategy and battle tactics of the other in the operational theatre of the Balkans between the years 1081 and 1108. Hence the topic encompasses the military organisation, the general concepts of war, the strategy and tactics and the way each of these cultures viewed its enemies as warriors, as well as how each perceived itself. The most crucial point is to establish how far this prolonged confrontation in the battlefields of Dyrrhachium, Ioannina and Thessaly led to changes or adaptations in their practice of warfare. Can

---

[4] *Alexiad*, I.4 (p. 25); Sewter, p. 38.

it be said that certain cultures undertook more tactical changes than others, and if so, what are the deeper reasons behind this phenomenon? How can we explain, for example, Alexius Comnenus' decision to fight a pitched battle in 1081, while choosing to impose a blockade on the Norman army twenty-six years later? Why did Bohemond not see through his enemy's tactics, letting his army fall into a trap?

The study of the Norman expansion in Italy and the Balkans also facilitates an in-depth examination of Norman strategy in each operational theatre of war (namely Italy, Sicily and Illyria) and question whether it can be characterised as Vegetian.[5] In relation to this issue, separate questions arise about the importance of military handbooks, such as Leo VI's *Taktika* and Nicephorus Phocas' *Praecepta Militaria*, for the Byzantine military establishment of the eleventh century and whether any of them were available to Byzantine commanders of this period, such as Alexius Comnenus. What sort of information about their enemies did these manuals provide to the Byzantine officers? What do they reveal about the place of literacy in the Byzantine command structure, the training of the officer class and professionalism? Do the manuals eventually become archaic, valued more as literary pieces rather than actual handbooks?

[5] J. Gillingham, 'Richard I and the Science of War in the Middle Ages', in *War and Government in the Middle Ages*, ed. J. Gillingham and J. C. Holt (Woodbridge, 1984), pp. 78–91; J. Gillingham, '"Up with Orthodoxy!" In Defence of Vegetian Warfare', *Journal of Medieval Military History* 2 (2004), 149–58; S. Morillo, 'Battle Seeking: The Context and Limits of Vegetian Strategy', *Journal of Medieval Military History* 1 (2003), 21–41; C. J. Rogers, 'The Vegetian "Science of Warfare" in the Middle Ages', *Journal of Medieval Military History* 1 (2003), 1–19.

Primary Sources and the Problems of Military History

The Norman campaigns in the Balkans were, from their inception, seen from many different points of view, and every account and reference in the sources must be interpreted in the light of where, when, by whom and in whose interests it was written. It is only natural to assume that Anna Comnena, being the daughter of the emperor and presenting his point of view, would have had a different perspective on the events that unfolded in Dyrrhachium from Geoffrey Malaterra, a monk who wrote his history at the request of Roger Hauteville, and in order to please him and his audience. This explains my focus on the chroniclers' social, religious and educational background, the date and place of the compilation of their work, their own sources and the way they collected their information from them, their biases and sympathies and thus their impartiality as historians.

Amatus of Monte Cassino

The *History of the Normans* was compiled by Amatus of Monte Cassino around the year 1080. It is the earliest chronicle we have for the Norman establishment in southern Italy and Sicily from its earliest stages in the 1010s to the death of Richard I of Capua on 5 April 1078.[1] The author provides little information about himself in his work; almost everything we know about Amatus comes from the continuator

---

[1] The classic edition of the work is *L'Ystoire de li Normant et la Chronique de Robert Viscart par Aimé, moine du Mont-Cassin*, ed. M. Champollion-Figeac (Paris, 1835). A modern translation of the work is Amatus of Monte Cassino, *The History of the Normans*, trans. P. Dunbar and revised with notes by G. Loud (Woodbridge, 2004). The main secondary works for Amatus' life and work are K. B. Wolf, *Making History: The Normans and their Historians in Eleventh-Century Italy* (Philadelphia, 1995), pp. 87–122; E. Albu, *The Normans in their Histories: Propaganda, Myth and Subversion* (Woodbridge, 2001), pp. 106–44; F. Chalandon, *Histoire de la domination normande en Italie et en Sicile*, 2 vols. (Paris, 1907), pp. xxxi–xxxiv.

of the *Chronica Monasterii Casinensis* up to 1139, Peter the Deacon, and a work he authored himself, *The Deeds of the Apostles Peter and Paul*, dedicated to Gregory VII and probably written just before the composition of the *History*, around 1078/9. He may have come originally from the area of Salerno, joining the monastery of Monte Cassino as an adult during the rule of Abbot Desiderius (1058–86) and witnessing first-hand the intellectual revival of the period.[2]

The original Latin text has been lost; Amatus' *History* survives only in a fourteenth-century French translation, where the translator has either omitted, summarised or paraphrased parts of the original text, or added comments of his own.[3] Amatus was contemporary with the events described in this book, and his monastery of Monte Cassino was close to the Norman principality of Aversa. He was, therefore, an eyewitness of the events he describes or, at least, he had access to people who were present at the events, while he must also have had access to Monte Cassino's archival material. From the dedication of his work to Abbot Desiderius we understand that Richard I of Capua (d. 1078) and Robert Guiscard (d. 1085) are the protagonists of Amatus' work.[4] In his *History* the Normans had launched a Holy War against the Muslims that were holding Christian lands (Sicily), while in the war against the Byzantines he viewed them as 'liberators who called on the assistance of God' against these 'effeminate' oppressors.[5] It is made clear through Amatus' writings that the Normans had received divine favour only because they trusted to their future in his hands.[6]

The *History of the Normans* is divided into eight books, beginning with a brief introduction on the Normans' identity and how and why they came to Apulia, and ending with Robert Guiscard's siege and capture of Salerno (1076/7) and the death of Richard I of Capua in 1078. Each book covers a period of seven to eight years but the dating in Amatus' work is problematic. He rarely provides us with any dates in his account and in the few cases where he does so, he simply mentions the day of the month and not the year. This problem becomes more acute as the author does not follow a strict chronological order in his narrative, but rather finishes an individual story by reaching its conclusion and then carries on with events that preceded it chronologically. One characteristic example is when Amatus narrates the victory of the Normans at Castrogiovanni in 1061 and immediately goes on to discuss the siege and capture of Bari, while between Bari and the capture of Palermo he interjects the first half of book VI.[7] This thematic approach makes Amatus' work difficult to use as a source by itself, and it needs to be examined in combination with two works of his contemporaries, William of Apulia and Malaterra.

---

[2]   Amatus, *The History of the Normans*, pp. 11–12; Wolf, *Making History*, p. 88.

[3]   Amatus, *The History of the Normans*, pp. 18–23; Albu, *The Normans in their Histories*, pp. 109–10.

[4]   'Dedication to the most Holy and Reverend Master Desiderius, Servant of His Servants': Amatus, *The History of the Normans*, pp. 41–2.

[5]   Amatus, I.21.

[6]   Amatus, *The History of the Normans*, pp. 24–5.

[7]   Amatus, V.24–8, VI.14; *The History of the Normans*, pp. 36–7.

William of Apulia

William of Apulia was the first of the Italo-Norman chroniclers who commemorated Robert Guiscard's campaigns in Illyria. His *Gesta Roberti Wiscardi* is the only work of the period that focuses on the achievements of the duke of Apulia.[8] Judging by his name, *Guillermus*, historians assume that he would have had Norman ancestors, although that name was known in Italy even before the coming of the Normans.[9] From letters that he wrote to Pope Urban II, it also becomes clear that he was French, although not necessarily from Normandy.[10] His last name, *Apuliensis*, suggests he was a Norman who was born in Apulia, probably at Giovenazzo.[11] It is certain that William wrote his work between the years 1088 and 1111, judging from the people to whom this work is dedicated, namely Pope Urban II (1088 to June 1099) and Guiscard's son and heir Roger Borsa (1085–1111). Certain textual references, however, help historians narrow down this period to 1095 to August 1099.[12]

He seems to have been a member of Roger Borsa's court and probably a layman, a fact inferred by the rare appearances of religious motifs in his work and his passionate interest in the art of war.[13] He was very much aware of the importance of certain military factors in campaigns, such as the composition of forces, battle plans and siege equipment as, for example, in the battle of Civitate and the sieges of Bari and Dyrrhachium.[14] Apart from this sparse evidence about his life, William of Apulia's full identity remains elusive. If he was indeed a member of Roger Borsa's court, he would have had access, like Anna Comnena, to high-ranking officials of the dukedom. He must have been able to talk to the veterans of Robert Guiscard's campaigns (or even to Roger himself) who had participated, for example, in the second Illyrian invasion of 1084. Unlike Anna, however, he does not mention where he gets his information from.[15]

William uses the first two of the five books of the *Gesta* as an introduction, dealing with the establishment of the Normans in Italy from 1012 up to the capture of Bari in 1071. The third book covers the period from 1071 to 1080, while the last two books focus on Guiscard's invasion of Byzantium (1080–5). In his description of the clash between the Normans and the Byzantines in Apulia, it is most likely that William was indeed an eyewitness of the events, but he cannot have known much of what was

---

[8]   The main secondary works on William are Chalandon, *Domination normande*, pp. xxxviii–xl; Wolf, *Making History*, pp. 123–42; H. Taviani-Carozzi, *La terreur du monde, Robert Guiscard et la conquête normande en Italie* (Paris, 1996), pp. 20–3; Albu, *The Normans in their Histories*, pp. 106–44.

[9]   *Gesta*, introduction, p. 17.

[10]   *Gesta*, introduction, p. 17.

[11]   Chalandon, *Domination normande*, p. xxxix.

[12]   *Gesta*, introduction, p. 11; Wolf, *Making History*, pp. 123–4; Chalandon, *Domination normande*, p. xxxix.

[13]   Albu, *The Normans in their Histories*, pp. 136–7.

[14]   *Gesta*, II.122–256 (pp. 139–47); II.480–573 (pp. 159–63); IV.235–448 (pp. 217–29).

[15]   *Gesta*, introduction, p. 26.

taking place in Campania or Sicily, as he is very brief on anything that did not concern his homeland.[16] Apart from the events that he had witnessed, he certainly used the lost *Annales Barenses*, which Lupus Protospatharius had also used in his *Chronicon*, and although it was generally believed that he consulted Amatus' *History* as well, more recent studies have shown that both wrote their works independently, with the material from the *Annales Barenses* being the only link between them.[17] William based his narrative of the Illyrian invasions on oral testimonies from eyewitnesses, but these sources are not identified and we cannot be certain whether he got his information from knights, footsoldiers or just followers of the army in the baggage train. The sole exception is his mention of a Latin envoy called Jean who was sent by the bishop of Bari to travel with the Norman army, a source which had also been used by Anna.[18]

The two people to whom William dedicated his work in the prologue and epilogue of the *Gesta* are Roger Borsa, duke of Apulia and Calabria (1085–1111), and Pope Urban II (1088–99). It is possible that Roger Borsa commissioned the writing of the work to solidify his claims as heir to the duchy of Apulia against those of his older half-brother Bohemond. As to why he chose William is not known, but the fact the latter was a Norman who might also have had Lombard roots and who had grown up in an area that was under Byzantine rule may have given him greater advantage over other candidates. Roger Borsa's influence in the *Gesta* is great and is manifested mainly through two matters: first, where William is referring to the legitimate succession of the dukedom of Apulia by Roger after the death of Guiscard at Cephalonia in 1085, thus strengthening his claims over Bohemond's,[19] and second, where the author narrates Guiscard's campaigns against Alexius, in which we can clearly see an attempt to make this part of the *Gesta* more pleasant to the ears of Roger.[20]

Although William was commissioned by Roger Borsa and was writing under the protection of Urban II, Marguerite Mathieu argues that 'his impartiality, his neutrality is remarkable' and that 'the author is generally objective, although certain tendencies for concealing things do exist'.[21] By contrasting William's narratives of the Sicilian and Illyrian campaigns, however, we gain a sense of strong disapproval of Robert Guiscard's quest across the Adriatic. We have to bear in mind that William was writing his work in a period of religious enthusiasm resulting from the launch of the First Crusade and at a time when the Byzantines were still considered as allies and the natural leaders of the crusade – William would not have been aware of Alexius' return to Constantinople from Philomelium in the spring of 1098. Unlike Malaterra, who

[16]   Chalandon, *Domination normande*, p. xl.
[17]   *Gesta*, introduction, pp. 26–38; Chalandon, *Domination normande*, pp. xxxix; Albu, *The Normans in their Histories*, p. 110.
[18]   *Gesta*, introduction, pp. 38–9; Chalandon, *Domination normande*, p. xl; F. Chalandon, *Essai sur le règne d'Alexis Ier Comnène, 1081–1118* (Paris, 1900).
[19]   *Gesta*, V.345–8 (p. 255).
[20]   For example, Roger's key role at the naval battle with the Venetians: *Gesta*, V.155–98 (pp. 245–7).
[21]   *Gesta*, introduction, pp. 22 and 27.

wrote shortly after the crusade, or Amatus, William does not accuse the Byzantines of being effeminate warriors who did not deserve to hold Apulia for themselves. In fact, he even deflates Guiscard's pretext of invading Apulia to restore Michael VII Ducas to the imperial throne.[22] Finally, William narrates the public anger over the conscription of footsoldiers from all over Apulia and Calabria, identifying them as a group set against the war with the Byzantines, contrary to Malaterra, who reports that fear of the unknown alone was troubling the minds of Guiscard's knights.[23]

Geoffrey Malaterra

Geoffrey Malaterra, a monk who bore the cognomen Malaterra from his ancestors, was the third chronicler who commemorated the conquest of Italy and Sicily by the Normans in the late eleventh century, and indeed the only one whose main focus is Roger Hauteville.[24] Although we know very little of Malaterra's life, he himself noted he had come from a region 'beyond the mountains', meaning the Alps, and that he had recently become a Sicilian.[25] It is possible that he was born in Normandy, although recent studies have cast doubt on Pontieri's conviction that Malaterra was indeed a Norman simply because the chronicler refers to the Norman knights as *nostri*.[26] It is, however, almost certain that he came to Sicily at the request of Count Roger, who wished to re-establish the power of the Latin Church on the island after its conquest from the Muslims in 1091. As Malaterra himself states, it was at Roger's specific request that he began writing his *De Rebus Gestis Rogerii Calabriae et Siciliae Comitis et Roberti Guiscardi Ducis Fratris Eius*.

Malaterra's sources for his work, for he was not an eyewitness to the events he describes in his history, were primarily oral, gathered from people who had witnessed the events, and we cannot be sure whether he had access to any archival material.[27] Like William of Apulia, he does not identify any of his sources and we do not know whether they were knights, footsoldiers or other followers of the Norman army. There is a debate as to whether Malaterra used the *Anonymi Vaticani Historia Sicula* in his work, a history of the Norman conquests in southern Italy and Sicily up to

---

[22]   *Gesta*, IV.246–63 (pp. 216–18).

[23]   *Gesta*, IV.128–33 (p. 210); Malaterra, III.24.

[24]   The modern translation of the work is Geoffrey Malaterra, *The Deeds of Count Roger of Calabria and Sicily and of his Brother Duke Robert Guiscard*, ed. and trans. K. B. Wolf (Ann Arbor, 2005). The main secondary works on Malaterra are E. Pontieri, *I normanni nell'Italia meridionale* (Naples, 1964); Chalandon, *Domination normande*, pp. xxxvi–vii; Wolf, *Making History*, pp. 143–71; Taviani-Carozzi, *La terreur du monde*, pp. 17–20; Albu, *The Normans in their Histories*, pp. 106–44.

[25]   Malaterra, *The Deeds of Count Roger*, preface, p. 42.

[26]   Malaterra, *The Deeds of Count Roger*, p. iv, and cf Wolf's introduction, pp. 6–7, especially n. 6. Taviani-Carozzi argues that Malaterra was almost certainly born in Normandy: *La terreur du monde*, p. 18.

[27]   Malaterra, *The Deeds of Count Roger*, preface, p. 41.

1091, written during the reign of Roger II, or whether these two sources for Robert Guiscard and Roger's lives were written independently.[28] Malaterra, however, would have been aware of the works of William of Jumièges or William of Poitiers, but it is not likely that he knew of William of Apulia's work, since the latter was writing between 1095 and 1099, just a few years before Roger's death in 1101.

The person that dominates Malaterra's work is Count Roger of Calabria and Sicily. Malaterra regarded Roger as a generous patron, the commemoration of whose deeds he could not eschew.[29] It is likely that Roger, very much aware that his life was about to end, commissioned Malaterra to write the history of the Norman conquests in Calabria and Sicily. One of the reasons was that he wanted his accomplishments to be transmitted to posterity; thus, Malaterra's writing was in 'plain and simple words' an attempt to magnify and glorify the warlike ventures of Robert and Roger, presenting them as part of a divine plan.[30] Roger, however, certainly wished to strengthen the claims of his sons, Simon and Roger, against those of their cousin Roger Borsa, the son of Robert Guiscard, to the island of Sicily. But despite Malaterra's intention of immortalising the count, he seems to have written his work with an eye to entertain him and his companions.[31] Given that he was commissioned to write the work, Malaterra was certainly partial in his narrative and we can note that he did indeed conceal certain events, as will be examined later.

Leo Marsicanus, Romuald of Salerno and Lupus Protospatharius

Other primary sources for the eleventh-century Norman infiltration include Leo Marsicanus and the continuators of his *Chronica Monasterii Casinensis*.[32] This work encompasses the history of Monte Cassino from the sixth century up to 1072, with greater emphasis on the events of the eleventh century. It was authorised by Abbot Oderisius I (1088–1105), probably around 1098, and it must have been completed by the time Leo was elected cardinal of Ostia by Pascal II in 1101. Leo's continuator was a certain Peter the Deacon, who carried the narrative up to the year 1139.[33]

Romuald, archbishop of Salerno 1153–81 and a leading prelate of the Norman kingdom of Sicily with political ambitions, was an important primary source for the Norman-Italian history of the eleventh century. He wrote numerous works, primarily of ecclesiastical interest, but his most important piece was his *Chronicon* from the

---

[28]   Chalandon, *Domination normande*, p. xxxvii–iii.

[29]   Malaterra, *The Deeds of Count Roger*, preface, p. 42.

[30]   O. Capitani, 'Specific Motivations and Continuing Themes in the Norman Chronicles of Southern Italy in the Eleventh and Twelfth Centuries', in *The Normans in Sicily and Southern Italy*, Lincey Lectures 1974 (Oxford, 1977), p. 6.

[31]   Malaterra, *The Deeds of Count Roger*, introduction, p. 9.

[32]   *Chronica Monasterii Casinensis*, MGH, SS, vol. 34; Chalandon, *Domination normande*, pp. xxxiv–v; Loud, *Robert Guiscard*, p. 6; Taviani-Carozzi, *La terreur du monde*, p. 16.

[33]   Chalandon, *Domination normande*, pp. xxxv–vi.

creation of the world up to the year 1178.[34] This marked the first attempt in Italy since antiquity to write a universal history. Romuald's sources for the eleventh century were Leo's *Chronica*, the *Annales Casinenses* and a lost chronicle from Salerno that was also used by the author of the *Chronicon Amalfitanum*.[35] Since he was not a contemporary of the events he describes, however, he is a less reliable source. Lupus Protospatharius' *Chronicon*, dealing with the history of the Mezzogiorno between 805 and 1102, also calls for mention.[36]

Orderic Vitalis

Valuable information concerning Norman affairs in southern Italy and Sicily can be found in the work of Orderic Vitalis, arguably one of the greatest chroniclers of his time. Born near Shrewsbury in 1075, he was the son of a clerk, Ordelarius, who had accompanied Roger Montgomery, earl of Shrewsbury, from Normandy to England in the wake of the Conquest. At the age of ten he was sent to the abbey of St Evroul in Normandy, where he was to spend his life until his death in or after 1141. The main body of Orderic's *Ecclesiastical History* was written between 1123 and 1137; it consists of thirteen books. In book VII, which was written probably after 1130, Orderic examines the period from the dethronement of Nicephorus Botaneiates in 1081, to the death of William the Conqueror in 1087. Orderic had used many written sources for his recapitulation of the events of William the Conqueror's reign, such as William of Poitiers and William of Jumièges, but for most of the events in Normandy, England and southern Italy between 1083 and 1095 and between 1101 and 1113 he relied mostly on oral sources, such as visitors to St Evroul or those he had met on his travels.[37] His dependence on oral testimonies, however, may have caused some confusion in his recollection of dates and events. Some events are presented in vague chronological terms, while at times his dating is also wrong, often by many years.[38] Orderic's use of military terms, as with most twelfth-century chroniclers, is also imprecise. For example, his use of *acies* may mean a line or a column, while *pedites* applies to both footsoldiers and dismounted knights. In general, Orderic's battle narratives become distorted by anecdotes from eyewitnesses, which are thrown into the narrative of the events.[39]

---

[34]   Romuald of Salerno, *Chronicon*, VII; D. J. A. Matthew, 'The Chronicle of Romuald of Salerno', in *The Writing of History in the Middle Ages: Essays Presented to Richard William Southern*, ed. R. H. C. Davis and J. M. Wallace-Hadrill (Oxford, 1981), pp. 239–74.

[35]   *Annales Casinenses*, MGH, SS, XIX; 'Chronicon Amalfitanum', in *Amalfi im frühen Mittelalter*, ed. U. Schwarz (Tubingen, 1978), ch. 23–41, pp. 204–21.

[36]   Lupus Protospatharius, *Annales*, MGH, SS, LX; W. J. Churchil, 'The *Annales Barenses* and the *Annales Lupi Protospatharii*: Critical Edition and Commentary' (unpublished Ph.D. thesis, University of Toronto 1979).

[37]   Orderic Vitalis, vol. VI, pp. xix–xxii.

[38]   Orderic Vitalis, vol. IV, pp. xxiii–iv.

[39]   Orderic Vitalis, vol. VI, pp. xxi–v.

Orderic refers to the campaign against Byzantium in 1081 at the beginning of book VII. Before that, however, he briefly mentions the dethronement of Michael Ducas (1078) and Nicephorus Botaneiates (1081) and Pseudo-Michael's appeal to Guiscard. For the campaign itself, however, Orderic's narrative is very brief. For the four-month siege of Dyrrhachium, he does not give anything more than a few brief comments of no particular importance, while for Alexius' army we only get a vague comment on its size and composition.[40] Orderic mentions just the outcome of the battle of Dyrrhachium, while following Guiscard's absence to Italy, our chronicler vaguely refers to one of the battles at Ioannina (1082).[41] He does not mention – whether deliberately we do not know – the Norman defeat at Larisa (1083), which caused Bohemond's retreat to Dyrrhachium. For Bohemond's invasion of 1107 in book XI, he relates a list of the knights that joined Bohemond from England, France and elsewhere and their preparations before crossing the Adriatic.[42] For the actual siege of Dyrrhachium and the Treaty of Devol (1108), however, Orderic offers nothing but some very general information about the course of the siege operation.

Orderic Vitalis is the main primary source to provide detailed information about members of great Norman families travelling to southern Italy, thus helping historians to establish the links between Normandy and the Norman infiltration into the south. Book III, which along with book IV examines events in England, Normandy and parts of the history of St Evroul, presents the internal history of several major Norman families in the first half of the eleventh century. We read about William of Giroie, originally from Brittany, who was to become a scourge of his enemies in Gaul, England and Apulia, while his grandson William III Giroie was known in Apulia as 'the good Norman'.[43]

William of Montreuil, another son of William I Giroie, is identified in the service of Richard I of Capua while Robert II Grandmesnil, a grandson of William I, was exiled in Italy for three years in 1061, along with Ralph III Tosny, Hugh of Grandmesnil and Arnold Echauffour.[44] William Echauffour, another member of the Giroie family, went to Apulia after receiving a knighthood from Philip I of France, where he took a noble Lombard wife and won thirty castles in the name of Robert of Loritello, nephew of Robert Guiscard.[45] These are just a few examples of how helpful Orderic is in establishing the origin of a number of Italian immigrants, and with additional help from Ménager's studies on French charter material of this period, historians are able to piece together the puzzle of the Norman/French descent into Italy.

---

[40] Orderic Vitalis, book VII, p. 19. Henceforth, the Latin number will be referring to the book of the *Ecclesiastical History* and not the volume, unless stated otherwise.

[41] No place or chronology are noted but we presume that Orderic must refer to the battles of Ioannina in 1082: Orderic Vitalis, VII, pp. 28–9.

[42] Orderic Vitalis, XI, p. 71.

[43] Orderic Vitalis, III, pp. 22 and 26.

[44] Orderic Vitalis, III, pp. 90, 98 and 106.

[45] Orderic Vitalis, III, p. 126 .

Anna Comnena

Anna Comnena, one of the most important and influential historiographers of the Byzantine literature, was the first-born child of Emperor Alexius I Comnenus. She was born on 1 December 1083 and at the age of eight was betrothed to Constantine Ducas, the son of the deposed emperor Michael VII Ducas. Anna's hopes, however, of ascending to the imperial throne were dashed by Constantine's death (some time before 1097), and from then onwards we can clearly see the emerging hatred she had for her younger brother and heir to the throne, John. After an attempted rebellion with her mother Irene, which followed the death of her father Alexius in 1118, she was sent into a comfortable exile at the monastery of the Theotokos Kekharitomenes until 1143, the year her brother died.[46]

Anna may have started compiling her work after the death of her husband Nicephorus Bryennius in 1137, but it seems more likely that she waited for her brother to pass away. Thus, the work was completed within five years, since we understand that the fourteenth of her fifteen books was finished in 1148. She writes: 'For thirty years now, I swear it by the souls of the most blessed emperors, I have not seen, I have not spoken to a friend of my father'. Since Anna was sent on exile in 1118, clearly she means the year 1148.[47]

As the daughter of an emperor, she was in daily contact with many distinguished figures of the state. She also acquired an education, and indeed a catholic one, that very few women had in that period.[48] As she writes in the preface of the *Alexiad*, she had 'fortified her mind with the Quadrivium of Sciences', meaning geometry, arithmetic, astronomy and music, while rhetoric, philosophy and dialectics certainly featured in her curriculum. She had also studied classical Greek history[49] and she had some knowledge, however vague, of the geography of the Balkans and Asia Minor. Her interest in theology was general, but her religious beliefs were strictly orthodox and she despised, if not hated, all non-Christians.[50] After the death of Constantine Ducas, Anna was married to Nicephorus Bryennius, a man with great education and with a passion for knowledge. Nicephorus had already started writing a work about Alexius' life at the request of the empress Irene, but at his death in 1137 left it unfinished. His work turned out to be a useful history of the empire from the times of Isaac I Comnenus (1057–9) to the middle of Botaneiates' reign (1078–81), rather than a biography of Alexius, and Anna summarised it in the first two books of her *Alexiad*.[51]

---

[46]   J. Chrysostomides, 'A Byzantine Historian: Anna Comnena', in *Medieval Historical Writing in the Christian and Islamic Worlds*, ed. D. O. Morgan (London, 1982), p. 35.

[47]   *Alexiad*, XIV.7 (II, p. 291); Sewter, p. 461.

[48]   G. Buckler, *Anna Comnena: A Study* (Oxford, 1968), pp. 178–87.

[49]   She cites the story of the deception of the Spartans by Themistocles at Salamis (480 BC): *Alexiad*, VI.10 (pp. 310–11); Sewter, p. 204.

[50]   Buckler, *Anna Comnena*, pp. 307–53; Chalandon, *Alexis I*, p. xix.

[51]   Buckler, *Anna Comnena*, pp. 230–1.

As already mentioned, Anna's position in the imperial court brought her into close contact with many leading figures of the empire. Apart from her father the emperor, she also had access to several other important officials such as her uncle and governor of Dyrrhachium, George Palaeologus, her husband and trusted senior official Nicephorus Bryennius, her grandmother and regent Anna Dalassena, Empress Irene, Taticius, who was Alexius' representative to the Latin Armies of the First Crusade, several ferry-men of the Bosphorus who were carrying messages and news to and from the capital and a 'Latin envoy sent by the bishop of Bari to Robert Guiscard'.[52] As she notes in her fourteenth book, 'I have often heard the emperor and George Palaeologus discussing these matters in my presence'.[53] Further, she gathered useful information from eyewitnesses, as she herself describes: 'My material [. . .] has been gathered [. . .] from old soldiers who were serving in the army at the time of my father's accession, who fell on hard times and exchanged the turmoil of the outer world for the peaceful life of monks'.[54] Finally, she was an eyewitness herself in a number of events at which 'most of the time [. . .] we were ourselves present, for we accompanied our father and mother. Our lives by no means revolved round the home'.[55]

There is a debate as to whether Anna used her own memories for the events prior to 1097, the year in which she describes in full detail the camping of the crusaders in Constantinople, something that might explain the confusion in her tenth book.[56] For earlier events, we know that she took extracts verbatim from the *Chronographia* of Michael Psellus, and she could have read the works of Attaleiates, Scylitzes, Zonaras and Leo the Deacon.[57] It has also been argued by Mathieu that Anna used William of Apulia's *Gesta* as a source; as she did not read Latin she would most likely have used a translator. For three episodes regarding Guiscard's siege of Dyrrhachium, Anna used brief passages of the *Gesta* nearly verbatim, and though their similarities are limited and brief this strongly suggests that Anna had somehow obtained William's work.[58] This argument, however, has been strongly criticised by Loud, who believes that it would have been impossible for Anna to have had access to a rare manuscript such as the *Gesta*. Instead, this simply points to a well-informed common source, probably Nicephorus Bryennius, who played an instrumental role in drawing up the Treaty of Devol.[59]

Other sources for the *Alexiad* include four main categories of documents. First, the memoirs that were written by war veterans who had chosen to spend the rest of

---

[52] For this Latin envoy named Jean, see G. A. Loud, 'Anna Komnena and her Sources for the Normans of Southern Italy', in *Church and Chronicle in the Middle Ages: Essays Presented to John Taylor*, ed. I. Wood and G. A. Loud (London, 1991), p. 47.

[53] *Alexiad*, XIV.7 (II, p. 291); Sewter, p. 460.

[54] *Alexiad*, XIV.7 (II, pp. 292–3); Sewter, p. 461; see also XIV.7 (II, p. 290); Sewter, p. 459.

[55] *Alexiad*, XIV.7 (II, p. 290); Sewter, p. 459.

[56] Chalandon, *Alexis I*, p. xi.

[57] Buckler, *Anna Comnena*, p. 231.

[58] *Gesta*, introduction, pp. 38–46.

[59] Loud, 'Anna Komnena', pp. 50–2.

their lives in the cloister, and whose works were compiled probably at the request of the emperor himself.[60] Second, she would have had direct access to the state archives in Constantinople, judging by the quotations that can be found in her work of a chrysobull (an official order by the emperor which was written down on parchment and then folded and sealed by the official secretary who was responsible for the emperor's seal) appointing Anna Dalassena as regent,[61] a letter to Henry IV of Germany,[62] the correspondence between the emperor, John Comnenus, and the inhabitants of Dyrrhachium in 1091,[63] and many other letters. Third, Anna must also have used the diplomatic correspondence between her father, or other high-ranking officials, and foreign leaders, including the passage of the crusaders from Constantinople, and letters written to the Seljuk chieftains Tutush and Kilij Arslan.[64] Finally, she must have had access to the documents of important treaties, like the Treaty of Devol (1108), which is the longest diplomatic document cited by Anna, along with Alexius' chrysobull to the Venetians (1082).[65]

Sadly, there are gaps in many places in the *Alexiad* where Anna Comnena omits to mention certain dates, places or names. This is either because her memory simply failed her or perhaps because she did not want to go into further details for various reasons (e.g. personal sympathies). One such example can be found in book V, where Anna describes Bohemond's campaign in Thessaly (1082–3). When describing the Byzantine army's course towards Larissa to meet up with the Normans, Alexius 'made his way to another small place commonly called Plabitza, situated near the River'.[66] There are also some inconsistencies between different parts of Anna's work, which have led historians to conclude that she probably did not compile the books of the *Alexiad* in chronological order.[67] For example, the fortifications of the city of Dyrrhachium are first mentioned by Anna at the end of book III, but the most detailed description of them can be found in book XIII, when she narrates Bohemond's siege of 1107–8.[68]

Anna, of course, had her prejudices (racial, social and personal) but that does not mean that she was necessarily trying to deceive her audience. Throughout her history, her love, affection and admiration for her father and his achievements are unshaken. As the ancient Greek historiographers, and especially Thucydides, served as her models, her stated objective was undoubtedly to tell the truth. Anna displays her remarkable concern for impartiality in history when, writing about the oral testimonies she had gathered, she noted: 'Most of the evidence I collected myself, especially in the reign of

[60] *Alexiad*, XIV.7 (II, pp. 292–3); Sewter, p. 461.
[61] *Alexiad*, III.6 (pp. 157–8); Sewter, p. 116 .
[62] *Alexiad* III.10 (pp. 174–7); Sewter, p. 126.
[63] *Alexiad* VIII.7 (pp. 413–14); Sewter, p. 262.
[64] *Alexiad*, I.2 (pp. 16–17); Sewter, pp. 33–4; see also IX.3 (p. 434); Sewter, pp. 274–5.
[65] *Alexiad* XIII.7 (II, pp. 228–46); Sewter, p. 424.
[66] *Alexiad*, V.5 (p. 245); Sewter, pp. 167–8.
[67] Buckler, *Anna Comnena*, pp. 253–6.
[68] *Alexiad*, III.7 (p. 185); Sewter, p. 133; ibid. XIII.3 (II, p. 190); Sewter, p. 403.

the third emperor after Alexius [Manuel I, 1143–80], at a time when all flattery and lies had disappeared with his grandfather'.[69] As she remarked in the preface of the *Alexiad*:

> Whenever one assumes the role of a historian, friendship and enmities have to be forgotten. [...] The historian, therefore, must shirk neither remonstrance with his friends, or praise of his enemies. For my part I hope to satisfy both parties, both those who are offended by us and those who accept us, by appealing on the evidence of the actual events and of eyewitnesses.[70]

Attaleiates, Psellus, Scylitzes and Zonaras

Michael Attaleiates was a senator and a judge who held the high court title of *proedros* and supported the party of the provincial aristocracy. He was born between 1020 and 1030 and died some time after 1085.[71] His most significant and influential work was his *History*, which examines the period 1034–79/80 and is based primarily on first-hand observations and oral testimonies from protagonists of the events.[72] His work is not as personal as Psellus' *Chronographia* but it is, indeed, considered a rhetorical panegyric for the old emperor Nicephorus Botaneiates, which makes him less impartial for this period than a modern researcher would wish.

Another important primary source of the eleventh century, the *Chronographia* of Michael Psellus, examines the years between 976 and 1078 and is structured around the reigns of emperors.[73] Psellus was one of the greatest intellectual figures of the eleventh-century Byzantine court. A writer, poet, philosopher and statesman with a career in civil administration, he was born in the capital in 1018 and died some time after 1081. He was one of the senior officials in the government of Constantine IX (1042–55), and he resigned only to return to the capital after 1059 as the 'senior philosopher'. His work was compiled in two parts, with the second section that deals with the period 1059–78 being written at the request of Michael VII (1071–8), thus being a panegyric of these emperors. Although the *Chronographia* has some serious deficiencies, such as the lack of dates, names and place names, and a vague geography, it is generally agreed that the work holds a very high place in the catalogue of medieval histories, as it is compiled by an educated man who not only recorded history but also helped make it.

John Scylitzes' life is rather obscure but we know he lived in the second half of the eleventh century and held the titles of *kouropalates* and *drungarius* of the Watch.[74] His *Synopsis Historion* encompasses the period between 811 and 1057 and he is viewed

---

69   *Alexiad*, XIV.7 (II, pp. 291–2); Sewter, p. 460.
70   *Alexiad*, 'Praefatio' (pp. 3–4); Sewter, p. 18.
71   *The Oxford Dictionary of Byzantium*, ed. A. Kazhdan et al., 3 vols. (New York, 1991), I, p. 229.
72   Michaelis Attaliotae, *Historia*, ed. I. Bekker, E. Weber, CSHB (Bonn, 1853), XLVII. The most recent translation into English is: Michael Attaleiates, *History*, ed. and trans. D. Krallis and A. Kaldellis (Cambridge MA, 2012).
73   Michael Psellus, *Fourteen Byzantine Rulers*, trans. E. R. A. Sewter (London, 1966); *Oxford Dictionary of Byzantium*, III, pp. 1754–5.
74   *Oxford Dictionary of Byzantium*, III, p. 1914.

as the continuator of Theophanes the Confessor.[75] Scylitzes uses a variety of sources and sometimes presents contradictory conclusions, while various sections differ stylistically as well. The major hero of the last part of Scylitzes' work is Catacalon Cecaumenus, and he must have been close to that senior general as Cecaumenus wrote his *Strategikon* between the years 1075 and 1078. Scylitzes' material is organised according to imperial reigns and as the work relies on sources which, other than Psellus, have not survived, it is of the greatest value for the history of the eleventh century. His work was extended up to the year 1078 by an unknown writer who may have used the *History* of Attaleiates.

Another valuable work is John Zonaras' *Epitome Historion*, a chronicle stretching from the creation to Alexius Comnenus' death in 1118.[76] It was written by the private secretary, and later commander (*drungarius*) of the imperial bodyguard (*Vigla*) in Alexius' court, some time in the middle of the twelfth century. The compilation of his chronicle began after he became a monk at the monastery of St Glyceria on Mount Athos. Zonaras largely copies Scylitzes, Attaleiates and Psellus, and manipulates his material in a somewhat mechanical, often superficial, manner with occasional errors. He criticised Alexius Comnenus' governance and monetary policy, and his work acts as a polemic against Anna Comnena's eulogy of her father.

The strengths and weaknesses of the principal narrative sources

In his introductory chapter to the classic *Art of Warfare in Western Europe during the Middle Ages*, the eminent medieval military historian J. F. Verbruggen analyses both the limitations and general value of medieval sources such as clerical and secular accounts.[77] Since my research includes a court layman (William of Apulia), monks (Malaterra, Amatus and Orderic) and a well-educated princess (Anna Comnena), a brief overview of these limitations is essential.

In many cases the clerical sources provide a narrative of battles, sieges or entire campaigns which is incomplete 'in order not to bore the reader', simply because reporting these events in the way modern war correspondents would was not their objective. It is undoubtedly an over-simplification to say that all clerics were ignorant of military affairs; Orderic Vitalis, for example, is one of the foremost sources for Anglo-Norman military history and much of his information came from contact with people who had seen active service. Nevertheless, many ecclesiastical chroniclers show little interest in recording details such as tactics and weaponry, or reporting in detail what really took place on the battlefield. Their accounts of battle are influenced by

---

[75]   John Skylitzes, *A Synopsis of Byzantine History, 811–1057*, trans. J. Wortley with notes by B. Flusin and J.-C. Cheynet (Cambridge, 2010).

[76]   Zonaras, *Annales*; *Oxford Dictionary of Byzantium*, III, p. 2229.

[77]   J. F. Verbruggen, *The Art of Warfare in Western Europe during the Middle Ages, From the Eighth Century to 1340*, trans. S. Willard and R. W. Southern (Woodbridge, 1997), pp. 10–18.

invention or borrowed from classical models, particularly in their terminology, while they tend to ascribe victories to a miracle or God's intervention.

Secular sources are, generally, more reliable in their accounts, especially when the author was an eyewitness to the events they describe, even though they have the tendency to glorify their heroes or certain groups of people depending on their sympathies (for example, when they report an inflated number for the enemy troops in order to enhance the victory of their patron in the eyes of the readers).[78] Additionally, as these sources were written in the vernacular they are extremely valuable since they provide a clear and distinct terminology. The fact that some of these writers may not have been experienced in military affairs, however, also highlights the risk of mistaken or inaccurate reporting of events.

The more general question about the dangers of chronicle material being used by modern military historians also needs to be addressed. This topic was first raised by Verbruggen in the mid-1950s and has been picked up since by John Keegan and, among others, Kelly DeVries, Stephen Morillo and Richard Abels.[79] In his introductory chapter 'Weaknesses of Modern Military Historians in Discussing Medieval Warfare', Verbruggen criticised representatives of the so-called old school of military historians – H. Delpech and the Prussian general Kohler – in producing works that lacked the critical appraoch which is indispensable to a study of the art of medieval warfare. He contrasted their work with that of other historians such as Charles Oman and Hans Delbrück. His main argument was that it is essential to check the military value of each chronicler's account, because even the best narratives may include inventions and legends, which can be spotted solely through reading the source in comparison with a multiplicity of other sources. Furthermore, his critique illustrated how Delpech and Kohler, who were experienced army officers but not professional historians, accepted all estimates of the numbers of troops and battle tactics and took great swathes of data at face value, without filtering it first. Their lack of historical criticism led to their work being discredited by modern historians.

Let us therefore examine Anna Comnena, Geoffrey Malaterra and William of Apulia as military historians and assess the accuracy of their descriptions of battles

---

[78]   H. Delbrück, *Numbers in History* (London, 1913), pp. 11–23. Although I agree with Delbrück's view, his methods have come under criticism by B. S. Bachrach, 'Early Medieval Military Demography: Some Observations on the Methods of Hans Delbrück', in *The Circle of War in the Middle Ages*, ed. D. Kagay, L. J. Andrew Villalon (New York, 1999), pp. 3–20. See also: J. Flori, 'Un problème de méthodologie. La valeur des nombres chez les chroniquers du Moyen Âge. À propos des effectifs de la première croisade', *Le Moyen Âge* 119 (1993), 399–422. For the use of numbers by modern historians of the Byzantine army see W. Treadgold, 'On the Value of Inexact Numbers', *Byzantinoslavica* 50 (1989), 57–61; W. Treadgold, 'Standardized Numbers in the Byzantine Army', *War in History* 12 (2005), 1–14.

[79]   Verbruggen, *Art of Warfare*, pp. 10–18; J. Keegan, *The Face of Battle, A Study of Agincourt, Waterloo and the Somme* (London, 2004 [1976]), pp. 27–36; K. DeVries, 'The Use of Chroniclers in Recreating Medieval Military History', *Journal of Medieval Military History* 2 (2004), 1–17; R. Abels and S. Morillo, 'A Lying Legacy? A Preliminary Discussion of Images of Antiquity and Altered Reality in Medieval Military History', *Journal of Medieval Military History* 3 (2005), 1–13.

and sieges. Some of the most important questions to be raised are: to what extent are the figures they provide for army sizes reliable, both in absolute numbers and in the ratios given between cavalry and infantry? What is the chroniclers' knowledge of the local geography where the military operations took place, including the terrain of the battles or sieges, and the army campaign routes that they describe? How accurate or detailed are their descriptions of castles and fortifications? Another major point is the extent to which these chroniclers provide dating for the major military events, and how far their narratives permit the accurate reconstruction of chains of events. Amatus of Monte Cassino has been consciously omitted because, even though his account is most valuable for the earlier period of the Norman infiltration into Italy, the *History of the Normans* concludes in the year 1078 and hence does not deal with the main events of this study, which concentrates on the Norman invasions of Illyria.

The question of numbers can be a tough one indeed. Even in modern warfare, it can be difficult for a general to be fully aware of the discrepancy between nominal troop numbers and actual combat-effective men. Such difficulties would have been much more acute for a medieval commander. For contemporary chroniclers who reported the size of an army or opposing armies in a battlefield, we cannot reasonably expect the provision of accurate or detailed information for a number of reasons. Their estimates were affected by the inherent tendency of such narratives to exaggerate; by biases towards friends or foes; and, unless the chronicler had taken part in an expedition, their reliance on oral testimonies from eyewitnesses, a method which always carries the risk of miscalculation or inflation. Other reasons may include the timing of a chronicler's writing of their account, like Anna Comnena's compilation of the *Alexiad*, which took place many decades after the events. Finally, confusion and mistaken identity always play their part, for instance when a number of knights might have dismounted or lost their horses for various reasons (battle casualties, fatigue, disease) and were counted as infantry by chroniclers inexperienced in military affairs.[80] Here is what the author of the early-seventh-century *Strategikon* had to say on the reporting of enemy numbers by inexperienced observers:

> The arrangement of cavalry and infantry formations and the disposition of other units cause great differences in their apparent strength. An inexperienced person casually looking at them may be very far off in his estimates. Assume a cavalry formation of six hundred men across and five hundred deep [. . .] If they march in scattered groups, we must admit that they will occupy a much greater space and to the observer will appear more numerous than if they were in regular formation [. . .] Most people are incapable of forming a good estimate if an army numbers more than twenty or thirty thousand.[81]

---

[80]   For all of these difficulties in reporting the figures of armies in the Middle Ages see Verbruggen, *The Art of Warfare*, pp. 5–9; J. France, *Victory in the East, A Military History of the First Crusade* (Cambridge, 1999), pp. 122–42; J. Haldon, *Warfare, State and Society in the Byzantine World, 565–1204* (London, 1999), pp. 99–106.

[81]   *Maurice's Strategikon: Handbook of Byzantine Military Strategy*, trans. G. T. Dennis (Philadelphia, 2010 [1984]), IX, pp. 102–3.

For the Norman campaigns of 1081 and 1084, we are more dependent on Latin sources for the numbers of Robert Guiscard's forces, while unsurprisingly Anna Comnena appears far better informed about the composition and size of her father's armies. Thus, Anna reports that the Norman army in 1081 comprised 30,000 men carried across the Adriatic in 150 ships of various sizes with – a rare detail – 200 men in each ship.[82] This was, however, a clear exaggeration in an attempt to magnify her father's victory over the Normans. But the *Alexiad*'s details for the composition of the Byzantine armies that were assembled in 1081 and 1107 are extremely valuable since the author includes the names of all the senior Byzantine officers. She does not, however, provide an estimate of their numbers, with the exception of the 2,800 Manichaeans and the Turkish force sent by Suleiman I.[83] Further, she reports that 13,000 men – a rather implausible figure – were drowned in the Norman-Venetian naval battle in the waters off Corfu in the autumn of 1084.[84] For the Norman host, Anna uses only adjectives like 'countless', 'innumerable', although she does provide us with a figure for the losses that the Normans suffered in 1085 as a result of an outbreak of malaria by quoting the excessive figure of 10,000 fatalities, of which 500 were knights.[85] It would thus appear that the numbers given by Anna are mostly as unreliable as they are rare, chiefly because the author is writing many decades after the events.

It is not surprising that William of Apulia was much better informed about Robert Guiscard's expeditions than Malaterra. He is in fact our only source for the participation of the Dalmatians in the 1081 expedition.[86] He writes that Guiscard's main army was transported in 'fifty liburnas' (small galleys). The author, however, does not discuss the composition of either the fleet or the army, nor the casualties inflicted on the Norman fleet by a storm before its arrival at Dyrrhachium. William is obviously less well informed about the Byzantine army than Anna, writing about a 'grand army' with 'different nationalities' both 'Greek and Barbarian', while he is also unaware of the size of the Venetian fleet in 1081.[87]

For Guiscard's second Illyrian campaign, William noted that the size of the Norman fleet was 120 ships.[88] Further, when he referred to the casualties of the severe cold in the Norman camp in the winter of 1084–5, he assessed that these amounted to five hundred knights in less than three months; the same figure quoted by Anna Comnena.[89] William also noted that Roger Borsa, along with Robert II, took part in this campaign, while Anna Comnena writes that the only son of Robert Guiscard who

[82]   *Alexiad*, I.16 (pp. 74–5); Sewter, p. 69.
[83]   *Alexiad*, IV.4 (pp. 198–9); Sewter, p. 141; XIII.5–8 (II, pp. 199–217); Sewter, pp. 408–13; V.5 (p. 244); Sewter, p. 167.
[84]   *Alexiad*, VI.5 (p. 285); Sewter, p. 190.
[85]   *Alexiad*, IV.3 (p. 196); Sewter, pp. 139–40.
[86]   *Gesta*, IV.200 (p. 214); IV.134 (p. 210).
[87]   *Gesta*, IV.322–4 (p. 222).
[88]   *Gesta*, V.143 (p. 244).
[89]   *Gesta*, V.215–19 (p. 248).

did take part was Guy, not mentioned at all by William.[90]

The focus of Malaterra's work is Roger Hauteville's conquest of Sicily, with Apulia and Illyria being but a mere sideshow in his narrative. Hence, we only gain some rough estimates of the opposing armies from Malaterra's narrative, although some useful exceptions include the 1081 invasion army, which figured some 1,300 knights, a reasonable size for a cavalry force.[91] For the siege of Castoria by the Norman forces in the spring 1082, the chronicler mentions that the numbers of the defenders included a contingent of 300 Varangians.[92] Nonetheless, for the crucial events of this period (the sieges and battles of Dyrrhachium and Larissa), Malaterra is silent when it comes to numbers. For example, he writes about the Byzantine forces mustered in October 1081: 'The emperor alerted the entire empire [...] and mobilised a large army [...] and thousands of soldiers'.[93] The Byzantine army was, indeed, larger than the Norman but these comments were probably intended to make Robert Guiscard's victory sound even greater to the ears of his patron, Roger Hauteville.

Even though all of our main sources let us down when it comes to giving accurate figures about the opposing armies, fortunately for modern historians other Latin chroniclers writing on this period seem much better informed and perhaps more reliable. There is the example of Malaterra's 1,300 knights for the 1081 campaign, which can be compared to the 700 horse given by Romuald of Salerno, although we must remember that Romuald was writing much later, in the second half of the twelfth century.[94] For Bohemond's army in 1107–8, none of our main sources venture any estimate as to its numbers and historians have to rely solely on other contemporary sources like the Anonymous of Bari, Fulcher of Chartres, Albert of Aachen and, although not a contemporary, William of Tyre in order to assess the size of the count's force.[95]

Another crucial point is the chroniclers' geographical knowledge and their degree of familiarity with the areas central to the events they described. Is their presentation of the battlefields and campsites detailed and accurate enough to track the route of each army? As far as the Latin sources are concerned, it is evident that both William of Apulia and Geoffrey Malaterra are not familiar with the geography of Illyria and Epirus. They rely on information passed on by eyewitnesses when it comes to toponyms, rivers, plains and, most importantly, the surrounding areas of Dyrrhachium and Larissa.

Although William of Apulia in many cases does mention particular locations relevant to the events, there is no detailed description of the surrounding areas and in some cases we are unable to identify these places on a modern map or follow the exact route of an army. For Guiscard's crossing of the Adriatic, he does mention the port of

[90]   *Gesta*, V.144, 151 (p. 244); *Alexiad*, VI. v (p. 282); Sewter, pp. 188–9.
[91]   Malaterra, III.24.
[92]   Malaterra III.29.
[93]   Malaterra III.26 and 27.
[94]   Romuald of Salerno, *Chronicon*, s.a. 1081.
[95]   See pp. 205–6.

Otranto as the gathering point for the embarkation of his army, but William is silent as far as the disembarkation point on the Illyrian coast is concerned.[96] Before the siege of Dyrrhachium, William informs us of the preparatory conquests on the Illyrian and Epirotic coastline, referring to the city of Aulon (Vlorë) along with 'certain others by the coast',[97] while before that, Bohemond is mentioned as having taken Corfu, Buthrotum (Butrint) and Vonitsa.[98] Furthermore, there is no description of the city or of the surrounding areas of Dyrrhachium, and the precise location of Guiscard's camp is probably the one given by William in his fifth book, where he described the starvation of many Normans at their camp near the River Glycys.[99]

Turning to the Byzantines, from the information we get from the *Gesta* it is impossible to track down the route of Alexius' army from Constantinople to Dyrrhachium or to identify the place where he pitched his camp. For the period between 1082 and 1084, the only details we find in the *Gesta* are the names of the places where the three battles took place: the cities of Ioannina, Larissa and Castoria.[100] Regarding Guiscard's second invasion in 1084, the duke embarked his army at Taranto and sailed for Greece from the port of Brindisi,[101] while the two Norman armies joined 'at the junction which was held by the other sons of the illustrious duke',[102] referring to the port of Buthrotum.

The *De Rebus* provides historians with even fewer details than the *Gesta*, among which are the port of Oricum (Hierichum), where the Norman fleet reached the shore, although its precise location is unclear, and that they moved their ships to a place where the Aous (Vjosë) River flows to the sea.[103] No further information is provided about the area around the city of Dyrrhachium or about the nature of the battleground, even though we do know that Alexius set up his camp at a distance of four stadia[104] from the Normans. Malaterra is also vague regarding the preparatory conquests before the major siege operations. After the battle of Dyrrhachium, he writes that: 'Various fortresses in the same province were unable to withstand the threat that the duke posed',[105] but he fails to be more specific. We detect the same vagueness when he describes the Norman siege of Castoria.[106] Finally, when Malaterra's narrative proceeds to Bohemond's campaigns on the Greek mainland, his brief chapter only deals with the battle outside Arta.

[96]   *Gesta*, IV.133 (p. 210).
[97]   *Gesta*, IV.232–3 (p. 216).
[98]   *Gesta*, IV.201–7 (p. 214).
[99]   *Gesta*, V.210 (p. 246).
[100]   *Gesta*, V.6, 26 and 76 (pp. 236 and 240).
[101]   *Gesta*, V.132 (p. 242).
[102]   *Gesta*, V.150–1 (p. 244).
[103]   Malaterra, III.24.
[104]   Pliny the Elder (*Natural History* II.85) wrote: 'A stadium corresponds to 125 of our paces, that is 625 feet', the Roman foot being slightly shorter than a modern foot. Four stadia amount to around 740 metres.
[105]   Malaterra, III.27.
[106]   Malaterra, III.29.

Anna Comnena's knowledge of the topography of the Balkans is another weak point in her work. More specifically, she gives valuable information about the point of embarkation and disembarkation of Guiscard's army in 1081,[107] although for Bohemond's invasion in 1107 she erroneously reports Bari as the port of embarkation while, in fact, it was the southern port of Brindisi.[108] For the area of Dyrrhachium, however, Anna's description is vague and wholly insufficient. She does mention some of the rivers, such as the Glycys where the Normans pitched their camp, or Charzanes (Erzen) where the Byzantines later pitched theirs, and she even mentions the name of the church of St Nicholas where the Varangians sought shelter after their retreat from the battle.

In her thirteenth book Anna becomes more accurate concerning the land blockade of the Norman army in 1107/8 – perhaps because she wrote that part of her work first. She identifies certain mountain passes (Petra), rivers (Charzanes, Diavolis, Bouses) or insignificant places where the imperial army spent the night (Mylus).[109] But all of the above would probably have been random eyewitness information rather than personal knowledge of the area. The only detailed description of the Dyrrhachium area can be found in her twelfth book during Bohemond's siege of the city in 1107/8.[110] As for Alexius' course from Constantinople to Dyrrhachium in 1081, we know next to nothing of the exact route that he followed, apart from his stop at Thessaloniki at an unknown date. It is very likely that the emperor would have followed the same route again to face Bohemond in 1108, and hence Anna's list of the stops the emperor made during his march: Geranium, Chirovachi, Mestus, Psyllus (on the River Hebrus) and Thessaloniki where he spent the winter.[111]

For the period 1082–3, Anna once more avoids giving us any specific details of the emperor's route until he reached Ioannina. There is also no description of the area around the city, especially where the two battles were fought, and after the defeat of the Byzantines Anna presents an account of Bohemond marching and countermarching over the Balkans in the most bewildering fashion.[112] For the actual siege of the city of Larissa and the battle that was fought in its vicinity, there is only a description for the place where Alexius chose to encamp his army.[113] While a few place names do appear later on in Anna's narrative they do not really help us construct a full and comprehensive picture of what really happened that day. For Guiscard's second campaign in 1084, the chroniclers provide information only about the places of embarkation (Otranto) and disembarkation (Aulon), the places of the triple naval battle with the Venetians (Cassiope and Corfu), the place of Guiscard's death and the port where the rest of Guiscard's fleet was anchored after the battle (Vonitsa).

---

[107] *Alexiad*, III.12 (p. 183); Sewter, p. 133.
[108] *Alexiad*, XII.9 (II, pp. 218–19); Sewter, p. 392.
[109] *Alexiad*, XIII.5–8 (II, pp. 199–217); Sewter, pp. 408–18.
[110] *Alexiad*, XII.9 (II, pp. 172–3); Sewter, p. 393.
[111] *Alexiad*, XIII.1 (II, pp. 177–8); Sewter, pp. 395–6.
[112] *Alexiad*, V.5 (pp. 242–3); Sewter, pp. 166–7.
[113] *Alexiad*, V.5 (pp. 244–5); Sewter, pp. 167–8.

Another striking drawback of our Latin chroniclers' accounts is the lack of dates. Starting with the *Gesta*, no indication of dates is given in any of William's books, and even references to seasons are rare. Even though William records the events in his story in a relatively straightforward chronological order, we need to confirm his account against those by Geoffrey Malaterra, Amatus of Monte Cassino or Anna Comnena and other contemporary chroniclers. For example, he writes that the shipwreck of Guiscard's fleet in 1081 happened 'in the summer'.[114] Of which year, however, William does not mention and historians have to read the *Alexiad* to confirm that it took place in June 1081. Further, William tells us about the 'occupation' of the city of Dyrrhachium by the Venetians (1083) some time during the winter and the fact that they stayed there for fifteen days.[115] For the second Illyrian campaign, the only dates given in book V are the number of months the Normans spent on the Illyrian coast, after their arrival from Italy – all units, except from the cavalry, spent the winter of 1085 at the camp near the River Glycys.[116]

Although Malaterra's history generally follows a solid chronological order, he provides only two specific dates in his third book, which focuses on Guiscard's Illyrian campaigns. For example, Guiscard is reported to have reached Otranto in May 1081,[117] but Malaterra does not give any further details concerning the actual siege of Dyrrhachium. He informs us that Alexius arrived at Dyrrhachium with his army before the surrender of the city to the Normans in October 1081,[118] but no more details are imparted about the day of the battle. For the subsequent period involving Guiscard's departure to Italy and Bohemond's whereabouts in the Greek mainland, Malaterra is surprisingly vague and brief, and any efforts to reconstruct the events lay mostly with the rest of the chroniclers of this period.

Anna Comnena has repeatedly come under criticism for the insufficient dating in her work. The reader, however, has to bear in mind two points. First, she was writing in the 1140s, that is several decades after the events had taken place, and as she was an elderly woman in her sixties, age might have affected her recollection of the events. Second, the different sections of her work were not composed in chronological order, a fact which inevitably leads to confusion and inconsistencies. For the part of her work dealing with the Norman campaigns in the Balkans, Anna writes that the first siege of Dyrrhachium began on 17 June,[119] and that the Normans were already encamped at Glabinitza for seven days to recover from their shipwreck; hence, we can trace their arrival at the Greek coast around 10 June.[120]

---

[114]   *Gesta*, IV.218 (p. 216).
[115]   William means the winter of 1083–4, see *Gesta*, V.96 (p. 240); V.84 (p. 240).
[116]   *Gesta*, V.207 (p. 246).
[117]   Malaterra, III.24.
[118]   Malaterra, III.27.
[119]   *Alexiad*, IV.1 (p. 187); Sewter, p. 135; see the interesting but unconvincing argument by Buckler that the battle of Dyrrhachium took place in 1082 and not in 1081: Buckler, *Anna Comnena*, pp. 406–14.
[120]   *Alexiad*, III.12 (p. 185); Sewter, p. 133.

For Alexius' departure from the capital, we only know that Pacurianus was despatched to Dyrrhachium in August along with an unknown number of men.[121] But since the emperor did not leave for Dyrrhachium 'until the disposition of the troops was complete', and bearing in mind that Alexius was reconnoitring the ground around Dyrrhachium by 15 October,[122] he would have left Constantinople around the end of August. Anna Comnena also notes that the battle of Dyrrhachium took place on 18 October,[123] but she does not report the city's surrender, and it is only from Anna's words that we presume it must have occurred some weeks after the Byzantine defeat, and certainly some time in early winter.

Anna's chronology is surprisingly weak for the following two-year period, for which she only provides two dates. After Bohemond had established his headquarters at Ioannina in spring 1082, Alexius left Constantinople with his troops to face him in May that year.[124] The other date that Anna provides involves Bohemond's arrival at Larissa and the beginning of the siege in full force (in November 1082, as I will show later).[125] Considering that the governor of Larissa, Leo Cephalas, dispatched an urgent letter to Alexius six months after the start of the siege (April 1083) and that shortly afterwards the emperor's army was on the move towards Larissa, it is assumed that Alexius must have arrived at the besieged city in May 1083.[126] For the rest of the period up until Guiscard's death at Cephalonia it is only the Latin sources that provide any kind of dates for the events.

Similarly sparse are the dates of Anna Comnena's narrative regarding Bohemond's invasion. Between the year 1105, when the emperor was notified about Bohemond's plans to invade Illyria, and the actual invasion two years later, there are only three indications for dates concerning Alexius' defensive measures. First, the emperor arrived at Thessaloniki in September 1105[127] to spend the winter in the Macedonian capital, as we find him there in March 1106 when a comet appeared in the sky, a premonition of the coming of the Normans.[128] The second date has to do with the emperor's attendance at a ceremony in Thessaloniki in honour of the patron of the city, St Demetrius, on 25 January 1107. But for the crucial period between Bohemond's invasion and the Treaty of Devol, Anna only notes the date of Alexius' departure from the capital on 1 November 1107.[129]

Even though Anna's accounts of the battles fought are not considered to be the

---

[121] *Alexiad*, IV.4 (p. 198); Sewter, p. 140.

[122] *Alexiad*, IV.5 (p. 203); Sewter, p. 143.

[123] *Alexiad*, IV.6 (p. 208); Sewter, p. 146.

[124] *Alexiad*, V.4 (p. 237); Sewter, p. 163.

[125] *Alexiad*, V.5 (p. 244); Sewter, p. 167.

[126] *Alexiad*, V.5 (pp. 245–6); Sewter, p. 167.

[127] It should read 'the twenty-fourth' and not 'the twentieth' year of Alexius' accession to the throne: *Alexiad*, XII.3 (II, p. 141); Sewter, p. 374.

[128] *Alexiad*, XII.4 (II, pp. 146–7); Sewter, p. 378.

[129] *Alexiad*, XIII.1 (II, p. 177); Sewter, p. 395.

best parts of the *Alexiad*, her descriptions 'though not the finest specimens of her art, are often lucid, instructive, and even interesting'.[130] Anna first examines the battles between the Norman and the Venetian fleets off the coasts of Dyrrhachium in June 1081. No number for the Venetian ships is given, although Anna notes that it 'comprised all types of ships'.[131] The Norman fleet had 150 ships of all types, but it remains unclear whether some units returned home after the disembarkation of the army, or if they all remained at Dyrrhachium. Anna tells us that the Norman fleet was very well protected by 'every sort of war machines', probably because they anticipated a confrontation with the Venetians. As for the description of the naval battle itself, unfortunately Anna does not give any details about the naval tactics employed or the chain of events that led to Bohemond's retreat.

The battle off Dyrrhachium between the Norman and Venetian fleets is described in detail by Malaterra, who gives a rather different version of what happened. In the *De Rebus* there is a vivid description of the events of the first and second day, including the preparation of the Venetian ships for the battle, a reference to the morale of the two armies and the deception of the Normans.[132] Malaterra also notes the use of Greek fire during the naval combat.[133] Although William of Apulia writes about the Venetian-Byzantine alliance, he does not go into more detail and gives the misleading impression of Venice being a satellite state of Byzantium.[134] After disclosing the reason why Alexius called for the Venetians to enforce a naval blockade,[135] William highlights the Venetian dominance in the Adriatic Sea.[136] No numbers, however, are given for the opposing fleets in the actual naval battle and the description of the three-day stand-off is too short and vague. Only the deception of the Normans by the Venetians is mentioned, along with the participation of the Dalmatians in Guiscard's fleet, which is another significant detail.[137]

Two of the most important land battles of this period took place close to Dyrrhachium and Larissa. Anna Comnena notes the exact date of the battle of Dyrrhachium as 18 October 1081, but again no numbers for the opposing armies are given apart from some estimates of their size and composition. Surprisingly, however, Anna takes her reader to her father's war council the day before the battle, where the battle plan is being finalised.[138] Her narrative for the day of the battle is relatively detailed, describing the battle lines drawn by first light and how the actual battle unfolded. For the battle lines, she notes the senior officers of the opposing armies and

[130]   Buckler, *Anna Comnena*, p. 417.
[131]   *Alexiad*, IV.2 (p. 192); Sewter, p. 137.
[132]   Malaterra, III.26.
[133]   Malaterra, III.26.
[134]   *Gesta*, IV.278–82 (p. 218).
[135]   *Gesta*, IV.286–90 (p. 220).
[136]   *Gesta*, IV.280 (p. 218).
[137]   *Gesta*, IV.300–11 (p. 220).
[138]   *Alexiad*, IV.5 (pp. 204–7); Sewter, pp. 145–6.

where exactly they were stationed but remains silent on the composition of each unit of the Norman army. The princess also notes the crucial tactical moves that decided the outcome of the battle, such as the attack of the Norman wing commanded by Amicetas, which was repulsed by the Varangians, and the Varangians' ill-thought advance far beyond the Byzantine line of attack and their retreat after they were attacked by a Norman infantry detachment.[139]

The author of the *Gesta* is no better informed about the events of 18 October than Anna, providing us only with the basic outline of the events of the day. William's description lacks some important details, like names and units, along with the description of battle tactics employed by the opposing armies. He is unaware of the composition of the opposing units, does not identify all of the senior commanders and fails to provide a description of the terrain. William tells us about the initial retreat of some Norman units, but Anna seems better informed when she writes that this was just the Norman flank commanded by Amicetas and not the entire Norman army as William noted.[140] William also ignores the retreat of the Varangians that led to the collapse of the Byzantine army's resistance, and he ends his narrative with the words: 'Alexius was defeated; his own [soldiers] had retreated. More than five thousand Greeks had lost their lives in that battle, and, between them, a multitude of Turks'.[141]

Anna Comnena once again takes us to Alexius' war council, which took place the day before the battle of Larissa.[142] She lists the leading officers of the army and gives details about Alexius' stratagem to deceive the Normans. As for the Byzantine battle lines, Anna only tells us that the generals 'were instructed to draw up the battle line according to the principles he himself [Alexius] had followed in former engagements'.[143] Anna's story, however, is even less detailed for the Normans than it is for the Byzantines, and before the beginning of the battle she writes nothing about Bohemond's battle plans or the composition of his army units. The description of the actual battle is realistic, but it lacks crucial information to reconstruct battle formations and the tactical movements of the two armies in the field.[144]

Unfortunately, our Latin sources are far less informed about Bohemond's achievements on the Greek mainland between the years 1082 and 1083, and it seems remarkable that the events in Castoria, Arta and Larissa are even mentioned in their histories. Malaterra probably chose not to refer to the turn of events in Greece after the Norman defeat at Larissa. William of Apulia's narrative of the battle of Larissa lacks any information on numbers for the opposing armies or any estimates for

[139]   *Alexiad*, IV.6 (pp. 209–11); Sewter, pp. 146–8.
[140]   *Gesta*, IV.366–76 (p. 224); *Alexiad*, IV.6 (p. 210); Sewter, p. 147.
[141]   *Gesta*, IV.413–16 (p. 226).
[142]   *Alexiad*, V.5 (pp. 169–70).
[143]   *Alexiad*, V.5 (p. 169).
[144]   Although there is a description of Bohemond trying to teach his men the phalanx formation on the second day of the battle: *Alexiad*, V.6 (p. 254); Sewter, p. 170; *Alexiad*, V.7 (pp. 253–6); Sewter, p. 172.

their composition,[145] although his history does contain the names of the opposing commanders and the Byzantine battle plan during the first day of fighting. As for the aftermath of this battle, the *Gesta* examines the main turn of events that led to the Norman retreat from the area of Larissa, the reasons why the latter had to retreat and the cities in which their officers sought refuge after their defeat in the field.[146]

For the actual siege operation against Dyrrhachium, Anna Comnena provides a description of the city's defences, although that given in her twelfth book is much more detailed and accurate, and of the siege equipment that the besieged army had at its disposal.[147] The *Alexiad* does not give any figures of the size of the army that was to defend the city of Dyrrhachium from the Normans, and it also lacks any comments on the losses inflicted upon the defenders of the city. As for the besiegers, Anna refers to the siege equipment that was brought from Italy, mainly wooden towers, as 'terrif[ying] the people of Dyrrhachium'.[148]

The siege of Dyrrhachium is the only military operation of its kind described by William of Apulia in his *Gesta*, and his is the most detailed account modern historians have about the events that unfolded during these ten months. Before the beginning of the siege, we read of the negotiations between George Monomachatus, the governor of Dyrrhachium, later replaced by George Palaeologus, and Robert Guiscard for the surrendering of the city to the Normans, a piece of information provided only by William.[149] There are also a few comments on the city itself, which was 'very well fortified' and 'surrounded mainly by brick walls' ('tegulosis obsita muris'), including a short paragraph on its history.[150] William notes that the city was besieged from all sides, while the Norman fleet took part in the attack by enforcing a blockade.[151] Much to our disappointment, Malaterra's study of the siege operation consists of only twelve verses of little value compared to the *Alexiad* or the *Gesta*.[152]

In Anna Comnena's narrative the whole operation for the siege of the city of Larissa was overshadowed by the battle itself. Historians can ascertain next to nothing about the city's fortifications or the course of the siege, with the exception of the urgent letter dispatched to the emperor from the governor of the city, Leo Cephalas.[153] Conversely, the siege of Castoria, which took place after the battle of Larissa, is recorded in the *Alexiad* in greater detail, although the dates for the siege and the surrender of the town are not given and we also do not have an estimate for the size of the besieged army. For Alexius' troops we only know that 'they were completely equipped for siege warfare

---

[145] William does mention that there were a number of Turks in Alexius' army: *Gesta*, V.70 (p. 240).
[146] *Gesta*, V.43–74 (pp. 238–40).
[147] *Alexiad*, III.9 (p. 172); IV.1 (p. 188); Sewter, pp. 126 and 135.
[148] *Alexiad*, III.12 (p. 182); IV.1 (p. 188); Sewter, pp. 131 and 135 .
[149] *Gesta*, IV.215–17 (p. 216).
[150] *Gesta*, IV.234–43 (p. 216).
[151] *Gesta*, IV.214 and 243 (p. 216).
[152] Malaterra, III.25.
[153] *Alexiad*, V.5 (pp. 245–7); Sewter, p. 168.

and for fighting in open country' but Anna does not say if he dismissed any of his units after his victory at Larissa. Also, there is a description of the city's natural defences, along with the siege equipment of the Normans and the Byzantines, which consisted mainly of catapults and *helepoleis* (siege towers).[154] In addition to the *Alexiad*, we can conclude from Malaterra's very brief narrative that Guiscard surrounded and attacked the city many times before its surrender, while in the meantime he was trying to convince the defenders to come to terms. Finally, Malaterra notes that Guiscard did not have siege engines with him but does not clarify what happened to those that were used at Dyrrhachium in 1081.[155]

Every medieval chronicler who reported a campaign had the tendency to inflate or deflate the numbers of soldiers for a variety of reasons. William and Geoffrey were much better informed about the composition and size of the Norman army, while the same can be said about Anna Comnena with respect to the Byzantines. The information that can be extracted from all three of the sources has to be treated with caution, however, as determining the size of armies was not one of the strengths of their narratives. As for the Byzantine army, the complete lack of charter or archival material, combined with the decline of the thematic armies in the eleventh century and the practice of raising mercenaries instead, makes any estimate of the size of the Byzantine units deployed at Dyrrhachium or Larissa very risky.

A similar deficiency in information (or interest) plagues our chroniclers' knowledge of the local geography relevant to Robert Guiscard's expeditions. None of our sources followed the armies in Illyria or Thessaly and, consequently, their descriptions of cities and battlegrounds are inaccurate. Few places, rivers, plains or the surrounding areas of Dyrrhachium and Thessaly are described adequately. Modern archaeology has managed to identify a number of the locations mentioned in our sources, including Dyrrhachium's fortifications, but there is still much to be done.

The absence of sufficient dates is also striking, even though we have to remember that all of our authors were writing many years after the events – and in the case of the *Alexiad* some five decades later. As for the description of the two major sieges and battles of Dyrrhachium and Larissa, Anna Comnena is our best source, even though her presentation of the battle tactics used reveals her limited knowledge of military affairs. William's description lacks some important details as well, such as names and units, along with any analysis of the battle tactics employed by the opposing armies, while Geoffrey Malaterra's account is too short to even be considered.

[154] *Alexiad*, VI.1 (p. 269); Sewter, pp. 181–2; I provide a detailed description of these machines below.
[155] Malaterra, III.29.

2

Norman Military Institutions in Southern Italy in the Eleventh Century

The political and social reasons behind the Norman descent upon Italy

A factor that encouraged contacts between France and Italy in the first quarter of the eleventh century was pilgrimage. Italy was the crossing point of every major pilgrimage route leading to the Holy Land, and the Normans appear as pilgrims in two of the three relatively different versions mentioning the coming of the Normans to Italy.[1] Amatus of Monte Cassino writes of a group of forty Norman pilgrims who witnessed a Muslim attack at Salerno while returning from Jerusalem 'before the year 1000' who were recruited by Gaimar IV to help the defenders.[2] On the other hand, William of Apulia and Lupus Protospatharius mention a group of Norman pilgrims who met with a Lombard noble named Melus while on pilgrimage on Monte Gargano in 1016, and promised to reinforce the latter's planned Apulian rebellion against the Byzantines.[3] In each case, the means to purify the soul from sin through pilgrimage significantly increased the religious and social ties between Normandy and Italy since the beginning of the eleventh century. The great religious site of the sanctuary of Monte Sant' Angelo sul Gargano, dedicated to Archangel Michael, served as an important religious link between Jerusalem, Italy and Normandy.[4]

Another contributing factor to the Norman migration to the south has been identified as the overpopulation of Normandy.[5] A characteristic example from this

[1] J. France, 'The Occasion of the Coming of the Normans to Southern Italy', *Journal of Medieval History* 17 (1991), 185–205; E. Joranson, 'The Inception of the Career of the Normans in Italy – Legend and History', *Speculum* 23 (1948), 353–96.

[2] Amatus, I.17–21; *Chronicon Casinensis*, II.37 (pp. 236–9).

[3] *Gesta*, I.11–57 (pp. 98–102); Lupus Protospatharius, *Chronicon*, s.a. 1017.

[4] J. C. Arnold, 'Arcadia Becomes Jerusalem: Angelic Caverns and Shrine Conversion at Monte Gargano', *Speculum* 75 (2000), 567–88.

[5] G. Duby, 'Les "Jeunes" dans la société aristocratique dans la France du nord-ouest au XII^c siècle', in

period is the sons of Tancred of Hauteville, whose reasons for venturing to Italy are discussed by Amatus of Monte Cassino, Geoffrey Malaterra and Orderic Vitalis. According to Amatus, 'these people [the Normans] had increased to such a number that the fields and orchards were not sufficient for producing the necessities of life for so many', with Malaterra adding that 'the sons of Tancred noticed that whenever their aging neighbours passed away, their heirs would fight amongst themselves for their inheritance, resulting in the division of the patrimony – which had been intended to fall to the lot of a single heir – into portions that were too small [. . .] Ultimately, with the guidance of God, they came to Apulia, a province of Italy'.[6] Overpopulation emerges as a reason for pushing Norman youth to abandon their homeland in the last speech that Orderic Vitalis puts into the mouth of Robert Guiscard, a few hours before his death in July 1085: 'We were born of poor and humble parents and left the barren country of the Cotentin and homes which could not support us to travel to Rome'.[7]

All of these accounts underline the fact that the division of the family patrimony was a serious issue in eleventh-century Normandy and that customs of inheritance dashed the aspirations of many younger sons of acquiring a piece of land for themselves. The type of joint tenure, where the younger sons were given a share of the patrimony under the control of their elder brother, which would satisfy the younger members of a family and discourage emigration, only became common towards the end of the eleventh century.[8] In the case of the Hauteville family, it should come as no surprise to see the departure from Normandy of William, Drogo and Humphrey, and gradually in the following decades of their half-brothers, Robert Guiscard, Mauger and Roger.

Apart from the issue of inheritance, which affected many young Normans, political factors also played an important role in the decision to leave for Italy. Many who did so were exiles, victims of ducal wrath as a result of their military or political opposition to William II, although some were later pardoned and reinstated.[9] Others were escaping the bitter conflicts between aristocratic families during the decades crucial to the rise of aristocratic power (1035–55), such as the Tosny and the Beaumont families.

The main driving force behind the expansion of the 1020s to 1050s, however, was the political and social disturbances in Normandy and many parts of northern France

---

Hommes et structures du Moyen Âge (Paris, 1973), pp. 213–25. For arguments against this reason see D. Bates, *Normandy before 1066* (London, 1982), pp. 244–8.

[6]   Amatus, I.1; Malaterra, I.5.

[7]   Orderic Vitalis, VII (p. 32).

[8]   E. Tabuteau, *Transfers of Property in Eleventh-Century Norman Law* (London, 1988); R. Bartlett, *The Making of Europe, Conquest, Colonization and Cultural Change, 950–1350* (London, 1994), pp. 47–50.

[9]   E. van Houts, 'L'exil dans l'espace Anglo-Normand', in *La Normandie et l'Angleterre au Moyen Âge*, ed. P. Bouet and V. Gazeau (Caen, 2003), pp. 117–27; L. R. Ménager, 'Pesanteur et étiologie de la colonisation normande de l'Italie', in *Roberto il Guiscardo e il suo tempo. Relazzioni e communicationi nelle prime giornate normanno-sueve (Bari, Maggio 1973)* (Rome, 1975), pp. 189–214 at pp. 209–13; C. H. Haskins, *The Norman Institutions* (Cambridge, MA, 1918), pp. 27–30.

after the breakdown of Robert II's regime in 1034, and especially during William II's minority.[10] These dramatic years between 1047 and 1057 appear in great contrast to the period of greater stability and peace of the late tenth and early eleventh centuries in the duchy, a situation which had attracted political exiles from Anjou and Brittany, including families like the Taissons or the Giroies, who would quickly become leading members of the Norman aristocracy. As Bates notes, the dramatic phase of the purely Norman expansion began when the same type of territorial fragmentation and reorganisation of family structures became pronounced within Norman society itself.[11] This point becomes even more significant if we compare the chronologies of the main events in Normandy and the immigration periods in Italy. There seems to be a link between periods of particular disturbance in the duchy of Normandy and periods of expansion in Italy. The period of the growing power of Rainulf of Aversa (second half of 1030s) and the establishment of the Normans at Melfi (1041) were preceded by the troubled reign of Richard III (1034–5) and the minority years of William II. The turbulent period of the two invasions of Normandy between 1053 and 1057 filled the ranks of the Normans in Italy just before the Calabrian, Apulian and Sicilian expansion in the decade between 1054 and 1064. The parallels that exist in this chronology of events in Normandy and Italy are more than coincidental.

One of the fundamental developments of Norman society in the first half of the eleventh century was the establishment of a number of families that gradually came to dominate the provincial administration of the duchy prior to the English invasion, and which would also come to provide the bulk of the Norman aristocratic elite in Anglo-Norman England. Exactly how this came about is uncertain, but the phenomenon has been the focus of a number of well-focused studies.[12] Here, however, I am more concerned with evidence of the existing links between families in Normandy and Italy in the eleventh century than with social changes in pre-conquest Norman society.

The first of these is the Norman family of the Tosnys, which exported one of its members to Italy around the mid-eleventh century.[13] Raoul Glaber gives us a story of how Ralph II fled from the duke's wrath after being entrusted with the defence of Tillières-sur-Avre (Upper Normandy) in the 1010s and reached Italy, only to return to Normandy after the defeat at Cannae (1018).[14] Another family that had migrated

---

[10]   D. C. Douglas, *William the Conqueror, The Norman Impact upon England*, 2nd edn (London, 1999), pp. 31–80; Bates, *Normandy before 1066*, pp. 46–93.

[11]   Bates, *Normandy before 1066*, p. 244.

[12]   Douglas, *William the Conqueror*, pp. 83–104; R. Allen Brown, *The Normans and the Norman Conquest* (London, 1969), pp. 35–60; Bates, *Normandy before 1066*, pp. 99–146.

[13]   L. R. Ménager, 'Inventaire des familles normandes et franques émigrées en Italie méridionale et en Sicile (XIᶜ–XIIᶜ siècles)', in *Roberto il Guiscardo e il suo tempo. Relazzioni e communicationi nelle prime giornate normanno-sueve (Bari, Maggio 1973)* (Rome, 1975), pp. 348–9; reprinted in *Hommes et institutions de l'Italie normande* (London, 1981).

[14]   Rodulphus Glaber, *Historiarum Libri quinque*, trans. and ed. J. France (Oxford, 1989), III, pp. 102; *Chronicon Casinensis*, II.37 (p. 239).

to Normandy, near Argentan in the southern marches, during the last decades of the tenth century, were the Giroies.[15] The family originally came from Brittany during the reign of Hugh Capet (987–96), and as vassals to the powerful Bellême family they participated in full in the civil disturbances of the second quarter of the eleventh century, managing to gain a significant number of lands, including Montreuil and Echauffour. Arnold of Echauffour, of the Giroie family, was deprived of his lands and went into exile in Apulia in 1060 for a period of three years before he was restored.[16] William of Montreuil, another famous Giroie, was established in Italy soon after 1050 and married the daughter of Richard of Capua, receiving as dowry the counties of Aquino, Marsia and Campania, while he was also pronounced duke of Gaeta.[17] Finally, Heremburge Giroire was married to a certain Walchelin of Pont-Echanfray, and their sons, William and Ralph, later joined Robert Guiscard's army fighting in Italy and Sicily in the 1060s.[18]

A family connected to the Giroies by blood was the Grandmesnils, which sent members of its lineage to Italy, the Holy Land, Constantinople and England.[19] Robert II Grandmesnil became a monk at St Evroul in 1050 and nine years later was elected abbot of the monastery. In 1061, after a serious disagreement with Duke William, he left St Evroul to take his case before Pope Nicholas II and he also paid a visit to Apulia.[20] Another member of the family who is reported to have been to Italy was Arnold of Grandmesnil, who is named by Orderic in a list of Normans along with the sons of Hauteville, William of Montreuil and three others.[21] Other sons and grandsons of Robert acquired secular lordships, such as William, who married one of Guiscard's daughters but later rebelled and found refuge in Alexius Comnenus' court some time in the 1090s. He is mentioned by Orderic Vitalis as participating in Guiscard's Illyrian campaign in 1084–5.[22]

Two other Norman families that greatly profited from their descent upon Italy from the mid-eleventh century onwards were the Blossevilles and the Moulins.[23] The first were the successors of the Ridels as dukes of Gaeta, while the Moulins, coming from Moulins-la-Marche in the Orne, gave their name to the area of southern Abruzzi, including Venafro, Isernia and Boianno.[24]

---

[15]   Ménager, 'Inventaires', pp. 362–3.

[16]   Orderic Vitalis, III (pp. 22 and 26); Ménager, 'Inventaires', pp. 309–13.

[17]   Amatus, IV.27; VI.1. 11; Orderic Vitalis, III (p. 58).

[18]   Orderic Vitalis, III (p. 30).

[19]   J. Decaens, 'Le patrimoine des Grentemesnil en Normandie, en Italie et en Angleterre aux XIᵉ et XIIᵉ siècles', in *Les Normands en Mediterranée dans le sillage des Tancrèdes*, ed. P. Bouet and F. Neveux (Caen, 1994), pp. 123–40; Ménager, 'Inventaires', pp. 316–17.

[20]   Orderic Vitalis, III (pp. 40, 74, 90, 96 and 98).

[21]   Orderic Vitalis, III (p. 58).

[22]   Orderic Vitalis, IV (p. 32) and VII (p. 32).

[23]   Ménager, 'Inventaires', pp. 299–300, 332–9 and 351–2.

[24]   A certain Raoul Moulin is mentioned by William of Apulia at Civitate: *Gesta*, II.135–6 and 170 (pp. 138–40); William of Poitiers, *Gesta Guillelmi of William of Poitiers*, ed. and trans. R. H. C. Davis and M.

Yet while the analysis of these families demonstrates the Norman origins or background of many of the high-profile adventurers to Italy, the Italian sources and charter evidence also contain numerous references to newcomers from other parts of France as well.[25] Amatus clearly distinguishes the Normans from the French and the Burgundians, while William of Apulia writes about the Norman tactic of assimilation by 'welcom[ing] anyone and then introducing them to their customs, their traditions and language'.[26] Four charters from Aversa for the years 1068–73 were issued by men calling themselves *Francus*, or *ex genere Francorum*, something that marks a clear distinction between Normans and French.[27] From a study of anthroponyms and cognomina of foreigners in eleventh- and twelfth-century south Italian documents, it is clear that approximately one in three of the invaders were of non-Norman origin. More specifically, charter evidence collected by Ménager reveals the origin of a number of non-Norman elements in Italy between the eleventh and twelfth centuries, of which eleven were Angevin, four were central French, three were Burgundian, thirty-one were Breton, two were from Champagne and five from Flanders.[28] This clearly reveals the significant role that Bretons, Flemings and other non-Norman elements played in the conquest of the south. An additional research of northern French charter evidence, collected by Musset, provides ten names for departures to the south, of which five are Norman, three are men from Chartres, one comes from Anjou and one from Maine.[29]

Another issue that has been debated amongst modern historians over recent decades has to do with so-called *Normannitas* (Norman-ness). R. H. C. Davis raised questions about the nature of the Norman expansion and compared the depiction of the *Normannitas* in works of chroniclers such as Dudo of St Quentin, William of Poitiers, William of Jumièges and Orderic Vitalis.[30] He drew a distinction between Dudo's work and that of William of Jumièges, based on the notion of the Frenchness identified by Dudo and the distinct Danish ancestry highlighted by William. Davis also underlined the unity and indivisibility of Normandy in Dudo's work and the

Chibnall (Oxford, 1998), I.28 (p. 42); Orderic Vitalis, III (p. 132, n. 1).

[25] G. A. Loud, 'How Norman was the Norman Conquest of Southern Italy?', *Nottingham Medieval Studies* 25 (1981), 13–34; S. Tramontana, *I normanni in Italia, linee di ricerca sui primi insediamenti* (Messina, 1970), pp. 83–95.

[26] Amatus, I.5; *Gesta*, I.165–8 (p. 108).

[27] *Codice diplomatico normanno di Aversa*, ed. A. Gallo (Naples, 1926), 386–7 (no. 43), 393–4 (no. 48), 396–7 (no. 50) and 399–401 (no. 53).

[28] L. R. Ménager, 'Pesanteur et étiologie de la colonisation normande de l'Italie', in *Roberto il Guiscardo e il suo tempo. Relazzioni e communicationi nelle prime giornate normanno-sueve (Bari, Maggio 1973)* (Rome, 1975), pp. 189–214, at pp. 202–4 and 368–86. See also J.-M. Martin, *La Pouille du VIe au XIIe siècle* (Rome, 1993), pp. 526–9.

[29] L. Musset, 'Actes inédits du XIe siècle. V. Autour des origines de St-Etienne de Fontenay', *Bulletin de la Société des antiquaires de Normandie* 56 (1961–2), 29–31.

[30] R. H. C. Davis, *The Normans and their Myth* (London, 1997), pp. 49–102; G. A. Loud, 'The "Gens Normannorum" – Myth or Reality?', *Anglo-Norman Studies* 4 (1981), 108–10.

identification of the Normans not as Vikings or French but as people or immigrants who belonged to the land of Normandy, a point developed further by Orderic Vitalis, who established the historical connection between Neustria and Normandy. This general notion of the Frenchness of the Normans is also supported by D. C. Douglas, who considered the Norman conquests of the eleventh century to have been made by men who were French in their language, culture, religion and political ideas.[31]

In a different approach to this issue, Bates thinks in terms of a fusion of cultures; a Scandinavian character stemming from their ancestral roots filtered with elements from the Carolingian character of the land they settled. He identifies both a tendency for political and economic assimilation, and also the clear self-assertiveness and independence of the Norman rulers. This view is shared by N. Webber, who argues that the assimilation of the Scandinavian and Frankish characteristics in Normandy, in conjunction with the adoption of the new ethnonym, *gens Normannorum*, marked the ethnogenesis of a new people with a distinct identity.[32]

But did the Normans consider their conquests in Italy as Norman as they did those in England? Both Norman and English chroniclers of the late eleventh and early twelfth century direct their attention to the south and several of them like to boast about the military achievements of their fellow countrymen. Davis draws attention to the examples of William of Malmesbury, Henry of Huntington and especially Orderic Vitalis.[33] But is there anything to suggest that this notion was reciprocated between the Normans and their chroniclers in the south? Several interesting points can be raised regarding the histories of our three Italian chroniclers: that these newcomers were identified predominantly as Normans, with the chroniclers giving their own version of the etymology of the term;[34] that the term Normans played a unifying role between the different bands operating in the south, having already encapsulated the cultural identity of the *gens Normannorum* long before 1016; that the leaders of the Normans personified *Normannitas* and possessed 'great martial valour'; and finally that several features are dominant in the Italian histories, such as the Norman energy (*strenuitas*), courage (*corage*), boldness (*hardiesce*) and valour (*vaillantize*).[35]

Although it is clear that the southern Normans were well aware of the deeds of their countrymen in the north and they recognised Normandy as their place of origin, none of them in fact saw the expansion into Italy as part of the wider achievements of the Norman race. *Normannitas* could only remain viable in Italy as a notion of identity and unity in a period of continuous territorial expansion. After the death of Robert Guiscard, and especially during the years of the monarchy after 1130, owing largely to the cessation of immigration from the north and the forces of intermarriage and

[31] Douglas, *The Norman Achievement*, pp. 22–9.
[32] Bates, *Normandy before 1066*, pp. 24–43; N. Webber, *The Evolution of Norman Identity, 911–1154* (Woodbridge, 2005), pp. 18–39.
[33] Davis, *The Normans and their Myth*, pp. 62–9 and 87–92.
[34] Amatus, I.1; Malaterra, I.3; *Gesta*, I.9–10 (p. 98).
[35] Bartlett, *The Making of Europe*, pp. 85–105; Webber, *The Evolution of Norman Identity*, pp. 60–71.

acculturation that were beginning to take effect, the identity of the Normans in the south was eventually redefined, with the Italian-Sicilian Normans not showing the slightest interest in appearing Norman.[36]

Military institutions in Normandy, France and England in the eleventh century and their links to southern Italy: service in the host

In Normandy and Anglo-Norman England of the eleventh and early twelfth centuries, there were two main categories of troops in the service of a senior lord. There were those who owed service in return for their lands (enfeoffed knights), and those who fought for pay, known as stipendiaries or mercenaries. The two most important military obligations of an enfeoffed knight were the duty in host and castle service. Host duty involved three types of military service in Normandy and France: the *arrière-ban*, the *service d'host* and the *service de chevauchée* (or *chevalchia*). Conversely, mercenaries were divided into three categories: members of the royal and baronial households that formed the core corps of every medieval army; professionals hired for a specific campaign or series of military operations, who lacked political or social ties to those who employed them and clearly fought for profit; and armies hired from neighbouring kingdoms or counties, serving the king or lord as allies or vassals.

Since the rarity of surviving records makes it almost impossible to draw a map of comital (military) responsibilities in southern Italy until the beginning of the twelfth century, I will discuss these two main categories of troops in eleventh-century Normandy and Anglo-Norman England and will draw some conclusions about military service in Norman Italy in the pre-monarchy period by way of analogy. After all, these bands of Norman and French youths that arrived in Italy in the first half of the eleventh century would have been influenced by the forms of lord–vassal relations, and the customs of tenure, military service and inheritance established in Normandy and other parts of France in the eleventh century, and it is expected that they would have attempted to enforce these norms, at least to some degree, in the areas which they came to control as the dominant minority.

Stipendiary knights

The core of most medieval armies from Charlemagne to Edward III was the household or *familia*, which can be divided into royal and baronial.[37] Although very

---

[36]   Davis, *The Normans and their Myth*, pp. 84–92; Webber, *The Evolution of Norman Identity*, pp. 71–84; J. H. Drell, 'Cultural Syncretism and Ethnic Identity: The Norman "Conquest" of Southern Italy and Sicily', *Journal of Medieval History* 25 (1999), 187–202; L. Musset, 'Les circonstances de la pénétration normande en Italie du sud et dans le monde méditerrannéen', in *Les Normands en Méditerranée aux XIᵉ–XIIᵉ siècles*, ed. P. Bouet and F. Neveux (Caen, 2001), pp. 41–51.

[37]   S. D. Church, *The Household Knights of King John* (New York, 1999), pp. 16–39 and 74–100; C. Warren Hollister, *The Military Organization of Norman England* (Oxford, 1965), pp. 167–76; M.

rarely mentioned in the primary sources, the *familiae* would have played a key role in the expansion of the Norman principalities in southern Italy between the 1040s and 1070s. In addition, the small number of Normans in Sicily before 1072 suggests that household troops would have formed the core of the armies that invaded the island from 1061 on. Malaterra, for example, refers to the role of Robert Guiscard's household in subduing Calabria in the late 1050s, although instead of the term *familia* he rather uses *sui* and *fideles*.[38] Geoffrey's history provides a typical example involving the robbing of a group of rich merchants travelling from Amalfi to Melfi in 1057 – the infamous incident with Peter of Bisignano, an operation which secured for Robert the services of a hundred knights for further plundering expeditions in Apulia that year.[39]

Around this period, Roger Hauteville entered Guiscard's household along with other newly arrived Normans. These troops, sixty according to Malaterra, were dispatched by Robert to Calabria 'to make war against many thousands of the enemy'.[40] Some 300 *iuvenes* are mentioned after the Norman victory at Castrogiovanni in the summer of 1061 under Roger's orders.[41] The same number of knights appears once more in 1063 when Roger returned to Calabria to collect supplies and to distribute lands to his followers before returning to Sicily.[42] Malaterra also notes that 'soldiers and mercenaries' ('milites et stipendiarii') garrisoned the cities of Troina and Petralia in 1061 after they surrendered to Roger.[43] Their numbers certainly would not have been great at that early stage; allegedly only 136 knights defeated the Muslims at Cerami in June 1063, while another small Norman force clashed with a Muslim army at Misilmeri in 1068.[44]

The Anglo-Norman royal *familia* was remarkably heterogeneous in its composition and included both landless, unenfeoffed knights and members of great aristocratic families with large estates that owed their rise to their close ties with the king or the great magnates. These *milites* were, in essence, well-trained and experienced troops in the personal service of the king or a great magnate, travelling with him and acting as a bodyguard, carrying messages, helping maintain law and order in his domains and, most importantly, forming a unit of troops that was combat-ready any time of the year at very short notice. When in service, the household knights would have been paid a daily wage, provided with food and compensated, if necessary, for the loss of any horses or equipment. An additional income would have been the spoils of any military operation.[45]

Prestwich, *Armies and Warfare in the Middle Ages: The English Experience* (London, 2006), pp. 38–48.
[38] Malaterra, I.17.
[39] Malaterra, I.23–5 and 26.
[40] Malaterra, I.19.
[41] Malaterra, II.16–17.
[42] Malaterra, II.29 and 30.
[43] Malaterra, II.20.
[44] Amatus, V.23; Malaterra, II.33 and 41.
[45] Prestwich, *Armies and Warfare*, pp. 84–5; P. Contamine, *War in the Middle Ages*, trans. M. Jones

These troops would have been particularly useful in times of unrest, for example during the Apulian rebellions in 1067, 1072 and 1078. The speed with which Robert Guiscard marched from Calabria to Apulia to suppress the 1067 rebellion seems remarkable, and Amatus' story strongly suggests that the duke had a combat-ready core of troops to besiege Geoffrey of Conversano's stronghold.[46] The quick surrender of the latter forced the rest of the ringleaders to seek terms. In 1079, Guiscard was in Calabria when the city of Bari was betrayed to the rebels, and again he had to march north with 460 knights, probably those of his ducal household along with mercenaries, in order to re-establish his authority.[47]

The professional mercenaries can be identified as a distinct group of elite mounted warriors who were hired to serve in a particular campaign or number of campaigns and were dismissed after the conclusion of the military operations.[48] When called for service they were often incorporated into the *familia* and would follow its command structure and regulations. Household knights were preferred to their enfeoffed comrades-in-arms because they could be recruited for long-term service and they were not subject to any feudal limitations. Both mercenaries and household knights were paid from the king's coffers but it is the way that these sums of money were raised that caused concern, public anger, protests and even rebellions. The main source of mercenaries for the Norman counts and their Anglo-Norman successors were the Low Countries and Brittany, and in many campaigns they would form a large part of the Norman or English armies in action. For example, William I relied heavily on his mercenaries for the campaign of 1066 and the establishment of his authority in England immediately after that.[49]

The noble households supplemented by the numerous bands of mercenaries played the most prominent role in the subjugation of the Byzantine outposts in Apulia and Calabria. Amatus writes about the recruiting tactics of the Normans in the region in the early stages of their infiltration into Apulia in the 1040s, while they were still relatively few in numbers despite immigration from France:

(Oxford, 2005), pp. 94–5.

[46]   Amatus, V.4; Malaterra, II.29.

[47]   *Gesta*, III.539–687 (pp. 194–202).

[48]   Hollister, *Norman England*, pp. 176–86; C. Warren Hollister, *Anglo-Saxon Military Institutions* (Oxford, 1962), pp. 9–24; E. Cuozzo, *La cavalleria nel regno normanno di Sicilia* (Melphite, 2002), pp. 71–211, especially pp. 159–74; M. Mallett, *Mercenaries and their Masters, Warfare in Renaissance Italy* (London, 1974), pp. 209–29; R. Abels, 'Household Men, Mercenaries and Vikings in Anglo-Saxon England', in *Mercenaries and Paid Men: The Mercenary Identity in the Middle Ages*, ed. J. France (Boston, 2008), pp. 143–65. For the problematic definitions of the term 'mercenary', see S. Morillo, 'Mercenaries, Mamluks and Militia, towards a Cross-Cultural Typology of Military Service', in *Mercenaries and Paid Men: The Mercenary Identity in the Middle Ages*, ed. J. France (Boston, 2008), pp. 243–59, 243–59.

[49]   *The Chronicle of John of Worcester*, 3 vols., ed. R. R. Darlington and P. McGurk (Oxford, 1995), II, pp. 604–7 and III, pp. 4–19; *The Carmen de Hastingae Proelio of Guy, Bishop of Amiens*, ed. and trans. F. Barlow (Oxford, 1999), p. 37.

The Normans did not cease to scour the principate [of Benevento?] for men strong and capable of fighting. They gave them, and had distributed, horses from the wealth of the Greeks whom they had conquered in battle, and they promised to give those who helped them against the Greeks a share in what they acquired in future. And so the people took heart and wished to fight against the Greeks.[50]

Sicily also offered some attractive opportunities for stipendiary troops, and it was probably they, along with household knights, who formed the core of the armies that repeatedly invaded the island from 1061 on, faced the Muslims in three pitched battles in the 1060s and manned a number of fortified towns in the north-east of the island. For example, we know of about 300 knights placed as a garrison in Messina in the late summer of 1061, another unit partly composed of paid troops garrisoned in Petralia in 1062, and a force of 250 knights under Roger that crossed to Sicily in December 1061 for a plundering expedition to the south-west and the city of Agrigento – all of these were probably stipendiary troops.[51]

Malaterra is the first of our sources to refer to the employment of a contingent of Slav mercenaries in the household of Robert Guiscard, when the latter was in the very early stages of subduing Calabria in 1057.[52] 'By giving them gifts and promising them even more in the future he had practically transformed them into brothers' – Malaterra's words reveal the fundamental idea behind Robert Guiscard's hiring of troops: no regular fixed pay would have been offered in this early period of expansion but rather numerous promises for future gifts, lands and booty.[53] As the overall leader of the Apulian Normans after 1057, Guiscard took great care to ensure the fair distribution of booty and ransom money to his followers: 'cherishing each of them equally and himself being cherished by all'.[54]

Such would have been the main source of (irregular) income for Robert Guiscard and Roger, which would come mainly in the form of cash, along with tribute money and profits from diplomacy: for example, the marriage negotiations between Guiscard and Constantine Ducas in the 1070s.[55] It is therefore no coincidence that a large number of knights abandoned Roger after 1064, when the Sicilian theatre of operations reached a standstill, as there were no further opportunities for enrichment and plunder. Guiscard's anxiety for regularly rewarding his followers with large sums of money is also understandable; referring to the great ransom gained from Peter of Bisignano in 1057, Malaterra noted that: 'After receiving such a large amount of

[50]   Amatus, II.25.
[51]   Malaterra, II.18 and 20.
[52]   Colonies of Slav settlers had existed in Bari, the Capitanata and Calabria, as well as in Sicily since the seventh century: Martin, *La Pouille*, pp. 504–9.
[53]   Malaterra, I.16.
[54]   *Gesta*, II.311–13 (p. 147).
[55]   On the monetary economy of southern Italy in the eleventh century see G. A Loud, 'Coinage, Wealth and Plunder in the Age of Robert Guiscard', *English Historical Review* 114 (1999), 815–43, especially pp. 829–39; Martin, *La Pouille*, pp. 401–85.

money, Guiscard strengthened his men's fidelity toward him by abundantly rewarding them'.[56]

The duke was supposed to request military service from vassals and *fideles* when large-scale operations were to take place, such as the sieges of Bari and Palermo and the invasion of Sicily in 1061. The first example of a large-scale mobilisation of the southern Italian magnates took place in 1067/8, just months before the beginning of the siege of Bari. Robert Guiscard would have needed all the troops he could get and it was this demand, along with Byzantine money (see the next chapter), that sparked a rebellion by some of his leading magnates in January 1067. Geoffrey of Conversano refused to provide his military obligations to the duke on the grounds that he did not owe any such assistance for lands he had conquered on his own. He was probably the wealthiest, and thus the most powerful, of the Apulian magnates who had arrived in Apulia in the early 1060s, and he had not taken part in the Melfi arrangements of 1042 between the twelve Norman captains. In theory, he should not have disputed Guiscard's authority as duke of Apulia and Calabria (as he was styled by Pope Nicholas II in 1059) and deny him military service for the Apulian lands where he had established himself. In reality, however, Robert Guiscard was (ducal title or not) still no more than a *primus inter pares* among the Norman leaders, who did not acknowledge that the members of the Hauteville kin-group had special powers over them.[57]

Enfeoffed knights

The *arrière-ban* can be seen as one of the most interesting obligations of this period. It concerned the general levy of all able-bodied freemen to defend their land in case of an emergency, commanded by the highest-ranking officials such as a prince or the king himself. It was not considered to be an obligation from a vassal to his lord or a kind of military service associated with tenures and fiefs, but it was based on the ancient sense of duty of all men to defend their nation from a foreign threat.[58] It also presented a great opportunity for the prince to call upon the full military power of his realm, by short-circuiting the feudal hierarchy. The term, probably stemming from the Carolingian *heriban* – a kind of military tax, which developed after Courtrai into a summons of all fief-holders regardless of whether they were subjects of the king, lay lords or ecclesiastical institutions.[59] For the later Anglo-Norman period, the mention of the *arrière-ban*, or of the *nomen proelii* under which it frequently appears in the records, can first be seen in the Bayeux Inquest of 1133.

The *service de chevauchée* (*chevalchia*) concerned the middle ranks of the feudal

---

[56] Malaterra, I.17 and 23.

[57] Malaterra, II.39; Chalandon, *Domination normande*, pp. 178–85; D. Matthew, *The Norman Kingdom of Sicily* (Cambridge, 2001), pp. 25–8.

[58] P. Guilhiermoz, *Essai sur l'origine de la noblesse en France au moyen âge* (Paris, 1902), pp. 289–99.

[59] Contamine, *War in the Middle Ages*, pp. 87–8 and 155–7.

hierarchy and was a more informal type of duty from a vassal to his lord.[60] Only those who possessed royal rights could summon the host, which is the fundamental distinction between the *chevalchia* and the service in the host. The military force, which was requested each time, was of modest size, since the intention of this institution was to engage in more localised objectives of limited scope, such as the siege of a castle, the pursuit of a fugitive or simply the escort of the lord. Whereas the general summons for a *service d'host* could only be issued by the king himself or by the prince and only for an important reason, the *service de chevauchée* could be ordered by a lesser lord. Although the service does not appear in the Norman records by name before 1066, there is little doubt that it must have been a significant obligation in post-Conquest Normandy, appearing in the inquests of 1133 and 1172.[61] If this is the case, and if we consider the widespread private warfare waged in the duchy of Normandy, especially during William I's accession and minority years, it is highly likely that the *chevalchia* was known in pre-conquest Normandy as well.

The king himself or one of the great princes of the kingdom of France, such as the duke of Normandy, could officially summon the feudal quotas of their realm. This military obligation shared by all the tenants-in-chief has been identified as the *service d'host* (*expeditio*). In comparison to the *arrière-ban*, the service in the host was more limited in numbers but its purpose was not restricted to cases of emergency. Enfeoffed knights serving under the king's banner, however, were theoretically limited to serving only within the frontiers of the realm, and in the case of Normandy they could not proceed outside the Norman frontiers. It was after the Conquest that a number of magnates were owed overseas service as a result of their holding lands in both sides of the Channel, with the most characteristic example being that of the dispute between King John and his northern magnates in 1213–14.[62] This limitation, however, could be overcome on the part of the suzerain and with a sharp reduction in the quotas, although there are cases to show that this rule was not so strictly enforced.[63]

There was also a time limit to the employment of the baronial *servitia debita*, with the knights being obliged to serve at their own expense in the lord's host for no more than forty days a year.[64] This specific number of days was first mentioned in Italy in 1095, while in Normandy it is found in the Bayeux Inquest of 1133, where it appears

[60] F. M. Stenton, *The First Century of English Feudalism: 1066–1166, Being the Ford Lectures Delivered in the University of Oxford in Hilary Term 1929* (Oxford, 1950), pp. 176–7; Hollister, *Norman England*, pp. 76–7 and 81–6.

[61] Hollister, *Norman England*, p. 82.

[62] Hollister, *Norman England*, pp. 81 and 101–11; J. C. Holt, *The Northerners* (Oxford, 1992), pp. 79–108, especially pp. 87–95; S. Painter, *The Reign of King John* (Baltimore, 1949), pp. 278–84.

[63] C. Cahen, *Le régime féodal de l'Italie normande* (Paris, 1940), p. 64; F. M. Powicke, *The Loss of Normandy*, 2nd edn (Manchester, 1961), p. 218.

[64] M. Chibnall, 'Military Service in Normandy before 1066', *Anglo-Norman Studies* 5 (1982), 74–5. For the debate on the term 'military service', see Hollister, *Norman England*, pp. 89–111; Hollister, 'The Annual Term of Military Service in Medieval England', *Medievalia et Humanistica* 13 (1960), 40–7.

as the regular period for the service due to the king of France, as well as for that owed to the duke within the confines of Normandy.[65] In the twelfth-century kingdom of Jerusalem, however, the service inside the kingdom was established by the *Haute Cour* at one year.[66]

Two known cases deviated from these limitations: the invasion of England by William I and Robert Guiscard's expedition in the Balkans in 1081. Before examining these two campaigns and the reasons why they are considered exceptional by medieval historians in terms of the military service demanded from the great magnates of each realm, I briefly consider the Byzantine expedition in Sicily (1038–41), when Gaimar V of Salerno, an imperial vassal, was asked to furnish troops for the campaign. Gaimar chose to send the 'restless' Normans, who had been his vassals since May 1038, under German recognition.[67] As Malaterra notes, Gaimar saw this 'as an opportunity to send away the Normans in his service without slighting them. In an effort to encourage the Normans to go, he [Gaimar V] made much of the gifts which had been promised to them [Normans] by Maniaces [the Byzantine general], enumerating them in his own words, even promising to add more of his own'.[68] In essence, what Malaterra is referring to is a bargain between the duke of Salerno and his vassal the count of Aversa, with promises of generous gifts and large sums of money being made if the Normans were enticed to serve overseas, although they would have been under no formal obligation to do so.

Although the chronicle material is scarce concerning William's preparations for his campaign in 1066, we are informed by Wace, writing about a hundred years after the Conquest, of the war councils William held with the most important magnates of his realm. We follow a dialogue between William Fitz Osbern, who reminds the rest of the leading magnates that they owed military service to the duke in return for their fiefs in the duchy, while the latter replied that they were not bound to serve beyond the sea.[69] We need to clarify at this point that in the pre-conquest period we cannot talk about fixed quotas for the senior magnates who were serving under William. Later, we find William Fitz Osbern suggesting to the duke that each magnate was 'willing' to provide at least double what they owed to him, with the Conqueror negotiating with each one of them separately for their 'contribution' of knight and ship service.

But in what way were the magnates persuaded to serve their duke beyond the Channel? The most satisfactory answer seems to be that the duke proposed to each of his men a minimum contribution to the English campaign, based on each one's

[65] 'per unumquemque annum unius militis per XL dies ei dare debeo servitium': F. Ughelli, *Italia Sacra*, 10 vols. (Venice, 1717–22), VI, p. 700; Haskins, *Norman Institutions*, pp. 19–20.
[66] D. Nicolle, *Crusader Warfare*, 2 vols. (London, 2007), I, pp. 14–15; R. C. Smail, *Crusading Warfare (1097–1193)* (Cambridge, 1956), p. 98, n. 3.
[67] Amatus, II.3; Malaterra, I.6; *Chronicon Casinensis*, II.63 (pp. 288–93).
[68] Malaterra, I.7.
[69] Wace, *The History of the Norman People: Wace's Roman de Rou*, trans. G. S. Burgess with notes by G. S. Burgess and E. van Houts (Woodbridge, 2004), pt III, pp. 158–9.

possessions, while leaving them free to contribute more, depending on their desire for rewards if the campaign was successful.[70] By doing this, William would have wanted to assess his strength and decide whether a campaign of such importance was feasible. William's army was, in short, an army of stipendiaries and fideles; although some among them owed military service to their suzerain, they were not following him overseas as a direct result of this obligation but rather as fellow adventurers seeking lands, booty and money.

Comparing William's Channel operation with that of his fellow countrymen in the south in 1081, Robert Guiscard had gathered according to Malaterra a 'poorly armed mob' ('imbecille vulgus'), while Anna Comnena describes these foot soldiers (Greeks and Lombards) as 'over age and under age, pitiable objects'.[71] It is most likely that these troops were ducal levies conscripted to serve overseas as a result of Guiscard calling for the *arrière-ban* – although no term of this kind appears in the primary sources – to be assembled for his expedition in 1081.[72] If the lords of the realm had no feudal obligation to serve in the Balkans, what would have changed their minds? We assume that a very similar pattern to the 1066 negotiations must have been followed.

Sadly, the chronicle material is silent about any formal or informal talks between the duke and his magnates and the promises which were almost certainly made, or about any further details concerning the rates of wages paid to the leading commanders of the Norman army. It is only Anna Comnena that writes about the long overdue wages owed by Bohemond to his vassal commanders after the siege of Larissa in the summer of 1083.[73] In order to make any expedition more lucrative for a greedy medieval nobleman, promises of a number of estates in the conquered regions would have been given.[74] It is only later, in the early twelfth century, that a fixed sum of money was promised to a lord or prince, paid either annually or quarterly, with the latter being obliged to recruit a fixed number of men and transport them to an agreed place at his own cost, as happened with Henry I and Count Robert of Flanders in 1101, an event from which the concept of contract service or money-fief (*fief-rente*) emerged.[75]

But were the quotas owed by the great magnates in pre-conquest Normandy to their lords definitively fixed or were they based on vague arrangements between the two parties? The prevalent view since the beginning of the twentieth century was Haskins's argument that fixed quotas of military service were imposed in ducal Normandy before 1050.[76] This notion, however, has been challenged by more recent

[70]   E. van Houts, 'The Ship List of William the Conqueror', *Anglo-Norman Studies* 10 (1987), 171–2.

[71]   Malaterra, III.24; *Alexiad*, I.14 (pp. 68–9); Sewter, p. 65; *Gesta*, IV.128–33 (p. 210).

[72]   This stands in contrast to the Anglo-Saxon fyrd that William took to Scotland in 1072 and into Maine the next year. See Hollister, *Norman England*, pp. 110–11 and 116–18.

[73]   *Alexiad*, V.7 (p. 256); Sewter, p. 173.

[74]   A useful comparison would be with William's promises to his troops in the campaign of 1069/70: Orderic Vitalis, II (pp. 234–5).

[75]   Hollister, *Norman England*, pp. 211–13; Mallett, 'Mercenaries', pp. 211–15.

[76]   Haskins, *Norman Institutions*, pp. 8–15; J. H. Round, *Feudal England* (London, 1895).

interpretations of the primary material, starting with an article written by Marjorie Chibnall[77] and works such as those by Yver, Bates and Douglas.[78] Douglas argues that the terminology of the Norman charters of this time is characteristic of an age in which feudal obligations have not yet been fully defined. In support of this there is an entire analysis of the use of the terms *feudum, beneficium, alodium* and *miles* which can be found in pre-conquest and post-conquest charters.[79] It is at least possible, according to Chibnall, that the services owed were either relics of older, Carolingian obligations, or the outcome of individual life contracts between different lords and their vassals, and that their gradual systematisation was the result of the intense military activity of the period of the Conquest.

From the information we can glean from our primary sources, it is highly likely that stipendiary household troops and mercenaries, under the command of Guiscard, Roger and other great magnates, played a prominent role in the territorial expansion in Apulia, Calabria and Sicily. In addition, military service from vassals and *fideles* was requested for large-scale operations like the siege of Bari and Palermo and the 1081 Illyrian campaign through institutions such as the *arrière-ban*, even if these are not clearly identified by our primary sources. A significant difference, however, from post-Conquest England of the period between 1070 and 1087 – when the entire country was claimed by William by right of conquest and lands were given to great magnates – was the precisely defined and rigidly enforced *servitium debitum*. In eleventh-century Norman Italy, just as in pre-conquest Normandy, the members of the powerful aristocratic families did not regard their holding of lands as a result of any ducal grant; thus, there was no specified number of knights that could be demanded for military service.

Well-established feudal quotas did not exist in southern Italy and Sicily before the compilation of the famous *Catalogus Baronum*. This was the register of the defence force levied during the years 1150 to 1168 by the Norman kings of Sicily in the mainland provinces of Apulia and Capua. It notes in detail the precise degree of each man's service owed to the king, which had been established in a series of provincial courts, and leaves no doubt about the difference between lands held *in demandio* and *in servitio*. The *Catalogus*, however, does not reflect the military situation of the Norman state before the 1150s. At that earlier time, the system that was imposed in Apulia and Calabria was not truly feudal in the sense that would have been recognised in Normandy, although it did contain elements imported from the country of origin of all these newcomers settling in the south. What evidence do we have about the introduction to Italy of military institutions found in pre-conquest Normandy and

[77] Chibnall, 'Military Service', pp. 66–77.
[78] J. Yver, 'Les premières institutions du duché de Normandie', in *I normanni e la loro espansione in Europa nell'alto medioevo 18–24 aprile 1968*, Settimane di studio del Centro italiano di studi sull'alto medioevo 16 (Spoleto, 1969), pp. 334–7 and 591.
[79] Chibnall, 'Military Service', 66–8; Douglas, *William the Conqueror*, pp. 96–8; Bates, *Normandy before 1066*, pp. 122–7 and 168–72.

in what way do these interfere with the continuity of previous administrative systems in the region?

We have already seen the main reasons behind the descent of the Normans to southern Italy and Sicily – reasons that varied from pilgrimage to social unrest in the duchy, and indeed how many of them were coming from other parts of France as well, places neighbouring Normandy like Brittany or Anjou. Coming from the same institutional background, we would expect that the Normans would introduce to Italy some elements of the administrative system of pre-conquest Normandy, as the creation of the Norman lordships in Italy had no precedent in Italian history. Indeed, it goes without saying that Italy was one of the few regions of the West that had not yet experienced the feudal institutions that were taking shape in other parts of Europe like France, England and Germany, but it would be this area that would attract youth gangs in search of land and booty.[80]

Even though the Norman conquest saw a brutal rupture with the previous administrative systems of the region, in the first decades of the Norman infiltration into Italy the elements of continuity did not entirely disappear. The Norman conquerors were only a small minority in a hostile land, which took many decades for them to subdue, and were too few to initiate a radical change in its society. Rather, it was their seigniorial institutions that had to be adapted to the existing society. In particular, as Falkenhausen has argued, their impact on the larger towns where the Lombard element was dominant, such as Amalfi, Bari, Benevento, Naples and Salerno, in which they rarely settled, was very limited.[81]

Continuity with the previous regime can be seen in the various aspects of government and, in particular, in the local officials of the Norman principalities and the land administration. The Normans were adopting into their service local dignitaries whose language skills were essential for the efficient running of the local administration, and their use was prevalent in all areas under Norman control. In Calabria and Sicily, Greek officials played a key role in every aspect of the local government and there are examples of important officials in Roger I's court to prove this point, such as the Greek 'protonotarius and chamberlain' Nicholas de Mesa and the *amiras* Eugenius, found in charters after 1092 and whose descendants were serving the Norman kings up to 1194. The same principle was also followed in Apulia and Capua, where local Lombard notaries were also employed by their Norman masters, and although they

---

[80]   Cahen, *Le régime féodal*, pp. 82–92; J. M. Martin, 'Éléments préféodaux dans les principautés de Bénévent et de Capoue (fin du VIIIe siècle – debut du XIe siècle) modalités de privatisation du pouvoir', in *Structures féodales et féodalisme dans l'Occident méditerranéen (Xe–XIIIe siècles)*, Collection de l'École française de Rome 44 (Rome, 1980), pp. 579–89.

[81]   Vera von Falkenhausen has contributed several valuable discussions on this issue. See, for example, *La dominazione bizantina nell'Italia meridionale dal IX all' XI secolo* (Bari, 1978); 'I Ceti dirigenti prenormanni al tempo della costituzione degli stati normanni nel Italia meridionale e in Sicilia', in *Forme di potere e struttura sociale in Italia nel Medioevo*, ed. G. Rossetti (Bologna, 1977), pp. 321–77, especially pp. 329 and 361.

disappear entirely following Jordan of Capua's government after the revolt of 1091, their pre-eminence in Apulia and Salerno carried on well into the twelfth century, where they remained indispensable for the management of the administration.[82]

The Norman conquest and the crumbling of Byzantine power in Italy left almost no remnants of the old Byzantine administrative organisation. The country moved abruptly towards the West, and the creation of Norman and French lordships, especially in areas formerly in Byzantine and Muslim hands (the interior of Apulia and Calabria, with the Capitanata in particular, present the greatest concentration of Transalpine settlers),[83] was strong for the larger part of the eleventh century. In William of Apulia's short description of the division of Apulian lands by the twelve Norman captains in 1042, a plan for future conquest rather than an actual division of the county, we understand that the Normans who had thus far infiltrated the country had been operating as different bands of mercenaries who now wished to reap the spoils of their success:

> They all met together and chose as their leaders twelve noblemen distinguished by their descent, good character and age. The others raised these to the rank of count: the name 'count' was given to them. They divided all the lands everywhere among themselves [which would be theirs] unless ill-fortune prevent them, proposing which places should belong to which leader and to whom tribute should be rendered.

The leaders of the Hauteville kin may have been the greatest of the landowners in southern Italy, while also retaining the control of major Apulian cities (Bari, Troia, Melfi etc.), but the Norman expansion in the south proceeded in an anarchic way. As William notes in his work, the normal title of a leader of a Norman band of the pre-monarchy period was *comes* (a count), ruling over conquered territories which were neither uniform nor homogeneous.[84] Cuozzo has made an important distinction between the pre-monarchy and the period that followed the establishment of a unified kingdom by Roger II; after 1130 the king reshuffled the territorial lordships and replaced the old dynasties, who were direct descendants of the small number of interconnected kin-groups that had developed by the time of Guiscard's death, with men of his confidence bound to the royal family.[85]

---

[82] V. von Falkenhausen, 'The Greek Presence in Norman Sicily: The Contribution of Archival Material in Greek', in *The Society of Norman Italy*, ed. G. A. Loud and A. Metcalfe (Leiden, 2002), pp. 253–88, at 259–69; Takayama, *Administration*, pp. 32–72; Takayama, 'The Great Administrative Officials of the Norman Kingdom of Sicily', *Papers of the British School at Rome* 58 (1990), 321–35; E. Jamison, 'The Norman Administration of Apulia and Capua: More Especially under Roger II and William I, 1127–1166', *Papers of the British School at Rome* 6 (1913), 383–481; Loud, *Robert Guiscard*, pp. 281–4.

[83] Martin, *La Pouille*, pp. 524–6.

[84] Martin provides an extensive study of all the comital families in Apulia and Calabria: *La Pouille*, pp. 719–43.

[85] E. Cuozzo, 'Quei maledetti normanni', in *Cavalieri e organizzazione militare nel Mezzogiorno normanno* (Naples, 1989), pp. 108–20; Loud, *Robert Guiscard*, pp. 246–60; D. Clementi, 'Definition of a Norman County in Apulia and Capua', in *Catalogus Baronum: Commentario*, ed. E. Cuozzo (Rome,

The counts were the leaders of a newly established social group that also appeared in Italy for the first time after the Norman infiltration – the *milites* or 'mounted knights' owing service. I have already examined the use of the terms *milites et stipendiarii* and *iuvenes* by Malaterra to identify the household and mercenary troops serving under Robert Guiscard and his brother in Italy and Sicily. Putting aside one not so convincing case in Cannes in 1054,[86] the term *miles* does not appear in the charters before the final years of the eleventh century, and more specifically in the towns of Gravina (1080),[87] Troia (1093) and Basilicata in the Capitanata region (1086).[88] In more central areas of mainland Apulia, the term is mentioned even later, as in the case of Bari (1107)[89] and Terlizzi (1123).[90]

In the pre-monarchy period, the term *milites* is often replaced by the terms *barons*, *boni homines* and *nobiles homines*. The term vassal (*vassallus*), in the sense of a person holding land that belongs to a lord to whom he owes loyalty, homage and military service also never appeared in Apulia in its traditional form. Rather, it was used to identify unfree or dependent peasants.[91] The term *fidelis*, however, appears in the charters relatively early: in 1077, three Normans are noted as the *fideles* of Peter, count of Trani, from whom the latter demanded the *consilium* the following year.[92] Finally, as Martin repeatedly notes, although the service owed by the Norman *milites* to their leaders in the regions of Apulia and Calabria during the eleventh century was, undoubtedly, of the feudo-vassal type, he points out that the first mention of the term *homage* (or *homagium, hominium*) only appears in the largely biographical work covering the reign of Roger II by Alexander of Telese. There, we read that the pope, after learning of Duke William's death, 'was invited by the citizens of Troia and on their request received their homage'.[93]

It can be argued that, as was the case with post-Conquest England, the systematisation of the services owed by vassals to their lords was to be a gradual procedure that extended beyond the Norman expansion in southern Italy and Sicily in the eleventh century. It was the intense military activity of the first half of the twelfth

1984), pp. 377–84; Martin, *La Pouille*, pp. 770–85.

[86]   *Codice diplomatico barese*, vol. VIII: *Le pergamene di Barletta, Archivio Capitolare (897–1285)*, ed. F. Nitti de Vito (Bari, 1914), p. 15.

[87]   *Regii Neapolitani Archivi Monumenta Edita ac Illustrata* (Naples, 1845–61), 6 vols., V, p. 443.

[88]   An unedited source cited by: Martin, *La Pouille*, p. 749, nn. 425 and 426.

[89]   *Codice diplomatico barese*, vol. V: *La leggenda della traslazione di S. Nicola di Bari. I Marinai*, ed. F. Nitti de Vito (Bari, 1902), p. 49.

[90]   *Codice diplomatico barese*, vol. III: *Le pergamene della Cattedrale di Terlizzi (971–1300)*, ed. F. Carabellese (Bari, 1899), p. 42.

[91]   Cahen, *Le régime féodal*, p. 42; Martin, *La Pouille*, p. 760.

[92]   *Codice diplomatico barese*, vol. IX: *I documenti storici di Corato (1046–1327)*, ed. G. Beltrani (Bari, 1923), 8; *Codex diplomaticus Cavensis*, ed. S. Leone and G. Vitolo (Badia di Cava, 1984–90), IX, p. 125.

[93]   Martin, *La Pouille*, pp. 756–7; Alexander of Telese, *The Deeds Done by King Roger of Sicily*, trans. with introduction by G. A. Loud, I.10 (unpublished translation accessed at http://www.medievalsicily.com/Docs/03_Norman_Conquest/Alexander%20of%20Telese.pdf).

century, a grave external threat from two empires and the firm leadership of a strong monarch that would lead to the creation of an organised system of military obligation in the Norman kingdom of Sicily and its epitome, the *quaternus magne expeditionis*, as the *Catalogus* should be referred to more accurately.[94]

Castles and castle service in Normandy, England and southern Italy

France and England

The period of Norman expansion in southern Italy coincides with a widespread phenomenon that had begun to appear in mainland Europe during that same period. The so-called *encastellation* of Europe took place between the tenth and the thirteenth centuries, and was of cardinal importance for the continent's political, social and military structure.[95] Even before the introduction of a new *castrum* in Europe, fortified sites had existed since the Roman times and before, such as the Anglo-Saxon *burg* and the Frankish *curtis* – administrative and economic centres enclosed by a large ditch, an earthen rampart and very often reinforced with a wooden palisade or a stone wall.[96] But around the end of the tenth century a new type of fortification emerged that would dominate Western Europe until the mid-twelfth century – the 'motte and bailey'.[97] This was significantly smaller – it covered an area of around 360 square yards, compared to 380 square yards of an Anglo-Saxon *burg* – and its main building material was earth and timber; it was seigniorial rather than communal, generally cheaper, involved much less work and could also be defended by just a few dozen soldiers. But it was clear that these originally earth-and-timber fortifications were inadequate to provide long-term security, mainly for maintenance reasons. Thus, more secure and impressive structures would come to replace them after the late eleventh century: what might be termed the 'keep and bailey' castles and the tower keeps, two types of fortifications where the main building material was stone.[98] There

---

[94] *Catalogus Baronum*, ed. E. Jamison (Rome, 1972); Cuozzo, 'Quei maledetti Normanni'; E. Cuozzo and J. M. Martin, *Cavalieri alla conquista del Sud. Studi sull'Italia normanna in memoria di Leon-Robert Menager* (Bari, 1998).

[95] Bartlett, *The Making of Europe*, pp. 65–70.

[96] For an introduction to the fortifications in England and the Continent before the late tenth century, see K. DeVries, *Medieval Military Technology* (North York, Ontario, 1992), pp. 174–201. For the Anglo-Saxon *burgh*, see R. Higham and P. Barker, *Timber Castles* (London, 1992), pp. 30–61; N. Pounds, *The Medieval Castle in England and Wales: A Social and Political History* (Cambridge, 1990), pp. 3–71; M. Strickland, 'Military Technology and Conquest: The Anomaly of Anglo-Saxon England', *Anglo-Norman Studies* 9 (1996), 369–82.

[97] J. R. Kenyon, *Medieval Fortifications* (London, 2005), pp. 3–39; R. Allen Brown, *English Medieval Castles* (London, 1954), pp. 23–34; M. Bouard, 'Quelques données françaises et normandes concernant le problème de l'origine des mottes', *Château Gaillard* 2 (1964), 19–26.

[98] Bartlett, *The Making of Europe*, pp. 68–9; Allen Brown, *English Medieval Castles*, pp. 35–7; DeVries, *Medieval Military Technology*, pp. 213–25; Kenyon, *Medieval Fortifications*, pp. 39–57.

is plenty of documentary evidence, however, to suggest that timber castles continued to be used until well into the fourteenth century.[99]

The numerous castles of the period can be divided into three main categories.[100] The first main division can be made between *a.* the royal and *b.* baronial castles, the former being in the exclusive disposition of the king and usually commanded by one of his entrusted officers or members of his family. The baronial castles can be also divided into two categories, those which the baron kept in his own hands and those which he entrusted, usually in the form of a fief, to one of his commanders or family members. Like regular land fiefs, the right to own a castle or castles was made hereditary by the end of the eleventh century.[101] Finally, there were *c.* the private castle-fortresses which were illegally erected and without the knowledge and consent of the local royal or baronial officer, usually by adventurers or powerful nobles.

Castle service was regularly demanded in areas of mainland Europe, mainly in northern France and Germany, and was a fundamental element of the tenurial obligations of a vassal to his lord long before its introduction into England after the Conquest. In France, it does not seem to have been demanded from an enfeoffed knight unless it was strictly mentioned in his contract, in a period when there was no clear distinction between host and castle service and they were both frequently joined in a single tenure.[102] In Germany, on the other hand, host and castle service were two distinct obligations, with the latter frequently owed by knights from poorer or inferior fiefs, which were specifically called *feoda castrensia*.[103] In pre-conquest Normandy, the castle guard was a typical obligation of the *vavassores* (rear-vassals or *milites minores – secundi*).[104]

The personnel responsible for manning a castle comprised either enfeoffed or household knights. The general idea was that service in the field was accompanied by some sort of castle service at a royal or baronial castle, although not in both.[105] There are great variations, however, in periods and areas of study and numerous examples where the castle service was accompanied with sharp reductions in the host service, or cases when the situation was reversed – where host duty was much heavier than the castle guard.[106] There are also cases where castle guard was demanded only in times of emergency, such as an invasion or rebellion. This is an element that proves the complexity and great variation of the castle service on the continent and in England, which was adapted to the needs of particular castles in specific regions.

---

[99] R. Highman, 'Timber Castles: A Reassessment', in *Anglo-Norman Castles*, ed. R. Liddiard (Woodbridge, 2003), p. 107.
[100] Contamine, *War in the Middle Ages*, pp. 45–6; Hollister, *Norman England*, pp. 136–66.
[101] Cahen, *Le régime féodal*, p. 74.
[102] Hollister, *Norman England*, p. 140.
[103] Guilhiermoz, *Essai*, pp. 298–309.
[104] Hollister, *Norman England*, pp. 129–35.
[105] Stanton, *English Feudalism*, pp. 206–9.
[106] Hollister, *Norman England*, pp. 142–4.

The length and frequency of service in a castle, and the number and type of men required to man it, also varied significantly. The main criteria for the selection of men for duty for a specific period of time were the strategic importance and size of the castle, its location (whether coastal or in the mainland, guarding an important bridge or crossroads) and the season of service.[107] Since evidence from the period of the Conquest is minimal, we can presume from evidence from the twelfth and thirteenth centuries that castle obligation was commonly performed in a rotating way, for forty days at the vassal's expense, with longer or shorter periods not being unusual. As with the host service, the payment of any castle-guard duty in excess of the usual forty days led to the tendency after the mid-twelfth century for all service to be paid. The process of commuting castle service was known and widespread at least by the reign of Henry I.[108]

In England, the greatest period of castle building relevant to the present study was during the reign of the Conqueror (1066–86), when fortifications were established throughout an undefended land and at great speed. The total number of known mottes and ring-works in England amounts to 625,[109] most of them concentrated in strategic areas like the Welsh marches, and the south-east and north-west of England.[110] A further thirty-six stone castles were built, out of which twenty-four were attached to major urban centres.[111] In brief, the Norman Conquest resulted in a radically new type of fortification: the *motte-and-bailey*; the introduction of the private castle as a new administrative system; and a dramatic increase in the number of fortified places.

This great increase in the number of castles built in England in the period following Hastings had to do with the Norman re-use and/or the modification of many pre-existing enclosures and fortified sites in England, either from the Anglo-Saxon or often the Roman periods – Pevensey (September 1066), Dover (October 1066) and Hastings (1066) are three typical examples.[112] What is striking is that during exactly the same period, meaning roughly between the 1060s and 1080s, the same phenomenon was taking place in southern Italy and Sicily. The intense military activity in the Italian peninsula in the previous two centuries, the rise of a great number of fortified rural communities in the late tenth century (*incastellamento*) and the long history of castle-

---

[107] Bradbury, *Medieval Siege*, pp. 74–5; J. Beeler, *Warfare in England, 1066–1189* (New York, 1996), pp. 303–4.
[108] Guilhiermoz, *Essai*, pp. 300–9; Hollister, *Norman England*, pp. 141–9, 154–61; Beeler, *Warfare in England*, pp. 300–5.
[109] Higham and Barker, *Timber Castles*, p. 47; Hollister, *Norman England*, p. 138, n. 1; R. Eales, 'Royal Power and Castles in Norman England', in *The Ideals and Practice of Medieval Knighthood III*, ed. C. Harper-Bill, R. Harvey (Woodbridge, 1990), pp. 54–63.
[110] In Shropshire, Herefordshire and Yorkshire alone mottes numbered 177: Higham and Barker, *Timber Castles*, p. 47; Beeler, *Warfare in England*, Appendices A and B, pp. 397–438.
[111] *The History of the King's Works*, ed. H. M. Colvin, 6 vols., HMSO (London, 1963–82), I, p. 22, fig. 5.
[112] Higham and Barker, *Timber Castles*, p. 59; B. English, 'Towns, Mottes and Ring-works of the Conquest', in *The Medieval Military Revolution*, ed. A. Ayton and J. L. Price (London, 1995), pp. 45–62; Pounds, *The Medieval Castle in England and Wales*, pp. 207–8.

building by the Byzantines and the Arabs can explain why the Italian Normans gladly settled for the occupation and/or modification of pre-existing fortified sites.

Turning to France, castles up to the late eleventh century were in the main primarily made of timber and stayed in use for a long period.[113] In Brittany, it is almost certain that the building of mottes was established around the beginning of the eleventh century, mostly in the southern marches, and went on through the twelfth century. It has also been suggested that the motte-and-bailey castle may be traced to Fulk Nerra of Anjou (987–1040) and his son Geoffrey Martel.[114] It is likely that in the southern marches of his county, on the borders with Maine and Anjou, William learned to appreciate the significance of these earth-and-timber castles. Another theory suggests that the castle has a Scandinavian origin, being the Frankish military response of the areas in the Loire and the Seine to the Viking raids.[115] Whatever the case, it is certain that the knowledge of building motte-and-bailey castles spread out from northern France to England, Italy and Sicily in the eleventh century.

In pre-conquest Normandy the construction of new fortifications, adding to the existing Carolingian examples, began in the early years of Richard II's reign (996–1026). Especially during the civil wars in Normandy in the 1030s to 1050s, a period which saw the rise of a new Norman aristocracy, the number of ducal or baronial castles rose rapidly, in striking contrast to their small numbers before the death of Robert I (1035). By the 1020s powerful ducal castles had been built in strategic locations in the duchy, like those of Mortain, Brionne-sur-Risle, Fécamp, St Lo, Ivry, Evreux, Eu and Exmes. All of these sites can be traced back to the late ninth century, while some of them played a significant defensive role not only during the Carolingian period but as early as the late Roman period.[116] Richard II added Tillières-sur-Avre, while Breteuil, Ambrières and Neufmarche were established by William II in this developing frontier barrier.[117] This list can be supplemented with numerous motte-and-bailey castles – twenty-four in total, either ducal or baronial – built in Normandy before 1066 and used in the civil conflicts of the period and in the wars against the count of Anjou.[118]

Apulia, Calabria and Sicily

Historians have identified two types of fortifications in Byzantine Apulia: the enclosed cities (castra, civitates) and a number of smaller fortified sites (castellia) –

[113]   Higham and Barker, Timber Castles, p. 94.
[114]   J. Le Patourel, The Norman Empire (Oxford, 1976), p. 304; B. Bachrach, 'Fortifications and Military Tactics: Fulk Nerra's Strongholds circa 1000', Technology and Culture 20 (1979), 531–49; B. Bachrach, 'The Angevin Strategy of Castle Building in the Reign of Fulk Nerra, 987–1040', American Historical Review 88 (1983), 171–207.
[115]   J. Bradbury, The Medieval Siege (Woodbridge, 1992), pp. 50–1.
[116]   J. M. Yver, 'Les châteaux forts en Normandie jusqu'au milieu du XIIe siècle', Bulletin de la Société des antiquaires de Normandie 53 (1955), 33–6 and 52–8.
[117]   Bates, Normandy before 1066, p. 57.
[118]   Higham and Barker, Timber Castles, p. 102; Yver, 'Les châteaux forts', pp. 52–9.

words which should not be translated as *castle* (the usual term for a castle in southern Italy was *palatium* and *rocca*) but rather as fortified inhabited centres.[119] There are also two periods when renovations of old Roman and Lombard fortifications and the new building of *castra* and *castellia* took place: at the end of the ninth century after the re-establishment of Byzantine power in the province, and at the beginning of the eleventh century during the empire's expansion north into the Capitanata.[120] In fact, the building of city-walls and fortifications (*kastroktisia*) was a public chore throughout the empire's provinces well into the eleventh century. The most striking element of Byzantine society in Longobardia, however, was the contradiction between the enclosed urban societies of the coastal areas and the undefended rural population of the mainland.[121]

The *castrum* in Byzantine Longobardia can be described briefly as a large city enclosed by walls, which formed the administrative centre and the seat of the bishop. Ancient cities that evolved gradually into sizeable and important administrative centres were Bari, Trani, Taranto, Montescaglioso, Cannae and Brindisi.[122] These cities, however, did not possess any more complex defensive fortifications than the ordinary stone city walls, which were usually two-fold (*muricinum, antemurale*), a ditch, flanking towers in the city's gates and possibly extra wall defences at the city's port.[123] In this fortified environment the *castra* were supplemented by the *castellia*, secondary smaller *castra* that were situated either in a strategic area or usually in the surroundings of a major fortified city, like the small towns of Troia, Fiorentino, Montecorvino, Dragonara, Civitate and Melfi.[124] All of these appear to have been foundations by the Byzantine catepan Basil Boiannes, built after the Byzantine victory at Cannae in 1018, which soon grew to become seats of bishoprics. In the year following the battle at Cannae, a Norman garrison was permanently established at the strong strategic fortress of Troia under Byzantine pay.[125]

During the period of Norman expansion in Apulia (1040s to 1070s), the first action taken by the newcomers after taking over a fortified site was to build an inner fortification in the town and man it with a Norman garrison, as in the cases of Troia (from 1080), Bari (from 1075), Melfi, Monte St-Angelo, Candela, Fiorentino and

---

[119]   von Falkenhausen, *La dominazione*, pp. 148–9; Martin, *La Pouille*, pp. 258–70.
[120]   Martin, *La Pouille*, p. 261.
[121]   Martin, *La Pouille*, pp. 268–70.
[122]   J. M. Martin, 'Modalités de l'"incastellamento" et typologie castrale en Italie méridionale (Xe–XIIe siècles)', in *Castelli. Storia e archeologia. Relazioni e comunicazioni al Convegno di Cuneo (1981)*, ed. R. Comba and A. A. Settia (Turin, 1984), pp. 96–8; *La Pouille*, pp. 258–66.
[123]   Martin, 'Modalités', p. 96.
[124]   Amatus, II.19; *Gesta*, I.245–53 (p. 112); Malaterra, I.9; Taviani-Carozzi, *La terreur du monde*, p. 170. For the site and plans of the town of Montecorvino: J. M. Martin and G. Noyé, 'La cité de Montecorvino et sa cathédrale', *Mélanges de l'École française de Rome – Moyen Âge – Temps modernes* 114 (1982), 513–49.
[125]   Romuald of Salerno, *Chronicon*, s.a. 1022; F. Trinchera, *Syllabus Graecarum Membranarum* (Naples, 1865), no. 18.

Montecorvino.[126] In addition, throughout the second half of the eleventh century the vast open *civitates* of the Byzantine period were enclosed and the smaller fortified sites (*castellia*) were also modified, probably by strengthening the walls and building a small château or a *donjon*, like the seven *castellia* surrounding Bari.[127] The contrast, however, between the building activity in the coastal areas close to Bari, Trani or Brindisi and the rest of the areas in the Apulian periphery, like the sensitive border areas with the Capitanata and the Lombard principalities, is striking, exactly as it was in the Welsh marches during William I's reign.[128] In general, there was no significant castle-building activity in the coastal areas, at least in the second half of the eleventh century, but in the same period the building of *castellia* in the Apulian periphery multiplied.[129]

What the Normans found in Calabria after 1056 was a very different situation from what they were about to face a few years later in Sicily.[130] Of the most significant ports of Calabria, Reggio, Cariati and Rossano, only the first was heavily fortified as the capital of Calabria, and in Rossano the Normans built a castle only in 1072.[131] Other major fortified cities in the north of the Val di Crati, those of Bisignano, Martirano and Cosenza were already paying tribute to Guiscard by 1056,[132] the cities of Nicastro and Maida were taken in 1057,[133] and others like Oppido,[134] St Martino,[135] Mileto, Gerace and Squillace between 1058 and 1059.[136] Sadly, the chroniclers provide us with no adequate details of their size, and Malaterra is vague or even silent when it comes to details about any renovations that might have taken place at these sites after the arrival of the Normans. Also, the prevailing idea amongst historians is that the motte-and-bailey type of fortification became common in mainland Italy only at the end of the eleventh century, when castle-building had spread more widely in a society affected by civil strife, although a small number of fortified sites built by wood can be seen as early as the late 1040s.[137]

---

[126] Martin, *La Pouille*, pp. 272–7; Martin, 'Modalités', p. 99; F. Nitti, *Le pergamene di S. Nicola di Bari, periodo normanno (1075–1194)* (Bari, 1968), n. 1 (1075).

[127] Martin, 'Modalités', p. 99, n. 88; *La Pouille*, pp. 277–82.

[128] Higham and Barker, *Timber Castles*, p. 46; Martin, *La Pouille*, pp. 278–82.

[129] Martin, 'Modalités', p. 99.

[130] For the Calabrian fortifications, see A. Bruschi and C. Miarelli-Mariani, *Architettura sveva nell'Italia meridionale* (Prato, 1975); J. M. Pesez and G. Noyé, 'Archéologie normande en Italie méridionale et en Sicile', in *Les mondes normands (VIIe–XIIe siècles), Actes du IIe congrès international d'archéologie médiévale (Caen, 1978)* (Tours, 1990), pp. 155–69; G. Noyé, 'Quelque données sur les techniques de construction en Italie centro-méridionale, Xe–XIIe siècles', in *Artistes, artisans et production artistique au Moyen Age*, ed. X. Barral (Rennes, 1983), pp. 275–306.

[131] Malaterra, III.1.

[132] Malaterra, I.17.

[133] Malaterra, I.18.

[134] Malaterra, I.32.

[135] Malaterra, I.32 and II.27.

[136] Malaterra, I.18, 36, 37 and II.23, 24.

[137] Higham and Barker, *Timber Castles*, pp. 78–9.

The two fortresses that were first established in Calabria by Guiscard's forces were Scribla and St Marco Argentano. Both were built in the strategically important Val di Crati during the first years following Guiscard's arrival in Italy (1047–8).[138] St Marco Argentano was built of timber,[139] not surprisingly if we consider Guiscard's economic status at the time and the abundance of timber in that particular area of Calabria. These first traces of earth-and-timber fortifications may ressemble the Norman motte-and-bailey type, but as Malaterra notes, the Normans eventually abandoned timber in favour of stone, as in Cosenza in 1091.[140] Scribla, on the other hand, should be considered one of the most distinctive examples of Norman castle-building activity in Italy, built in a highly strategic place and, possibly, on a previous Byzantine defensive site.[141] Constructed in the mid-eleventh century, it is one of the earliest castles built by the Normans in Italy, and it bears strong similarities to the castles of that period in Normandy and France. The castle was surrounded by a ditch and a double stone wall, and it is believed to have been reinforced by flanking towers, although the exact dating can be very difficult.[142] The stone tower (*donjon*) of Scribla was square-based and it dominated the land-platform on the west side of the castle. It had four levels and served both as a defensive site and a residential place.

Although Scribla has suffered much destruction since the first period of the Norman occupation of the site, historians and archaeologists are able to distinguish the Norman characteristics of that first period and compare them to the various influential elements imported from Sicily during the second period of the occupation of the site after 1064. As in Sicily, but to a much lesser degree, the Normans were able to re-use the existing Byzantine fortifications or modify them with wooden superstructures. Archaeological evidence, however, indicates that motte-and-bailey type of fortifications became widespread in Calabria only at the end of the eleventh century. As for the typical sample of early Italian-Norman castle architecture, a reconstructed flanking tower and *donjon*, along with traces of a primitive ditch and a stone curtain wall, can be found in Scribla.

What the Normans found in Sicily after the 1060s, in terms of influence from other cultures, was distinct from what they had dealt with so far in Normandy and mainland Italy.[143] Two completely different civilisations, the Byzantine and the Arab,

---

[138]   A. M. Flambard-Hericher, 'Un instrument de la conquête et du pouvoir: les châteaux normands de Calabre. L'exemple de Scribla', in *Les Normands en Mediterranée aux XIe–XIIe siècles*, ed. P. Bouet, F. Neveux (Caen, 2001), p. 95.

[139]   Amatus, III.7.

[140]   Malaterra, IV.17.

[141]   Flambard-Hericher, 'Instrument', p. 99; G. Noyé, 'Problèmes posés par l'identification et l'étude des fosses-silos sur un site d'Italie méridionale', *Archaeologia medievale* 8 (1981), 421–38.

[142]   Flambard-Hericher, 'Instrument', pp. 100–1 and 104.

[143]   For the Sicilian fortifications, see H. Bresc, 'Terre e castelli: le fortificazioni nella Sicilia araba e normanna', in *Castelli. Storia e archaeologia*, pp. 73–87; F. Maurici, *Castelli medievali in Sicilia. Dai bizantini ai normanni* (Palermo, 1992).

had left their mark in that part of the Mediterranean, both influenced by each other and about to influence the Normans as well. Historians and archaeologists have come across three main types of fortified sites in Sicily between the ninth and the eleventh centuries.[144] First, there were the highly crowded and heavily fortified ports, which also were the most important commercial centres of the island, such as Palermo and Messina, or smaller ones such as Termini, Cefalu, Girgenti and Syracuse. There were also the well-defended cities situated in closed valleys, and if coastal, usually built at a certain distance from the coast for security reasons,[145] like Trapani, Mazara and Rametta. Third come the *castra*, built in isolated and naturally defended locations, like Castrogiovanni, which dominated a strategic crossroads of the island from east to west.

Among this last type, the *castra*, we find a great number of highly fortified Byzantine sites, which had to be overcome by the Arabs during their expansion and settlement in Sicily throughout the ninth century. And it was probably these Byzantine *castra* that served as a model for future Arab castle-building on the island. The list is filled with names, either Greek/Latin or Arabic, like Castronuovo (831), Caltabellotta and Platani (840), Ragusa (848), Caltavuturo (852), Butera (854), Qasr al-Harir (857), Castrogiovanni (859), Noto (864) and Syracuse (878), to mention but a few.[146] Around 990, the Arab geographer Muqaddasi listed some thirty names of fortified places, either newly built or reoccupied, while the number of fortified sites rose to around ninety after the *incastellamento* of the second half of the tenth century.[147]

Because of the insufficient numbers of troops during the Sicilian expansion and to prevent any rebellious activities, the Normans inevitably demolished a number of smaller *castra*, although the exact figure would be impossible to estimate. They were, however, also quick to seize and modify either old and abandoned or newly conquered ones, mostly by building overstructures and/or inner fortifications, something that proves once more their ability to adapt to new environments. Consequently, the building activities of the Normans increased drastically in the 1060s to 1070s in places like Messina (1061),[148] St Marco di Alunsio (1061),[149] Troina (1062),[150] Petralia (1066),[151] Palermo (1071),[152] Mazara and Paterno (1072),[153] Mount Calascibetta

---

[144]   H. Bresc, 'Les normands constructeurs des châteaux', in *Les Normands en Mediterranée aux XIe–XIIe siècles*, pp. 64–5; 'Terre e castelli', pp. 73–4 and 79.

[145]   Muslim pirate activities had pushed the inhabitants of Calabria further inland around the 960s.

[146]   In parentheses are the dates when these *castra* were captured by the Arabs: Maurici, *Castelli*, p. 44; Bresc, 'Terre e castelli', p. 73.

[147]   Bresc, 'Terre e castelli', pp. 74–5 and 78; Bresc, 'Les normands constructeurs des châteaux', pp. 65–6.

[148]   Malaterra, II.13.

[149]   Malaterra, II.17.

[150]   Malaterra, II.20.

[151]   Malaterra, II.38.

[152]   Malaterra, II.45; *Gesta*, III.337–9 (p. 182).

[153]   Malaterra, III.1.

(1074),[154] Trapani and Castronuovo (1077).[155] In the Val di Mazara in the west we find twelve further names of *castra*, either conquered or newly constructed, which were given to *milites* by Roger,[156] while in 1086 Malaterra writes about eleven *castra* that surrendered to the count after the submission of Agrigento.[157]

As a consequence of the repeated use of many fortified sites over the centuries, archaeologists cannot confirm the building of any mottes on the island of Sicily.[158] What they can observe, however, for eleventh-century Sicily is the lack of need for earth and timber in the fortifications, although this was still probably used in superstructures, and the turn to stone instead.[159] Apart from the variety of new features that the Normans introduced in their Sicilian architecture, such as different kinds of ramparts,[160] ditches – which were rarely found in Byzantine fortifications – or baileys,[161] the Normans were greatly influenced by two categories of *castra* from previous historical periods; the Muslim palace of Calathamet, built during the reign of the Fatimid Caliph Al-Hakim (996–1020) in the predominantly Muslim Val di Mazara, and the Byzantine *castrum* in Caronia, in the north-west of the Christian Val Demone.[162]

The originality or the success of the Norman administration in Sicily, which was based on Western standards and was enriched by Byzantine and Arab elements, was not a direct result of Norman ingenuity but rather of their ability to adapt to the new environment and combine the existing knowledge that they had carried from France with what they found in Sicily for their interest and needs. An additional proof of this is the establishment of some sort of a technical school, or more precisely a corps of *studiosi magistrati*, who were brought to Messina 'from all around' in 1082: a clear sign of the Norman desire to take advantage of inherited knowledge.[163]

---

[154] Malaterra, III.7.

[155] Malaterra, III.11 and 12.

[156] Bresc, 'Les normands constructeurs des châteaux', p. 69; Taviani-Carozzi, *La terreur du monde*, pp. 382–3.

[157] Malaterra, IV.5.

[158] Bresc, 'Les normands constructeurs des châteaux', p. 71.

[159] At Trapani (1077): 'urbem [. . .] castro et caeteris munitionibus ordinat, militibus et iis, quae necessaria erat, munit, turribus et propugnaculis undique uallans', Malaterra, III.11; at Agrigento (1086): 'urbem itaque pro uelle suo ordinans, castello firmissimo munit, uallo girat, turribus et propugnaculis ad defensionem aptat', Malaterra, IV.5; at Petralia (1066): 'turribus et propugnaculis extra portam accuratissime firmavit', Malaterra II.38; Bresc puts the *propugnaculis* of Petralia into a different category, see Bresc, 'Les normands constructeurs des châteaux', p. 72.

[160] See the comparison of Messina, Palermo and Petralia: Maurici, *Castelli*, p. 162; Bresc, 'Les normands constructeurs des châteaux', p. 72.

[161] See the comparison of Monte San Giuliano and Castellammare del Golfo: Maurici, *Castelli*, p. 162; Bresc, 'Les normands constructeurs des châteaux', p. 72.

[162] Bresc, 'Les normands constructeurs des châteaux', pp. 72–5; J. M. Pesez and J. M. Poisson, 'Le château du castrum sicilien de Calathamet (XIIe siècle)', in *Castelli. Storia e archeologia*, pp. 63–72.

[163] 'Cui operi studiosos magistratus, qui operariis praeessent, statuit': Malaterra, III.32.

3

The Byzantine Army of the
Tenth and Eleventh Centuries

The Byzantine army constantly evolved throughout its history. A worthy successor to the vast mechanism set up by the Romans, its most remarkable trait was the degree of adaptability that characterised it as an institution, along with the open-minded attitude of its officers and the tactics they applied in the battlefield. Numerous military manuals, such as Maurice's *Strategikon*, Leo VI's *Taktika*, the *Praecepta Militaria* of Nicephorus Phocas, the *Taktika* of Nicephorus Uranus and the *Strategikon* of Cecaumenus, offer us a thorough look into the way Byzantine officers thought and how they faced their enemies in each operational theatre. They had two distinct but mutually supportive mechanisms, which had been established since the eighth century: the *themata*, armies which were defensive in nature and whose main objective was to intercept and harass any invading army, and the *tagmata*, professional units trained to deliver the final blow to the enemy on pitched battle.

The army that Alexius Comnenus deployed against the Normans in 1108 was different in both structure and make-up from that which Romanus IV Diogenes had gathered for his Turkish campaigns that culminated in the battle of Manzikert in 1071. The old thematic and tagmatic units (indigenous troops that formed the backbone of the army's structure for centuries) were largely replaced by mercenaries.[1] Alexius Comnenus depended on the hiring of large bodies of paid troops of any ethnic background for long-term military service, like the Varangian Guard (largely comprised of Anglo-Saxons after 1081), the German Nemitzi and several Frankish regiments. There were also units from neighbouring client or allied states that were hired for short-term periods, usually for a number of campaigns or just for a single campaigning season, like the Seljuks of Nicaea, the Pechenegs, the Cumans and the Venetians. Finally, there were some indigenous troops, organised into battalions that

---

[1] For reasons that will be mentioned but not analysed in depth here, as this goes beyond the focus of this study.

resembled the old tagmatic structure and bearing the name of their place of origin, such as the Macedonians, the Thessalians and the Thracians, who constituted a large part of Alexius' armies in 1081 and 1108.

The establishment and development of the themata from the Heraclian to the Macedonian dynasties (610–1025)

By the term *themata* historians have identified the peculiar provincial organisation, prompted by the conditions of the time, whose distinguishing feature was the concentration of both military and civil authority in the hands of the military governor (*strategos* – general) of each province.[2] *Themata* were introduced in Asia Minor during the years of Constans II (641–68), successor of the great Heraclius (610–41),[3] as a response to the Slavic and Persian threat at the time. *Thema* derives from the ancient Greek verb *tithemi*, which means to place, and it originally denoted the military formations that were stationed in the newly created provinces. It was only later that it came to mean the actual province where the troops were stationed. and, as Haldon has argued, the older civil *eparkhai* or provinces continued to exist well into the eighth century, while some significant aspects of the late Roman civil administrative apparatus (the praetorian prefect, *dioiketes*) survived until the early ninth century.[4]

The individual parts of this defensive mechanism consisted of the native soldiers (*stratiotai*) who were settled in the provinces as farmer-soldiers and were entered in the military registers as owing hereditary military service to the state in exchange for lands from the imperial demesne.[5] They were attached to the lands surrounding a specific fort,

---

[2]   A. A. Vasiliev, *History of the Byzantine Empire*, 2 vols. (Madison, 1928), I, p. 275; J. Haldon, *Byzantium in the Seventh Century: The Transformation of a Culture*, 2nd edn (Cambridge, 1997), p. 208. Haldon's revision of the abovementioned terminology to 'where the civil administration was subordinated to military priorities and interests' is more correct: J. Haldon, 'Military Service, Military Lands, and the Status of the Soldiers: Current Problems and Interpretations', *Dumbarton Oaks Papers* 47 (1993), 11.

[3]   Treadgold traces the period of the introduction of the *themata* in the East in the years 659–62: W. Treadgold, *Byzantium and its Army, 284–1081* (Stanford, 1995), pp. 24–6; Haldon, 'Military Service', pp. 3–7.

[4]   H. Ahrweiler, 'Recherches sur l'administration de l'empire byzantin aux IXe–XIe siècles', *Bulletin de correspondance hellénique* 84 (1969), 1–109; reprinted in: *Études sur les structures administratives et sociales de Byzance* (London, 1971); Haldon, *Byzantium in the Seventh Century*, pp. 215–32. See also W. E. Kaegi, Jr, 'Changes in Military Organization and Daily Life on the Eastern Frontier', in Η καθημερινή ζωή στο Βυζάντιο (Athens, 1989), pp. 507–21.

[5]   W. Treadgold, 'The Military Lands and the Imperial Estates in the Middle Byzantine Empire', *Harvard Ukrainian Studies* 7 (1983), 619–31; M. F. Hendy, *Studies in the Byzantine Monetary Economy, c. 300–1450* (Cambridge, 1985), pp. 634–40. Haldon has argued that there was no connection between land and military service and that the provision of soldiers with land (as opposed to the acquisition by soldiers of land through other means) can at best have been a slow and partial process: Haldon, 'Military Service', pp. 18–29.

a military camp or an important town, and these lands provided the economic means for the maintenance of themselves, their families and their military equipment. It was the responsibility of the local *strategos* and his subordinates to select, from the total of those registered, those who were actually capable of carrying out their duties. The fundamental principle was that these military lands would eventually become inalienable and remain in the possession of the same family as hereditary (*stratiotikos oikos*).[6]

The soldiers were recruited by the *strategos* of the *thema* and were obliged to report for duty when their officers sent for them, either for defensive or offensive campaigns, or for regular training.[7] As far as the primary sources let on, there were no geographic limitations concerning their service or a time limit of any kind. The soldiers received a fixed pay (*rhoga*) of a modest size, delivered on a four-yearly rotational cycle (described by Constantine VII in the tenth century as 'the old system')[8] which varied, of course, throughout the centuries and with regards to the categories of soldiers (for example, the tagmatic units were paid on a monthly basis for their food and equipment, as well as fodder for their animals).[9] The troops were also supported with the *annonae* (rations) and *capitus*, sources in kind or converted into a cash equivalent (according to a fixed tarif), and the cash rewards issued on the occasion of an imperial accession and every fifth year thereafter. They also enjoyed exemption from all but the standard fiscal burdens, the *synone* (land tax) and the *kapnikon* (tax on household property).[10]

The *strateia* (military service) for the soldier was hereditary and personal (it was attached to an individual and his family),[11] and by the early tenth century it was perceived as attached to the land, as well as to the person registered on the military rolls as its holder. The most significant difference from the Western European knights was the absence of the *homage* and the *investiture* binding the two parts together. The Western knight was indeed of a much higher status than a Byzantine thematic soldier, who resembled more closely the old Roman legionary.

[6]   Ahrweiler, 'Recherches', pp. 11–12.

[7]   For examples of forced conscription: Ahrweiler, 'Recherches', 13; Haldon, *Warfare, State and Society*, p. 120. For their military training: E. McGeer, *Sowing the Dragon's Teeth: Byzantine Warfare in the Tenth Century* (Washington, DC, 1995), pp. 217–22.

[8]   *De Cerimoniis*, CSHB, pp. 493–4.

[9]   Treadgold, *Byzantium and its Army*, pp. 118–57; W. Treadgold, *The Byzantine Revival: 780–842* (Stanford, 1988), pp. 349–51; Haldon, *Warfare, State and Society*, pp. 126–8; Haldon, *Byzantium in the Seventh Century*, pp. 224–6; N. Oikonomides, 'Middle-Byzantine Provincial Recruits: Salary and Armament', in *Byzantine Warfare*, ed. J. Haldon (Aldershot, 2007), pp. 151–66.

[10]   Ahrweiler, 'Recherches', pp. 6–8; Haldon, *Byzantium in the Seventh Century*, pp. 142–6.

[11]   J. Haldon, *Recruitment and Conscription in the Byzantine Army c. 550–950: A Study of the Origins of the Stratiotika Ktemata* (Vienna, 1979), pp. 47–58. Gorecki has argued that the holder of a strateia was, in theory at least, still the one who carried out the military service, although force of circumstance had already by the later ninth century allowed for a replacement or representative of the registered stratiotes to carry out the actual soldiering (*strateuomenoi* in contrast to the *stratiotai*): D. Gorecki, 'The Strateia of Constantine VII: The Legal Status, Administration, and Historical Background', *Byzantinische Zeitschrift* 82 (1989), 157–76.

For the first century and a half, the *themata* were used only in Asia Minor, but as the empire expanded throughout the ninth century, new *themata* were created, extending the power of the emperor from Antioch to the Danube and Calabria in Italy. In addition, Emperor Theophilus (829–42) introduced the *kleisourai* around 840; these were military districts established to guard the mountain passes of the Taurus Mountains in Cilicia against the Arabs, usually dominated by a small fortress.[12] John I (969–76) united the thirty small frontier *themata* of Asia Minor into three *ducates* (Chaldea, Mesopotamia, Antioch), with each duke's authority being superior to the local generals. With this new command structure John wished to create a protective curtain in the sensitive frontier zones of the empire in East and West. This move, however, seriously affected the in-depth defensive capabilities of the empire in the frontiers, prompting strategy to become more and more localised and able to respond to threats of equal status rather than large field armies.

Finally, the number of men in each *thema* is difficult to determine. As can be expected, the numbers varied significantly throughout the centuries but the trend towards round and even numbers was to be found in all the *themata* of the empire, at least in theory.[13] Thus, there were the small 800-strong *cleisurae* in the east, the 1,000-strong smaller *themata* such as Nicopolis and Cephalonia, the 2,000-strong *themata* such as Sicily and Hellas and the 10,000-strong Thracesian *thema*.[14]

The professional units of the tagmata

Constantine V's reign (741–75) is marked by one of the greatest military innovations in the Byzantine army's history, the introduction of the *tagmata* or regiments. The fundamental distinction between the old thematic and the new tagmatic units was that the members of the *themata* were part-time soldiers – this qualification is no reflection on their fighting abilities, merely indicating that they represented a kind of peasant militia scattered in large numbers across the Byzantine countryside. The soldiers of the *tagmata*, however, were professional, highly trained, experienced and very well equipped and paid. As opposed to their thematic counterparts, they were recruited by the *themata* close to the capital and equipped by the state.[15]

Constantine established six *tagmata*, the three most senior of which were the cavalry regiments named Scholae, Excubitores[16] and the Watch (Vigla); the first

---

[12] Treadgold, *Byzantium and its Army*, pp. 32 and 69. Haldon believes that the *cleisurae* were established as early as the reign of Heraclius: Haldon, *Warfare, State and Society*, p. 114.

[13] Treadgold, 'Standardized Numbers', pp. 1–14; Treadgold, 'Inexact Numbers', pp. 57–61.

[14] Treadgold, *Byzantium and its Army*, pp. 43–86; Haldon, *Warfare, State and Society*, pp. 67–106.

[15] Treadgold, *Byzantium and its Army*, pp. 179–86; J. Haldon, 'The Organisation and Support of an Expeditionary Force: Manpower and Logistics in the Middle Byzantine Period', in *Byzantium at War (9th–12th Century)*, ed. K. Oikonomides (Athens, 1997), pp. 111–51.

[16] The term *excubitores* is used by the sources up to 772, while the term *excubitae* starts from 813, with the exception of some Lives of Saints of the seventh century, such as that of St Theodore of Sykeon:

two derived from the guard units of the late Roman emperors, while the Vigla was a contraction of the Vigiles of Rome.[17] Nicephorus I (802–11) set up a fourth cavalry *tagma*, named Hicanati, while John I founded the cavalry *tagma* of the Athanatoi (Immortals) in the early years of his reign. The three junior *tagmata* were infantry regiments, with the Numera and Walls serving as garrison troops for the capital, while the Optimates manned the baggage train on a campaign. The commander of each *tagma* was called *domesticus* and was assisted by a *topoteretes*, with the *domesticus* of the Scholae appearing as the commander-in-chief of the imperial army when the emperor was not leading the campaign.

During the period of the Epigoni, but mainly on the second half of the eleventh century, additional *tagmata* were created, which are mentioned by contemporary chroniclers: the *homoethneis*, the *stratelatai*, the *hesperioi arithmoi*, the *megathymoi* and the *arkhontopouloi*, probably 2,000-strong and stationed in the capital. These *tagmata* had already started to replace the original *tagmata* after the defeat at Manzikert, a period for which historians find fewer and fewer references to them in the contemporary chronicles.[18]

Before the mid-tenth century the *tagmata* were stationed in the vicinity of the capital. It was during the reign of Romanus II (959–63) that they were divided into eastern and western commands. This decision was taken after many decades of experience of the western and eastern armies fighting different enemies in the Balkans and Asia Minor respectively. Detachments of the *tagmata*, however, were also sent to certain key frontier regions, like Macedonia and Illyria in the Balkans or the Anatolian and Armenian regions in Asia Minor; a clear sign of the empire's offensive policy. These tagmatic sub-units formed an autonomous organisation inside the thematic structure and they were under the command of the *strategos* only during campaigning periods. Before Romanus' reforms, the three cavalry *tagmata* had 4,000 troops each and the three infantry *tagmata* had 2,000 men each, while following the reforms the numbers of the cavalrymen in the Scholae and the Excubitores increased by 2,000; each *domesticus* of the east and west having 3,000 at his disposal. The Hicanati, the Watch and the Immortals retained their total of 4,000 troops each.[19]

The basic structural unit of both the thematic and tagmatic armies was the *bandum* of 200 men, retaining its numbers at least until the mid-tenth century.[20] These *banda* could easily be combined to form larger units, such as the 1,000-men *drungus* (or taxiarchy, commanded by a *drungarius* or taxiarch), which was also the minimum number of troops that each *thema* had, and the 4,000-men *turma* led by a *turmarch* (*tourmarkhes*). Although these numbers kept changing throughout the centuries, the

---

Oxford Dictionary of Byzantium, II, pp. 646–7.

[17]   Haldon, *Warfare, State and Society*, p. 68.

[18]   Ahrweiler, 'Recherches', pp. 28–9.

[19]   Treadgold, *Byzantium and its Army*, pp. 64–86 and 113–15.

[20]   Treadgold, *Byzantium and its Army*, pp. 93–117; W. Treadgold, 'The Army in the Works of Constantine Porphyrogenitus', *Rivista di studi bizantini e neoellinici* 29 (1992), 77–162.

basic principle of keeping the structural units of the army to round numbers remained the same. Another important structural unit, set up by Leo VI in an effort to expand the cavalry, was the office called *tribune*, commanding fifty men. This may seem of little importance, but if we read the *Praecepta Militaria* of Emperor Nicephorus II, we will notice the use of the cavalry *bandum*, denoting a fifty-man unit as part of a 200-man *bandum*, in a period when the emperor had raised the ratio between cavalry and infantry from a fifth to a quarter.[21]

The landed aristocracy and the decline of the themata

During Leo VI's reign (886–912), the landed aristocracy of the provinces, which had emerged in Asia Minor around the mid-eighth century, gathered immense power in its hands. Well before the reign of Leo, emperors had placed those close to them in key positions of command over the army and had made them into state officials. The fact that small-holders, the backbone of the thematic organisation of the empire, were rapidly being transformed into dependants (*paroikoi*)[22] of the landed aristocracy can be interpreted as an attempt to acquire capital in landed property independently of the central government. Up to that period, imperial donations were a very significant source of aristocratic wealth and social status in each generation of *eugeneis*, with the latter inevitably willing to break this chain of dependence on the emperor.[23] This was first recognised as an immediate threat by Romanus I Lecapenus (920–44) and historians have identified four distinct periods of crisis associated with the changing pattern of the legislation targeting the *dynatoi*.[24] Legislative documents (*nearai*) represented a series of imperial responses to the changing political and economic circumstances of these periods.[25] The already established power of the landed aristocracy, however, and the excessive taxation of the small-holdings, which was a great burden for the *stratiotai*, doomed the imperial legislation to almost complete failure.[26]

---

[21] *Praecepta Militaria*, IV.1–2 (p. 38).

[22] Men who either sold or willingly gave their land to a patron-aristocrat, and in exchange for freedom, escaped military service and the paying of state taxes.

[23] J.-C. Cheynet, 'The Byzantine Aristocracy (8th–13th Centuries)', in *The Byzantine Aristocracy and its Military Function* (Aldershot, 2006), pp. 25–6.

[24] The term *dynatos* is described throughout the tenth century in terms of rank denoting all those who held the titles of *patrikios* and *magistros* and all the members of the military and bureaucratic hierarchies.

[25] G. Ostrogorsky, *Quelques problèmes d'histoire de la paysannerie byzantine* (Brussels, 1956); P. Lemerle, *The Agrarian History of Byzantium from the Origins to the Twelfth century. The Sources and the Problems* (Galway, 1979), pp. 85–115. Both these scholars, though they differed in their translation of the key terms *penetas*, *ptokhos* and *dynatos*, agreed that evidence pointing to a conflict of interests existed, whatever interpretation might afterwards be placed on its precise nature. The four distinct periods of crisis have been examined by: R. Morris, 'The Powerful and the Poor in Tenth-Century Byzantium: Law and Reality', *Past & Present* 73 (1976), 3–27.

[26] The Byzantine tax system was regressive, meaning that the richer you were the less taxes you had to pay: M. Angold, *The Byzantine Empire, 1025–1204* (London, 1997), pp. 88–9.

A clear indication of the rapidly rising power of the families of Anatolia was the two civil wars early in Basil II's reign (976–9, 986–9). The military aristocracy of Asia Minor, taking advantage of the Byzantine reconquest which allowed them to greatly expand their lands and earn significant reputation, would not easily have given away its privileges to the legitimate representative of the Macedonian dynasty. Thus, according to Psellus' claims, Basil targeted the foundations of their power, namely the control over their lands and consequently over the *stratiotai* as well, along with their important offices in the army and provincial administration (e.g. the rebel Bardas Sclerus had become *dux* of Mesopotamia).[27] The real conflict of interest was played out between the emperor and the *dynatoi*, not between the *dynatoi* and the *penites* as identified in the legislative documents – this was an artificial creation of the emperor's closest advisers. Hence, Basil not only revived the old legislation set by Romanus I and Constantine VII, but further re-introduced the *allelengyon*, a law that made the powerful responsible for paying the outstanding taxes of the small-holders.[28]

In order to deal with the rebellious tendencies of the armies of the east, Basil II also introduced the commuting of military service to allow him to hire mercenaries loyal to him.[29] This reform, however, was not regularised by the government until the mid-eleventh century.[30] It has also been suggested that even during the reign of Basil II several thematic units in Asia Minor were disbanded because of their poor performance, with the emperor moving towards the tagmatisation of the *themata*.[31] The timing of the introduction of these measures was not a coincidence, as they took place in a period of intense military activity when Basil desperately needed the money to finance his Bulgarian wars, which lasted up to the year 1018.

In the Epigoni period, although imperial power was controlled by the bureaucrats of the capital who wished to diminish the power of their antagonists in Asia Minor, no measures were taken to reverse the decline of the *themata*. Laws such as the *allelegyon* and the *epibole* were revoked by Romanus III Argyrus (1028–34), and the final blow came during the reign of Constantine IX (1042–55) with the introduction of the new ministry of *epi ton kriseon* under the office of the judge-praetor.[32] This was the first

[27]   C. Holmes, 'Political Elites in the Reign of Basil II', in *Byzantium in the Year 1000*, ed. P. Magdalino (Leiden, 2003), pp. 44–56. In the same volume: J.-C. Cheynet, 'Basil II and Asia Minor', pp. 76–9.
[28]   Angold, *The Byzantine Empire*, pp. 26–7; Holmes, 'Political Elites', pp. 35–69; T. E. Gregory, *A History of Byzantium* (Oxford, 2005), pp. 203, 230. For the centralisation of the Byzantine government in the last two decades of the tenth century: H. Ahrweiler, 'Recherches sur la Société byzantine au XIe Siècle: nouvelles Hiérarchies et nouvelles Solidarités', *Travaux et Memoires* 6 (1976), 99–124. In the same volume: N. Oikonomides, 'L'évolution de l'organisation administrative de l'empire byzantine au XIe siècle', pp. 125–52.
[29]   The imperial government had begun asking for money in return for military service since the first half of the tenth century. See Treadgold, *Byzantium and its Army*, pp. 138–9; Haldon, 'Military Service', 28; Lemerle, *The Agrarian History of Byzantium*, pp. 124–5.
[30]   H. Ahrweiler, *Byzance et la mer* (Paris, 1966), pp. 144–9.
[31]   Cheynet, 'Basil II and Asia Minor', pp. 82–8.
[32]   After 1025 it had become common for the *strategos*'s authority to be limited to military matters,

office to be abolished by Alexius Comnenus in his struggle to reunite the civilian and military authorities of the provinces under the duke-catepan, who, in turn, would be under the unified command of the ministry – *logothesion* of the *stratiotikon*.[33]

The collapse of the military institution of the *themata* was the result of the gradual erosion of its foundations, namely the military lands and the farmer-soldiers. On the whole, the decrees issued by the emperors of the tenth century, although they can be considered a significant effort to limit the powers of the great landholders of Asia Minor, accomplished very little, and even though they should have been strengthened and further enhanced by the successors of Basil II, they were abandoned and gradually forgotten. The emperors of the eleventh century, however, are not solely to blame for the failure to act in favour of the small-holders because, as we saw, the transformation of small-holders into dependants had already begun in the early tenth century. The change of policy, which appeared to originate with the Epigoni, was a sad reality that was no longer possible to control and finally sealed the death of the *themata*. Fortunately for the empire, the tagmatic units seemed to have suffered much less throughout the same period because their organisation was not based on military lands; rather, they were paid and equipped by the central government. It was the economic crisis of the second half of the eleventh century that affected them more than any row between the emperors and the provincial aristocracy.

The administrative-economic system of the *pronoia*[34] can be seen as the innovative solution to two of the most pressing problems of Alexius' reign, the disintegration of the army and the collapsing economy. The *pronoia* was the piece of land handed over from the imperial demesne to imperial favourites, usually from the lower levels of the provincial aristocracy, to administer (*eis pronoian*), and during the reign of the Comneni the grantee of a *pronoia* had to offer military service to the state in exchange for that land. Having inherited an economy with no reserves of money in the imperial treasury, a debased coinage and a large army of mercenaries from the Balkans and Western Europe, the system of distributing *pronoiai* in return for military service, a system which much resembled Western feudalism,[35] seemed to have provided an answer to the pressing needs for more troops that Alexius was facing. This measure

with the judge (*praetor*) of the *thema* being responsible for the thematic administration: M. Angold, 'Belle Époque or Crisis? (1025–1118)', in *The Cambridge History of the Byzantine Empire c. 500–1492* (Cambridge, 2008), ed. J. Shepard, pp. 598–601.

[33]   Ahrweiler, *Byzance et la mer*, pp. 199, 203 and 207–8; Angold, *The Byzantine Empire*, pp. 149–53.

[34]   For an introduction into the theme of *pronoia*: P. Magdalino, 'The Byzantine Army and the Land: from Stratiotikon Ktema to Military Pronoia', in *Byzantium at War (9th–12th Century)*, ed. N. Oikonomides (Athens, 1997), pp. 32–6; T. Maniati-Kokkini, 'Μία πρώτη προσέγγιση στη μελέτη του βυζαντινού θεσμού της πρόνοιας: οι προνοιάριοι' ['A First Approach to the Study of the Institution of the Pronoia: the *Pronoiarioi*'], *Hellenic Historical Company. 9th National Historical Conference, May 1988* (Thessaloniki, 1988), pp. 49–60.

[35]   For this debate, see J. Haldon, 'The Feudalism Debate Once More: The Case of Byzantium', *Journal of Peasant Studies* 17 (1989), 5–40.

only had short-term effects, however, and was not developed on a large scale. It was after the 1090s that Alexius had the time and the resources to finance the revival of a strong and centralised land and naval armies that would give him the opportunity to recover imperial territories in Asia Minor and the Balkans.

The Byzantine infantry in the tenth and eleventh centuries

In understanding the structure and battle tactics of the Byzantine army of the tenth century our most detailed primary source for this task, and one that is also closer chronologically to the Comnenian period, is the *Praecepta Militaria*, a military manual attributed to Emperor Nicephorus II Phocas (963–9) that contains useful advice based on experience in fighting the Muslims in Cilicia, Mesopotamia and Syria in the second and third quarters of the tenth century. The structure, consistency and tactics of the Byzantine army must certainly have evolved during the Epigoni period, but the extent to which this happened eludes historians. The *Praecepta* and the rest of the military treatises of the period set rather strict guidelines, but they allowed the commander a great deal of discretion in the field. They reflect the practice of older and well-established strategies and tactics, along with a number of innovative practical ideas. The task of the historian is to distinguish between the two. As the author of the mid-tenth-century work *On Skirmishing* notes: 'We have acquired this knowledge not simply from hearing about it [from the old military manuals] but also from having been taught by a certain amount of experience'.[36]

Another crucial point is the composition of the imperial army. When modern historians refer to the Byzantine Empire as a predominately Greek empire, they are making the same mistake as thinking of the 1914 Habsburg empire as Austrian or the empire of Queen Victoria as British.[37] Hence, one of the major contributing factors to the adaptability of the Byzantine army over the centuries was its ability to incorporate effectively several ethnic groups into its ranks. Numerous peoples such as Kurds, Christian Arabs (the Khurramites, the Mardaites and the Maronites of today's Lebanon), Vlachs, Armenians, Bulgars, Slavs, Rus and Illyrians (Albanians) were recruited into the army, either as individuals or in larger groups.[38] Discipline was the rule among the ethnically diverse units of the Byzantine army, although exceptions were noted by chroniclers, such as the suspicion which often developed into open hatred by the Byzantines towards the heretical Paulicians.

The Byzantine infantry units of the tenth century were divided into heavy and light. The composition of an infantry 1,000-man *drungus* was 400 infantrymen (*hoplitai*), 300 archers (*toxotai*), 200 javeliners (*akontistai*) and slingers (*sphendobolistai*) and 100

---

[36] *On Skirmishing*, XIII–XV (p. 146).

[37] D. C. Smythe, 'Insiders and Outsiders', in *A Companion to Byzantium*, ed. L. James (Oxford, 2010), pp. 67–80.

[38] Nicolle, *Crusader Warfare*, I, pp. 163–75.

spearmen to conduct sorties (*menaulatoi*).[39]

> The formation of the infantrymen under discussion is to be a double-ribbed square, thus called a 'four-sided formation' by the ancients, which has three units on each side so that all together there are twelve units on the four sides. In case the cavalry force is large and the enemy does not bring along a similar number of infantry, twelve intervals should be left open. If, on the other hand, the cavalry force is not large and the enemy does bring infantry along, eight intervals should be left open.[40]

The basic infantry formation was a quadrilateral one which had small intervals on each of the four sides, and depending on the numbers of cavalry and their ratio with the infantry units, along with other significant factors like the terrain and the composition of the enemy's units, could either form a square, thus having two intervals on each side, or a rectangle, with three intervals at the front and two at the flanks. Variations depending on the nature of the terrain and the deployment of the troops, either broad or narrow front, can also be found in the sources.[41] This square formation, however, was relatively recent in the history of Byzantine warfare. Although square formations existed since ancient times, this particular hollow square where the cavalry could take refuge and regroup is first mentioned by Nicephorus Phocas and can be attributed, with the necessary caution, to the defensive frontier wars in Cilicia in the second quarter of the tenth century under John Curcuas. Hence, historians can identify another sign of Byzantine adaptability to the Arab encircling manoeuvres experienced in this period.[42]

Nicephorus also uses the term *parataxis*, identifying the basic structural unit of the *drungus*. But what was the deployment of each man in a *drungus*? 'The heavy infantrymen must be deployed two deep in a double-faced formation, and keep two infantrymen at the front and two at the back. Between them are three light archers, so that the depth of the formation is seven men".[43] Thus, the infantrymen and the archers stood seven lines deep and a hundred across. In acknowledgement that the intervals on each side of the square formation presented a weak point to the whole square formation, the 200 javeliners and slingers were deployed to guard these points, positioned alongside the last two lines of the infantrymen.[44] The remaining 100

[39] *Praecepta Militaria*, I.75–84 (p. 16). An indicative bibliography on the equipment of the infantry: T. G. Kolias, *Byzantinische Waffen. Ein Beitrag zur byzantinischen Waffenkunde von den Anfangen bis zur lateinischen Eroberung* (Vienna, 1988); J. Haldon, 'Some Aspects of the Byzantine Military Technology from the Sixth to the Tenth Centuries', *Byzantine and Modern Greek Studies* 1 (1975), 30–47; T. Dawson, 'Syntagma Hoplon: The Equipment of Regular Byzantine Troops, c. 950 to c. 1204', in *A Companion to Medieval Arms and Armour*, ed. D. Nicolle (Woodbridge, 2002), pp. 81–90.

[40] *Praecepta Militaria*, I.39–51 (p. 14); cf. *On Strategy*, XV.1–117 (pp. 46–52).

[41] *Praecepta Militaria*, II.151–75 (pp. 30–2).

[42] McGeer, *Sowing the Dragon's Teeth*, pp. 257–65; M. Bennett, 'The Crusaders' "Fighting March" Revisited', *War in History* 8 (2001), 5–11.

[43] *Praecepta Militaria*, I.62–5 (p. 16).

[44] *Praecepta Militaria*, I.89–94 (p. 16).

menaulatoi, the elite spearmen of the infantry, were to take their place in front of the infantrymen, thus increasing the depth of the taxiarchy's formation to eight men.[45]

The role of the infantry units of the Byzantine army in a period of intense military activity in Asia Minor and the Balkans reflects the empire's need for professional soldiers to be deployed alongside elite tagmatic cavalry units, with discipline, high morale and excellent training being paramount. This, however, stands in sharp contrast to the view of foot soldiers before that period. From the establishment of the *themata* and their *stratiotai* in the mid-seventh century up to the mid-tenth century the empire was on the defensive against its enemies both in the Balkans and Asia Minor, with only brief respites, and the missions undertaken by infantry soldiers involved mainly the manning of strategic towns, forts and outposts and the occasional frontier guerrilla warfare. Hence, the view of the foot soldiers of the pre-conquest period as relatively undisciplined, poorly trained peasant militias whose role in warfare was overshadowed by the heavy cavalry prevailed – a situation that the generals of the tenth century desperately tried to change.

It is crucial to understand when reading the *Praecepta* and the rest of the military treatises of the tenth century that although they provide valuable information on the equipment and the battle tactics of the imperial armed forces, they may give us a false idea about the status of these units and the general strategic role played by foot soldiers in the battlefields of the period of the Epigoni, where a return to somewhat pre-conquest tactics can be observed. Although they still played an integral part in the defence of the empire's borders, the decline of the *themata*, the economic crisis in the middle of the century which resulted in budget cuts, the fiscalisation of the military service and the increasing employment of mercenaries – indigenous or foreign – had seriously undermined the foot soldiers' overall battlefield effectiveness by the second half of the eleventh century.[46]

The Byzantine cavalry in the tenth and eleventh centuries

The tenth century was a period when the cavalry units of the *tagmata* and *themata* dominated the battlefields of the Balkans and Asia Minor and their use sometimes overshadowed even the mentioning of any provincial foot soldiers by the contemporary primary sources. The three major types of cavalrymen were the *procursatores*, the thematic levies and the heavily armed tagmatic troops (*kataphraktoi*). The *procursatores* were a reconnaissance unit of lightly armed cavalry numbering 500 men – 110–20 of whom would have been horse archers and the rest lancers. The regular cavalry of the *themata* wore sleeveless waist-length cuirasses or waist-length mail shirts, similar to the *procursatores*, along with conic-shaped iron helmets and carrying round, oval or

---

[45] *Praecepta Militaria*, I.94–5 (pp. 16–18).
[46] Haldon, *Warfare, State and Society*, pp. 197–228.

kite-shaped wooden shields.[47] Although they had swords, it is specifically noted in the *Praecepta* that they either fought as lancers or as mounted archers (with a ratio of three to two).

The *kataphraktoi* were by far the most elite unit of the Byzantine army when it came to training, experience and equipment. Nicephorus' *Praecepta*, along with the famous graffito of a third-century *klibanarios* from Dura Europus,[48] gives us a good idea of the defensive[49] and offensive equipment of a *kataphraktos*. Each cavalryman was wearing a *klibanion*, a short-sleeved, waist-length lamellar cuirass, supplemented by extra cuirass sleeves, while the arms and forearms were protected by thick gauntlets (*manikelia*). Under the *klibanion* there were the *zabai*, which usually meant sections of chain mail, or plates of leather, supplemented by the *kremasmata*, which were skirt-like coverings of the area from the waist to the knees.[50] The head were protected by an iron helmet with two or three additional layers of thick *zabai*.

The *kataphraktos*' main combat weapon was the iron mace, and a second weapon was the *paramerion*, a type of single-edged curved sword of Avar influence. An extra sword is described as a *spathion* (a double-edged sword for a hand-to-hand combat carried over the left shoulder).[51] Teardrop shields are not the only ones shown in middle Byzantine pictorial sources; round and oval shields are just as prevalent. They are generally depicted as being of modest size, approximately 50 to 80 cm in diameter for the cavalry, as opposed to infantry shields, which were around 100–20 cm.[52]

The numbers of *kataphraktoi* serving in the Byzantine army must have been low, simply because acquiring and maintaining such equipment must have been difficult for the state's budget. For that reason their formations had to be supplemented by mounted archers and lancers numbering perhaps even more than half of a single 504-strong cavalry unit.[53] These elite soldiers must have disappeared by the time of the Norman invasion in 1081, because the last time the term *kataphraktos* is mentioned in the sources is in the *Taktika* of Nicephorus Uranus (written c. 999–1005). It seems likely that after the stabilisation of the empire's frontiers in the 1020s to 1030s they fell under strength and were stood down by the middle of the century.[54]

---

[47] *Praecepta Militaria*, IV.7–11 and 36–9 (pp. 38–40); Haldon, 'Byzantine Military Technology', 30–47; Kolias, *Waffen*, pp. 88–131.

[48] For Dura-Europos, see the classic studies: M. I. Rostovtzeff, *Dura-Europos and its Art* (Oxford, 1938); R. Ghirshman, *Iran: Parthians and Sassanians* (London, 1962).

[49] *Praecepta Militaria*, III.26–37 (pp. 34–6).

[50] McGeer, *Sowing the Dragon's Teeth*, pp. 69–70 and 215–16; T. G. Kolias, 'Ζάβα, ζαβάρετον, ζαβαρειώτης', *Jahrbuch der österreichischen Byzantinistik* 29 (1980), 27–35.

[51] *Praecepta Militaria*, III.53–60 (p. 36). J. Howard-Johnston, 'Studies in the Organization of the Byzantine Army in the Tenth and Eleventh Centuries' (unpublished D.Phil. thesis, Oxford University, 1971), pp. 286–90.

[52] T. Dawson, '"Fit for the Task": Equipment Sizes and the Transmission of Military Lore, Sixth to Tenth Centuries', *Byzantine and Modern Greek Studies* 31 (2007), 3–4.

[53] *Praecepta Militaria*, III.50–3 and 69–70 (pp. 36–8).

[54] Haldon, *Warfare, State and Society*, p. 223.

The *Praecepta* gives direct instructions concerning the cavalry's formation.[55] The first of the three lines of the cavalry force had three units, two of them consisting of light cavalrymen and the middle one of *kataphraktoi*. The two light cavalry units had a total force of 500 men in five lines, with the basic structural unit being the 50-man *bandum*. These two units were supposed to consist of 300 mounted lancers and 200 archers, in a double-faced formation 'for a possible attack from the rear'. The third unit consisted of the *kataphraktoi* in their triangular formation and a full complement of 504 men.[56] Supplementing the first line of the cavalry formation were the units of the outflankers (*hyperkerastai*) and the flankguards (*aposobetai*), each having two 50-man *banda* of both mounted archers and lancers. Finally, Nicephorus notes that the first line of the cavalry formation was supposed to be supported by another two lines, at a bow-shot distance, consisting of four and three units of light cavalry respectively.[57] Galloping ahead of the outflankers and flankguards were the *procursatores*.

But what caused the addition of a third line of cavalry as rearguard in the first half of the tenth century and what does that tell us about the adaptability of Byzantine military thinking? Since the late Roman period, the deployment of a cavalry force in the battlefield took place in two parallel lines of three and four units respectively.[58] It is in the *Praecepta* that we read for the first time about a third line of three units that was supposed to be added as a rear-guard to deal with the encircling tactics of the Bedouin auxiliaries of the Hamdanid armies (*Arabitai*),[59] which are clearly distinguished from the main Muslim body of the *Agarenoi*.[60] This third line is specifically identified with its Arabic name – *saqat*,[61] and is a striking reminder of the addition of the second line of cavalry (rear-guard) that we read of in the seventh-century *Strategikon*.[62]

The corps of the *procursatores* was also introduced in this period (mid-tenth century). This unit is first mentioned in the Byzantine treatise *On Skirmishing* (written c. 969) as the unit of the *trapezitai* or *tasinarioi*.[63] Nicephorus, however, greatly expanded his analysis of the use of this unit during a campaign and the fact that this unit is established in the middle of the tenth century while its role in the battlefield was very similar to the Bedouin units of the Arab armies. This is another indication of Arab influence on the Byzantine armies of the period.

---

[55] *Praecepta Militaria*, IV.24–6 (p. 40); cf. *On Strategy*, XVII, XVIII (pp. 56–60).

[56] *Praecepta Militaria*, IV.47–50 (p. 40).

[57] *Praecepta Militaria*, IV.52–6, 65–7 and 69 (p. 42).

[58] Maurice, *Strategikon*, II.1 (pp. 23–5).

[59] For these Bedouins: McGeer, *Sowing the Dragon's Teeth*, pp. 225–46; Nicolle, *Crusader Warfare*, II, pp. 19–193.

[60] *Praecepta Militaria*, II.101–10 (p. 28).

[61] A. Dain, 'Saka dans les traités militaires', *Byzantion* 44 (1951), 94–6.

[62] Maurice, *Strategikon*, II.1 (pp. 23–4).

[63] *On Skirmishing*, II.23–5 (p. 152).

Byzantine fighting methods against the 'Franks'

It would be better for every man to lose his head than to flee even half a foot before the heathen.[64]

A sense of honour dominated the behaviour of the Western knight in his life, forbidding any flight before the enemy as the utmost shame and cowardice.[65] And what more perfect example of this notion of heroism and noble deeds that dominated Western Christianity in this period than the *chansons de geste* (French for 'songs of heroic deeds')? But what was the difference between the military feeling in the East and West during the Middle Ages? How did the Byzantine officers view war?

The great difference between East and West was, indeed, the chivalric ideals of fair and honourable battle that dominated the West, but were considered somehow impractical in the East.[66] In brief, the Byzantine officer was a professional who saw battle as the chance to achieve his objective using every means possible, fair or unfair, chivalric or unchivalric.[67] Military manuals like the *Strategikon*, the *Taktika* and the *Strategikon* of Cecaumenus all praise the use of varied stratagems to deceive the enemy and bring back the army with as few casualties as possible, considering it absurd to lose experienced soldiers and money to draw a campaign to a violent and uncertain end. The Byzantine mentality can be summarised in the following extract by Cecaumenus:

And only when you know everything about your enemy, only then must you stand and fight them, but do not let your army perish for no reason. Fight in such a way by applying tricks and machinations and ambushes to humiliate your enemy, and only when it is the last choice of all, and in the utmost need, only then stand and fight.[68]

Why do these manuals praise the use of fraud and deception to win a battle? It all comes down to Byzantium's geographical position and its economic situation. Throughout its history, the empire was doomed to fighting in two operational theatres, the Balkans (including Italy and Sicily) and eastern Asia Minor. The emperors had to allocate their limited resources in money and manpower in the most effective way; thus, they were very rarely able to afford any unnecessary losses. More so, if we take into account the state's agricultural economy, which was barely able to support the soldiers' wages: 'The financial system [. . .] is principally concerned with paying the

[64] *Chanson d'Antioche*, ed. P. Paris, 2 vols (Paris, 1848), II.i, viij, c. 24, vv. 557–8, p. 227.
[65] M. Strickland, *War and Chivalry: The Conduct and Perception of War in England and Normandy, 1066–1217* (Cambridge, 1996).
[66] For an introduction into the idea of chivalry, see M. Keen, *Chivalry* (London, 2005), pp. 1–18; S. Painter, *French Chivalry, Chivalric Ideas and Practices in Mediaeval France* (London, 1940).
[67] C. W. C. Oman, *A History of the Art of War in the Middle Ages AD 378–1485*, 2 vols. (London, 1991), I, p. 201. Oman's old-fashioned view has been revised by modern scholars: W. Treadgold, 'Byzantium, The Reluctant Warrior', in *Noble Ideas and Bloody Realities*, ed. N. Christie, M. Yazigi (Leiden, 2006), pp. 209–33; W. E. Kaegi, Jr, *Some Thoughts on Byzantine Military Strategy* (Brookline, MA, 1983), pp. 1–18; Haldon, *Warfare, State and Society*, pp. 34–46; G. T. Dennis, 'The Byzantines in Battle', in *Byzantium at War (9th–12th Century)*, ed. N. Oikonomides (Athens, 1997), pp. 165–78.
[68] Cecaumenus, pp. 9–10.

soldiers. Each year, most of the public revenues are spent for this purpose.'[69]

Because these manuals were written in a period when the empire was on the defensive, struggling to keep or, to put it more vividly, to lose as few lands as possible in the Balkans and Asia Minor, we can understand the Byzantine reluctance to fight pitched battles unless it was a case of utmost need. The *Strategikon* was written in the early seventh century, a period when Spain, Africa and Italy were being viciously attacked by Visigoths, Berbers and Lombards respectively. More than three centuries later, the compilation of the *Taktika* coincided with Leo VI's struggle with Symeon of Bulgaria (893–927) and the Arab advances in Cilicia and Armenia. Although tactical offensives did occur, they were only to preserve or retrieve lost grounds and they did not resemble Justinian's expansionist wars or the period of the reconquest.

This is what a late-ninth-century officer was advised to do instead of engage his enemy on a pitched battle. According to Leo:

> Unless there is some advantage or urgency in taking some action, you must not place yourself at risk. Those who undertake such dangers do not differ from men who are caught when gold is used as bait; looking only at the beautiful colour, they struggle to gain possession of it.[70]

> It is well to harm the enemy by deceit, by raids, by hunger, and to hurt them for a long time by means of very frequent assaults and other actions. You should never be enticed into a pitched battle. For the most part, we observe that success is a matter of luck rather than of proven courage.[71]

Leo VI and Maurice add three ancient tricks to apply against an enemy:

> You should furnish the enemy with cause to suspect betrayal and to distrust deserters from you to them so they will either not believe them or will kill them, if you send letters by such conveyance that they will fall into the enemy's hands.[72]

> You may sow dissension and suspicion against the distinguished men among the enemy. When you conduct raids in enemy territory, do not burn the estates of those men; instead, leave behind some sign of friendship with them, either in writing or in some other way.[73]

> Some commanders have welcomed embassies from the enemy and replied in gentle and flattering terms, sent them on their way with honours, and then immediately followed along and attacked them unexpectedly.[74]

All of the aforementioned principles agree with the recommendations of the late Roman author Flavius Vegetius Renatus, who between 383 and 450 wrote the single

---

[69]   *On Strategy*, II.18–21 (pp. 12–13).

[70]   Leo VI, *Taktika*, XX.36 (p. 550).

[71]   Leo VI, *Taktika*, XX.51 (p. 554).

[72]   Leo VI, *Taktika*, XX.29 (p. 546).

[73]   Leo VI, *Taktika*, XX.22 and 161 (pp. 544 and 592).

[74]   Leo VI, *Taktika*, XX.24 (p. 544); Maurice, *Strategikon*, IX.1 (p. 93); Maniaces applied this trick in 1030 against 800 Arabs at Teluch: Scylitzes, II (p. 494).

most important theoretical work on warfare available to medieval commanders, although historians cannot establish with certainty whether the writings of Vegetius were known to Byzantine commanders or not:

> For good generals do not attack in open battle where the danger is mutual, but do it always from a hidden position, so as to kill or at least terrorise the enemy while their own men are unharmed as far as possible.[75]

It is preferable to subdue an enemy by famine, raids and terror, than in battle where fortune tends to have more influence than bravery.[76]

For the purpose of comparison and in order to highlight the continuity of these basic principles, it is worth mentioning the writings of the Chinese general, Sun Tzu (c. 500 BC):

> A skilful leader subdues the units of an enemy without offering a battle. He conquers his [enemy's] cities without laying siege to them. He conquers his kingdom without long-term military operations.[77]

These already ancient tricks of bribing the enemies, sending spies to bring back important information on enemy morale and numbers, along with the despatch of friendly letters to the enemy officers, seem up to date in Alexius' dealings with the Norman invasion of 1107. We read in the *Alexiad*'s thirteenth book:

> The general (I think) should not invariably seek victory by drawing the sword; there are times when he should be prepared to use finesse [...] and so achieve a complete triumph. So far as we know, a general's supreme task is to win, not merely by force of arms; sometimes, when the chance offers itself, an enemy can be beaten by fraud.[78]

Setting aside the morality of these stratagems, in what way were they employed against the enemies of the empire, and specifically the Franks? What did the Byzantines know about their enemies' tactics and the ways to combat them? The *Taktika* of Emperor Leo VI serves as a key study for the entire military thinking of a high-ranking Byzantine officer, devoting an entire chapter on how to combat the enemies of Byzantium. Three centuries after the compilation of the *Strategikon*, Leo presents an in-depth examination of the Frankish warrior of the post-Carolingian period in ch. XVIII of his *Taktika*, entitled 'On the study of several national and Roman battle arrays':

> The Franks and the Lombards are bold and daring to excess; they regard the smallest movement to the rear as a disgrace. So formidable is their charge with their broadsword, lance and shield, that it is best to decline a pitched battle with them until you have put all the opportunities on your side. You should take advantage of their indiscipline and disorder; whether fighting on foot

---

[75] Vegetius, *Epitome*, III.9 (pp. 83–4).

[76] Vegetius, *Epitome*, III.26 (p. 116).

[77] Sun Tzu, *The Art of War*, trans. into Greek by K. Georgantas (Thessaloniki, 1998), III.6 and 17a (pp. 31–2).

[78] *Alexiad*, XIII.4 (II, pp. 194–5); Sewter, p. 405.

or on horseback, they charge in dense, unwieldy masses, which cannot manoeuvre, because they have neither organisation nor drill. Nothing succeeds better against them than a feigned flight, which draws them into an ambush; for they follow hastily, and invariably fall into the snare. They are impatient from hunger and thirst, and after a few days of privation they desert their standards and return home as best they can. Nor are their chiefs above the temptation of taking bribes; a moderate sum of money will frustrate one of their expeditions. On the whole, therefore, it is easier and less costly to wear out a Frankish army by skirmishes, protracted operations in desolate districts, and the cutting off of its supplies, than to attempt to destroy it at a single blow.[79]

The *Taktika* was the most detailed and most recent examination of Frankish military tactics at the time of the Norman invasion of 1081. But even though the author of the early-seventh-century *Strategikon* describes the infantry armies of the early Merovingian period and Leo refers to the Frankish chivalry in the early stages of the development of the feudal cavalry, historians are able to find some common features in both works. Something that can be easily gleaned is the bravery of the Frankish soldiery, with special attention being paid to the chivalric nobility of the post-Carolingian era. Philippicus, the probable author of the *Strategikon*, calls them daring and impetuous, as if they were the only people in the world who were not cowards. This courage and stubbornness, however, was to be their downfall because both authors strongly encourage the Byzantine general not to confront them in pitched battle but rather to resort to guerrilla tactics and stratagems.

Leo placed much attention on the Frankish battle-charges, specifically mentioning how undisciplined a Frankish attack is, with the Franks advancing in dense cavalry masses that could not manoeuvre easily on the battlefield. This weakness, however, is debatable and the supposition that they were fighting in one single formation could simply have been the result of the way they were observed.[80] In Charlemagne's period the men who had joined the royal army from the provinces formed their own contingents, so it is likely that they also fought in the same formations.[81] Another feature of the Frankish warrior that was again singled out and used against them was their 'greedy and easily corrupted nature' that would turn the soldiers against their officers, and the officers against their generals and kings.

According to the *Taktika*, in order to sustain a heavy Frankish cavalry attack, the best thing for a general to do was to avoid battle at all costs until all the opportunities were in his favour. If he could not avoid battle, he should use the feigned flight tactics that might draw the Franks into an ambush, or attack their unprotected flanks. He should take advantage of the terrain and the weather conditions and impose a land-blockade that would lead to a shortage of food, water and, most importantly, wine, flaring up discontent amongst the soldiers. Finally, a Frankish campaign could easily be brought to an end by bribing the enemy officers with a 'moderate' amount of money. In any case, Leo considers being drawn in a pitched battle against the Franks as a last and

---

[79] Leo VI, *Taktika*, XVIII.76–92 (pp. 464–8).
[80] J. F. Verbruggen, *L'armée et la stratégie de Charlemagne* (Düsseldorf, 1965).
[81] Contamine, *War in the Middle Ages*, pp. 22–9; Oman, *The Art of War*, I, pp. 84–8.

desperate resort that should be avoided at all costs. In Italy, the Byzantines followed Leo's strategy of avoiding battle only after the three consecutive defeats of 1041 and the failed Sicilian expedition of 1038–41. The deeper reasons behind this lie in the fact that Longobardia was a secondary operational theatre compared to Asia Minor or the Balkans, and after the 1050s no significant reinforcements could be spared for that distant province. Thus, all the catepans could do was to use the heavily fortified Apulian landscape to their advantage and deny battle to the Normans.

The geopolitical instability of the period of the Epigoni (1025–71) – the battles at Manzikert (1071) and Kalavrye (1078)

The death of Basil II marked a turning point in the history of the Byzantine state. After the magnificent achievements of the three emperors of the Reconquest (963–1025), what followed was a period of relative stability and peace, which the empire had hardly ever known. Unfortunately, this breathing space was not spent in conservation and consolidation, in an attempt to secure and expand what had already been achieved, but it resulted in a period of internal relaxation, which gradually broke up the military system that had been carefully managed up to Basil's reign, leading to significant ground-losses for the empire in all fronts. But what were the military defeats inflicted on the Byzantine army in this period in both Asia Minor and the Balkans? Was the result of any of these defeats significant enough to destroy a large part of the imperial forces and cause any major geo-political changes?

   In order to fully understand the collapse of imperial control on the frontiers of the Balkans and in Asia Minor in the mid-eleventh century, it is important to examine the principal cause that eroded these foundations. Crucial to the issue are the buffer states of Bulgaria and Armenia.[82] Before the final annexation of the Armenian kingdom of Ani by Constantine IX, the elite Armenian soldiers served as a protective shield for the empire's north-eastern borders in Asia Minor and were an invaluable source for the Byzantine infantry.[83] The same was true of the kingdom of Bulgaria, which was an effective buffer state between the imperial lands of Macedonia and Thrace and the areas north of the Danube that were dominated by the nomadic tribes of the Turkic Pechenegs.[84]

   The Pechenegs had served the Byzantine emperors on several occasions, either as vassals or paid mercenaries against the Russians to the north or the Hungarians to the west. But the subjugation of Bulgaria by Basil II in the 1010s, along with the pressure by the Uzes and Cuman Turcoman tribes, caused the Pechenegs to cross the Danube in 1047 and invade imperial territories, while the Arabs in the East were replaced by a

[82] Angold, *The Byzantine Empire*, pp. 37–44.
[83] E. McGeer, 'The Legal Decree of Nicephoros II Phocas concerning Armenian Stratiotai', in *Peace and War in Byzantium*, ed. T. Miller, J. Nesbitt (Washington, DC, 1995), pp. 123–37.
[84] *De Administrando Imperio*, CSHB, pp. 49–53.

far more dangerous enemy, the Seljuks. The collapse of the imperial frontiers seemed imminent, mostly because the army and, most importantly, the treasury could not support the demand for soldiers from both theatres of war, let alone more distant provinces like Longobardia where the Normans had already begun their expansion.[85] After the 1050s, the increasing pressure on the empire's borders both in the East and West, combined with the civil wars of the period that diverted large numbers of soldiers away from the external threats, proved too much.

In the Balkans, the most significant geo-political development was the invasion of imperial territory by the Pecheneg tribes in the winter of 1046/7 and a settlement of about 800,000 of them in areas of Bulgaria and northern Macedonia, roughly between Sofia and Nis.[86] The fact that the empire had to accept the settlement of the Pechenegs on imperial soil and employ them as garrison troops and thematic levies reveals its military inability to block their passage south of the Danube. In the following decade, the Byzantines were twice forced to mount large-scale campaigns to pacify them, in 1052 and 1059. In both cases the Byzantines were beaten back by guerrilla-war tactics and the weather. Thus, in order to use these fine mounted archers in its own interests, the central government attempted to turn their territories into buffer zones against the Uzes and the Cumans, in coordination with several key Byzantine garrisons in the area, and employ them as mercenary troops. The Byzantines were up against a much more formidable enemy, the Seljuks, and they needed all the help they could get.

In Asia Minor, Turkish troops had become familiar to the Byzantines as a result of their employment by the Arabs.[87] The Fatimids of Cairo, the Hamdanids of Aleppo and the Abbasids since the reign of Mu'tasim (833–42)[88] had allowed them to infiltrate their armies, usually as an elite corps of slave-soldiers (*ghulam mamluk*), initially forming the ruler's or general's personal retinue but eventually coming to represent the nucleus of Muslim armies.[89] The nomadic tribes of the Seljuks, however, first appeared on the eastern Byzantine frontiers in the second quarter of the eleventh century and on the early 1050s the Turkish pressure on the Armenian lands, recently annexed by Byzantium, resulted in the sack of the key city of Kars in the heartland of Iberia

[85]   Angold, *The Byzantine Empire*, pp. 81–91; M. Whittow, 'The Middle Byzantine Economy (600–1204)', in *The Cambridge History of the Byzantine Empire c. 500–1492*, ed. J. Shepard (Cambridge, 2008), pp. 465–92.

[86]   Angold, *The Byzantine Empire*, pp. 37–40.

[87]   D. A. Korobeinikov, 'Raiders and Neighbours: The Turks (1040–1304)', in *The Cambridge History of the Byzantine Empire c. 500–1492* (Cambridge, 2008), pp. 692–710.

[88]   For Mu'tasim's important but largely neglected victory upon the Byzantines at Dazimon in 838, with the crucial help of 10,000 Turkish mounted archers, see W. E. Kaegi, Jr, 'The Contribution of Archery to the Turkish Conquest of Anatolia', *Speculum* 39 (1964), 99–102.

[89]   J. Waterson, *The Knights of Islam, the Wars of the Mamluks* (London, 2007), pp. 33–53, especially pp. 37–44.

in 1053.[90] Two years later, the much weakened but spiritually significant Buwayhid Caliphate of Baghdad also fell to the Seljuks. Although the Fatimids of Cairo probably posed a more serious threat to the sultan, in order to protect his northern borders, he diverted a large number of mounted Turkish nomads (Islamicised Turks of the Oguz tribe) to conduct large-scale raids in the sultanate's northern border areas, including Armenia.[91] As a result of these raids the entire Byzantine defence system in the eastern border areas collapsed in just two years (1058–9), with the Turkish nomads sacking the key cities of Melitene (1058), Sebasteia (1059) and several others in Syria and Mesopotamia throughout the 1060s.

A key question is what caused this sudden collapse of the Byzantine defence system in the East in just two years.[92] It would be wrong to consider the decline of the thematic army that manned these key border cities as one of the reasons, since this process of erosion had been taking place for many decades, and yet the defence of these areas seemed to work well enough before the Seljuk invasion, with the area experiencing only minor incursions for nearly two centuries. Certainly the absence of the Armenian buffer state should be considered one cause, with the Seljuk raids being directed against Byzantine territories and not against any other allied state. In addition, Constantine IX's decision to disband the 10,000-strong thematic army of the ducate of Iberia in 1053 and subject the soldiers to tax instead was seen as unprecedented. According to contemporary chroniclers like Attaleiates and Scylitzes, who were senior officials in the capital, this had catastrophic consequences for the empire's eastern defences,[93] while it also entrusted professional but unreliable troops with the defence of these border areas. In the end, the lightly armed but highly mobile Turkish nomads were able to penetrate deep into Byzantine territory by simply bypassing the highly fortified places, while the imperial forces were unable to intercept them because of their poor mobility and leadership.[94]

What Romanus IV Diogenes found in the army when he was pronounced emperor on 1 January 1068 was shocking: the thematic armies had fallen into decay, the tagmatic forces had lost a percentage of their strength and their morale was shattered by their involvement in civil wars, while the small mercenary units were unable to stand up to the emperor's expectations in taking the offensive against the Turks. By the winter

---

[90]   Matthew of Edessa, *Armenia and the Crusades: Tenth to Twelfth Centuries: The Chronicle of Matthew of Edessa*, trans. A. E. Dostourian (London, 1993), 47–50 and 92, pp. 44–6 and 76–7.
[91]   C. Cahen, 'La première pénétration turque en Asie Mineure', *Byzantion* 18 (1948), 5–67; J. T. Roché, 'In the Wake of Manzikert: The First Crusade and the Alexian Reconquest of Western Anatolia', *History* 94 (2009), 135–53.
[92]   General works include P. Charanis, 'The Byzantine Empire in the Eleventh Century', in *A History of the Crusades*, ed. K. M. Setton, M. A. Baldwin (Philadelphia, 1956), I, pp. 177–219; M. Angold, 'The Byzantine State on the Eve of the Battle of Manzikert', *Manzikert to Lepanto: The Byzantine World and the Turks 1071–1571* (Amsterdam, 1991), pp. 9–34.
[93]   Scylitzes, II (p. 608); Attaleiates, pp. 44–5; *The Chronicle of Matthew of Edessa*, XCII, p. 76.
[94]   Kaegi, 'The Contribution of Archery', pp. 104–6.

of 1070/1, the emperor was preparing for his third and final expedition against the Seljuks, in an attempt to re-establish control over lower Armenia and the important Armenian fortresses, apparently to block the Turkish invasions bypassing the Taurus Mountains.[95]

The numbers in the army that the emperor gathered in Armenia are difficult to estimate, but the chroniclers do indicate its make-up. For the mercenary forces, Romanus was accompanied by a detachment of the Varangian Guard, although not the full contingent of 6,000 men;[96] a detachment of Frankish heavy cavalry of unknown size, led by the 'Latin from Italy' named Crispinus, who had been sent to Abydus earlier in the campaign;[97] a German mercenary battalion serving as the emperor's personal guard, called the Nemitzi, was also sent to a distant post in the Balkans because of its rebellious behaviour;[98] a contingent of Franks under Roussel of Bailleul, again of unknown size but probably no more than 1,000;[99] and detachments of Pechenegs and Oguz Turks, whose exact number is unknown.[100] An Arab source also mentions a unit of Russian mercenaries of unknown size, distinct from the Varangian Guard.[101]

The indigenous units included both tagmatic and thematic troops. Since 1069, Romanus had called in the five *tagmata* of the East for training and to fill in their ranks with new recruits.[102] Theoretically, these units should have numbered 12,000 men in total, but it is highly unlikely that Romanus was able to bring their numbers back to their original strength. In the spring of 1071 Romanus called for further reinforcements from his western tagmatic units, raising the number to an additional 12,000 men.[103] For the thematic armies of Asia Minor, the primary sources specifically refer to detachments from the *themata* of Armeniacum, Cappadocia, the Armenian heavy infantry from Theodosiopolis and the *thema* of Anatolicum (units from Pisidia and Lycaonia are mentioned), while it is almost certain that the neighbouring *themata* of Antioch (ducate), Chaldea (ducate), Sebasteia, Charsianum and Colonia also contributed troops to the imperial army.[104] Trying to assess the exact numbers of these units seems hopeless, with the margin of error being high, but in theory the

---

[95]   Attaleiates, p. 136. For the fragmented landscape of the Pontic and Transcaucasian mountains, see M. Whittow, 'The Political Geography of the Byzantine World – Geographical Survey', *The Oxford Handbook of Byzantine studies*, ed. E. Jeffreys, J. Haldon, R. Cormack (Oxford, 2008), pp. 223–5.
[96]   Scylitzes, II (p. 668).
[97]   Attaleiates, pp. 122–5 and 170–1; Scylitzes, II (pp. 702–3).
[98]   Attaleiates, p. 147; Zonaras, *Annales*, III (pp. 696–7); for more on this German battalion, see Haldon, *The Byzantine Wars*, p. 114.
[99]   Attaleiates, pp. 148–9.
[100]   Attaleiates calls them indiscriminately Scyths, pp. 127 and 148; Scylitzes mentions them as 'the Uzes and the other neighbouring nations', II (p. 668).
[101]   C.Cahen, 'La campagne de Manzikert d'après les sources musulmanes', *Byzantion* 9 (1934), 613–42.
[102]   Attaleiates, pp. 103–5.
[103]   The western *tagmata* would have sustained fewer losses throughout the decades than their eastern counterparts. See Attaleiates, p. 123; Scylitzes, II (pp. 678–9).
[104]   Attaleiates, pp. 122–4 and 148–9; Scylitzes, II (pp. 668–9 and 678–81); Bryennius, p. 35.

numbers for the small *themata* like Lycaonia were 800 men, while larger ones like Armeniakon could have provided a contingent of 5,000 men. Further, detachments of unknown strength were brought from mainland Greece, specifically from the *thema* of Bulgaria and Macedonia.[105] The grand total of mercenaries and indigenous troops that Romanus brought with him in the early summer of 1071 can be put at around 40,000 men, and this was by no means the full military strength of the empire, considering all the garrison troops that were left in other sensitive border areas like Italy, the Balkans and Syria, although both the loyalty of the mercenaries and the training and equipment of many of the thematic units has to be seriously questioned.

The imperial army seems to have escaped relatively unscathed from the day's fighting on 26 August 1071, with the political consequences of the defeat at Manzikert being far more significant than the losses on the battlefield.[106] The rearguard and reserve units under the treacherous command of Andronicus Ducas, consisting probably of some of the eastern *tagmata* along with the contingents of the Pechenegs and the Oguz Turks, escaped back to the capital without suffering any casualties. Bryennius' left wing, which included the five western *tagmata*, also escaped with relatively few losses, with these units reportedly defending the Balkans against the Pechenegs the following years. Concerning the units of the right wing under Alyates, and especially the Armenian and Cappadocian forces, the sources tell us that a significant number of them managed to escape to Trapezus, Theodosiopolis and Doceia (an important fortress on the main route to Constantinople, north-east of Amaseia).

No great military figure is said to have died in the battle.[107] If we add the elite units of Tarchaniotes and Roussel, which retreated to Melitene before the battle, a significant number of around 20,000 men,[108] it seems clear that the actual losses incurred during the battle were limited to the emperor's immediate retinue, the Armenian infantry and the *tagmata* close to him, around 5 to 10 per cent of the campaigning army.[109] The Manzikert campaign may have been a strategic failure but it was not a tactical disaster as has been carelessly noted by some contemporaries, like Attaleiates, and modern historians.

The defeat at Manzikert and the civil wars of the early 1070s that followed the usurpation of the throne by Michael VII Ducas (1071–8), marked the collapse of the empire in both the East and West. In Italy, Bari fell to the Normans in 1071, while between 1072 and 1077 the Byzantine authority in the Balkans was also seriously shaken. A Bulgarian revolt broke out in 1072, which was suppressed with great difficulty by local generals, while in 1075 Croatia, a vassal state since the times of Basil

---

[105] Scylitzes probably means the ducate of Thessalonica and the small *themata* of Strymon and Beroea: Scylitzes, II (pp. 668–9).
[106] A. Friendly, *The Dreadful Day: The Battle of Manzikert, 1071* (London, 1981).
[107] Attaleiates, p. 167.
[108] Attaleiates, pp. 155 and 158; Zonaras, *Annales*, III (p. 697).
[109] Haldon, *The Byzantine Wars*, p. 126; J.-C. Cheynet, 'Manzikert: un desastre militaire?', *Byzantion* 60 (1980), 410–38, at p. 431.

II, declared its independence and loyalty to Rome. This period is also characterised by numerous Pecheneg and Hungarian raids that spread havoc in the southern and western Balkans respectively.

In Asia Minor, the treaty agreed between Alp Arslan and Romanus was abandoned, thus giving the Turks an excuse to invade imperial territories. The severity of the Turkish raids, conducted by various Turkish chieftains and concentrating mainly on the north-western Anatolian plateau, along with Constantinople's tactic of eliminating key local landowners responsible for the defence of their localities for fear of rebellions, led to the loss of key cities like Dorylaeum (Eskişehir), Ancyra (Ankara), Iconium (Konya), Amaseia (Amasya) and Caesarea in Cappadocia (also known as Caesarea Mazaca; Turkish Kayseri) upon which lay the control of the entire Anatolian plateau. In 1078, according to Anna Comnena, 'It is true that in this area [Anatolia] the empire was reduced to its last men. Turkish infiltration had scattered the eastern armies in all directions and the Turks were in almost complete control of all the districts between the Black Sea and the Hellespont, the Syrian and Aegean waters'.[110]

Finally, the last major battle before the rise of Alexius Comnenus to the imperial throne was the one that took place at Kalavrye, in 1078.[111] In March 1078, the incompetent Michael VII was forced to abdicate by a representative of the military aristocracy, the old *strategos* of the *thema* of Anatolikon, Nicephorus Botaneiates. The latter, however, was soon challenged by the *dux* of Dyrrhachium, Nicephorus Bryennius, a general with a glorious military career as *dux* of Bulgaria since 1074, who marched from his base at Dyrrhachium against the capital, and established himself at Hadrianopolis (Edirne), his home city. The emperor sent the experienced *domesticus* of the west, Alexius Comnenus, to suppress the rebellion with all the troops he could muster.

The rebel general, taking advantage of his office, managed to gather an army of mercenaries and indigenous troops from Macedonia, Thessaly and Thrace.[112] The three divisions drawn by Bryennius for the battle included the right wing under the command of Bryennius' brother John, who had a contingent of 5,000 men including Frankish mercenaries, Normans from Italy and, according to Anna, the Maniacati, who had taken part in George Maniaces' Sicilian expedition (1038–41),[113] cavalry units from Thessaly and troops from the *hetaireia*, the emperor's personal guard, which consisted of foreign troops.

It is clear that Bryennius had taken full advantage of his position at Dyrrhachium to call for reinforcements from the other side of the Adriatic. On the left wing Catacalon

---

[110]   *Alexiad*, I.4 (p. 25); Sewter, p. 38.

[111]   N. Tobias, 'The Tactics and Strategy of Alexius Comnenus at Calavrytae, 1078', *Byzantine and Modern Greek Studies* 6 (1979), 193–211.

[112]   *Alexiad*, I.4–6 (pp. 23–38); Sewter, pp. 39–48; Zonaras, *Annales*, III (pp. 716–17).

[113]   *Alexiad*, I.5 (p. 27); Sewter, p. 40; Attaleiates, p. 242; these Maniacati were most likely the sons of the former soldiers of George Maniaces who had settled in Illyria after the defeat of their commander in 1042.

Tarchaniotes commanded some 3,000 troops from Macedonia and Thrace while the centre, consisting of 3,000–4,000 men from Macedonia, Thessaly and Thrace, was under the orders of Bryennius himself. Further, there was a contingent of Pecheneg mercenaries of unknown size situated a mile's distance from the main rebel army, ready to outflank the imperial units. Opposing this rebel army of about 13,000 men, Alexius had about 2,000 Turkish troops, provided by Suleiman-ibn-Qutalmish, who was a vassal of Botaneiates, a few hundred mounted Franks[114] and the cavalry *tagma* of the Immortals[115] numbering around 1,000, both of which he commanded in person, as well as the indigenous troops from Choma (a place close to the river Maeander in Phrygia); probably around 2,000-men-strong or less.

Several conclusions can be drawn from analysing the composition of the two armies in 1078. First, it is clear that the role of the mercenaries is crucial, with Turkish, Pecheneg and Frankish troops being employed by both sides and in large numbers. At the same time, the role of the indigenous troops had become less significant. The indigenous troops of the east, both thematic and tagmatic, had virtually disappeared, with Alexius being capable of mustering only a few thousand Phrygians from Choma, who must already have been withdrawn to the capital a few years earlier by Michael VII. We must also add the factor of time, which the central government scarcely had in abundance in order to raise extra troops from the remnants of the *themata* of the East. Another aspect that draws attention, however, is the absence of the *tagmata* of the west from this battle. Was Alexius unable to contact them? Perhaps, but most of the original *tagmata*, like the Scholae, the Excubitae and the Watch, had in any case declined to such a degree after Manzikert that they were increasingly rarely mentioned by contemporary chroniclers.

The Varangians and Franks in the Byzantine army of the eleventh century

It is common knowledge among historians of the Byzantine Empire that non-Greek mercenaries were employed by the emperors from the late Roman period onwards, in response to the occasional needs of the imperial army for additional high-quality manpower. Within the period of the Reconquest (963–1025), there are numerous examples of non-Greek troops finding their way onto the imperial pay-roll, not yet termed *misthophoroi* (recipients of pay) but rather 'allies' (*symmakhoi*) or 'foreigners' (*ethnikoi*). Throughout this period, considerable numbers of Rus, Bulgarians, Armenians, Abkhazians and Hungarians joined the imperial forces in Asia Minor or in the Balkans, with typical examples being the Arab campaigns of Nicephorus Phocas and John Tzimisces and the Bulgarian wars of Basil II. These troops were supplied by countries that were either in cordial relations with Constantinople, were

---

[114]   Zonaras, *Annales*, III (p. 717).
[115]   This *tagma* has nothing to do with John Tzimisces' *tagma* of the Immortals which was established in 969.

dependent upon their trading agreements or were simply satellite or vassal states. In order to raise these sizeable units, Constantinople had to have the permission and active cooperation of their respective lords or overlords. What then was the difference between these large units of foreign mercenaries and the Westerners that first appeared at the imperial court in the middle of the eleventh century?

A typical example of the old pattern is the Byzantine expedition to Sicily in 1038, when a contingent of 300 mounted Normans took part in the campaign, sent by Gaimar of Salerno, who was the suzerain of the Normans of Aversa and a vassal of the empire. The case of the Normans fits in with the already established pattern of the Byzantines employing large units of mercenary soldiers to cover their occasional needs for troops, a very common practice for the central government and for local commanders. But the Frankish troops that first arrived at Constantinople in the mid-eleventh century, although they received a fixed wage and could easily desert their employers if their reward was not satisfactory, differed mainly in that they were employed as individuals – they were materialistic volunteers who had travelled a long way in search of sufficient pay and the opportunity to pillage and destroy, living up to the term 'soldiers of fortune'. Furthermore, contingents of troops served the emperor for a limited number of campaigns, while a large number of Franks served under imperial generals for many decades, either for or against the emperor. The 300 Normans of the 1038 campaign, although they were sent by Gaimar of Salerno, who was a vassal of Byzantium, were not his native subjects and were serving George Maniaces under their own leaders, namely William and Drogo Hauteville. A significant number of them were still referred to as 'Maniacati' by Anna Comnena in 1078.

A key date, however, for the mercenary forces in the Byzantine Empire is the year 988, which marks the arrival of the Scandinavian regiment of 6,000 Varangians in the capital. Upon their arrival, the Varangians relieved the Excubitae (the elite unit of the Scholae responsible for the defence of the imperial palace) and they were divided into the 'Varangians of the City', who guarded the emperor and escorted him in his tours outside the palace, either within the capital or in his campaigns, and the 'Varangians outside the City', who were stationed in key posts in the provinces.[116] Undoubtedly, the Varangian Guard would have formed the spearhead of Basil's expansionist policy, from the Syrian expedition of 999[117] and the Armenian campaign of 1000[118] to the bloody and destructive Bulgarian wars that culminated in the battle of Clidium (1014).[119]

During the time of the Epigoni, a key date for the leadership of the Varangian Guard was the year 1034, when the younger half-brother of the Norwegian king Óláfr II and

[116]   Sigfús Blöndal, *The Varangians of Byzantium*, trans. and ed. B. Benedikz (Cambridge, 2007), p. 45.
[117]   G. Schlumberger, *L'épopée byzantine à la fin du dixième siècle: guerres contre les Russes, les Arabes, les Allemands, les Bulgares: luttes civiles contre les deux Bardas*, 2 vols. (Paris, 1896–1905), II, pp. 152–3.
[118]   Asochik, *Histoire universelle*, trans. E. Dulaurier and F. Macler (Paris, 1883–1917), p. 165.
[119]   Scylitzes, II (p. 348). P. Stephenson, *The Legend of Basil the Bulgar-Slayer* (Cambridge, 2003), pp. 11–49; P. Stephenson, *Byzantium's Balkan Frontier: A Political Study of the Northern Balkans, 900–1204* (Cambridge, 2000), pp. 47–80.

future king Haraldr III Sigurðarson (Hardrada) endeavoured to enter the Varangian Guard. From this year onwards, our main primary sources for the Varangians consist mainly of numismatic and other archaeological evidence, along with Scandinavian sagas, which relate the life story of Haraldr. These sagas were written down in Iceland as much as two centuries after the events and they can be misleading. *Haralds saga Sigurðarsonar* ch. 3 relates that after an audience with the empress Zoe, Haraldr and his mercenaries served on the galleys with the soldiers that went out into the Greek Sea.[120] It is reasonable for the empire to have used those experienced mercenaries in policing duties in the Aegean Sea, an area that was ravaged by Arab raids in the previous centuries, even more so if we consider the grand naval strategy that had started taking shape as early as the reign of Romanus III (1028–34), and involved the revival of the imperial fleet and the expulsion of the Muslims from Sicily.[121] Whether the Varangians were used as crews of some sort of privateer ships or they actually manned imperial ships, thus being under the direct command of the *drungarius* of the fleet, is not made entirely clear by the sources, although the last case seems much more likely. Furthermore, it is important to note that in this early period Haraldr was still in command of the Varangians outside of the City, which probably had its winter quarters in the Thracesian *thema*.[122]

The campaign that made Haraldr's Varangian Guard famous, however, was their participation in the 1038 campaign against the Kalbite Muslims of Sicily, under the command of the famous George Maniaces.[123] In this campaign a contingent of Varangians, probably around 500 under the command of Harald, was sent to Italy to take part in the expulsion of the Kalbites, along with units from the Greek mainland and 300 Normans from Aversa.[124] The specific role played by the Varangians in this campaign is rather obscure, although *Heimskringla* implies that they were used to man the imperial naval squadron sent to patrol the coastline of eastern Sicily. It is also highly likely that they were sent to reduce a number of fortified sites in the east and south-east of the island.[125] The fact that they manned imperial ships during this campaign is further supported by their role in patrolling the Apulian coasts between 1066 and 1068, and defeating a Norman fleet off Brindisi, according to contemporary

[120] Snorri Sturluson, *Heimskringla*, ed. Bjarni Aðalbjarnarson (Reykjavík, 1941–51), vol. III, p. 71.

[121] Ahrweiler, *Byzance et la mer*, p. 123.

[122] Scylitzes, II (pp. 508–9).

[123] A. Savvides, Γεώργιος Μανιάκης. Κατακτήσεις και υπονόμευση στο Βυζάντιο του 11ου αιώνα, 1030–1043 μ.Χ. [*Georgios Maniaces. Conquests and Subversion in 11th Century Byzantium, 1030–1043*] (Athens, 2004).

[124] Cecaumenus, p. 97; Malaterra, I.7; Amatus, II.8; *Gesta*, I.203–6 (p. 110); Scylitzes mentions 500 Normans: Scylitzes, II (p. 545).

[125] *Haralds saga Sigurðarsonar* ch. 6–10 (within *Heimskringla*) tells us about the siege of four unidentified castles: Snorri Sturluson, *Heimskringla*, vol. III, pp. 76–81. Could it be that two of these were Messina and Syracuse, for which the rest of our sources talk about? See Malaterra, I.7; Amatus, II.8 and 9; Scylitzes also mentions the capture of thirteen more cities: Scylitzes, II (p. 520). For the course of the campaign: Amari, *Storia dei Musulmani di Sicilia*, II, pp. 438–55.

chroniclers; this was a very similar operational theatre. It is regrettable, however, that *Heimskringla*, an unreliable saga written centuries later, is our only source concerning the siege-tactics of the Varangians in Sicily.[126] These included the enforcement of a land-blockade, the digging of tunnels to undermine the city-walls, and other unchivalric tricks employed to capture an unidentified castle.

The Varangians were further involved in all the major expeditions that took place during Constantine IX's reign, throughout the 1040s and 1050s, in both Asia Minor and the Balkans. A force of 3,000 Varangians participated in the annexation of the Armenian kingdom of Ani (1045), while three years later they were called to the Balkans to fight the Pechenegs as they penetrated south of the Danube.[127] In the mid-1050s, a large unit of Varangians and Normans was called to defend the imperial fortresses in Armenia against Seljuk raids, with much success.[128] During the civil conflicts after Constantine IX's death in 1055 we have the first case of the rare phenomenon of Varangians facing each other in battle. The fact that Isaac Comnenus, the leader of the *coup d'état* against Michael VI (1056–7), had employed Varangian troops as well as Normans is attested by Psellus, who was an eyewitness of the events as the emperor's ambassador to his rival.[129] It is more likely, though, that the emperor's units were the Varangians of the City, the personal guard of Michael, while Isaac must have employed the Varangians outside the City, who would have been in the Armenian *thema* fighting the Seljuks just before Isaac's *coup d'état*.[130]

In the 1060s the Varangians were dispatched to the distant province of Longobardia primarily for garrison duties in strategic fortresses. In 1066, a contingent of them was sent to Bari, under the command of Leo Mauricas, to take the offensive against the Normans in Apulia. He succeeded in retaking Taranto, Brindisi and Castelanetta, with a number of Varangians being posted in Brindisi to defend it against the Normans.[131] It is possible that they were not withdrawn from Italy until the Norman siege of Bari in 1068. During the siege they were probably employed in one of their usual tasks, the naval patrolling of the Apulian coasts. Indeed, Lupus Protospatharius and Scylitzes refer to a naval engagement off Brindisi in 1070, where the Byzantine fleet consisting of Varangians defeated Robert Guiscard's inexperienced fleet.[132] Also, Cecaumenus clearly distinguishes between the infantry units of the Rus, who are identified as *kontaratoi*, and the Varangians, who were *ploimoi* (marines).[133]

[126] Scylitzes, II (pp. 520–3 and 545); Zonaras, *Annales*, III (pp. 590–4); the 'Italian-Norman' sources are Malaterra, I.7 and I.8; *Gesta*, I.196–221 (pp. 108–10); Lupus Protospatharius, *Chronicon*, s.a. 1038.
[127] Scylitzes, II (pp. 572–3); Attaleiates, pp. 31–43; Cecaumenus, pp. 22–3.
[128] Matthew of Edessa, *Chronique*, trans. E. Dulaurier (Paris, 1858), pp. 99–102; *The Chronicle of Matthew of Edessa*, II.3 (p. 87); Scylitzes, II (p. 606).
[129] Psellus, *Chronographia*, VII.25 (p. 289).
[130] Scylitzes, II (p. 624).
[131] Anonymus Barensis, *Chronicon*, s.a. 1066.
[132] Lupus Protospatharius, *Chronicon*, s.a. 1071; Scylitzes, II (pp. 722–3).
[133] Cecaumenus, p. 30.

Other foreigners that came to dominate the Varangian Guard in the last quarter of the eleventh century and gradually replaced the Rus were the English, both Anglo-Saxons and Anglo-Danes.[134] The first mention of English warriors in the Byzantine court comes from Anna Comnena when she narrates her father's rebellion against Botaneiates in the spring of 1081. She mentions the 'Varangians from Thule', a term which – in the case of the *Alexiad* – may be taken to mean warriors from the British Isles.[135] The second primary source for the English migration is Orderic Vitalis who refers to 'some of them [the English] who were still in the flower of their youth travelled into remote lands and bravely offered their arms to Alexius, emperor of Constantinople'.[136] At another point in his work, when examining Robert Guiscard's invasion of Illyria, in 1081, he refers to the emperor Alexius, who 'received into his trust the English who had left England after the slaughter of King Harold [. . .] and had sailed across the sea to Thrace [Greece]. He openly entrusted his principal palace and royal treasures to their care, even making them guards of his own person and all his possessions.'[137] Here, Orderic implies that the English newcomers replaced their Rus counterparts as the emperor's personal bodyguard, but we have no idea whether they were numerous enough to dominate the Varangians outside of the City as well.

In addition, Geoffrey Malaterra writes for the first time about the 'Angles – whom they [the Byzantines] called Varangians' when describing the opposing forces right before the battle of Dyrrhachium.[138] Finally, Scylitzes refers to the Varangians who took part in Isaac Comnenus' rebellion against Michael VI in 1057, as of clearly Celtic origin.[139] Since it is highly improbable that the Varangian guard would have become English by the mid-1050s, historians presume that the chronicler, who writes around the end of the eleventh century, is confused and apparently refers to the post-1081 composition of the Guard. The aforementioned extracts from four contemporary

[134]   The Rus were an amalgamation of Scandinavian – mainly Swedish – settlers and Slavic and Finno-Ugrian nomads. The term Rus is used here mainly as a geographical term that includes Russians of both Slavic and Scandinavian origin, unless specified otherwise. For more on the debate concerning the origin of the ninth and tenth century Rus see G. Vernadsky, *The Origins of Russia* (Oxford, 1959), pp. 198–201; Sigfús Blöndal, *The Varangians of Byzantium*, pp. 1–14; H. R. E. Davidson, *The Viking Road to Byzantium* (London, 1976), pp. 57–67.

[135]   Alexiad, II.9 (p. 120); Sewter, p. 95. In her work, Anna describes the boundaries of the Roman Empire in its heyday and she clearly differentiates between the island of Thule and 'all the people who live in the region of the North'. Alexiad, VI.11 (p. 312); Sewter, pp. 205–6. For more on the interpretation of this term used by Anna see Buckler, *Anna Comnena*, p. 438; S. Blöndal, 'Nabites the Varangian', *Classica et Mediaevalia* 2 (1939), 145–7; Sewter, p. 392, n. 33.

[136]   Orderic Vitalis, IV (p. 202).

[137]   Orderic Vitalis, VII (p. 16).

[138]   Malaterra, III.27; Blondal believes that Malaterra might have been carried away by the presence of separate English regiments amongst the mainly Russian-Norse Varangian Guard at Dyrrhachium. It does seem possible to me, however, that this was contrived too. See Blöndal, 'Nabites', 151–2 and 157; Blöndal, *The Varangians of Byzantium*, p. 21.

[139]   Scylitzes, II (p. 613).

and historically reliable chroniclers, combined with a chrysobull issued by Alexius Comnenus in 1088, where the foreign mercenaries serving in the imperial army were: 'Russians, Varangians, Kulpingians, English, Franks, Germans, Bulgarians, Saracens, Alans and Abasgians',[140] lead us to the conclusion that after the first few years of Alexius' reign the Rus had come to be replaced as the dominant element in the Varangian Guard. Thus, the year 1081 must be seen as a *terminus ante quem* for the incorporation of Anglo-Saxons into the Varangian Guard; but do we have enough evidence to trace when this immigration to Byzantium began.

Two other chrysobulls issued by Michael VII and Nicephorus Botaneiates, in 1075 and 1079 respectively, providing an almost identical list, do not mention the term English.[141] Matthew of Edessa does refer to some 'inhabitants from distant islands' at Manzikert, but this does not constitute enough evidence to verify the existence of distinct English units for the 1068–71 periods.[142] The year that is most appealing as a *terminus post quem* is the fatal year 1066. The fact that they are not mentioned as distinct units in the imperial army until 1081, however, is probably because the main wave of mercenaries did not come before the complete conquest of England by William I, his crushing of the local rebellions and the defeat of Denmark's king, Svein Estrithson, in the spring of 1070.[143]

Another mercenary group in the Byzantine army that came to play a vital role in the empire's politics in the second half of the eleventh century were the Franks, who first appear as individual mercenaries in Byzantine service in the year 1047, during the revolt of Leo Tornicius. Like the Varangians, the Franks were most likely used for purposes of defence, manning towns like Manzikert on the Armenian borders. After Tornicius' rebellion they were recalled, along with the rest of the eastern *tagmata*, to the Balkans to repel the Pecheneg invasion of 1049. This time they also had their own leader, Hervé (surnamed Phrangopulus, 'the son of a Frank').[144] He was a veteran of Maniaces' Sicilian campaign and had commanded the left wing of the imperial army in the battle against the Pechenegs.[145]

---

[140]   Zachariae a Lingenthal, *Jus Graeco-Romanum* (Lipsiae, 1867), III, p. 373.

[141]   C. Sathas, *Bibliotheca Graeca Medii Aevi* (Venice and Paris, 1872–94), I, p. 55.

[142]   Matthew of Edessa, *Chronique*, pp. 166–9. K. Ciggaar, 'England and Byzantium on the Eve of the Norman Conquest (The Reign of Edward the Confessor)', *Anglo-Norman Studies* 5 (1982), 87–8. I do not agree with Ciggaar that Matthew's comments constitute enough evidence to identify English units at Manzikert.

[143]   The predominance of the English in the Guard after 1081 is supported by a number of scholars: A. A. Vasiliev, 'The Opening Stages of the Anglo-Saxon Immigration to Byzantium in the Eleventh Century', *Annales de l'Institut Kondakov* 9 (1937), pp. 39–70; J. Shepard, 'The English and Byzantium: A Study of their Role in the Byzantine Army in the Later Eleventh Century', *Traditio* 29 (1973), 53–92; Chalandon, *Alexis I*, p. 76; J. W. Birkenmeier, *The Development of the Komnenian Army* (Leiden, 2002), pp. 64–5; J. Godfrey, 'The Defeated Anglo-Saxons Take Service with the Eastern Emperor', *Anglo-Norman Studies* 1 (1978), 68–70.

[144]   E. van Houts, 'Normandy and Byzantium', *Byzantion* 55 (1985), 554–5.

[145]   Scylitzes, II (p. 597–605 and 616).

The unit commanded by Hervé is described by Scylitzes as the wing of the 'Roman phalanx', consisting of mounted Frankish mercenaries who were Hervé's fellow-countrymen. If we accept, however, the possibility that Hervé's men were all Franks, their numbers should have been substantial if they made up an entire wing of the imperial army's battle-line – probably a few hundred, judging by Scylitzes.[146] Hervé also possessed the court titles of *magister* and *stratelates* of the East, which put him in charge of not only Frankish, but also Byzantine tagmatic units in Asia Minor, thus replacing Catacalon Cecaumenus.[147]

In the 1050s the Franks were to be found in all the major operational theatres of the empire. Scylitzes mentions the presence of Franks (this time they are specifically put on horseback) sent to Upper Armenia by Michael VI to fight back a Seljuk raiding party in 1056, again under the command of Hervé.[148] This Frankish contingent not only managed to push back the Seljuks but, indeed, successfully pursued the retreating Turks, although as we have already seen that was a very dangerous battle tactic. Perhaps they were still unfamiliar with the Seljuk way of fighting.

During Isaac Comnenus' rebellion against Michael VI, 'two Frankish battalions and one Russian who were spending the winter in these areas [the Armenian *thema*]' were reported, probably after their successful fighting-back of the Seljuks in the previous summer (1056).[149] For these significant events, there is an eyewitness description from Psellus, who was one of the ambassadors sent by Michael VI to negotiate with Isaac:

> There were Italians, and Scyths from the Taurus, men of fearful appearance, dressed in fearful garb, both alike glaring fiercely about them. The one [the Franks] made their attacks as their spirit moved them, were impetuous and led by impulse, the other [the Varangians] with a mad fury; the former in their first onslaught were irresistible, but they quickly lost their ardour; the latter, on the other hand, were less impatient, but fought with unsparing devotion and a complete disregard for wounds.[150]

Again, we see in this description by Psellus the whole theme that dominated the Byzantine military manuals, from the *Strategikon* to the *Taktika*, whereby the Franks were characterised by the tremendous impact of their cavalry charge and their limited stamina.

In the late 1040s and the 1050s, the Franks would have been permanently established in areas pointed out by the government in order to live off the land. The places where we read of them being quartered for the winter in Asia Minor were in the Armenian

---

[146] Scylitzes, II (pp. 597–605 and 617).
[147] J. Shepard, 'The Uses of the Franks in Eleventh-Century Byzantium', *Anglo-Norman Studies* 15 (1993), 275–305, at pp. 296–7. For the significance of these court titles and their evolution since the seventh century, see J. B. Bury, *The Imperial Administrative System in the Ninth Century* (London, 1911), pp. 20–36.
[148] Scylitzes, II (pp. 617–19).
[149] Scylitzes, II (p. 624).
[150] Psellus, *Chronographia*, VII.25 (p. 289).

thema, while many of them must have been stationed in the neighbouring *themata* of Chaldea and Iberia, along with a number of Varangians.[151] One valuable source to trace their whereabouts is the exemption acts (the chrysobulls), granted to landowners or monastic houses, relieving them from the obligation of providing shelter and all the necessary supplies to the imperial army's troops. Since it was an obligation for every citizen of the empire (even of great monastic houses) to supply the imperial troops with quarters and all the residential necessities, there were special taxes imposed on the local population termed *mitaton, phrangomitaton, haplekton, mesaplekton, phrangiatikon*. Thus, a great number of exemptions relating to Varangians or Franks indicate their winter quarters and establishments.[152] This might be considered an attempt not only to settle these restless warriors, especially in a sensitive frontier area like the north-east of Asia Minor, but also to avoid paying by cash in a period when the collapse of the economy seemed imminent and the coinage had already been significantly debased by Constantine IX.

The second of the three Frankish commanders to be found in Byzantium in our period of research was Robert Crispin. He had followed a similar career pattern as Hervé, having sailed to Constantinople 'to become a noble (*chevalerie*) at the emperor's court',[153] probably around the mid-1060s. After his arrival, Attaleiates writes that Robert was immediately sent east to the Frankish camps to spend the winter, probably in 1068/9, along with the rest of his followers.[154] It is not possible to estimate the number of his troops at this early stage, but Matthew of Edessa does mention a strong garrison of 200 Frankish knights at Sewawerat, north of Edessa in northern Mesopotamia, defending the castle against a Seljuk raid in 1065/6.[155] Information from Scylitzes, Attaleiates, Bryennius and Zonaras puts this number at four hundred, since all of these sources link the numbers that Roussel of Bailleul took over with that which Robert Crispin commanded before him.[156] After Manzikert, Crispin took part in a campaign with his Frankish contingent against the former emperor Romanus.[157]

The fact that Crispin commanded the Byzantine army's left wing in a battle against Romanus would have raised great resentment and discontent from the Byzantine generals, both against Crispin and the emperor. And this is duly noted by Cecaumenus in his *Strategikon*:

> Do not raise foreigners, if they do not come from the royal family of their land, to great offices nor trust them with significant titles, because if you honour the foreigner with the office of

---

[151]   Scylitzes, II.789 (p. 606).

[152]   *Actes de Lavra*, ed. G. Rouillard and P. Collomp (Paris, 1937), 1, 28 and 80; Sathas, *Bibliotheca Graeca*, pp. 1 and 55.

[153]   Amatus, I.8.

[154]   Attaleiates, p. 122; Scylitzes, II (p. 678).

[155]   *The Chronicle of Matthew of Edessa*, II.27 (pp. 107–8); Matthew also notes the presence of a Frank in the garrison of Edessa in the same year, II.28 (p. 109).

[156]   Attaleiates, p. 183; Scylitzes, II (p. 708); Bryennius, p. 147; Zonaras, *Annales*, III (p. 709).

[157]   Bryennius, p. 135; Psellus, *Chronographia*, VII.31–2 (pp. 363–4); Attaleiates, pp. 173–4.

primikerios[158] or *strategos*, then what is the point of giving the generalship to a Roman [i.e. Byzantine]? You will turn him [the Roman] into an enemy.[159]

The precedent of a Frank commanding a large division of the Byzantine army had already been set by Hervé in 1049. The fundamental distinction, though, between these two cases is that Hervé commanded a division of fellow Franks under the command of a Byzantine general against foreign invaders (the Pecheneg invasion of 1049). Crispin, on the other hand, participated in civil conflicts, having the full support of an emperor that the rest of the Byzantine generals possibly would not have had, and apparently he was the dominant figure in Andronicus Ducas' army in 1072, inspiring admiration not only from his own men but from Byzantine troops as well.[160]

The most famous of the Franks to have been employed by Constantinople in the second half of the eleventh century was Roussel of Bailleul. Along with Geoffrey Ridel, the duke of Gaeta from 1068, he was Count Roger's principal lieutenant in his Sicilian campaign. The fact that he is no longer mentioned by the Italian chroniclers after Cerami suggests that around the period of standstill in the Sicilian theatre of operations he decided to pursue a more profitable career across the Adriatic. Initially, Roussel managed to take advantage of the desperation of the local inhabitants of the areas of Lycaonia and Galatia in the Armenian *thema* for protection against the Seljuk raids.[161] His ambitions were clearly high from the beginning of his establishment in imperial territories, but whether he had designs on the imperial throne from the outset is uncertain.

For the Manzikert campaign, Attaleiates informs us of the presence of a Frankish contingent under Roussel, probably of around 500 knights, although no numbers are provided.[162] In the winter of 1073/4 he openly challenged the Ducades in open battle, defeating Isaac Comnenus and taking him prisoner, while also managing to capture John Ducas, who was sent with a large army against him. Before being bought off by Michael VII and sent back to his estates in the Armenian *thema* to defend the empire's collapsing borders, he had managed to raise John Ducas as a rival claimant to the imperial throne.[163] By that time, his estates and thus his power had been greatly increased and he was seen as one of the most powerful nobles in north-eastern Asia Minor.

Roussel found in Alexius Comnenus a cunning and much more formidable rival. Alexius was sent in Amaseia (autumn 1075) in the Armenian *thema* with a meagre

---

[158] *Primikerios*: a title given to heads of administrative departments in the Byzantine government and to officials in the imperial court (*primikerios tou kaboukleiou*).

[159] Cecaumenus, p. 95.

[160] Attaleiates, pp. 173–4; Psellus, *Chronographia*, VII.30 (p. 364).

[161] Shepard, 'The Uses of the Franks', p. 300; A. Simpson, 'Three Sources of Military Unrest in Eleventh Century Asia Minor: The Norman Chieftains Hervé Frankopoulos, Robert Crispin and Roussel of Bailleuil', *Mesogeios/Méditerranée*, 9–10 (2000), 194.

[162] Attaleiates, pp. 148–9.

[163] Roussel's army must have comprised around 2,700–3,000 men: Attaleiates, pp. 183–93; Scylitzes, II (pp. 708–9).

force, probably a few hundred strong, to deal with Roussel once and for all.[164] The young general resorted to the plundering of Roussel's estates and the besieging of the principal cities under his control, thus denying him his source of revenue while avoiding a pitched battle.[165] Having very few soldiers at his disposal to even consider a battle, his choice of reducing the enemy's strongholds must have been his only option at the time, and although it seemed to work for a while, at least according to the *Alexiad*, the key to victory lay with the Seljuks and with the side that would manage to buy them off as allies.[166]

Eventually, Roussel was captured by the Turks and handed over to Alexius, with Anna Comnena writing about the famous incident with the inhabitants of Amaseia, where the imperial force had been stationed, rioting and even trying to set the captured Frank free.[167] Was it because the Frankish army provided better protection for the local population than the official Byzantine authorities, or maybe because the locals were accustomed to doing business with the foreigners? Probably both, if we consider Alexius' precautionary measure of sweeping away the remaining Frankish garrisons from the neighbouring areas before returning to the capital with his valuable prisoner. This was done in case the province fell back into the previous *status quo* as a result of the extensive support Roussel had enjoyed in the area from the local Byzantine and Armenian element.[168] It is significant that Roussel had not confiscated or plundered any of the domains of the wealthy nobles of the Armenian *thema*,[169] fearful that they would turn against him and call on either the emperor or, even worse, the Seljuks.

The period of Alexius' maturing years, namely the period of collapse in the 1070s, when he was a young officer in the service of the Ducas family, must have taught him a great deal about how to deal with mercenaries, and especially Westerners. In a significant change of tactics towards them, he may have allowed some of them to have their own commander after becoming an emperor. For example, Constantine Humbertopulus, a nephew of Robert Guiscard, had been living in Byzantium for a long time, and judging by his Orthodox name he was not a newcomer who had raised his own followers in a distant imperial province, but rather a trusted imperial officer who actively assisted Alexius' rise to the throne.[170] Humbertopulus also took part in the 1081 campaign against Robert Guiscard's siege of Dyrrhachium, commanding a 'regiment of Franks'.[171]

The increasing dependence of the central government of Constantinople on mercenary forces can be seen as the response to a combination of factors whose

---

164   Bryennius, p. 185.
165   *Alexiad*, I.2 (p. 16); Sewter, p. 33.
166   *Alexiad*, I.2 (pp. 16–17); Sewter, pp. 33–4. See also Bryennius, pp. 187–9; Attaleiates, pp. 199–200.
167   *Alexiad*, I.2 (pp. 17–19); Sewter, pp. 34–5.
168   *Alexiad*, I.4 (pp. 24–5); Sewter, pp. 36–7.
169   Bryennius, p. 187.
170   *Alexiad*, II.4–5 (pp. 93–104); Sewter, pp. 81–2.
171   *Alexiad*, IV.4 (p. 199); Sewter, p. 141.

detailed examination is beyond the scope of this study. The extensive frontier areas subjected to seven decades of expansionist policy had to be manned by seasoned, professional and well-trained soldiers, a task which the thematic troops had proved incapable of performing. Western mercenaries – it was the Franks who were employed on a permanent basis – were the cheapest and most efficient solution to a period of economic troubles and coin debasement. Since their first appearance outside the walls of Constantinople in 1047, they served the emperors in all operational theatres, most frequently by manning castles and strategic towns in Armenia, Cilicia and Bulgaria, crucial frontier regions of the empire. They were predominantly cavalry, numbering a few hundred, and since the early 1050s they had their own leaders, the most renowned of them being Hervé, Robert Crispin and Roussel of Bailleuil. The long-established view of them being the main cause for numerous rebellions over the centuries, however, has been challenged by a recent series of studies.[172] Indeed, as we have seen in this chapter, there were Frankish leaders whose ambitions extended far beyond that of a faithful employee. If we look carefully at the political context of those rebellions, which would have included indigenous troops as well, then the situation becomes different. Would any rebellions have been mounted if Nicephorus Phocas or Basil II was on the throne? Probably not. The Varangian Guard had not rebelled against an emperor since the 980s and were, in fact, the most elite unit of the Byzantine army. These mercenaries filled crucial gaps in the Byzantine army's battlefield effectiveness: the Franks by providing elite cavalry battalions that seemed to gradually replace the tagmatic units of the *kataphraktoi*, and the Varangians by manning strategic towns in Armenia and the Balkans against important enemies of the empire, a task that had been assigned since the seventh century to the thematic soldiers but was now seriously neglected by the central government.

[172] Shepard, 'The Uses of the Franks'; Haldon, *Warfare, State and Society*, pp. 85–93.

4

The Byzantine Naval Forces of the Tenth and Eleventh Centuries

Strive at all times to have the fleet in top condition and to have it not want for anything. For the fleet is the glory of Romania [Byzantium].[1]

The resurgence of Byzantine naval power in the Aegean and the Mediterranean in the tenth century is in contrast to the significant territorial losses the Byzantine Empire sustained in the ninth century, such as the fall of Sicily to the Aghlavids of Tunisia by the year 878 and the conquest of Chandax by the Umayyad Muslims from Spain in 824. Several expeditionary armies were assembled and fleets were gathered from all the maritime and coastal *themata* of the empire against the Muslims of Crete in 911, 949 and again in 960, with the island's capital falling to the imperial forces in March 961, while Cyprus became an effective administrative province of the empire in 965. Hence, the pacification of the eastern half of the Mediterranean basin that came as a result of the conquest of Crete, Cyprus, Cilicia and northern Syria, the securing of the naval routes to and from Constantinople and the increasing presence of the Byzantine authority in its Italian provinces marked a new era of *pax Romana* on the high seas that was to last for nearly a century.[2]

The structure of the Byzantine navy allowed it to play both a defensive and an offensive role, depending on the policy shaped by the central government. The three major units of the imperial navy, established in the early eighth century, consisted of the imperial fleet, an elite unit based primarily at Constantinople and commanded by a *drungarius* of the fleet; the fleets of the marine *themata* of the Cibyrrhaeots, Samos and Aegean Sea, each under its own *strategos*; and the provincial fleets of the rest of the coastal *themata* of the empire, small squadrons that had as their main duty the policing of the coasts and major ports, each under a turmarch or an *arkhon*.

---

[1]   Cecaumenus, *Logos nouthetikos*, in *Strategikon*, §87.
[2]   J. H. Pryor and E. Jeffreys, *The Age of the Δρόμων, The Byzantine Navy ca 500–1204* (Leiden, 2006), pp. 50–76.

The imperial fleet was established in the aftermath of the first Arab siege of Constantinople (674–8) and thereafter played a very similar operational role to that of the tagmatic units of the army. Since its operational role up to the middle of the ninth century was auxiliary to the land armies (providing them with transportation and security), the imperial fleet consisted primarily of large transport ships manned by oarsmen with no fighting units of marines on board. It was the serious territorial losses of the empire in Crete and Sicily that prompted Basil I to introduce marines into the imperial fleet, thus upgrading it to the most elite naval unit under its direct command at the time. From that period onwards, its squadrons were responsible for the defence of the coastal areas neighbouring the capital, as well as for its port and maritime traffic, for the policing and monitoring of the traffic in the major maritime routes of the empire, for providing assistance to the provincial fleets of the non-maritime coastal *themata*, for the neutralisation of enemy pirate activity, for providing transportation for the land armies in large-scale campaigns and for undertaking naval expeditions against enemy naval bases.[3]

Like the *tagmata* of the land armies, the imperial fleet was built and equipped in the capital. It formed part of its garrison, and during the reign of Leo VI it had some 4,000 marines and 19,600 oarsmen.[4] Prior to the period of the Epigoni, the crews of the imperial fleet were recruited, like their thematic counterparts, from the areas surrounding the capital and mainly the *thema* of the Opsicium and the coastal areas of Thrace – mariners from this latter region were called *stenitai* after the narrow pass of the Bosporus.[5] Mercenaries were also frequently used, From the proto-Byzantine period, in times of serious external threat or for large-scale operations, such as the Cretan expeditions of 845 and the 'the army of forty coins' (*sarakontarios stratos*) after each soldier's pay).[6] These were either natives, mainly from areas famous for the quality of their marines like the coastal areas of the Greek mainland and the Aegean islands, or foreign allies (*symmakhoi*), the latter being recruited in groups or as individuals and having the option of remaining in the service of the empire after the end of the campaign, like the Rus and the Varangians.[7]

The structure of the imperial fleet followed the same pattern as that of the *tagmata*.[8] Hence, the *drungarius* of the fleet was the supreme commander of the

---

[3] Ahrweiler, *Byzance et la mer*, pp. 46–7; K. Papasoteriou, Βυζαντινή υψηλή στρατηγική, 6ος–11ος αιώνας (Byzantine High Strategy, 6th–11th century) (Athens, 2001), pp. 199–202.

[4] Treadgold, *Byzantium and its Army*, p. 76 and especially Table 2 on p. 67.

[5] *De Administrando Imperio*, LI (p. 246).

[6] Theophanes Continuates, in Theophanes Continuates, Ioannes Cameniata, Symeon Magister, Georgius monachus, Οι μετά Θεοφάνην [The continuators of Theophanes], CSHB, vol. 33, ed. I. Bekker and E. Weber (Bonn, 1838), p. 81. A later example is the Cretan expedition of 949, with many details available in *De Ceremoniis*, pp. 651–71.

[7] Ahrweiler, *Byzance et la mer*, Appendix I, pp. 403–5.

[8] Basileios Patrikios, 'Ναυμαχικά που συντάχθηκαν με εντολή του πατρικίου και παρακοιμώμενου Βασιλείου' ['Naumachika compiled under the order of the patrikios and parakoimomenos Basileios'],

imperial fleet stationed in the capital, being appointed by and held accountable solely to the emperor himself.[9] Like his counterparts in the *tagmata*, he had a *topoteretes* as lieutenant-in-chief and an extended staff, with the lieutenant being in charge of a naval detachment when the *drungarius* was unable to leave the capital.[10] The commander of a small flotilla of 3–5 dromons (ships) was an *arkhon* called 'count' who received direct commands from the admiral, the *drungarius* of the fleet. Under the count there was the office of the centarch, responsible for the command of a single dromon.

Among the first maritime *themata* to be established in 674 was that of the Carabisiani, renamed as the Cibbyrrhaeots by Leo III in 727. Its base was initially in Samos and its boundaries included almost the entire southern Anatolian coast, the islands of the Aegean Sea along with the eastern Peloponnese, Attica and Euboea. Following the failed expedition to retake Crete in 843, Michael III (842–67) introduced the *thema* of the Aegean Sea, which included all the islands of the Greek archipelago that formerly belonged to the Cibbyrrhaeots' jurisdiction. After the *thema* of the Aegean Sea was separated from the Cibbyraeots, each one of the new *themata* would have had about 1,000 marines and 6,000 oarsmen. In the early years of Basil I's reign (867–86) the *thema* of Samos was separated from that of the Aegean Sea, including the opposite Anatolian coasts and the important ports of Smyrna, Adramyttium (Edremit) and Ephesus. The *thema* of Samos would have had 600 marines and 4,000 oarsmen, while the manpower of the Aegean Sea would have been diminished to 400 and 2,000 men respectively.[11] The *themata* of the Cibbyraeots, the Aegean Sea and Samos were the only clearly maritime *themata* (*themata ploima* or *ploimothemata*), contrary to the land *themata* (*kaballarika themata*) and the rest of the coastal *themata*.[12]

The operational role of the thematic navy was the defence and policing of the coastal areas and ports under their jurisdiction, much like their counterparts in the land *themata*. Their main tasks were to keep the sea routes safe for navigation, to neutralise whatever pirate activity occurred in their patrolling area (something which inevitably included mounting small-scale campaigns against enemy bases) and to secure and control trading activities in all the major ports of the *thema*. The thematic fleet was built and equipped in the province itself, with the marines and the oarsmen

in Ναυμαχικὰ Λέοντος ϛ, Μαυρικίου, Συριανοῦ Μαγίστρου, Βασιλείου Πατρικίου, Νικηφόρου Οὐρανοῦ [*The Naumaukhika of Leo VI, Maurice, Syrianos Magister, Basileios Patrikios, Nikephoros Ouranos*], introduction, translation and commentary by I. X. Dimitroukas (Athens, 2005), pp. 152–73, IV.2–3 (pp. 166–8); Leo VI, *Taktika*, XIX.26–7 (p. 512).

[9]   R. Guillard, 'Le drongaire de la flotte, le grand drongaire de la flotte, le duc de la flotte, le megaduc', in his *Recherches sur les institutions byzantines*, 2 vols. (Amsterdam, 1967), I, pp. 535–62.

[10] The *topoteretes* was in command of the imperial fleet during the Sicilian campaign of 1038–40: Scylitzes, II (pp. 522 and 524).

[11] Treadgold, *Byzantium and its Army*, p. 76.

[12] These terms appear in *De Ceremoniis*, pp. 656, 662 and 668; J. and P. Zepos, *Jus Graecoromanum* (Athens, 1931), XIII, p. 223.

being recruited locally and having their own lands to support and the responsibility to equip themselves (*autostoloi* or *auteretai*).[13]

The command structure of the three maritime *themata* was very similar to that of the land armies, for obvious reasons. The highest command-post of the *thema* was held by a *strategos*, directly appointed by the emperor, who was the admiral-in-chief and responsible for both the civil and military administration of the *thema*. The *drungarius* was in command of a thematic sub-division (for example, the Cyclades or the Dodecanese islands in the Cibbyraeots *thema*) and, like the *strategos*, he was responsible for both the civil and military administration of his area. He was inferior to the *strategos* only in rank and was held accountable for his actions, not by the *strategos* of the *thema*, but directly by the emperor who appointed him. Below the *drungarius* and in command of a number of small squadrons of 3–5 dromons or *khelandia* was the turmarch.[14]

Coastal *themata* that were never upgraded to the level of a maritime one were the *themata* of Hellas (689), Peloponnese (800s), Cephalonia (800s), Thessaloniki (before 836), Nicopolis (before 845), Dyrrhachium (before 845) and Longobardia (902), with about 2,000 men each.[15] The non-maritime coastal *themata* maintained their own naval squadrons for the security of their coasts, ports and maritime commerce, thus operating a flotilla of light ships not suitable for open-sea expeditions. These ships were built in Constantinople and controlled by the central government. The crews of the provincial fleet were recruited from all parts of the empire, though mainly from the coastal areas of the Aegean and southern Asia Minor, for obvious reasons. These were also equipped and paid by the central government.[16] Apart from the *drungarius* and the turmarch, two offices which were, theoretically, inferior to the office of the *strategos*, there was also the command of the *arkhon-abydikos*. This middle-ranking official was in command of an important naval base or a major thematic port, such as Dyrrhachium, Thessaloniki, Corinth or Chandax. He commanded a small squadron of light ships to control maritime traffic.[17]

---

[13] For the two *themata* of Samos and the Aegean Sea, because of the lack of sufficient lands within their localities, marines in the tenth century were probably recruited mainly from the Thracesion and Opsikion *themata* on the mainland of Asia Minor: *De Thematibus*, pp. 83 and 105.

[14] Leo VI, *Taktika*, XIX.25–7 (p. 512). See the next section for definitions of the dromon and *khelandion*.

[15] In parentheses I have put the date of their establishment as *themata* or, in the case of Dyrrhachium and Nicopolis, their mention in the *Taktikon Uspenskij* (845–56). See G. Ostrogorsky, 'Taktikon Uspenskij und Taktikon Benesevic, Zur Frage ihrer Entstehungszeit', *Zbornik radova* 2 (1953), 39–59. Ferluga dates the establishment of the *thema* of Dyrrhachium as early as the 820s: J. Ferluga, 'Sur la date de la création du thème de Dyrrhachium', in his *Byzantium on the Balkans, Studies on the Byzantine Administration and the Southern Slavs from the VIIth to the XIIth Centuries* (Amsterdam, 1976), pp. 215–24; G. Ostrogorsky, *History of the Byzantine State* (Oxford, 1989), pp. 210–17; Ahrweiler, *Byzance et la mer*, pp. 71–92.

[16] Ahrweiler, *Byzance et la mer*, p. 110.

[17] Ahrweiler, *Byzance et la mer*, pp. 54–62, 85–93 and 163–70.

The Byzantine warships and their tactics

The typical high-seas elite warship of the empire in the period was the *dromon* (from the Greek *dromeas*, meaning 'the runner'). This was a two-masted fully decked bireme with two banks of oars, one rowed from below the deck and one from above it. There were twenty-five oarsmen on each side of each deck, thus raising the total number of oarsmen to a hundred, all fully seated.[18] The marines and the officers of the ship numbered around fifty men, while the *ousia*, the standard complement of a war galley (its crew excluding the marines and the officers), totalled 108 men.[19] Another type of warship that had the same features as the dromon was the *khelandion*; both Ahrweiler and Pryor consider these two types of vessel to be almost identical.[20] However, although the Greek primary sources used these two terms indiscriminately, it is interesting to mention that Theophanes identifies the *khelandia* primarily as horse-transports.[21] The Arabic primary sources, however, use only the term *khelandion* to describe Byzantine warships.[22]

A smaller but much faster type of ship compared to the dromon and the *khelandion* was the *galea*. It derived from the same design mentality for a war ship and it had two sails (the one amidships being smaller by a third) and probably one bank of oars on the deck.[23] Because of its speed, however, this type of ship was used primarily for courier service and, during campaigns, for the transport of orders. There is also mention of *galeai* being used in espionage.[24] Other types included the supply and carrier ships like the *pamphylos*, which was 'like a baggage-train, which will carry all the equipment of the soldiers, so that the dromons are not burdened with it; and especially in time of battle, when there is need of a small supply of weapons or other materiel, [these]

[18]   Basileios Patrikios, Ναυμαχικά, II.7 (p. 162); Leo VI, *Taktika*, XIX.8–9 (pp. 504–6).
[19]   Pryor and Jeffreys, *The Age of the Δρόμων*, pp. 123–34 and 254–5; Th. Korres, «Ὑγρὸν πῦρ», Ἕνα ὅπλο τῆς βυζαντινῆς ναυτικῆς τακτικῆς (*'Holy Fire', A Byzantine Naval Tactical Weapon* (Thessaloniki, 1995), pp. 83–90; K. Alexandris, Η θαλάσσια δύναμις εἰς τὴν ἱστορία τῆς Βυζαντινῆς Αὐτοκρατορίας (*Sea Power in the History of the Byzantine Empire*) (Athens, 1956) p. 79.
[20]   Ahrweiler, *Byzance et la mer*, Appendix II, pp. 412–13; J. H. Pryor, 'Byzantium and the Sea: Byzantine Fleets and the History of the Empire in the Age of the Macedonian Emperors, c.900–1025', in *War at Sea in the Middle Ages and the Renaissance*, ed. John B. Hattendorf and Richard W. Unger (Cambridge, 2003), pp. 83–105, at pp. 85–6; D. Agius, *Classic Ships of Islam, From Mesopotamia to the Indian Ocean* (Leiden, 2008), pp. 334–8; V. Christides, 'Arab-Byzantine Struggle in the Sea: Naval Tactics (7th–11th Centuries AD): Theory and Practice', in *Aspects of Arab Seafaring*, ed. Y. Y. Al-Hijji and V. Christides (Athens, 2002), pp. 87–106; V. Christides, 'Byzantine *Dromon* and Arab *Shini*: The Development of the Average Byzantine and Arab Warship and the Problem of the Number and Function of the Oarsmen', in *Tropis III. Proceedings of the Third International Symposium on Ship Construction in Antiquity*, ed. H. Tzalas (Athens, 1995), pp. 111–22.
[21]   Theophanes Continuates, p. 471.
[22]   Ahrweiler, *Byzance et la mer*, Appendix II, p. 412, n. 3.
[23]   Basileios Patrikios, Ναυμαχικά, III.2, p. 166; Leo VI, *Taktika*, XIX.10 (p. 506); XIX.81 (p. 534).
[24]   Ahrweiler, *Byzance et la mer*, Appendix II, p. 414; Pryor, Jeffreys, *The Age of the Δρόμων*, pp. 190 and 396.

undertake the distribution'.[25]

In the non-tidal waters of the Mediterranean war galleys, like the dromons and the *khelandia*, would have been suitable for any sort of landing on a hostile beach, unlike the heavy and round-hulled *pamphylos*, which required a dock. The horse-transport units of the Byzantine fleet had been equipped with a *climax* since at least the early tenth century, which was a ramp used for the loading and unloading of the horses from the ship's gunwales, either from the stern or usually from the bow. This term is mentioned in the *De Ceremoniis* for the Cretan expeditions of 911, 949 and 960/1[26] and reveals the necessary modifications to the ships when they had to carry horses, such as hatches not just to the sides but also on the decks, leading down into the holds, while further modifications would have been engineered in the hulls of the ships concerning the stabling of the horses.[27] According to Pryor, the *khelandia* were indeed specialised horse transports, able to carry between twelve and twenty horses.[28] But these must have been built differently from dromons when it comes to the dimensions of the ship's beam, which would have been much wider to accommodate both the lower bank oarsmen and the horses.[29] A significant structural difference between the tenth-century Byzantine transport ships and their Italian counterparts in the twelfth century was that the latter placed both banks of oarsmen on the upper deck, thus making more room for the horses in the ship's hull.

Turning to the battle tactics of the Byzantine navy, the existence of an above-water beak in the larger warships reveals a fundamental difference between the ancient Greek and Roman naval tactics and those used by the Byzantines, at least after the early tenth century. This beak, replacing the below-water ram, possibly as early as the sixth century, indicates a change in the objectives of naval engagements, from penetrating the enemy ship's hull below the water line to damaging the ship's oars and upper hull and bringing it to a stop in order to board it and capture or burn it.[30]

What is obvious in all contemporary treatises of naval warfare is the same spirit of avoidance of battle at all costs, identified as Vegetian strategy by modern historians, which characterised the Byzantine attitude towards warfare on land. The basic idea of Byzantine warfare at sea follows the simple *dicta* by Syrianus Magister (c. 830–40s) that 'if the enemy is overwhelmingly stronger than us and a great danger hangs over

---

[25] Leo VI, *Taktika*, XIX.11 (p. 506).
[26] *De Ceremoniis*, pp. 658–9; Leo the Deacon, *The History of Leo the Deacon: Byzantine Military Expansion in the Tenth Century*, trans. A. M. Talbot (Washington, DC, 2005), 7 (pp. 60–1).
[27] Pryor and Jeffreys, *The Age of the Δρόμων*, pp. 309–10.
[28] Pryor and Jeffreys, *The Age of the Δρόμων*, pp. 325–30. For the sake of comparison, fourth century BC Greek horse transports (*naus hippagogos*) were rowed by 60 oarsmen, and could carry up to 30 horses: L. Casson, *Ships and Seamanship in the Ancient World* (Princeton, NJ, 1971), p. 93.
[29] Pryor, Jeffreys, *The Age of the Δρόμων*, pp. 315–25.
[30] Basileios Patrikios, Ναυμαχικά, VI.2 (p. 170); Pryor and Jeffreys, *The Age of the Δρόμων*, pp. 134–52 and 382–4; V. Christides, 'The Naval Battle of Dhat as-Sawari AH 34 / AD 655–656. A Classical Example of Naval Warfare Incompetence', *Byzantina* 13 (1985), 1331–45.

our cities, then we should avoid war and overcome the enemy by wisdom rather than might'.[31] Leo VI also strongly urges an admiral that:

> You must indeed deal with the enemy through attacks and other practices and stratagems, either with the whole of the naval fleet under you or with part of it. However, without some urgent compelling reason for this, you should not rush into a general engagement. For there are many obstacles [in the workings] of so-called Tyche [Luck] and events in war [are] contrary to expectation.[32]

When a decision to engage the enemy was taken by the senior officers, then the fleet would deploy its squadrons in several formations depending on a series of factors such as 'time, by attacking the enemy at a moment when we have the winds as allies, as happens frequently with off-shore winds; place, [by using] the sea between two pieces of land, or a river, [areas] in which the numbers of the enemy are useless because of the narrowness of the sea'.[33] The author of the *Taktika* provides his readers with a variety of naval formations to engage the enemy (§§50–6); the two most commonly used were the crescent-shaped and the straight line:

> Sometimes [you should draw up] a crescent-shaped or sigma-shaped [i.e. C-shaped] formation in a semi-circle, with the rest of the dromons placed on one side and the other [i.e. of the flagship] like horns or hands and making sure that the stronger and larger [ships] are placed on the tip. Your Gloriousness [should be positioned], like a head in the deep of the semi-circle [. . .] The crescent arrangement should be such that, as the enemy attack, they are enclosed within the curve. Sometimes you will form the ships on an equal front in a straight [line], so that, when the need calls, [you can] attack the enemy at the prow and burn their ships with fire from the *siphones*.[34]

The tactical objective of the crescent-shaped formation was for the stronger ships on the sides of the formation to overwhelm the enemy ships and then turn around and attack the rest of the formation on their exposed flanks where they were most vulnerable. Once the opposing units came into close proximity with each other they would attack the enemy ships and their crews with bows and arrows, snakes, lizards and other dangerous reptiles, pots with burning lime or tar and, of course, with Greek fire,[35] projected either through the ship's *siphones*, through small hand-

---

[31] Syrianus Magister, 'Οι ναυμαχίες' ['Naval Battles'], in Ναυμαχικά Λέοντος ϛ,' Μαυρικίου, Συριανού Μαγίστρου, Βασιλείου Πατρίκιου, Νικηφόρου Ουρανού [*The Naumakhika of Leo VI, Maurice, Syrianus Magister, Basileios Patrikios, Nikephoros Ouranos*], pp. 112–43 IX.12 (p. 124).

[32] Leo VI, *Taktika*, XIX.36 (p. 516).

[33] Syrianus Magister, IX.12 (p. 124).

[34] Leo VI, *Taktika*, XIX.50–1 (p. 522). Compare with Syrianus Magister, IX.30–41 (pp. 134–40). *Siphones* were tubes used to propel Greek fire.

[35] A selected bibliography on Greek fire: J. R. Partington, *A History of Greek Fire and Gunpowder* (London, 1999), pp. 1–41; J. Haldon, 'Greek Fire Revisited: Recent and Current Research', in *Byzantine Style, Religion, and Civilization: In Honour of Sir Steven Runciman*, ed. E. Jeffreys (Cambridge, 2006), pp. 290–325; J. Haldon and M. Byrne, 'A Possible Solution to the Problem of Greek Fire', *Byzantinische Zeitschrift* 70 (1977), 91–9; H. R. Ellis-Davidson, 'The Secret Weapon of Byzantium', *Byzantinische Zeitschrift* 66 (1973), 61–74.

siphons or thrown against the enemies in a form similar to small hand-grenades.[36] The importance of the proper management of the preliminary missile phase was indicated by the emperor's insistence on using the projectiles effectively, not wasting them against an enemy protected by shields, and ensuring that neither supplies were exhausted nor the crews exhausted themselves in hurling them. When the ships were close enough, boarding detachments were sent to the enemy ship and the result of the naval battle largely depended on the courage and the fighting abilities of the boarding teams. For that reason,

> apart from the soldiers or the upper oarsmen, [all others] however many there might be, from the *kentarkhos* down to the last [man], should be *kataphraktoi* – having weapons such as shields, pikes, bows, extra arrows, swords, javelins, corselets, lamellar cuirasses, helmets, vambraces – especially those engaged in fighting hand to hand in the front line of attack in battle.[37]

Finally, if we follow the writings of Leo VI, a potentially decisive weapon that came to the fore at this point of the naval engagement were the '*gerania* [cranes] or some similar contrivances, shaped like a gamma [Γ], turning in a circle, to pour either wet flaming pitch or the processed [fire] or anything else into the enemy ships when they are coupled to the dromons when the *manganon* is turning over them'.[38] This technique was coupled with the thrusting of pikes from the lower bank of the dromons through the oarports, a tactic that Leo claims had only recently been devised.[39]

The Byzantine navy in the eleventh century

During the Reconquest, the empire had managed to expand its borders to a degree unprecedented since the times of Justinian. Even though the tagmatic armies were the primary weapon of the emperors on the Syrian and Danube frontiers capable of launching large-scale campaigns, for the fleet it was a period of serious neglect and decline. The *pax Romana* that had been established in the Byzantine seas turned the attention of the central government away from the sea, with severe consequences, especially for the units of the imperial fleet. After the death of Basil II in 1025, the role of the navy was to police the coastline and control maritime traffic rather than to launch large-scale offensive operations against enemies like the Muslims. Consequently, the dromon fleets were steadily neglected in favour of the provincial light-ship squadrons. The empire, relying on its land armies, lost the opportunity to control effectively the

---

[36] Leo VI, *Taktika*, XIX.59–64 (pp. 526–8). Greek fire could only be used effectively against enemy ship formations when the fleet was staging a frontal attack. For the ideal conditions that allowed the use of this weapon at sea see Th. Korres, «Υγρόν πύρ», ένα όπλο της βυζαντινής ναυτικής τακτικής [*'Holy Fire', A Byzantine Naval Tactical Weapon*] (Thessaloniki, 1995), p. 88.

[37] Leo VI, *Taktika*, XIX.14 (p. 508).

[38] *Manganon*: this could either mean a stone or a fire-arrow thrower, or a block-and-pulley device.

[39] Leo VI, *Taktika*, XIX.67–9 (pp. 528–30).

international maritime routes and dominate the Mediterranean.[40]

Throughout the first half of the eleventh century, the Byzantine navy's history is linked with the empire's distant province of Langobardia, with two large-scale expeditions being sent to expel the Kalbite Muslims from Sicily. The degree of decline of the imperial fleet in this period is clear if we look at the units from the *themata* of Cephalonia and Samos, which were mobilised for the 1025 Sicilian expedition instead of the dromons and the *khelandia* from Constantinople.[41] It was not until the accession of Romanus III (1028–34) that a long-term strategy against the Muslims began to take shape and, as a consequence, the construction of a high-seas fleet seemed imperative.[42] This policy, however, took a serious blow when, as Scylitzes writes, a fire took hold in the capital's naval base that burned all the dromons that were stationed there (1035).[43] The collapse of the imperial fleet was so serious that there were practically no ships to defend the capital from Vladimir's boats in 1043.[44]

For the fleets of the naval *themata* (Cibyrrhaeots, Aegean Sea and Samos), we observe a steady decline in their crews and numbers throughout this period. The 1040s contain the last mention of the Cibbyraeots in the primary sources, when they participated in the crushing of a revolt in Cyprus in 1042, and fought against the Russian fleet in the waters of Constantinople in 1043, a naval battle that virtually depleted their strength.[45] In the same period, the two other naval *themata* of Samos and the Aegean Sea, like the Cibbyraeots, were transformed into civil administrative provinces, as was the case with the land *themata* of Asia Minor.

During the second half of the eleventh century, the central government failed to build and organise an imperial fleet that could act independently from their tagmatic counterparts. Equipped with Byzantine or Varangian mercenaries, the units of the imperial fleet were in the service of the land armies as their transport units and nothing more, with the provincial fleets policing the immense coastline of the empire.[46] The situation seemed so bad that the Byzantine navy may be said to have reverted to early Byzantine tactics, to a time when commercial ships were modified and used for transport purposes, as Theophanes Continuates confirms for the third quarter of the eleventh century.[47]

After his accession on 1 April 1081, Alexius Comnenus had to deal with two enemies in two different parts of the empire, the Normans in the Balkans and the Seljuks of Rum in Asia Minor. Alexius wisely chose to deal with the Normans first, after concluding a peace treaty with the Turks, recognising that the former posed

[40]   Ahrweiler, *Byzance et la mer*, pp. 117–18.
[41]   Scylitzes, II (p. 457).
[42]   Ahrweiler, *Byzance et la mer*, p. 123.
[43]   Scylitzes, II (p. 529).
[44]   Zonaras, *Annales*, III (p. 632); Psellus, *Chronographia*, VI (pp. 199–203).
[45]   Scylitzes, II (pp. 550 and 554).
[46]   Ahrweiler, *Byzance et la mer*, pp. 129 and 155.
[47]   Theophanes Continuates, p. 479.

a much more serious threat to the empire and had to be dealt with for the long term. The role of intercepting any Norman invasion fleet would probably have been assigned to the provincial fleets of Dyrrhachium, Cephalonia and, perhaps, Nicopolis. But the major naval bases in Cephalonia, Dyrrhachium and Corfu had been abandoned, thus allowing only a small squadron of ships to patrol the area with no immediate effect.[48]

In the Aegean Sea and the Bosphorus, the large naval bases of the imperial navy in Crete (Chandax), the Cyclades and the Dodecanese islands were either severely undermanned or deserted, and Alexius Comnenus did not have any ships at his disposal when he attempted to reclaim from the Turks the Bithynian coasts opposite the capital in 1081. Anna Comnena only mentions a number of random small boats or skiffs being used to transfer the troops onto the opposite coast of the Bosphorus.[49] By the beginning of the 1090s the situation had become even worse with the establishment of a number of semi-independent Turkish emirates on the Aegean coast of Asia Minor; the most notable was that in Smyrna under the ambitious Tzachas, who had been a prisoner of Nicephorus III (1078–81) in the capital and, probably, was familiar with the tactics of the Byzantine navy. Tzachas had allied himself with the Pechenegs in a failed attack against Constantinople in 1090/1,[50] but it seems that this very serious threat of a joint land and naval attack, along with a series of revolts in the important naval bases of Crete and Cyprus the following summer (1091),[51] alerted the government and for the first time we see long-term plans for the revival of the imperial navy. This new fleet was to have a new command under the *logothesion* of the fleet.[52]

The fleet was ready in the summer of 1094 and it was placed under the overall command of the grand *drungarius* of the fleet, John Ducas. The firm hold of the imperial authority was re-established in Crete and Cyprus, along the west coast of Asia Minor and the islands of the eastern Aegean like Chios, Samos, Mitylene and Rhodes, marking an era of relative peace in the Aegean Sea.[53] This new Byzantine fleet was also patrolling the Illyrian coast in the summer of 1097 during the crossing of the crusaders' army from Apulia. These naval units were under the command of John, the duke-catepan of Dyrrhachium, and the grand duke Nicolaus Maurocatacalon, and although we cannot be sure of their numbers or types of their ships, they performed well in their duties assigned by the emperor.[54]

[48]   Ahrweiler, *Byzance et la mer*, pp. 179–81.
[49]   *Alexiad*, III.11 (p. 179); Sewter, p. 129.
[50]   *Alexiad*, VII.8 (pp. 361–9); Sewter, pp. 233–6.
[51]   P. Frankopan, 'Challenges to Imperial Authority in Byzantium: Revolts on Crete and Cyprus at the End of the 11th Century', *Byzantion* 74 (2004), 382–402.
[52]   Ahrweiler, *Byzance et la mer*, p. 203.
[53]   Ahrweiler, *Byzance et la mer*, pp. 186–7.
[54]   For the new offices of duke-catepan and grand duke see Ahrweiler, *Byzance et la mer*, pp. 199–210; Angold, *The Byzantine Empire*, pp. 149–51.

The difference between the naval forces that Alexius Comnenus could mobilise in 1081 and those of fifteen years later, when his squadrons enforced an efficient naval blockade of Bohemond's camp in the vicinity of Dyrrhachium, is significant and can be attributed, in a grossly oversimplified manner, to the stability in the empire's political affairs, which further allowed commerce and hence the economy to recover to a certain degree.[55] The empire was now firmly in control of the waters and the maritime routes of the Ionian, the south Adriatic, the Aegean and the eastern Mediterranean Seas and with the Fatimid caliphate in serious decline at least for the last half a century (it was to be revived by Saladin later in the twelfth century) it was only the rise of other maritime powers in Italy that could threaten its dominance.[56]

The city that posed the most serious threat to Alexius' plans for naval supremacy was Pisa, whose massive naval expedition to the Levant in the summer of 1099 was to attract Alexius' attention. Some 900 ships that were bound for Syria plundered the islands of Corfu, Zante, Leucas and Cephalonia and later clashed with a Byzantine naval squadron off Rhodes.[57] This threat led to the construction of a second fleet, which was to be commanded by the experienced Lombard Landulf, which significantly reinforced the imperial forces at Constantinople and the oriental squadrons in Crete and Cyprus against the Norman-Genoese alliance of 1101–4.[58] What would thus characterise Alexius' strategy from the 1090s onwards was to be a combination of the policy from the times of the Isaurian (717–802) and Macedonian (867–1025) dynasties, namely an offensive policy for the reconquest of old imperial territories, the predominance of army officers in the central and provincial administration and the revival of strong, centralised land and naval armies.

---

[55] For more details on this topic, see Chalandon, *Alexis I*, pp. 277–320; A. Harvey, *Economic Expansion in the Byzantine Empire, 900–1200* (Cambridge, 1989); M. Whittow, 'The Middle Byzantine Economy (600–1200)', in *The Cambridge History of the Byzantine Empire c. 500–1492* (Cambridge, 2008), ed. J. Shepard, pp. 473–6.

[56] Ahrweiler, *Byzance et la mer*, pp. 192–3; A. Lewis and T. Runyan, *European Naval and Maritime History, 300–1500* (Bloomington, 1985), pp. 32–3 and 52.

[57] The number 900 is surely an exaggeration by Anna Comnena. It is more likely that the Pisans would have gathered 120 ships, according to Albert of Aachen and the *Annales Pisani: Alexiad*, XI.10 (II, p. 115); Sewter, pp. 360–1; Albert of Aachen, *Historia Ierosolimitana, History of the Journey to Jerusalem*, ed. and trans. S. B. Edgington (Oxford, 2007), VI.55 (p. 476), although Albert erroneously talks about both the Pisans and the Genoese; *Gli Annales Pisani*, RIS, VI, pt II, ed. B. Maragone and N. Zanichelli (Bologna, 1930), s.a. 1099 (p. 7); Andrea Dandolus, *Chronicon*, RIS, XII, s.a. 1100 (pp. 221–2).

[58] Ahrweiler, *Byzance et la mer*, p. 193.

5

The Establishment of the Normans in Southern Italy and Sicily

Southern Italy before the Normans

Regional strategy is shaped to a great extent by the geography of an operational theatre; hence, the study of the topography of southern Italy is essential for a the better understanding of the factors that affected Norman and Byzantine strategic thinking in the region and for explaining the course of events that unfolded in the decades after the coming of the Normans. Apulia's northern limits are fixed by the lower Fortore River, with the area between the Fortore and the Ofanto, known by its Byzantine name of Capitanata (modern Foggia). To the east, the Capitanata forms a fertile lowland peninsula, the Gargano. Situated between the Ofanto and the Brindisi-Taranto line is central Apulia, which is blocked to the west by the southern Apennines.

Most of the cities in Apulia were, and still are, situated on the shoreline, not just for reasons of commerce with other Mediterranean ports, but most importantly because of the rough limestone terrain and the absence of any rivers in the Apulian interior.[1] The Via Appia, one of the oldest and most strategic military roads built by the Romans in the late fourth century BC, connected Rome with Brindisi via the Apulian countryside and along with the Via Traiana, an extension of the Via Appia through Benevento and coastal Apulia, is strategically connected to the Via Egnatia that reached Constantinople.[2] The Basilicata (modern Lucania) between the River Bradano to the north and the Monte Pollino massif in the south is the most mountainous region of southern Italy, an inhospitable terrain with unreliable rainfall and dry rivers for half the year.[3] Finally, the Terra d'Otranto (modern Lecce province) is a rock of limestone that divides the Adriatic from the Ionian Sea.

[1]   D. S. Walker, *A Geography of Italy* (London, 1967), pp. 204–5.
[2]   N. H. H. Sitwell, *Roman Roads of Europe* (London, 1981).
[3]   A. Guillou, 'La Lucanie byzantine: étude de géographie historique', *Byzantion* 35 (1965), 119–49.

Calabria, like Apulia, has similar contrast between inland and coastal areas. There are two dominant plateaus, the Sila between the valleys of the Rivers Crati and Amato (1,929 metres), and the Aspromonte plateau (1,956 metres) on the southern tip. The plateaus were for the most part forested with black pine and oak. Most of northern Calabria and the Tyrrhenian and Adriatic coastline were ideal for agriculture because of their terrain – clay and sand – and mild climate, contrary to the severe winters of the plateaus.[4] Thus, all the major towns in our period were built either in the valleys of the Rivers Crati and Amato or in the southern coastal areas.

Throughout the tenth century the borders between the Byzantine territories in Apulia and Calabria and the Lombard principalities of Capua-Benevento (one state between 900 and 975) and Salerno remained relatively stable. This was mostly because of the lack of resources directed by Constantinople to Italy and the inability of the Lombard princes to destabilise Byzantine rule in Apulia; periodic expeditions led by the Byzantine *strategoi* (956, 969) only achieved short-term recognition of the Byzantine authority. The only territorial gain for the empire came in the Capitanata during the first decade of the eleventh century.

On the eve of the Norman arrival in southern Italy Byzantine holdings comprised two principal areas. The first was the province of Sicily, which was made up of the territories under Byzantine rule in Sicily (up to 902) and the Calabrian peninsula. Then, there was the newly established province of Longobardia, which was separated from the naval *thema* of Cephalonia by Leo VI in 902. Longobardia had a mixed population, with the southernmost tip in the Terra d'Otranto being predominantly Greek, but the rest of the province was mostly Lombard, especially in the areas bordering the Abruzzi. Calabria was mainly Greek, with the exception of the Basilicata in the north-east, which included some scattered Lombard elements.[5]

Despite the fact that Longobardia and Calabria were seen as a distant and not so important frontier area of the empire, they formed a part of a highly centralised governmental organisation. Hence, there is no evidence to suggest that these two provinces were not organised as *themata* in more or less the same fashion as all the other provinces of the empire.[6] Both military and administrative authority was exercised by the *strategos* of the *thema*, who was based in Bari. He was liable only to the emperor who had appointed him to his command, and he was awarded with the

[4]   Walker, *A Geography of Italy*, p. 213.

[5]   Martin, *La Pouille*, pp. 489–532; G. A. Loud, 'Byzantine Italy and the Normans', in *Proceedings of the XVIII Spring Symposium of Byzantine Studies*, ed. J. Howard-Johnston (Amsterdam, 1988), pp. 215–33.

[6]   J. Gay, *L'Italie méridionale et l'empire Byzantin depuis l'avènement de Basile Iᵉʳ jusqu'a la prise de Bari par les Normands (867–1071)* (Paris, 1904), pp. 178–81; von Falkenhausen, *La dominazione*, pp. 23–7; A. Pertrusi, 'Contributi alla storia dei temi bizantini dell'Italia meridionale', in *Atti del terzo congresso internazionale di studi sull'Alto Medioevo (Benevento, Montevergine, Salerno, Amalfi, 14–18 ott. 1956)* (Spoleto, 1959), pp. 495–517; G. M. Ioannides, Στρατολογία και έγγεια στρατιωτική ιδιοκτησία στο Βυζάντιο [*Recruitment and the Ownership of Military Lands in Byzantium*] (Thessaloniki, 1989).

high-ranking court title of *patrikios, anthypatos* or *protospatharios*.[7] The second in command and a governor of a smaller administrative area was the turmarch,[8] while other local offices are also occasionally mentioned in Apulia like the Lombard *gastald*, the *topoteretes* and the *ek prosopou* (literally, a representative).[9] The *ek prosopou* was the officer responsible for all civil and administrative duties of the *thema* after the second half of the eleventh century, when the *themata* were eventually transformed into civil administrative provinces.[10]

Emperor Nicephorus Phocas upgraded the *thema* of Longobardia to a catepanate in 969; this came as a response to Otto I's invasion of Apulia and Calabria in 968 and recognition of the significance of the south-eastern coasts of Italy in controlling the entrance to the Adriatic and Ionian Seas, and in particular Bari's importance as a commercial centre for the southern Adriatic.[11] Technically, the role of the catepan in the military and civil administration of the region remained the same as with his predecessors, the generals of Longobardia.[12] There is no evidence to suggest that the *strategos* of Calabria was under the jurisdiction of the catepan of Bari.[13] Probably in the early eleventh century, the region of Lucania was also upgraded to a *thema* under the command of a *strategos*.[14]

Estimating the actual numbers deployed in an average Byzantine *thema* after 1025 is a very challenging task. But even trying to assess the numerical strength of Longobardia at the beginning of the tenth century also poses problems, mostly because of the lack of primary material, although the evidence is much better for the western rather than the eastern provinces of the empire. The *thema* of Sicily, the predecessor of the *thema* of Calabria, must have been one of the typical western *themata*, which means that it should have had at least a 1,000-men *drungus*. Bearing in mind that the *Taktikon Uspensky* ranks it between the *themata* of 2,000-men, it is likely that Sicily

[7]   Gay, *L'Italie méridionale*, p. 160.
[8]   Gay, *L'Italie méridionale*, p. 415; V. Zakhou, Ἡ διοίκηση των δυτικών Βυζαντινών επαρχιών (100ς-110ς αιώνας), Ιόνιος Λόγος 3 (2011), 190–1.
[9]   Martin, *La Pouille*, pp. 705–6. For more on these titles and ranks: von Falkenhausen, *La dominazione*, pp. 76–107 and 129–44; K. Plakogiannakis, Τιμητικοί τίτλοι και ενεργά αξιώματα στο Βυζάντιο [*Honorific Titles and Active Offices in Byzantium*] (Athens, 2001).
[10] Zakhou, 'Διοίκηση', p. 189.
[11] S. Lampakis, 'Ἡ τελευταία εκατονταετία' ('The Final Century'), in Βυζαντινά στρατεύματα στη δύση (50ς-110ς αι.) [*Byzantine Armies in the West (5th–11th c.)*], ed. S. Lampakis (Athens, 2008), pp. 393–8; Gay, *L'Italie méridionale*, pp. 348–9. For the significance of Longobardia's military and civil upgrade: V. von Falkenhausen, 'Between Two Empires: Byzantine Italy in the Reign of Basil II', in *Byzantium in the Year 1000*, ed. P. Magdalino (Leiden, 2003), pp. 135–59, at p. 140. For more on Bari and its commerce: P. Skinner, 'Room for Tension: Urban Life in Apulia in the Eleventh and Twelfth Centuries', *Papers of the British School at Rome* 65 (1998), 159–77.
[12] Ahrweiler, 'Recherches', pp. 61 and 64; Martin, *La Pouille*, p. 702.
[13] Gay, *L'Italie méridionale*, p. 347; Pertusi, 'Contributi alla storia', p. 504
[14] Von Falkenhausen, *La dominazione*, pp. 116–17.

and Calabria had a 1,000-men *drungus* each by the end of the ninth century.[15] The significant losses inflicted by the Arab naval raids in Calabria during the second half of the tenth century may have been balanced by the redeployment of troops from Sicily; thus, speculation that the *thema* of Calabria may have had a 1,000-man *drungus* by the turn of the eleventh century seems sensible.

Longobardia was established by the 870s by combining the few territories the empire possessed in the Terra d'Otranto. Administrative and political offices such as that of the *strategos* were handed out, until the second quarter of the tenth century, to Lombard elements of the local nobility, like Prince Landulf of Capua-Benevento, who was appointed *strategos* of Longobardia in 921.[16] This practice, however, was to last only until the middle of the century.[17] Officially, Longobardia was separated from the *thema* of Cephalonia in 902; if we consider that Cephalonia had a 1,000-man *drungus*, and had lost half of its manpower six years earlier (896) because of the establishment of the *thema* of Nicopolis, it is difficult to ascertain whether it would have had more than 1,000 men available to be deployed to mainland Italy during that period.[18] These soldiers would have been Sicilian veterans, and it is almost certain that settlers from Asia Minor and the Balkans were dispatched as well.[19]

There were two distinct military obligations that the local population owed to the Byzantine authorities. The first was naval service, and judging by Longobardia's status as a non-maritime coastal *thema*, we are to understand that in theory the provincial fleet of Apulia and Calabria would have been built in Constantinople and thus controlled by the central government. According to the incident of the Calabrian *strategos* Nicephorus Hexacionites in 965, however, the Byzantine government expected local communities to provide a small number of ships sufficient for the defence and patrolling of the coasts.[20] Whether this was a well-established 'exception to the rule' or simply an isolated incident, we cannot be certain. It may have been an attempt by the local authorities to replace the losses inflicted on the imperial squadrons in the failed attempt to conquer Sicily the previous year. Whatever the case, I have not found any other example of naval squadrons from coastal *themata* being built locally rather than in the capital. In addition, a regularly imposed military tax termed *drungaraton* is attested in this period. Judging by its name it must have been raised in support of the local naval forces.[21]

The Byzantine government had also established a system of land service owed by members of the rural communities in the form of local militias, which is first attested

---

[15]   Treadgold, *Byzantium and its Army*, pp. 66–7, especially Table 2 in p. 67.
[16]   Von Falkenhausen, *La dominazione*, pp. 34–6.
[17]   Martin, *La Pouille*, pp. 696–7.
[18]   Martin, *La Pouille*, pp. 76–8.
[19]   Loud, *Robert Guiscard*, p. 19.
[20]   *Vita Sancti Nili Iunioris*, Patrologiae Cursus Completus. Series Graeca, ed. J.-P. Migné, 161 vols (Paris, 1855–67), vol. 70, cols. 105–7.
[21]   Martin, *La Pouille*, p. 712.

in the region in 980.²² This system greatly resembles the old Lombard military and administrative system of the *gastalds*, with the *gastald* being placed as the high official of the state, demanding military service from the rural populations of his area, the *milites*, who belonged to the social class of the *mediani*.²³ The Lombard *milites* did not own any fiefs, military equipment or horses, which were rather provided by the state as a kind of patrimony. This is as deep as modern historians can probe into the similarities between these two systems.²⁴ We know, however, that there was a strong relationship between the possession of land and military service well into the eleventh century, although the criteria for someone to be called for military service are not clear.²⁵ It is hard to believe, however, that there would have been a re-organisation or redistribution of lands, as in the case of the rest of the Byzantine *themata* in the seventh and eighth centuries, where the norm was for state lands to be given to the *stratiotai* in exchange for military service. Finally, the commuting of the *strateia* (military service) is also attested in the last years of the tenth century and into the first decades of the eleventh.²⁶

The typical Italian soldiers under Byzantine command were the *kontaratoi*, with the most likely derivation of the term coming from the Greek *kontarion* ('spear'), meaning that these soldiers were probably armed with short spears.²⁷ These were locally raised militiamen of Lombard origin who were lightly armed, poorly trained, undisciplined and rarely trusted by the Byzantine authorities.²⁸ They were fighting mostly on foot, which can explain the elite role that the Norman cavalry played in the first four decades of their infiltration in the south. Basil Boeoannes chose the Normans and not the locals to man his new, powerful fortress of Troia in 1019, undoubtedly aware of the fighting capabilities of the Lombard troops under his orders. Their poor performance at Civitate in 1053 and in the three battles of 1041, when their ranks were easily broken by the Norman cavalry, is characteristic. It should also be noted that, even though in

²² G. Coniglio, *Le pergamene di Conversano (901–1265)* (Bari, 1975).
²³ Cahen, *Le régime féodal*, pp. 28–30.
²⁴ The only studies on this subject so far are by B. M. Kreutz, *Before the Normans: Southern Italy in the Ninth and Tenth Centuries* (Philadelphia, 1991), pp. 10–16 and 26–31, 56–8 and 97–155; Martin, *La Pouille*, pp. 226–35.
²⁵ Chalandon, *Domination normande*, pp. 35–7; Gay, *L'Italie méridionale*, p. 367.
²⁶ Three acts established at Conversano (980), Bari (1017) and Cannes (1034): Martin, *La Pouille*, pp. 703–4.
²⁷ Leo VI, *Taktika*, XII.31 (p. 234); XII.36 (p. 236); XII.94 (p. 268). The author of the *Taktika* uses the term *kontaratoi* to identify the heavy infantry soldiers placed in the first two lines and the rear of an infantry phalanx. Nicephorus Phocas uses the term *hoplitai* instead, while the *Sylloge Taktikorum* names them as *aspidephoroi* (shield-bearers): *Praecepta Militaria*, I.62–5 (p. 16); *Sylloge Taktikorum*, XLV (p. 73). Cecaumenus uses the term *kontaratoi* in contrast to the *ploimoi* (marines): Cecaumenus, pp. 30 and 73. Other Latin derivations vary: *conterranei* (fellow-countrymen) or *contracti* (those employed by contract): Gay, *L'Italie méridionale*, p. 454, n. 5.
²⁸ Chalandon, *Domination normande*, pp. 35–6; Loud, *Robert Guiscard*, p. 36; Gay, *L'Italie méridionale*, p. 454.

the three battles of 1041 the Byzantines had brought with them reinforcements from the mainland, including a Varangian contingent, the Lombards probably formed the nucleus of the Byzantine force.

In the decades that followed the defeats of the imperial forces in 1041 and the subsequent establishment of the Normans at Melfi, the basis of the military system of the militias, the land, was eroded by the continuous expansion of the Norman principalities. Thus, the central government could only count on either the reinforcements sent from the Balkans or on one of the most formidable weapons at the disposal of any Byzantine government throughout the empire's history, diplomacy. However, with the Byzantine army and navy unable to launch any serious counter-offensive in Italy, Byzantine policy was confined to diplomatic manoeuvres. After the defeat of the papal army at Civitate and the deterioration of the diplomatic relations between the Eastern and Western Churches the following year, the next step in Byzantium's diplomatic game in Italy was to try to buy off the leading Norman counts. Eventually, this tactic was only to prove effective in the short term, and it could not avert the inevitable, which was the loss of all imperial lands in Italy.

The coming of the Normans

The main primary sources for the period present the Normans as having been moved by piety and persuaded to join the cause of Lombard insurgents against the Byzantine government in 1016, for it was allegedly while visiting the holy shrine of St Michael on Mount Gargano that they first came into contact with the rebel leader, Melus. Piety or not, the Normans were drawn into a conflict they had not started and they proved themselves, in due course, to be cunning enough to play into the confused political situation in the region. To give a detailed analysis of the political background in Italy and Sicily prior to the Norman appearance in Salerno in the year 1090 would be unnecessary as this has been examined in detail in many previous studies.[29] It suffices to say that it was the political conditions in Apulia, Campania and Sicily, and the insecurity that they fuelled, which provided a fertile ground for the offering of military help by the Normans in the first half of the eleventh century, help which was greatly appreciated by all the regional political powers (including the Holy Roman emperor), who were oblivious to the Norman ambitions, which were in any case rather unformulated and largely unshaped in the third decade of the eleventh century.

To begin with, the first insurrection against Byzantine authority after the arrival of the Normans in Apulia was reported in the area of the Capitanata, in the late spring of 1017. This was not only because the predominantly Lombard element in the region was drawing support from Capua but also because the area had been conquered by the Byzantines less than a decade ago and their power had not been firmly established yet.[30]

---

[29]   See my introduction.
[30]   Gay, *Italie méridionale*, pp. 403–4.

The Norman troops that were employed by the rebellious Lombard forces numbered just 250 horsemen; thus, we assume that their role would have been auxiliary to the rebel forces that were mainly composed of infantry units.[31] In contrast to the last rebellion of 1009, the Lombards did not manage to drive the Byzantines out of their positions in the Capitanata, with a period of standstill giving the opportunity to the authorities in Bari to send for help.[32]

In the intervening period between the initial stalemate in the Capitanata theatre and the arrival of the Byzantine reinforcements, the rebels managed to overcome Byzantine resistance in three pitched battles.[33] At first, the Byzantine general Leo Passianus led a massive army, probably composed of local militia and some Byzantine troops based in Bari, against Melus in the area of Arenula, close to the River Fortone, resulting in an indecisive outcome that forced the Byzantine general to fall back and regroup (May 1017). The second confrontation took place on 22 June, close to the now lost village of Civita, where Passianus' troops were routed and he himself lost his life.[34] Unsurprisingly, Melus tried to profit from his early success and launched a third attack further south and close to Troia, at a village called Vaccaricia, which ended up in a renewed Byzantine defeat and with the rebels gaining control of the areas between the River Fortore and the town of Trani in the following months.[35] Sadly, because of the sparse chronicle information available, it is impossible to reconstruct these three battles in detail and to understand the role the Normans played in these military operations. We suspect, however, that they served as auxiliary cavalry within the main rebel army of the Lombards.

By the end of 1017, Byzantium had almost completed the conquest of Samuel's Bulgaria and had managed to put an end to one of the bloodiest wars the empire had experienced in the Balkans for nearly a century.[36] As a result, ample reinforcements were released from the Balkans to resume action across the Adriatic, led by one of the ablest generals of the empire at the time, Basil Boeoannes, who immediately after his arrival began undermining the support that Melus was getting from the Lombard princes of Capua.[37] The first major confrontation between Melus' rebel forces and the revitalised Byzantine armies took place at Cannae, on the right bank of the River Ofanto in October 1018. Again, none of our primary sources allows us to reconstruct the battle in much detail, but we do know that Boeoannes won a decisive victory over

---

[31] Amatus, I.22.

[32] *Gesta*, I.57 (p. 102).

[33] Amatus erroneously mentions five battles: I.21. See also Loud's comments on *The History of the Normans*, n. 26, p. 52.

[34] *Gesta*, I.67–79 (p. 102); Lupus Protospatharius, *Chronicon*, s.a. 1017.

[35] Amatus, I.22; *Chronicon Casinensis*, II.36–7 (pp. 235–40).

[36] Stephenson, *Byzantium's Balkan Frontier*, pp. 47–80.

[37] He was *protospatharios* and *Catepan* of Longobardia between 1017 and 1028. See *Oxford Dictionary of Byzantium*, I, p. 303.

the rebel army.[38] It is in this period that Boeoannes took the decision to build a series of fortified towns to defend the north-western borders of Apulia, which included Troia and Melfi, as we read of a Norman garrison of unknown numerical strength being established at the strong strategic fortress of Troia under Byzantine pay.[39]

Although the Normans may have suffered significant casualties that year at Cannae, the defeat brought ample opportunities for the surviving bands of mercenaries to offer their services to other employers like the Lombard principalities of Campania, the Byzantines and even the German emperor. During the next fifteen years, after Henry II's descent to Italy to restore his influence over the Lombard principalities in the spring of 1022, a number of serious disputes emerged between the Lombard principalities in Campania.[40] During these turbulent years a host of Normans were employed by Gaimar III of Salerno and Pandulf III in the siege operations against Capua (1024–6) and Naples (1028–9).[41] Other Normans were installed by Henry II at Comino, north of the Terra Sancti Benedicti, an area that was probably granted to the principality of Capua by the German emperor in 1022.[42] The ranks of the Normans at Comino included Toustain (or Thorsteinn) of Begue, Gilbert, Osmund Drengot, Asclettin, Walter of Casiny and Hugh Falluca.[43]

Other survivors of Cannae were employed by the prince of Benevento, while Abbot Atenulf of Monte Cassino had manned the fortress of Pignetano with a Norman garrison to oppose the count of Aquino.[44] In the decade between the fall of Naples (1029) and the Byzantine expedition in Sicily (1038), a certain Rainulf would eventually become the greatest of all the lords in Campania and a member of the local Lombard aristocracy. Being invested in 1030 by Sergius IV of Naples as his vassal in the fortified town of Aversa, some 15 kilometres north of Naples, he soon after allied himself with Pandulf of Capua by marrying his niece, the princess of Amalfi in 1034.[45] Four years later he switched his allegiance again, helping Gaimar V of Salerno against Pandulf, thus being installed at Aversa as an imperial vassal in May 1038, after Conrad II's descent into Italy.[46] It was in this turbulent period in the mid-1030s that the three sons of Tancred of Hauteville rode down to Italy.

[38]   *Gesta*, I.91–4 (p. 104); Amatus, I.23; *Chronicon Casinensis*, II.36 (p. 235); Lupus Protospatharius, *Chronicon*, s.a. 1019.
[39]   Romuald of Salerno, *Chronicon*, s.a 1022; Trinchera, *Syllabus*, no. 18, pp. 18–20; Chalandon, *Domination normande*, p. 62; Taviani-Carozzi, *La terreur du monde*, p. 143.
[40]   Chalandon, *Domination normande*, pp. 59–66.
[41]   *Chronicon Casinensis*, II.38 (pp. 240–1); Amatus, I.31 and 34; *Gesta*, I.136 (p. 106).
[42]   Amatus, I.29; *Chronicon Casinensis*, II.41 (p. 245).
[43]   Amatus, I.31; William of Jumièges, *The Gesta Normannorum Ducum of William of Jumièges, Orderic Vitalis, and Robert of Torigni*, 2 vols., ed. E. van Houts (Oxford, 1992–5), VII.30; *Chronicon Casinensis*, II.41 (p. 245). For the Scandinavian origin of these names and their traces to Normandy, see Ménager, 'Pesanteur et étiologie', pp. 196–200.
[44]   Loud, *Robert Guiscard*, p. 74.
[45]   Kreutz, *Before the Normans*, pp. 87–93.
[46]   Amatus, II.3; Malaterra, I.6; *Chronicon Casinensis*, II.63 (pp. 288–93).

The two decades that passed between Cannae and the second German expedition to Italy under Conrad II in the spring of 1038 brought the increasing involvement of the Normans in the politics of the Lombard principalities of Campania. At the same time, the control of Constantinople over its subjects and its neighbours was declining rapidly. This political instability in mainland Italy was taken advantage of by the Kalbite Muslims of Sicily, who initiated an aggressive policy of raids during the first three decades of the eleventh century, bringing chaos and destruction to the coastal cities of Apulia, Calabria and the Tyrrhenian and Adriatic Seas, thus severely affecting the commercial sea routes and the income of the Italian traders.[47] As the Byzantine Empire had never ceased to consider Sicily as part of its *imperium*, the two expeditions to conquer the island that were launched in 1025 and again in 1038 can be seen as the product of the renewed confidence on the part of the Macedonian dynasty to reclaim these lands from the Muslims. Some 300 Norman troops took part in the military operations extending from Messina to the Val di Noto between the years 1038 and 1041, but they were certainly not numerous enough to have influenced the military operations significantly. The experience of marching for two years with a well-disciplined army, however, and participating in at least one major battle against an enemy they had not yet faced on their own ground (Syracuse), including one siege operation (Messina), must have been an extremely useful experience for the Normans of Aversa and their leaders.

Following the Norman settlement at Aversa (1030), the event that had a most significant impact on the Norman settlement in Italy was their establishment in the strategic fortress-town of Melfi on the Apulian-Campanian border in 1041. The city was betrayed to them by a Milanese officer of the Byzantine forces in Apulia called Arduin who, after commanding the Norman forces in Sicily, was placed as *topoteretes* (commander) of the town of Melfi. He would have hoped for a widespread rebellion against the Byzantine authorities when he called for the Normans from Aversa to seize power, but he was soon to be disappointed.[48] The 'twelve Norman captains' and an unspecified number of their followers established themselves in one of the most strategic towns in mainland Apulia, a geo-political event with major long-term consequences for the *status quo* in the region.

In the short term, however, the Byzantine catepan Michael Duceianus reacted sharply and confronted the united Lombard-Norman forces in two pitched battles. Both battles, however, at Olivento (17 March 1041) and Ofanto (4 May 1041) ended with the Byzantine forces in a shameful retreat and the spreading of the rebellion to other parts of Apulia and the Capitanata. The Byzantines were swift to renew hostilities with the rebels and the third and final battle took place at Montepeloso on

[47]   A. Ahmad, *A History of Islamic Sicily* (Edinburgh, 1975), pp. 34–5; M. Amari, *Storia dei Musulmani di Sicilia*, 3 vols. (Catania, 1935), II, pp. 424–6; A. Metcalfe, *The Muslims of Medieval Italy* (Edinburgh, 2009), pp. 79–80.
[48]   *Gesta*, I.234–40 (pp. 110–12); Malaterra, I.9.

the 3 September, concluding in the final defeat of the Byzantine army.[49] What has to be borne in mind, however, is the fact that the role of the Normans at this early stage of their expansion in Apulia was still auxiliary and they were far from playing a leading role in the outcome of that insurrection.

Even by the mid-1040s, the exact figure of the Normans in Aversa and Melfi is not known. As will be explained below, the numbers given for the Norman army that had fought the Byzantines in 1041 were around 500, a reasonable number for two decades of almost continuous fighting and recruiting from parts of France. The fact, however, that many territories in the north and west of Apulia surrendered to William Hauteville does not necessarily imply that this came as a result of their numerical strength or was part of a well-prepared plan. At this early stage of the Norman infiltration into Italy, these newcomers had not yet established a coherent political identity. They were still divided, with the two most powerful groups being those in Aversa and Melfi, with other smaller bands operating independently in the Capitanata and northern Campania.

Throughout this period, from the establishment at Melfi (1041) to the battle at Civitate (1053), the Norman counts of Melfi and Aversa systematically conquered large areas of Apulia from the Byzantines, who seemed powerless to respond. By 1047–8 almost all of the mainland area of northern and western Apulia belonged to the Normans, including Bovino, Lavello, Venosa, Montepeloso and Materra, while over the next two years they began their incursions further to the south and east, reaching as far as Lecce and Scribla. The greatest opportunity the Byzantines and the papacy had to stop this systematic erosion of their territories by the Normans presented itself in 1053, when three years of diplomatic negotiations between Pope Leo IX and the Lombard principalities, Germany and Byzantium, ended in one of the most crucial confrontations in medieval Italian history. The Normans were on their own against almost all of their former friends and enemies in Italy and their future in the peninsula depended on the outcome of this battle.

Leo IX's defeat at Civitate, apart from the obvious political consequences that it had on all the political powers of southern Italy, opened the way to the Normans for further conquests in all directions, including Capua, Salerno, Capitanata, Apulia and Calabria. From this period onwards, the Normans were taking full advantage of their success and by the end of 1055 large areas of the heel of Otranto came under their strategic control, including Oria, Nardo, Lecce, Minervino, Otranto and Gallipoli, while many others were paying tribute like Troia, Bari, Trani, Venosa and Acerenza.[50] Furthermore, Count Humphrey went as far as to besiege Benevento in 1054, an attempt that ended in a failure that revealed the Normans' inexperience in conducting effective siege warfare. In the late 1050s, the most remarkable Norman advances were made in the province of Calabria by Robert Guiscard, leader of the Apulian Normans

---

[49]   Amatus, II.23; *Gesta*, I.322–3 (p. 116).
[50]   *Gesta*, II.293–6 (p. 148).

since 1057. By 1056, several of the most important strongholds in northern Calabria were paying tribute to him, such as Bisignano, Martirano and Cosenza, while in late 1059 he was under the walls of Reggio, the capital of Byzantine Calabria, and it submitted to him in the early summer of 1060.

The invasion of Sicily

> Noticing how narrow the sea was that separated it [Sicily] from Calabria, Roger, who was always avid for domination, was seized with the ambition of obtaining it. He figured that it would be of profit to him in two ways – that is, to his soul and to his body.[51]

By reading Malaterra's view of the motives behind the Norman invasion of Sicily, we understand that the decision to invade the island had been planned by Roger just a few months before the actual invasion, which is surely not the case. In fact, From the synod at Melfi in August 1059, Robert Guiscard had been invested by Pope Nicholas II as 'future duke of Sicily', thus laying the foundation for the conquest of the island which would serve both parties. The Normans would profit from the conquest of an island as fertile and rich as Sicily, while the Catholic church would reap the fruits of glory for taking the island away from the infidels after almost two centuries and not allowing it to fall under the jurisdiction of Constantinople – Sicily, along with Calabria and Illyria, had been brought under the authority of the patriarch of Constantinople by Constantine V (741–75), whose creation of Orthodox metropolitan sees there was seen as a result of the iconoclastic crisis of the period. The Norman invasion of Sicily, from the period between 1061 and the conquest of Palermo in 1072, consisted primarily of three major pitched battles between Norman and Muslim armies, two major sieges and one great amphibious operation conducted by a hybrid Norman fleet.

Sicily is covered with mountains (25 per cent) and hills (61 per cent). Etna dominates the geography of the island on the east coast (3,263 metres), while in the north there are three granite mountain groups, covered with forest, just short of 2,000 metres. These cover a zone from Milazzo to Termini and spread as far inland as Petralia and Nicosia. The coastlands of the northern part of the island, from Taormina to Trapani, present an alternation of narrow alluvial plains and rocky spurs which significantly hinders communications. The interior of Sicily is dominated by impermeable rocks and rounded hills separated by open valleys, with the harsh climate characterised by long summer droughts and low rainfall, creating a sharp contrast with the coast. Finally, along the southern shore, low cliffs alternate with alluvial plains, while between Mazara and Trapani a series of broad marine platforms can be identified.[52]

The enemies that the Normans were to face in Sicily were the Muslim dynasty of the Aghlavids, who by the beginning of the ninth century had overwhelmed all of modern Tunisia and Libya and were launching numerous raids on Calabria and Sicily itself.

---

[51]   Malaterra, II.1.
[52]   Walker, *A Geography of Italy*, pp. 215–22.

They established themselves permanently on the island in 827 when, taking advantage of a local rebellion by the governor Euphemius, they landed in full strength and stormed Palermo in 830. Their progress was slow, a prelude to the Norman pace of conquest; in fact, it took them five decades to subdue the island, which eventually capitulated because of poor leadership and the empire's much more pressing wars in the East against the Arabs. The Aghlavids were eventually ousted in 909 by the Fatimids, who directly ruled the island for almost four decades. In 947, they dispatched a governor from Ifriqiya to crush a local rebellion at Palermo, and his governorship was to lead to the establishment of the local Muslim dynasty of the Kalbites, which ruled for more than ninety years. Nominally still vassals of the Fatimids and, practically after 972, of the Zirid viceroys in Ifriqiya, the Kalbites enjoyed a significant degree of autonomy and self-sufficiency.

The breakdown of the political consensus at the beginning of the eleventh century and the emergence of separatist forces were also combined with a great migration from North Africa, because of civil-religious conflicts between Sunni and Shi'a factions.[53] Several Muslim naval raids also took place, aiming at southern Italy and western Greece. When the last Kalbite emir, al-Hasan, was assassinated in 1052, the island was divided into three contending principalities: the south and centre was ruled by Ibn al-Hawas, who also commanded the key fortresses of Agrigento (in the west coast) and Castrogiovanni (in the centre), the west by Abd-Allah ibn Manqut and the east by Ibn al-Timnah, based in Catania. Ibn al-Timnah emerged in the Sicilian political scene in 1053 and in the following years he established himself in Syracuse. His conflict with al-Hawas and his gradual loss of power in the east of the island forced the Muslim emir to contact Roger Hauteville in February 1061. Al-Timnah actively assisted the Normans in their invasion of the island by providing troops, guides, money and supplies until his death in 1062, in the vain hope that his allies, once defeating al-Hawas, would hand the island back to him.[54]

Prior to the main invasion of the island of Sicily in May 1061, two other reconnaissance missions took place, one conducted by Roger with a force of sixty knights who landed close to Messina in the summer of 1060, and a second taking place two months before the main invasion and led by Guiscard, who targeted the surrounding areas of Messina.[55] For the main amphibious operation in May 1061, Roger landed his troops in the Santa-Maria del Faro, just a few kilometres south, in order to avoid the Muslim ship-patrols which were sweeping the coasts. His advance guard took the Muslim garrison of Messina by surprise and overran them.[56]

---

[53]   Metcalfe, *The Muslims of Medieval Italy*, pp. 92–3.
[54]   Ahmad, *A History of Islamic Sicily*, pp. 25–40.
[55]   Malaterra, II.1 and 4; Amatus, V.9 and 10.
[56]   Both the Byzantines and the Muslims used to alert their naval centres for an imminent campaign by land or sea, and they both used more or less the same signalling techniques of smoke and fire: *On Strategy*, VIII (p. 26); P. Pattenden, 'The Byzantine Early Warning System', *Byzantion* 53 (1983), 258–99; H. S. Khalilieh, 'The Ribât System and its Role in Coastal Navigation', *Journal of the Economic and Social*

Malaterra notes a military tactic employed by Roger to enter the city by force, according to which his troops performed a feigned retreat in order to draw the Muslim garrison out of the city, and then turned back and attacked them fiercely.[57] Whether this was, indeed, a military tactic well practised and employed by Roger or was just presented that way by the chronicler we will never know for sure; what is certain, however, and has to be underlined, is the frequency with which Normans were using this particular tactic, with the most characteristic examples being those of Hastings and Dyrrhachium, as I will examine in detail in a later chapter.

Following Roger's success at Messina, Guiscard crossed the straits of Scylla and Charybdis with the main Norman force of 1000 knights and 1000 infantry.[58] The Norman army marched west, capturing Rometta with no great difficulty, but then failed to take Centuripe because of the city's strong fortifications, the lack of time and the danger of a relief army arriving.[59] Their next target was Castrogiovanni, the headquarters of the local emir, Ibn al-Hawas, and of great strategic importance for the control of the central plateau of the island, situated as it was west of Mount Etna and Val Demone in central Sicily. As the Normans were far away from their bases in the north-east and in hostile territory, largely relying on the local Christian Orthodox population for supplies, and because of the menacing approach of winter, they could not afford to stay in Sicily for long. In their usual non-Vegetian tactics, Robert and Roger were active in seeking battle with their enemy, who was nowhere to be found, pillaging their way down to Castrogiovanni and killing many of the inhabitants in order to provoke the emir to face them in pitched battle.[60]

In the summer of 1061 the first of the major pitched battles between the Normans and the Muslims took place close to the fortress of Castrogiovanni and on the banks of the River Dittaino. The heavily outnumbered force commanded by Robert Guiscard inflicted a heavy defeat on the Muslim army, a tremendously important victory for Norman morale, considering that the Norman conquest of Sicily was still in its very early stages. There were no significant gains for the Normans, because with the escape of many Muslims (including Ibn al-Hawas) back to their base and with the campaigning season almost over, they could not afford to stay in hostile territory any longer. Hence, we are informed of Roger's decision to retire back to Messina after a successful pillaging expedition to Agrigento.[61]

Despite such a promising beginning, the conquest of Sicily proved a very lengthy process. By the end of 1061, the Normans had managed to take control of most of the areas of the north-east of the island, mainly inhabited by Greek Orthodox Christians.[62]

History of the Orient 42 (1999), 212–25.

[57] Malaterra, II.1.

[58] Amatus, V.20.

[59] Malaterra, II.15; Amatus, V.21.

[60] Malaterra, II.16.

[61] Malaterra, II.17 and 18.

[62] Von Falkenhausen, 'Norman Sicily', pp. 253–88.

The anti-Muslim feeling amongst the local population had emerged as a decisive factor from the Byzantine expedition of 1038–41, owing to the aggressive Kalbite policy of extending the Muslim colonies in the south and east of the island.[63] But once the Muslims had recovered from their initial shock, they resisted stoutly for many more years. The main reason for the difficulty in conquering the island was certainly the scarcity of occasions when the Normans could deploy enough of their forces to Sicily, with Roger having just a few hundred knights to maintain his dominions and launch plundering expeditions when necessary. Throughout the year 1062, no major conflicts between the Normans and the Muslims occured, mostly because of Roger's strife with his brother.

In order to understand why Robert Guiscard could ill-afford to send many troops to his brother in Sicily, apart from their strife in 1062, one has to consider how Apulia was a far more important operational theatre than Sicily. Looking at Guiscard's operations in the region, he had to deal with the conquests of Brindisi (recaptured by the Byzantines soon after) and Oria in 1062, along with a serious rebellion at Cosenza in Calabria in 1064–5, which took several months to suppress. Robert's attention turned to Apulia once again after 1065, capturing Vieste and Otranto by the end of 1066. Soon afterwards, however, he was about to face the most dangerous rebellion against his power in Apulia, headed by Amicus, Joscelin of Molfetta, Roger Toutebove and two of his own nephews, Geoffrey of Conversano and Abelard.[64] The way in which the operational theatres of Apulia and Sicily are connected is clear. Thus, in order to examine properly the Norman invasion of Sicily a close eye should be kept on the political and military developments across the straits of Messina.

After the settlement of the strife between Robert and his brother Roger in the spring of 1063, we can observe a slight change of tactics used by Roger to conduct his warfare in Sicily. In order to diminish his disadvantage of having a very small number of stipendiary knights at his disposal, he used the mobility and speed of the horses to ambush the Muslims, with the most characteristic example being that of the Norman victory at Cerami, in the early summer of 1063. Important as it was, however, the victory at Cerami did not bring the Normans closer to conquering the island but merely confirmed their hold on the north-eastern part. Roger simply maintained his army on a hand-to-mouth basis, relying on plundering raids in the south and south-west of the island, with his brother very rarely being able to send reinforcements from Apulia.

Following the events at Cerami in 1063, we have very little information on what took place in Sicily over the next four years. This suggests either that Roger had only a few troops at his disposal, or that the Muslims were putting up a vigorous resistance to

[63]   Metcalfe, 'The Muslims of Sicily under Christian Rule', in *The Society of Norman Italy*, pp. 289–95.
[64]   Although Chalandon has noted that the rebellion began in 1064, recent studies by Loud have shown that this Apulian rebellion only stretched from the autumn of 1067 to the early spring of 1068: Chalandon, *Domination normande*, pp. 178–85; Loud, *Robert Guiscard*, pp. 133–4.

the Norman expansion. Nonetheless, we are informed that Roger maintained pressure on his enemies and carried on with his advance, albeit gradually, along the north coast towards the capital. The town of Petralia, which had been abandoned in 1062, was reoccupied and converted into Roger's main base in Sicily, with its fortifications being improved in 1066; in fact, Roger's attention to the west and north is marked by his moving of his main base from Troina to Petralia.[65] By 1068, the raids conducted by Roger were affecting the entire northern coast, reaching close to Palermo itself and, in that year, he was able to inflict a bloody defeat on the Muslims at Misilmeri, only 12 kilometres south-east of the Muslim capital of the island, Palermo.

The conquests of Bari (1071) and Palermo (1072)

His enemies entirely subdued and all their fortresses captured, he prepared to besiege the people of Bari. There was no city in Apulia which exceeded the opulence of Bari. He besieged it, wealthy and strongly defended, that by overcoming the rulers of so great a city he might therefore terrify and subject the lesser towns, for of all the cities along the Apulian coast Bari was the greatest. (William of Apulia on the duke's plan of conquering Bari)

By the end of August 1068, Robert Guiscard was ready to begin the most ambitious military operation he had yet undertaken – the siege of Bari. There is no doubt of the significance of this military operation. Even though the Byzantines had been dislodged from their bases elsewhere in Italy, Bari was still the largest and wealthiest city, the most important port of the southern Adriatic and the seat of the catepan of the Byzantine province of Longobardia, or what was left of it.[66] By the year 1068, the Normans had enjoyed a significant number of victories against all of their enemies in both Italy and Sicily. Their record was admirable, indeed; however, their major weakness at this stage remained their lack of experience in conducting siege and naval warfare.

During the siege of the city, Guiscard did his best to exploit the internal divisions among the inhabitants of Bari. On the part of the Byzantine government, two attempts were made to relieve the city with shipments of supplies and money. One took place in 1069, when Bari officials returned from Constantinople with a supply fleet, but, as Amatus tells us, 'this small amount of money was quickly consumed'.[67] The second, early in 1071, was led by Joscelin of Molfetta, a Norman rebel who had fled to Constantinople after the suppression of the Norman rebellion in 1068.[68] In between the two attempts, Guiscard made an expedition with his fleet further south to Brindisi in 1070, which eventually surrendered shortly before Bari's capitulation. He probably wished to create a diversion, which however ended in the defeat of his

---

[65] Malaterra, II.38.
[66] Skinner, 'Room for Tension', 159–77.
[67] Anonymous Barensis, *Chronicon*, s.a. 1069; Amatus, V.27.
[68] Amatus, V.4.

fleet by the Byzantine naval officer and commander of a naval squadron, Leo Mauricas, while his land forces were ambushed by the governor of Brindisi.[69] Unfortunately, the sources do not provide us with much information on how Guiscard managed to recover from his defeat in Brindisi to capture Bari a few months later.

Bari's surrender on 16 April 1071 was a tremendous success for the Norman duke, who now possessed the last Byzantine stronghold not only in Apulia but in the entire Italian peninsula. Not for the first time, luck did indeed favour him. We do not know with certainty whether Robert was aware of the geo-political events that were taking place in Asia Minor, but his timing in launching this operation could not have been better. Since his climb to the throne of Constantinople in 1068, Romanus IV Diogenes was preoccupied with the fight against the Seljuk Turks in Asia Minor, which included a multitude of provinces far more important to the empire than Longobardia. Hence Romanus, an old and experienced Byzantine general, chose the eastern theatre as his main priority and, consequently, could not spare any reinforcements for the besieged people of Bari. Guiscard may have been informed about these events by the Franks who were serving in the imperial army, but we cannot be entirely sure.[70] Thus, the speed with which the Normans cleared Apulia and Calabria of the Byzantine presence can be largely attributed to the lack of substantial reinforcements sent by the central government.

The duke would have certainly realised the strategic role of Palermo for his military operations on the island of Sicily, launching a siege of the city from 1064, but that expedition failed because of the lack of resources, manpower and naval support. In Bari he managed to overturn these inefficiencies, with the naval blockade imposed by his navy being the key move that won him the city. Palermo was a large coastal city-port, like Bari, and Guiscard could do nothing else but to apply, once more, the same strategy. The siege, however, was preceded by a diversion expedition to southern Sicily, conducted by Roger, to draw the attention of the Zirids of Tunisia towards Malta rather than Palermo. This is clearly suggested by Malaterra, who also notes the capture of Catania as a 'trophy' of this campaign.[71] Sicily was very important for the Zirids, mostly for importing large quantities of wheat and grain, and although they had officially withdrawn from Sicily a few years earlier, they still had forces on the island, as William of Apulia reports the presence of Muslim ships that later engaged the Normans.[72] Thus, the diversion attack was wisely orchestrated by Robert.

---

[69]   Lupus Protospatharius, *Chronicon*, s.a. 1071; Scylitzes, II (pp. 722–3); Cecaumenus, pp. 66–7.

[70]   G. Theotokis, 'Rus, Varangian and Frankish Mercenaries in the Service of the Byzantine Emperors (9th–11th c.) – Numbers, Organisation and Battle Tactics in the Operational Theatres of Asia Minor and the Balkans', *Byzantina symmeikta* 22 (2012), 126–56.

[71]   Malaterra, II.45; Amatus, VI.14.

[72]   *Gesta*, III.225–34 (p. 176).

The Norman strategy of expansion in Apulia, Calabria and Sicily

It was the geography of castle-building in Italy that dictated the direction of the strategic expansion of the Normans, along with their limited manpower, money, experience and equipment – something which can be confirmed by their failed attempts to besiege Bari (1043) and Benevento (1054). The Norman expansionist strategy in the 1050s had to do rather with the extraction of tribute from the majority of the cities and the establishment of outposts in order to have an effective control of the countryside. Norman tactics appear to have included the seizure of a smaller fortified place, or the building of a fortification in a strong natural position (like San Marco Argentano or Scribla in northern Calabria), using it to raid and spread terror to the surrounding areas and force the local population into submission, thereby forcing them to swear fealty, pay tribute, provide some sort of military service, and hand over hostages, but not necessarily surrender the town or its castle (if there was any) into the hands of a garrison. Here is what Malaterra writes about Robert Guiscard's tactics in Calabria in the 1050s:

> After receiving such a large amount of money [ransom paid by Peter of Bisignano, a wealthy inhabitant], Guiscard strengthened his men's fidelity toward him by abundantly rewarding them. He launched attacks against the Calabrians, assailing the inhabitants of Bisignano, Cosenza, and Martirano with daily attacks, and forcing the adjacent region to enter into a peace treaty with him, that is, a pact whereby they retained their fortresses while paying tribute and rendering some sort of service to Robert. This agreement was secured with oaths and hostages.[73]

As stipendiary household troops and mercenaries would have played a prominent role in the territorial expansion in Apulia, Calabria and Sicily, relations between the Norman counts and the local population depended on the military service demanded by the Normans and the ways in which the latter sought to maintain and increase the numbers of the stipendiary soldiers in their service. Extracting money from the local population and living off the fertile lands of the Apulian and Calabrian valleys served two purposes for the Normans: economic and psychological.[74] Ransom money, as in the case of Peter of Bisignano, would have served to maintain and increase the number in Guiscard's and Roger's households, and persuade the soldiers to fight for extended periods. But the consequences on the local Greek and Lombard populations were much more devastating, as the sources confirm:

> He [Drogo Hauteville] went to the very limits of Calabria where he found a very secure mount which was well supplied with timber [San Marco Argentano in the Saline Valley] and gave it to his brother. He [Robert] looked at the land and saw that it was vast, had rich cities, and many towns, and that the fields were full with many animals. Because he was poor and he had only few knights and there was little money in his purse he became a brigand. [...] Wherever it pleased him, he kept plundering the land and he began to seize men whom he ransomed for bread and wine and golden bezants.[75]

---

[73] Malaterra, I.7. See also II.13 and II.20.
[74] Loud, 'Coinage, Wealth and Plunder', pp. 825–35.
[75] Amatus, III.8–9. See also: Malaterra, I.16 and 36.

But it is Malaterra's graphic description of the Normans contributing to the social instability of eleventh-century Italy that we should particularly note:

> In the year 1058 there was a great disaster, a heaven-sent scourge from an angry God, made necessary – or so we believe – by our sins. It afflicted the entire province of Calabria for three months [...] to the point that, seeing that death was imminent in three different forms, scarcely anyone figured that he would succeed in evading all three of these dangers. The first of these threats was the raging sword of the Normans that spared virtually no one. The second was the famine that consumed the weak, once their strength had been exhausted. The third was the stroke of disease that, spreading horribly, permitted virtually no one to escape untouched, rushing about like a fire raging freely in a dry cane field.[76]

In Malaterra's account we can identify the cause of social instability as undoubtedly a serious drought that would have been responsible for failed crops and the ensuing famine and pestilence, decimating the local population of Calabria. What is rare and even more remarkable is that the chronicler directly links the Normans with this situation by accusing them of contributing to this disaster, obviously by pillaging and demanding money and tribute from the suffering Calabrians.[77] By associating the Normans with famine and pestilence as the three scourges from God to punish the people for their sins, we may think that there was a link in Malaterra's mind with the Four Horsemen of the Apocalypse, representing Conquest, War and Famine (with the final horseman identified as Death).

The combination of negotiation, tolerance, fear and diplomacy can be more clearly identified in the following stages of the Norman expansion in Sicily. We saw that in this period, Sicily was also fragmented politically with three competing emirates, and it was the disaffection of a local emir, Ibn-al-Timnah, that would prove invaluable for the Normans, as he would actively assist them by providing troops, guides, money and supplies for the first two years of their invasion. As was the case with Ardouin and the capture of Melfi, and the favouring of the pro-Norman party at Bari, the Normans were always keen to take advantage of local rivalries to serve their interests, and they were also prepared to instill fear and terror in the local population or be flexible and tolerant in equal measure when it suited them, i.e. when it came to securing the submission of strategic strongholds.

Although Muslim allied troops would have played a key role in the Norman expansion in Sicily, at least until the assassination of Ibn-al-Timnah in 1062, the main source of manpower under Guiscard and Roger's command was household troops and mercenaries, such as Slavs from the Balkans. Thus, fortresses were built in strategic locations to serve as bases to subjugate the surrounding regions, for example at Gerace, Troina, Petralia, Paterno and Mazara, and the same pattern of looting and devastation that we saw in Calabria was followed in Sicily as well:

---

[76]   Malaterra, I.27; 'La theotokos de Hagia Agathe (Oppido) (1050–1064/1065)', in *Corpus des actes grecs d'Italie du Sud et de Sicile* 3, ed. A. Guillou (Vatican City, 1972), pp. 29–30.

[77]   Malaterra, I.27.

Count Roger led three hundred *iuvenes* [young landless, un-enfeoffed knights] in the direction of Agrigento to plunder and reconnoitre the land, devastating the whole province by putting it to the torch. When he returned, he supplied the whole army abundantly with spoils and booty.[78]

Fear and brutality were also powerful psychological weapons in the hands of the Normans:

Finding the city of Messina undefended, he [Guiscard] captured the city and stormed its towers and ramparts, killing all those whom he found within, except those who managed to flee to the Palermitan ships. [...] The terrified citizens of Rometta [just west of Messina], in order to avoid having the same thing happen to them, sent envoys to meet the advancing army and sue for peace.[79]

Among those who tried to flee was a certain youth, one of the most noble among the citizens of Messina, who had a very beautiful sister whom he tried to take with him as he fled. But the girl, a slight young woman, weak by nature and unaccustomed to such effort, began to lose heart [...]. The brother tenderly encouraged her to flee, but when his words had no effect and he saw that she was physically exhausted, he fell upon her with his own sword and killed her so that she would not have to live among the Normans and be corrupted by any of them.80

Although this anecdotal incident is possibly fictional, it encapsulates the fear and sheer terror that the populations that came across these Norman soldiers would have experienced. It is certain that speculations over the fate of conquered populations in Italy would have reached the ears of the Muslims in the port cities of Messina and Palermo that were in direct contact with the mainland ports, and fear for their own lives would certainly have driven people to extreme measures, like suicide. Particularly in a society where the possibility of a female member of a family being defiled by a Norman soldier 'who did not live his life according to it [Quran]', would have been too much for the honour of the family, and incidents like that described in the anecdote would certainly have taken place. This may not have been a reputation that the Normans would have considered as 'noble and chivalric', but it had the desired psychological effect on the conquered populations. Finally, both fear and bluff on Roger's part are evident in his alleged speech to the people of Gerace in 1063:

Do you think that I will be incapable of taking control of this little bit of land [Gerace]? I am not someone whom you can put off with evasions. If you delay any longer, your vines and olives will be torn up before your very eyes. Your besieged city will provide no protection from us once we have prepared our machines.[81]

The people of Gerace seem to have taken the bait; the fear of the consequences of resisting his army and Roger's bluff of bringing his siege machines brought him the result he wanted. The threat of the repercussions for not surrendering was real enough – the Geracians would have heard what happened to the citizens of Messina two years

---

78   Malaterra, II.17.
79   Malaterra, II.13.
80   Malaterra, II.11.
81   Malaterra, II.26.

earlier – but Roger's threats of bringing his siege machines were empty words because, at that early stage of the Norman infiltration in the south, the Normans were still relatively inexperienced in siege warfare, as I will show in the following section of this chapter.

Guiscard and his brother, however, were well prepared to show the necessary tolerance and negotiate with both the Christian and the Muslim populations of Sicily. As their limited resources both in manpower and money did not allow them to take every Sicilian town by force or to install a garrison in each and every one of them, the Normans accepted the surrender of several Sicilian towns without inflicting any damage on the local population, sometimes only taking an oath of fealty and a number of prisoners. Examples include the towns of Rometta, Centuripe, Petralia and Troina, along with what we read in Malaterra about the surrender of Aiello and Palermo, a Christian and a Muslim city respectively:

> The people of Aiello, knowing that if they resisted they would eventually be taken by force and everyone in the town would be pitilessly killed, sued for peace. The duke, though most eager to avenge the killing of his men, nevertheless made peace with the people of Aiello, so that, needing to be elsewhere, he would not be delayed there any longer. He accepted the fortress which they handed over to him and disposed of it as he saw fit.[82]

> The people of Palermo said that they were unwilling to violate or relinquish their law [Quran] and wanted assurances that they would not be coerced or injured by unjust or new laws, and they had no other choice but to surrender the city, to render faithful service to the duke [Guiscard], and pay tribute. They promised to affirm all this with an oath to their holy books. Rejoicing, the duke and the count accepted what was being offered to them.83

Finally, regarding the kind of service promised to the Normans by the Sicilians and the Calabrians, if we return to the example of the people of Bisignano in the late 1050s, we understand that the great need of Robert Guiscard and Roger for locally raised troops would have developed into some sort of an agreement with the local Christian and Muslim communities for a quota of militias, most likely non-fixed, in addition to the expected tribute.[84] Non-fixed quotas of military service would have been demanded from the people of Iato, in the Muslim Val di Mazara in 1079, as we understand from Malaterra's comments: 'the people of Iato came to despise the yoke of our people and renounced their previous agreement to provide service and tribute.'[85] That year we also find the first mention of Roger Hauteville having distributed lands to 'Sicilian' (Muslim?) knights from the areas of Corleone and Partinico (in the Val di Mazara) 'to whom he had already distributed lands in the areas that he had conquered', and whom he called for service against the people of Iato. Amatus writes that Guiscard

[82] Malaterra, II.37.
[83] Malaterra, II.45.
[84] Metcalfe, *The Muslims of Medieval Italy*, p. 95; R. Rogers, *Latin Siege Warfare in the Twelfth Century* (Oxford, 1992), pp. 100–2.
[85] Malaterra, III.20; indeed, an almost identical statement is made by Malaterra regarding the people of Calabria for the year 1058: I.28.

had used Muslim sailors in his blockade of Salerno in 1076;[86] but the most significant deployment of Muslim troops came during the siege of Capua in 1098, when Muslim troops – both stipendiary and owing service – constituted the largest part of Roger's army.[87]

Major siege operations in Italy and Sicily

The Normans took up the offensive in Italy directly after their victory at Civitate, with the most remarkable advances taking place in Calabria, mostly between 1056 and 1059, a period when all the Byzantine strongholds in the peninsula surrendered to Guiscard. The siege of the city of Reggio, which began in late 1059, marked an important chapter in Norman military expertise, not only because it was the first major confrontation in a city in which the Normans fought themselves, but also because it was the first recorded case where the Normans actually used siege engines of such size and scale.[88] The garrison of Reggio was eventually forced to surrender in the early summer of 1060, and as Malaterra tells us: 'when they [Byzantines] saw the siege machines being pulled up towards it [fortress], they lost confidence in their own strength and came to terms.'[89]

In Apulia during the same period, Troia fell to Robert in 1060 after a land blockade forced the defenders to surrender because of hunger, while in early 1068, during Robert's siege of his nephew Geoffrey's stronghold at Montepeloso, following the latter's rebellion against his uncle a few months earlier, the city capitulated when the Normans bribed the local castellan.[90] At Messina, the only city where the Normans had to force themselves in, they were favoured by luck as most of the garrison had already been put out of action in a previous sortie and the remaining defenders were caught by surprise. Conducting an effective land and naval blockade in a large and well-fortified city, such as Bari, however, surely presented a formidable task for Guiscard's newly established navy and relatively inexperienced army in siege operations.

The siege of Bari began in August/September 1068 and the necessity of a wide-scale mobilisation of all the Italian vassals of Robert was clear. This must have triggered the rebellion in Apulia and Calabria a year earlier, when Guiscard demanded military service from his vassals. The rebellion was provoked by the refusal of a number of them to offer military service for lands they had conquered on their own – a rebellion that was fuelled by Byzantine money.[91] Even though the Normans must have brought all the soldiers they could spare, along with Calabrians (predominantly Greeks) to man

---

[86]   Amatus, VIII.14.
[87]   Eadmer, *The Life of St Anselm*, ed. R. W. Southern (Oxford, 1962), pp. 106–13; Malaterra, IV.26.
[88]   Some siege engines were used in 1041 during the battle of Montepeloso. But Malaterra is too vague in his terminology, see Malaterra, I.10.
[89]   Malaterra, I.34.
[90]   *Gesta*, II.459–73 (pp. 156–8).
[91]   Chalandon, *Domination normande*, pp. 178–85.

their ships, none of the chroniclers provides us with an estimate of the numbers of either of the opposing armies.[92] The Byzantines were quick to realise that they were impregnable behind their high walls, and so they were reluctant to offer the Normans what they really wanted – a pitched battle. Thus, Guiscard immediately ordered his fleet to block the entrance of the city's port and bring siege engines 'of different types' before the city, ready to make full use of them.[93] The siege dragged on for more than two and a half years, a clear sign of Guiscard's decisiveness and (financial) ability to keep large numbers of troops in the field for long periods, during which reinforcements also arrived from Sicily under Roger. The determination of the inhabitants of Bari, however, appeared equally strong.

Something striking that needs to be mentioned at this point is the absence of local units of the Byzantine navy in the area. None of the chroniclers mention the presence of any Byzantine ships in the initial stages of the siege and Robert Guiscard was left, apparently, unopposed to impose his naval blockade on the city. We cannot be sure what may have happened to the Italian units of the Byzantine provincial fleet, but we presume that either they had been evacuated to Dyrrhachium, a much safer base, or they were patrolling the southern Adriatic coasts of Apulia, from Bari to Otranto. The latter seems more likely, since we saw a naval squadron of unknown strength defeating Robert Guiscard's units off Brindisi in 1070 under Leo Mauricas, a senior naval officer who was to be seen again off the Dyrrhachian coast in 1081.

Once Bari had capitulated on 16 April 1071, a major expedition to Sicily was ordered since the campaigning period had just begun. After staying for a few days at Bari, Robert ordered his army to move to Reggio,[94] while his brother was already on his way to Sicily for his task of diverting the Muslims' attention elsewhere. We do not have any specific numbers, either for the Muslim garrison at Palermo or for the Normans, but we know that Guiscard ordered all of his troops that had taken part at the Bari campaign to follow him to Reggio. Guiscard's fleet is estimated by Amatus as at least fifty ships, while Lupus Protospatharius takes the number up to fifty-eight.[95] This was an important increase in the Norman fleet capacity that probably came from the captured Bariot ships, in comparison to the naval operation at Messina only twelve years earlier when Robert only had thirteen transport ships. This significant increase in the number of ships suggests that there was a plan of overcoming Bari first in order to obtain more ships for the siege of Palermo. The mariners that manned the Norman ships were Calabrians, Bariots and, according to William of Apulia, captive Greeks, while the marines were definitely Normans.[96] Finally, we have to mention a

[92]   *Gesta*, II.485–6 (p. 158).
[93]   *Gesta*, II.517–19 and 522–7 (p. 160); Amatus, V.27.
[94]   *Gesta*, III.166 (p. 172).
[95]   10 'catti' and 40 'other ships', probably galleys as Bennett suggests, see M. Bennett, 'Norman Naval Activity in the Mediterranean, 1060–1108', *Anglo-Norman Studies* 15 (1992), 13; Amatus, VI.14; Lupus Protospatharius, *Chronicon*, s.a. 1071.
[96]   *Gesta*, III.235–6 (p. 176–7).

great strategic move by Robert, who, in order to secure his rear from any relief army, installed the son of Serlo in the region of Cerami and Castrogiovanni with orders to harass the enemy.[97]

The siege of Palermo lasted for five months and, although the chroniclers' accounts are contradictory, we are able to reconstruct the basic chain of events. It is clear that the city was blockaded by land and sea and that there were sorties and sharp engagements between Norman and Palermitan detachments under the city's walls. As time went on, hunger and disease quickly became a major problem for the besieged, a clear sign that the city was not adequately prepared for a siege and that perhaps Roger's diversionary expedition to Catania had indeed brought results.[98] Regarding naval engagements, William of Apulia talks about a battle between the Norman and a mixed Kalbite-Zirid fleet of unknown size outside the port of Palermo, when the Normans forced their enemies to retreat to the port.[99] Finally, Guiscard entered the city by applying a simple trick of diverting the enemy in one place of the city, while an elite unit climbed the walls elsewhere. The last line of defence, in the original old-city quarter of al-Kazar, lasted only a few days, eventually falling on 10 January 1072. The defenders agreed to surrender their city to Guiscard, on the condition that he spared their lives and allowed them to continue to practise their religion unimpeded.[100]

In the 1070s, the Normans conducted two major siege operations, one at Salerno in 1076 and the other at Naples one year later. The key point in both these cases is that Richard of Capua joined forces with Robert Guiscard against papal territories in Campania. At Salerno, the Norman army consisted of 'three different peoples, Latins, Greeks and Saracens, and he [Guiscard] ordered many ships to come to Salerno to guard the harbour', although no specific number is given, while all the necessary fortifications were built around the city to block its approaches.[101] In this case, as in many others, the Normans' main weapon was famine, which did not take long to show its first serious effects on the inhabitants. The city, however, did not choose to surrender but was rather betrayed to Robert on 13 December 1076, almost eight months after the beginning of the siege.[102] Even by the mid-1070s, the Norman besieging techniques were still largely famine and treason from within instead of costly siege operations that could not guarantee the desirable outcome.

After the taking of Salerno, Richard of Capua ordered his forces to assemble and march against Naples in the early spring of 1077, while asking Robert's help for a naval blockade. According to Amatus, Guiscard sent help in the form of a naval squadron of unknown numerical strength from Amalfi – which had surrendered to Guiscard

---

[97] Malaterra, II.46.
[98] Amatus, VI.17.
[99] *Gesta*, III.225–54 (pp. 176–8).
[100] *Gesta*, III.324 (p. 182).
[101] Amatus, VIII.14.
[102] Amatus, VIII.24; *Gesta*, III.424–55 (pp. 186–8); Romuald of Salerno, *Chronicon*, s.a. 1076; Lupus Protospatharius, *Chronicon*, s.a. 1077; *Chronicon Casinensis*, III.45 (pp. 422–3).

in 1073 – and Calabria, while the necessary fortifications to blockade the city by land were also erected.[103] There were frequent attacks on the city by the Normans, either by land or sea, that were repulsed successfully, and numerous attempts by the defenders to counter-attack and face the Normans outside the city walls. But even in this case, the Normans were waiting for famine to force the defenders to consider surrendering their city. The siege, however, was prolonged for many more months, when finally Richard's death in April 1078 forced the Normans of Capua to abandon the operation.[104]

Major naval operations – the crossing to Sicily

> The Norman race had up to this point known nothing of naval warfare. He [Robert Guiscard] greatly rejoiced at the novelty of this naval victory, hoping that he and the Normans might in the future engage in battle at sea with more hope of success.[105]

Transporting an armed force by sea, which included large numbers of horses and heavily armoured knights, would turn out to be one of the greatest challenges that the Normans had to face since their arrival in Italy almost four decades earlier. Despite being descendants of Scandinavians, it is unlikely that any of them had ever set foot on a warship before, let alone organise a massive amphibious operation in a hostile territory like the one Robert and his brother were planning. Between 1060 and 1076 the possibility of the Normans having built their own ships can be clearly discounted, not only because the chroniclers give no indication of it but also because there are no halts in their operations, which could be explained by their engagement in ship-building. The significance, therefore, of the Norman landings in the coasts near Messina in May 1061 is tremendous in regard to the evolution of military thinking, not just for Italy but for England as well.

The Normans not only lacked the necessary experience in conducting naval operations; they did not have the knowledge or skills to build a fleet of warships and, especially, horse-transport ships. As the possibility of having shipwrights in their train is not supported by the chroniclers' material, all they probably did was use the ships of their conquered subjects for any military operation that required the support of a fleet, especially since the Greeks and the Apulians were experienced sailors and the Byzantine fleet was accustomed to carrying cavalry units, with the most recent examples being the 1025 and 1038 Sicilian campaigns. By conquering some of the most important Byzantine ports in southern Italy following the capture of Bari, such as Cariati, Rossano, Gerace and Otranto by 1066, they had the opportunity of using the Greek ships and crew for their own military purposes.

Although the primary sources avoid detailing whether the tribute paid by certain coastal cities, either Italian or Sicilian, was accompanied by any supplementary

[103]   Amatus, VIII.25; Malaterra, III.3.
[104]   Amatus, VIII.32; *Chronicon Casinensis*, III.45 (p. 423).
[105]   *Gesta*, III.132–8, p. 170.

military service, historians like Waley and Pryor agree that the ships and their crews were hired by the Normans to be used in Sicily and, later on, in Bari and Palermo.[106] Stanton, however, has raised some concerns about the nature of the tribute paid by the Italians, arguing that the Normans demanded an undefined quota from each major port. This undoubtedly resembles the naval equivalent of the feudal service owed by the Cinque Ports in England, established since the years of Edward the Confessor (1042–66).[107]

Information about the types of vessels employed by the Normans in their amphibious operation is scarce, with the chroniclers frequently employing the vague term *naves*.[108] In general terms the ships captured in the aforementioned ports must have been mostly long, open galleys, heavy round-hull merchant ships and small fishing vessels which could have been adapted for naval use, as well as Venetian and Amalfitan ships of various types, encompassed under the terms *khelandion*, *pamphylos*, *sandalion*, *katina*, *tarida* (Arabic *tarrada*, the horse-transport ship of the Muslims in the tenth century that had a square stern with two stem-posts, which enabled the positioning of a ramp that could be lowered to unload the horses) and *sagena*.[109]

The invasion army that Guiscard and Roger landed in Sicily in 1061 numbered, according to Amatus, some 270 knights that were transferred across the straits in thirteen ships, followed by another wave of 166 some hours later.[110] The immediate operational aim was to capture Messina and secure the transportation of the rest of the army from the opposite Calabrian coast. The ratio of one to one (twenty men and their horses in each ship) for men and horses being transported to the island suggests that Guiscard was able to pack his ships with the maximum number of horses for this short-distance crossing; the distance was, undoubtedly, a significant parameter if we compare Messina with Roger's crossing to Malta thirty years later, carrying just fourteen horses in his flagship. The number of men and horses also confirms the fact that the ships used were not designed primarily for transportation, like their Byzantine equivalents, which had a loading capacity of about 105–10 men and around 12–20 horses.[111]

---

[106] D. P. Waley, 'Combined Operations in Sicily, AD. 1060–78', *Papers of the British School at Rome* 22 (1954), 121; J. H. Pryor, 'Transportation of Horses by Sea during the Era of the Crusades: Eighth Century to 1285 A.D.', *Mariner's Miror* 68 (1982), pp. 12–13.

[107] C. D. Stanton, 'Naval Power in the Norman Conquest of Southern Italy and Sicily', *Haskins Society Journal* 19 (2008), 132–4. For the service owed by the Cinque Ports see N. A. M. Rodger, *The Safeguard of the Sea*, I *(660–1649)* (London, 1997), pp. 23–7; Hollister, *Anglo-Saxon Military Institutions*, pp. 103–26.

[108] Malaterra mostly uses *naves*. In the very rare occasion when he becomes more specific, he uses terms like *germundi, galea, catti, golafri* and *dromundi* (from the Byzantine *dromon*): Malaterra, II.8.

[109] J. H. Pryor, *Geography, Technology, and War, Studies in the Maritime History of the Mediterranean, 649–1571* (Cambridge, 2000), pp. 25–39 and 60–3; V. Christides, *The Conquest of Crete by the Arabs (ca. 824): A Turning Point in the Struggle between Byzantium and Islam* (Athens, 1984), pp. 42–50; Agius, *Classic Ships of Islam*, ch. 12, esp. pp. 334–42; Bennett, 'Norman Naval Activity', pp. 41–58; Stanton, 'Naval Power', pp. 130–1.

[110] Amatus, V.15; Malaterra, II.10.

[111] Pryor and Jeffreys, *The Age of the Δρόμων*, pp. 123–34, 254–5, 307 and 325–30.

At first glance, there seems to be no immediate connection between the two expansion theatres of the Normans in the middle of the century: Sicily and England. Historians, however, have found strong indications that the knowledge and experience gained in Sicily in 1061 significantly contributed to the success of the naval operation conducted by William I five years later.[112] Waley notes that the technical problems were the same in the north and south (although Gillmor has argued that the landing ground in Sussex required ships with shorter hulls) and there have been many instances of Mediterranean influence on shipping in the north, like the master of the English king's ship in the early twelfth century who was an Italian.[113] Even if we dismiss the enigmatic line in the *Carmen de Hastingae Proelio* that specifically puts Italian-Norman soldiers at the forefront of the construction of William's fleet in 1066, charter evidence does confirm that relations between members of families in Normandy and Italy were maintained.[114]

It seems more likely that the real contribution of the Normans lies not in the ship-building process but rather in the modification of the existing ships from Flanders or Normandy. These would have been either warships similar to their Viking predecessors or merchant vessels that would have been modified to transport William's army across the Channel. Given that the Italian Normans had not witnessed the construction of any Byzantine or Italian vessel, or at least their presence in any shipyard in Italy is not recorded, they are unlikely to have put into practice any supposed ship-building knowledge that they simply had never acquired. These Normans, however, had seen first-hand how a merchant vessel could be modified to transport horses, and they could communicate this experience to their counterparts in northern France. This argument can be further strengthened by the fact that, although William of Poitiers tells us that ships were ordered to be constructed for the English invasion, it is highly unlikely that a large number of them were built in the few months before the landing at Pevensey.

---

[112]   Waley, 'Combined Operations', pp. 121–2; B. S. Bachrach, 'On the Origins of William the Conqueror's Horse Transports', *Technology and Culture* 26 (1985), 505–31; B. S. Bachrach, 'Some Observations on the Military Administration of the Norman Conquest', *Anglo-Norman Studies* 8 (1985), 7; F. Neveux, 'Quelques aspects de l'impérialisme normand au XIe siècle en Italie et en Angleterre', in *Les Normands en Méditerranée aux XIe–XIIe Siècles*, pp. 60–3. Bennett disagrees with the link between the Mediterranean and the Channel, rather pointing towards Scandinavia for the influence on William's invasion fleet: M. Bennett, 'Amphibious Operations from the Norman Conquest to the Crusades of St. Louis, c. 1050 – c. 1250', in *Amphibious Warfare 1000–1700*, ed. D. J. B. Trim and M. C. Fissel (Leiden, 2006), pp. 52–3. Bennett based his argument on a series of studies edited in: *The Earliest Ships: The Evolution of Boats into Ships*, ed. R. Gardiner (London, 1996), ch. 5, 7 and 8.

[113]   C. M. Gillmor, 'Naval Logistics of the Cross-Channel Operation, 1066', *Anglo-Norman Studies* 7 (1984), 105–31; Haskins, *Norman Institutions*, pp. 121–2; Prestwich, *Armies and Warfare in the Middle Ages*, p. 265.

[114]   *Carmen de Hastingae Proelio*, p. 16; Loud, 'How Norman was the Norman Conquest of Southern Italy?', 13–34; G. A. Loud, 'The Kingdom of Sicily and the Kingdom of England, 1066–1266', *History* 88 (2003), 540–67.

Major pitched battles fought in Italy and Sicily

The three battles fought in 1041 against the Byzantines were of cardinal importance for the future of the Norman establishment in Italy. For the first pitched battle on the banks of the River Olivento on 17 March 1041, the rebel force consisted of 500 infantrymen and 700 cavalrymen, placing the Normans in the centre of the formation as the most elite and well-equipped unit, and keeping the infantry on the sides to protect its flanks. The total number of the Byzantine troops under Doceianus' command is unknown too, and we should not believe William of Apulia's comments that they were numerous enough; however, he does let us know of their battle tactic not to let their entire army engage the enemy in one wave of attack. Instead, they preferred sending one battalion at a time in repeated attacks until the enemy's front had been broken.[115] The Byzantine units that engaged the rebel forces at Olivento were comprised largely of locally raised militias with very limited or no military experience, poor equipment and low morale, a force that would not have made an impression on the experienced and heavily armed Norman cavalrymen. This is precisely why it is unlikely that an elite and numerous army could have been deployed from Sicily, where the army was still based since Maniaces' campaign, to Apulia at such a short notice (maybe less than two weeks). Also, Scylitzes does not mention the presence of elite troops at Olivento, but for the next battle at Ofanto a few weeks later he specifically writes about troops from the Greek mainland that were escorted by units of Varangians.[116]

The second battle took place at the River Ofanto further south on 4 May. After receiving the necessary reinforcements from Sicily, the Byzantines faced the rebels in a battle of which we know next to nothing apart from the Byzantine army's retreat after repeated attempts to break the enemy's front, during which it suffered heavy casualties.[117] The numerical strength of the opposing armies is not known, but the rebel army is unlikely to have suffered many casualties at Olivento. If they did, it could not have been difficult to replace them with new recruits joining their army after their previous victory. For the third and final battle of the year, fought at Montepeloso on 3 September, Amatus tells us that the new catepan, Boeoannes, had brought with him Varangians from the capital,[118] and William talks about reinforcements called from Sicily.[119] It is more likely, however, that Boeoannes had to rely on the forces that his predecessor had gathered, along with newly recruited Apulian troops; on this last point, Scylitzes is adamant that no reinforcements were sent from the mainland.[120] For the rebel force, Amatus' comments on their recruiting tactics imply that they were

---

[115] *Gesta*, I.255–6 (p. 112); Amatus, I.21; Malaterra, I.9.
[116] Scylitzes, II (p. 546).
[117] Amatus, II.23; *Gesta*, I.297–308 (p. 114); Malaterra, 1.10, although Malaterra confuses Ofanto with Montepeloso; *Chronicon Casinensis*, II.66 (pp. 298–301).
[118] Amatus, II.24.
[119] *Gesta*, I.328–30 (p. 116).
[120] Scylitzes, II. (p. 546).

hard-pressed and low in numbers, probably only a few hundred strong. The initiative on the battlefield belonged to the rebels who, being aware of the position of the enemy camp, sent a small force in an attempt to steal horses, an indication that they still did not possess enough mounts, and force their enemies to come out of the camp and fight them in a pitched battle. This they did and they succeeded in inflicting a third and final defeat on the Byzantines.[121]

By the year 1040, the Normans had already established a permanent base at Aversa, but it was only in 1041, when they allied themselves with Lombard rebels, that they seriously challenged the Byzantine authority in a key fortress in Apulian territory. As in the previous decades, the numbers of Norman cavalry units engaged in the Lombard rebellion are not mentioned, with a figure between 500 and 1000 cavalry being the most likely. The Norman cavalry would have constituted the most elite unit of the rebel army and so it would have been deployed in the centre of the formation in order to take full advantage of its cavalry charge to overrun the Byzantines. Any information on the impact of the Norman cavalry charge on the opposing Byzantine formations would be extremely valuable, especially whether they had engaged infantry units of the Varangian Guard, a prelude to the battle of Dyrrhachium in 1081. Unfortunately, our primary material lets us down on this count.

The most crucial battle, however, for the future of the Norman presence in Italy took place at Civitate on 17 June 1053. The army that Pope Leo had managed to gather after his trip to Germany in March and his descent into southern Italy in May was indeed substantial. It consisted of troops from Capua, the Abruzzi and the Lombard areas of northern Capitanata, with some troops arriving also from Benevento and Spoleto. The southern Italian leaders that actively participated in the anti-Norman coalition were Duke Atenulf of Gaeta, his brother Count Lando of Aquino and the counts of Teano, Guardia and Campomarino from the Biferno Valley on the Adriatic coast.[122] This force was further augmented by reinforcements from Germany, probably freebooters, prosecuted criminals or just men who had been influenced by the pope, even though Henry III had recalled his imperial troops earlier in March. These troops consisted of an infantry force of several hundred (700 according to William of Apulia who is our most detailed source for this battle, but in fact probably not more than 300) from Swabia with a certain Garnier and Albert as their leaders.[123]

Faced with this threat, the Normans were also forced to reconcile whatever differences and tensions they may have experienced in the past. Humphrey of the Hautevilles, who had succeeded his brother Drogo as leader of the Melfi Normans two years earlier, had the overall command of the army, having with him Peter and Walter, the sons of Amicus, the Hautevilles' principal competitors, and the Beneventan

---

[121]   Amatus, II.25 and 26; *Gesta*, I.373–95 (pp. 118–20); *Chronicon Casinensis*, II.66 (pp. 298–301); Malaterra, I.10.
[122]   *Gesta*, II.148–76 (p. 140).
[123]   *Gesta*, II.151–63 (p. 140).

Normans, Gerald of Buonalbergo, Count Richard of Aversa (since 1049) and Robert Guiscard from Calabria. William estimated their number at 3,000 cavalry and a few infantry. This seems to be large by the standards of the period; it is more reasonable to assume force about half of that in number as more likely.[124]

The Normans divided their forces into three main divisions: the centre was commanded by Humphrey, the right wing by Richard of Aversa and the left was entrusted to Robert Guiscard. Opposite him, Humphrey had the Swabian infantry, while the rest of the Italian forces were placed in the wings.[125] Most of the armies of this early Norman period were divided into three or four units called battles or divisions (*acies*), being lined up one behind the other. There are many examples from this period where the battles were put in the field directly facing the enemy, with Civitate, Tinchebray, Hastings and Dyrrhachium being just a few examples. It seemed more reasonable, when an army consisted of more than one nation, when it had more than one general or if they wished to increase the length of their formation, as in the case of Civitate, to be arrayed in three parallel divisions all facing the enemy. But there was no well-established model to follow for battle-array and it was up to the general to choose the right battle formation for his army.

At the battle of Civitate Richard's cavalry units directly attacked the enemy's left wing, which melted away almost immediately and was pursued by the advancing Norman horsemen. While this pursuit was under way, the rest of the Norman cavalry was already engaging the enemy, who, according to William, chose to retreat, apart from the Swabians, who put up a vigorous resistance and refused to leave their position. At this crucial point, Richard returned from the pursuit of the Italians to attack the Swabian infantry. His manoeuvre ended up at once in a massacre and one of the most decisive victories of the eleventh century.[126] In this case, although the Normans were numerically inferior to the papal army, the key to victory lay in their use of their traditional heavy cavalry charge against a heterogeneous infantry army. Even the mere sight of a Norman cavalry charge must have been terrifying to the poorly armed Italian militia that would have made up the bulk of the papal army. Their onslaught and retreat from the battlefield was the direct outcome of this intimidation.

At this point we must also stress that although the cavalry was undoubtedly the weapon that dominated the battle of Civitate, the example of the Swabians also demonstrates the power of heavy infantry. Even though the Germans were heavily outnumbered, their discipline and experience allowed them to put up a stout resistance. The retreat of the Lombard units of infantry cannot in any case diminish the importance of heavy infantry on a battlefield of this period and we can very well imagine that the result would have been rather different if the papal army consisted of more units like the Swabians. Cavalry operating alone stood no chance against heavy

[124]   *Gesta*, II.122–38 (p. 138).
[125]   *Gesta*, II.183–91 (p. 142); Amatus, III.40; *Chronicon Casinensis*, II.84 (pp. 331–3).
[126]   *Gesta*, II.211–56 (pp. 142–6); Amatus, III.40.

and well-disciplined infantry – only when the formation is disrupted is it possible to carry on with a heavy charge.[127] But this issue will be analysed in more detail when I examine the battle of Dyrrhachium.

In Sicily, the first battle in the Norman quest to subdue the island occurred close to the fortress of Castrogiovanni and on the banks of the River Dittaino (summer 1061). Robert Guiscard had taken some 700 knights onto the field, and maybe the same number of infantry. Amatus gives the number of 1,000 for cavalry and infantry, but Guiscard had undoubtedly left some of his men to garrison Messina, as Malaterra tells us, and so the number 700 must be closer to reality.[128] The Muslim army facing the Normans allegedly had 15,000 horsemen and 100,000 infantry, a surely exaggerated number given by Amatus.[129] It is almost certain, however, that the Normans were heavily outnumbered. In this battle, they did not put their army in the field in three separate battalions, forming one attack-wave as in their victory at Civitate, but Roger was rather chosen to command the first wave and Robert was to follow him with the second if necessary. Also, the Muslims too had formed three battle lines. Unfortunately, the course of the battle is unknown to us, but it is suggested that the Norman cavalry charged once again upon their enemies in their usual manner, forcing the Muslims to retreat to the castle of Castrogiovanni with heavy casualties. The result of the battle, although it brought no significant military gains for the Normans, was a tremendous boost for their morale and fame as warriors throughout Sicily and Italy.

After almost a year of no large-scale fighting between the Normans and the Muslims, the newly arrived North African army, along with the regrouped Kalbite Muslims, marched towards the Norman strongholds in June 1063 and met their enemies on the banks of the River Cerami, some 10 kilometres from Roger's base at Troina. After a standstill of three days, the Normans won a confrontation at the castle of Cerami, where Serlo, commanding only thirty-six knights, forced an enemy contingent of about 3,000 cavalry and many infantrymen to retreat. After this initial success, Roger's force of a hundred knights engaged the enemy by forming two battles (vanguard and rearguard). The re-grouped Muslim army, however, managed to repel the first Norman attack and move against the rearguard, which was commanded by Roger. At this point, however, according to Malaterra, who is our only source for this battle, the intervention of St George along with Roussel of Bailleul's exhortations saved the day for the Normans, who counter-attacked and forced their enemies into

---

[127] J. Gillingham, 'An Age of Expansion, c. 1020–1204', in *Medieval Warfare*, 64 and 76–8; M. Bennett, 'The Myth of the Military Supremacy of Knightly Cavalry', in *Armies, Chivalry and Warfare in Medieval Britain and France, Proceedings of the 1995 Harlaxton Symposium*, ed. M. Strickland (Stamford, 1998), pp. 310–16; S. Morillo, 'The "Age of Cavalry" Revisited', in *The Circle of War in the Middle Ages*, pp. 45–58.
[128] Malaterra, II.17; Amatus, V.23. The number for Guiscard's cavalry (700) is also confirmed by Ibn al-Athir. See Amari, *Storia dei Musulmani di Sicilia*, III, n. 1, 75.
[129] Amatus, V.23. Malaterra is careful to distinguish between the local Sicilian Muslims and reinforcements that had arrived from Tunisia: II.17.

retreat. For the outcome of the battle, Malaterra gives a number of 15,000 dead and 20,000 Muslim prisoners, which even if grossly exaggerated, confirms the assumption that the 136 Norman knights were vastly outnumbered by their enemies.[130]

Only a few months prior to Guiscard's most ambitious military operation until that time, the siege of Bari, the last major pitched battle fought against the Muslims took place at Misilmeri (1068), some 12 kilometres south-east of the capital Palermo. The information given by Malaterra is sparse, but we are able to reconstruct the main chain of events. After launching a plundering expedition to the Palermo area, Roger's cavalry force came upon a sizeable mixed Zirid and Kalbite army at Misilmeri, which was arranged in battle order awaiting their arrival. We are unaware of the exact size of the two armies, but as usual, the Normans must have been many times outnumbered. Roger did not hesitate this time, as in Cerami, and after arranging his army's battle lines and having surprise on his side, launched an attack upon the enemy. Once again, the Muslims were unable to withstand a Norman cavalry attack and Malaterra reports that hardly anyone survived to carry the news to Palermo.[131]

A number of important conclusions can be drawn regarding the Norman strategy and battle tactics in Italy and Sicily in the eleventh century. First of all, we have to draw a clear distinction between two periods, with the turning point being the battle at Civitate (1053), perhaps the most significant battle in the medieval history of the area. In the pre-Civitate period the Normans were mere auxiliary units, playing no significant role in the development of the political *status quo* of the region. Numbering a few hundred, they were bands of elite cavalry mercenaries employed by the highest bidder, which included Lombards, Byzantines, the German emperors and great ecclesiastical institutions in the Abruzzi.

Two key points were the establishment of the two Norman bands in Aversa (1030) and Melfi (1041/2). The first attempt to dislodge the Normans from Italy took place at Civitate in 1053, and the failure of the papal army of Leo IX marked the beginning of the end for the Lombards and the Byzantines in the region. Calabria and great parts of mainland Apulia had been conquered by the end of the decade, and in 1061 Robert Guiscard and his brother invaded Sicily. The conquest of the island, however, was to prove a far tougher affair than the Normans could have anticipated. Owing to the lack of forces available and internal problems in Apulia, Palermo fell eleven years later and the last Muslim garrison was expelled in 1091.

In the pre-Civitate period, pitched battles were relatively rare and the numbers involved did not exceed a few thousand. Only at Civitate did the Normans play a protagonistic role in the events that unfolded, although they were heavily outnumbered by the predominantly Italian troops of the papal coalition army. The Normans, having fought with and against their Lombard adversaries, were aware of their weaknesses and chose to apply their heavy cavalry charge, which had a tremendous effect on

---

[130]   Malaterra, II.33.
[131]   Malaterra, II.41.

the enemy foot soldiers. After Civitate, pitched battles continued to be rare but this does not necessarily mean that the Normans were pursuing a Vegetian strategy, or the avoidance of battle unless the chances were overwhelmingly in their favour. As the aggressors in the two operational theatres of the period, Apulia and Sicily, they actively pursued battle but it was only in Sicily that they got what they wanted.

In the three pitched battles fought in Sicily between 1061 and 1068, we see the Normans once more adjusting their battle tactics to the enemy they had to face, being aware of the quality of troops they had to fight (i.e. their discipline, morale and, of course, their equipment). In order to compensate for their numerical inferiority, they chose not to deploy their forces in three cavalry divisions side by side, as at Civitate in 1053, but one behind the other, forming two or three attacking waves, a tactic which makes the front of the army shorter but increases the depth of the formation, thus giving greater impetus to the cavalry. Furthermore, they chose relatively broken, hilly or marshy terrain, which was also dominated by a river or an uphill castle, in order to diminish the numerical advantage of their enemies and the mobility of their cavalry.

Two conclusions can be drawn at this point: first, military tactics play a much more significant role than numbers in a pitched battle, with the Normans using their cavalry charge to counterbalance their numerical inferiority in the battlefield four times in fifteen years. Second, the Norman victories in the battlefields of Italy and Sicily could not by themselves determine the course of events. Italy and Sicily were heavily fortified regions with numerous stone castles wherein their adversaries, the Byzantines and the Muslims (mainly after 1072), could lock themselves and refuse battle, thus denying the Normans their advantage of heavy cavalry attack.

Until the 1060s, the key characteristics of the Norman expansionist strategy in the south included negotiation and tolerance. The paying of tribute was agreed, along with the building of outposts to control and raid a specific area, but no massacre of populations is reported or any garrison installed – except, of course, in strategic cities. It seems as if the Normans were trying to conquer Apulia, Calabria and Sicily as quickly and as economically as possible. After the Normans had expelled the Byzantines from the interior of Apulia, Bari stood as the ultimate stumbling block to their predominance in Italy. To overcome the Norman numerical inferiority and their inexperience in siege operations, Duke Robert chose to conduct a naval blockade of the city and cut off the city's supply lines with Dyrrhachium, hoping for an eventual surrender because of starvation. The newly established Norman navy, that had previously carried hundreds of knights across to Sicily in the first Norman amphibious operations of the period, proved capable of the task, and the city surrendered in the early spring of 1071. Palermo was next in line, and exactly the same siege strategy was deployed with equally successful results.

A final point that needs to be addressed has to do with the role of religion and the religious enthusiasm displayed by the Normans during their invasion of Sicily in the 1060s. Although we cannot characterise the Norman invasion of Sicily as a crusade, we can identify it as a holy war and place it among other holy wars of the eleventh century, like the Spanish Reconquista.[132] We have already seen the role played by Rome in encouraging the Normans to invade the island, but what specific examples of religious enthusiasm can we identify in the histories of Amatus and Malaterra?

Amatus notes that 'he [Guiscard] called his knights to take Sicily, saying, "I should like to deliver the Christians and Catholics who are bound in servitude to the Saracens [. . .] and wreak vengeance for this injury to God"'.[133] In his exhortation before the battle at Castrogiovanni in 1061, Amatus puts the following in Guiscard's mouth: 'The strength of our faith has the flame of the Holy Spirit, because in the name of the Holy Trinity we shall take this mountain of the dung of heresy and accumulated perversity. God is powerful enough to give us victory over the multitude of infidels.'[134] But the most important evidence comes from Malaterra regarding the battle of Cerami in 1063. In his attempt to encourage the heavily outnumbered Normans to attack the Muslims, Roussel of Bailleuil is reported to have said: 'It is certain that, with God leading us, the enemy will not be able to stand before us. This people [Muslims] has rebelled against God, and power which is not directed by God is quickly exhausted.'[135] It was while rushing against their enemies, inspired by this speech as they were, that the Norman knights witnessed St George leading the charge on his white horse and carrying a white standard with a cross tied to the tip of his lance; hence their battle-cry 'God and St George'. Saint George is the best known warrior-saint of Christianity and the white banner with the cross may be a reference to Constantine's *labarum* carried at the battle of the Milvian Bridge in 312. The point that should most draw our attention is what Malaterra writes about the aftermath of the Norman victory at Cerami: 'The pope [Alexander II] sent both his apostolic blessing and absolution from sin to the count [Roger] and to all others who were helping him to win Sicily from the pagans. The pope also sent a banner from the Roman see [. . .] under which the count and his men were to rise up and wage war against the Saracens.' Absolution from sins was a significant development, although not a novelty, as it was used by Leo IV and John VIII as early as the ninth century, while the banner of St Peter reminds us of William the Conqueror's invasion of England three years later.[136]

What is interesting about our chroniclers' accounts of the Norman expansion in Sicily is that, even though they stress numerous times the religious toleration that was demonstrated by Guiscard and Roger's men throughout the conquest of the island, one can clearly notice their struggle to highlight the religious nature of their fight

[132]   C. Tyerman, *God's War, A New History of the Crusades* (London, 2006), pp. 43–57; J. Riley-Smith, *What were the Crusades?*, 4th edn (Basingstoke, 2009), pp. 1–26; I. S. Robinson, *The Papacy, 1073–1198* (Cambridge, 1990), pp. 324–44.

[133]   Amatus, V.12.

[134]   Amatus, V.23.

[135]   Malaterra, II.33.

[136]   C. Erdmann, *Die Entstehung des Kreuzzugsgedankens* (Stuttgart, 1955), pp. 23, 139–40, 172–3 and 181–3. There exists an English translation: *The Origin of the Idea of Crusade*, trans. M. W. Baldwin and W. Goffart (Princeton, 1977).

against the infidels. Of course, these pre-battle speeches that dominate in Amatus' and Malaterra's narratives are a topos, even if similar morale-boosting speeches might actually have been delivered. The exact words, however, reflect how the Italian-Norman chroniclers perceived the fight against the Muslims – as a holy war to recover lands that were once Christian.

6

Robert Guiscard's Invasion of Illyria

Diplomatic relations in Italy on the eve of the invasion of Illyria

In order to elucidate the political and diplomatic significance of the conference at Ceprano (June 1080) that saw the reconciliation of the pope with the Norman leaders, I begin by giving a brief description of the papal–Norman relations in the age of Gregory VII (1073–85).[1] Gregory, almost as soon as he was elected in the papal curia, became openly hostile towards the Normans, thus returning to the papal policy of the pre-1059 period, when the Normans were regarded as enemies of St Peter.[2] During the years of the reformist papacy, and especially of Leo IX (1049–54), the growing numbers and political significance of the Normans in southern Italy compelled Rome to make a decision as to whether the Normans were potential allies to be recruited for pay, or dangerous enemies to be controlled, or even completely subdued. After Leo's election to the see of Rome in 1048, he and his successors chose the option of open hostility.[3] What came to weigh on Rome's policies were the continuous inroads made by Norman troops into the Abruzzi area and specifically around Benevento, territories under papal overlordship since the summer of 1073.[4] The protagonist of the Norman depredations in this area since the mid-1060s was Robert of Loritello, and although Robert Guiscard may not have been directly involved in the inroads, Robert of Loritello was after all the duke's nephew.

Relations with Rome, however, were not always hostile; in 1059, when Pope Nicolas II was in desperate need of political and military support against his rival John Mincio, cardinal bishop of Velletri (known as Benedict X), an alliance with Richard of Capua

[1]   H. E. J. Cowdrey, *Pope Gregory VII* (Oxford, 1998), pp. 425–39; Robinson, *The Papacy*, pp. 367–97; *The Register of Pope Gregory VII, 1073–85*, trans. H. E. J. Cowdrey (Oxford, 2002).
[2]   Robinson, *The Papacy*, p. 369.
[3]   H. E. J. Cowdrey, *The Age of Abbot Desiderius, Montecassino, the Papacy, and the Normans in the Eleventh and Early Twelfth Centuries* (Oxford, 1986), pp. 108–9.
[4]   *The Register of Pope Gregory VII*, I.18a (pp. 20–1).

and Robert Guiscard seemed very attractive. Indeed, this was an alliance with both political and ecclesiastical repercussions for the region; after the treaty of Melfi, the Norman military muscle provided the necessary protection to the reformist papacy in its attempts to reassert its influence over the bishoprics of Apulia and Calabria. However, relations with the pope, although amicable, were not Guiscard's priority throughout most of the 1060s because of his preoccupation with events in Apulia and Sicily; thus, he proved unable (or perhaps unwilling) to curb the territorial ambitions of his counts in the Abruzzi and the Roman Campania.[5]

It was when the Norman inroads into papal lands began to incur serious damage in the second half of the 1060s, with Richard of Capua capturing Ceprano and raiding a substantial area reaching to the outskirts of Rome, that we see a gradual transformation of papal policy towards the Normans.[6] Pope Alexander II (1061–73) appeared to inaugurate a policy that was to be followed until the end of the 1070s: instead of a Norman *entente* between Richard and Robert, Rome now favoured the fomenting of divisions among them as the most efficient way to exert some sort of control over the Norman lords.[7] Relations between the Normans and Gregory VII (1073–85) in the first four years of the latter's pontificate were the most strained, with the root of the problem surely being the Norman incursions into territory under papal overlordship. The abbot of Monte Cassino can be seen playing a significant mediator's role, as Desiderius (abbot, and later Pope Victor III, 1086–7) saw the Normans as his principal benefactors and allies.[8] Attempts to set up a meeting between the two parties at Benevento in the summer of 1073, however, came to nothing, and during the following winter Gregory took a step further.[9] In February 1074 he called upon William I of Burgundy for help against Robert Guiscard, specifically directing the 'faithful of St Peter' towards a campaign to 'bring the Normans to peace and then cross to Constantinople to bring aid to Christians'.[10] Even though this expedition failed to materialise, it represents the first example of the manipulation of a crusade for political purposes, this time openly directed against the Apulian Normans.[11]

The continuous depredations of the Normans in the Abruzzi and the combined operations of Richard of Capua and Robert Guiscard against Salerno (1076), Naples (1077) and Benevento (1078) resulted in both being excommunicated

[5] Loud, *Robert Guiscard*, pp. 186–97; Cowdrey, *The Age of Abbot Desiderius*, pp. 108–22.

[6] *Chronicon Casinensis*, III.23 (p. 389).

[7] This point is well argued by: D. Whitton, 'Papal Policy in Rome, 1012–1124' (unpublished D.Phil. thesis, Oxford University, 1979).

[8] Cowdrey, *The Age of Abbot Desiderius*, pp. 120–3. For a different view on the events, see G. A. Loud, 'Abbot Desiderius of Montecassino and the Gregorian Papacy', *Journal of Ecclesiastical History* 30 (1979), 305–26.

[9] Amatus, VII.9.

[10] *The Register of Pope Gregory VII*, I.49 (pp. 54–5).

[11] H. E. J. Cowdrey, 'Pope Gregory VII's "Crusading" Plans of 1074', in *Outremer, Studies in the History of the Crusading Kingdom of Jerusalem*, ed. B. Z. Kedar, R. C. Smail (Jerusalem, 1982), pp. 27–40.

twice by Gregory, in Lent 1075 and again in February 1078. It is paramount at this point to understand that diplomatic relations in the Italian peninsula were largely dependent upon a third party that, theoretically, regarded southern Italy as part of its *imperium* – the German emperors. Diplomatic (and personal) relations between Gregory and Henry IV in the first two years of the former's pontificate were cordial, judging by the pope's correspondence with the duke of Swabia in September 1073.[12] Matters broke down, however, in 1075, mainly because of the excommunication of two of Henry's court advisors accused of simony and, most importantly, the German emperor's involvement in the election of the archbishop of Milan (1075). Lombardy and the metropolis of Milan were central in Gregory's dealings with Henry, with the former finding a hostile environment of what he called 'heresies' of simony, clerical marriage and incontinence, which were coupled with Milan's claims to independence from Rome.[13] Relations reached breaking point when Henry declared Gregory deposed through a council of German bishops at Worms, with the pope retaliating by excommunicating him a few months later (spring 1076).[14]

It was this breach of alliance between Rome and Germany that was to see a brief rapprochement between Gregory and the Normans. Gregory had opened hostilities in two distant fronts, something he could ill afford, let alone risk an alliance between Henry and the Normans, which came close to materialising in the summer of 1076.[15] What caused relations to deteriorate once again was the combined Norman siege operations against Salerno, Naples and Benevento, which resulted in Guiscard's second excommunication in February 1078. Even though by that time the pope's relations with Germany had improved significantly, with Henry submitting to Gregory at Canosa in January 1077, a solution to the internal problems facing the emperor reached a dead end about a year later. Faced with a rival claimant to the throne in a country that was divided and devastated by civil war, Henry received another excommunication by the pope in November of the same year (1078).

Once again, Gregory was facing enemies on two fronts and it was obvious that an alliance with the Normans would be sought. Thus, after the conference at Ceprano between Gregory VII, Robert Guiscard and Jordan of Capua, which took place in June 1080, we have the final settlement between the Normans and Rome. That settlement saw the lifting of the excommunication and Robert's investment with the lands that he had held since 1059, even those which he had 'taken in defiance of the pope', meaning the disputed lands of Salerno, Amalfi and the Abruzzi area.[16] This agreement was crucial, not only for the pope, who desperately needed Norman military support against Henry IV's army, but also for the Norman duke, who was

[12]   *The Register of Pope Gregory VII*, I.21a (pp. 25–6).
[13]   Cowdrey, *Pope Gregory VII*, pp. 75–158.
[14]   *The Register of Pope Gregory VII*, III.10a (pp. 187–93).
[15]   Amatus, VII.27.
[16]   *The Register of Pope Gregory VII*, VIII.1a, b and c (pp. 364–5).

anxiously preparing for his Illyrian campaign. The latter could not afford to have such an enemy back home while he was fighting on the other side of the Adriatic, bearing in mind that the last rebellion in Apulia had taken place only a year before (winter 1078/9).[17] For both Gregory and Robert, their alliance was dictated by the current political climate which none could possibly ignore. Peace with Gregory VII, after six years of almost continuous strife between them, left the Norman duke free to consider his most ambitious plan to date: his campaign against the Byzantine Empire.

The Norman preparations that began in Salerno in the summer of 1080 saw the appearance of the deposed emperor Michael VII at the Norman court, something which provided Guiscard with the pretext he needed to justify his campaign as a 'restoration mission'. Of course, this convenient story is far from true and was merely what Guiscard hoped the Byzantines would most easily fall for, and thus follow him against the usurper of the imperial throne, Nicephorus Botaneiates. For this, he also had the full support of Rome that had officially recognised his expedition as an effort 'to restore Emperor Michael VII to the Byzantine throne'. On 25 July 1080, Gregory VII called upon the bishops of Apulia and Calabria and all the 'faithful of St Peter' to go 'resolutely in true faith with no differences of mind to the help and defence of the aforesaid emperor', offering absolution from their sins as the heavenly reward for their actions.[18] But how far back do the relations between Robert Guiscard and Michael VII date?

Michael VII was not the first emperor to have sought a Norman alliance. The negotiations between the duke of Apulia and Constantinople can be traced back to the years of Romanus IV, who had also sought to conclude an alliance treaty some time in 1071, although it is not clear precisely when.[19] The civil conflict in the capital and the coming of Michael VII interrupted the negotiations, but the new emperor was quick to acknowledge the significance of an alliance with the Apulian Normans, mainly for the provision of ample bodies of mercenaries for the Byzantine army. Thus, he reopened talks with Robert Guiscard by sending a letter, either at the end of 1071 or the beginning of 1072. This treaty, however, which was to be ratified by a marriage alliance between Guiscard's daughter and Michael's brother Constantine, was not to be on equal terms. In this letter it becomes clear that the Byzantines were attempting to draw the Normans into their own world by lavishly giving away titles and accepting a 'barbarian' girl into the imperial *gynekonete* (women's quarters) in exchange for readily enlisting able-bodied troops at their disposal and a faithful ally on their western borders. According to the terms of the marriage treaty, Robert Guiscard would promise to respect and defend the imperial territories with all the forces he

[17]   Loud, *Robert Guiscard*, pp. 241–3; Chalandon, *Domination normande*, pp. 254–5.

[18]   *The Register of Pope Gregory VII*, VIII.6 (pp. 371–2); I. S. Robinson, 'Gregory VII and the Soldiers of Christ', *History* 58 (1973), 182–3.

[19]   Sathas, *Bibliotheca Graeca*, V, p. 387; W. B. McQueen, 'Relations between the Normans and Byzantium, 1071–1112', *Byzantion* 56 (1986), 429.

could muster against the enemies of the emperor.[20] This was just the kind of strategy favoured by the Byzantines in winning over their neighbours, as is stated in the works of Constantine Porphyrogenitus, Leo VI and others.

Robert Guiscard proved intelligent enough not to be drawn into this trap and turn himself into a vassal-duke of the empire. The negotiations continued throughout the following year, with another letter being sent probably at the end of 1072 or the beginning of 1073.[21] It was the chrysobull of August 1074, however, that finally ratified the alliance between the Normans and Constantinople, with Michael's newly born son being offered as a stronger footing.[22] What actually persuaded Guiscard to give in to Michael's proposals was the immense political pressure applied by Gregory VII, triggered by Michael's exhortations for a military campaign against the Seljuks to save the empire 'after the Normans [Guiscard] have been pacified'.[23]

If Guiscard's pretext of acting in favour of the deposed emperor Michael VII is put aside, what we have to delve into in more detail is the deeper reasons behind Robert Guiscard's expedition.[24] Undoubtedly, given the marriage alliance between Robert and Michael, and the fact that the latter's deposition must have brought shame to Robert's daughter and would have been a blow to Robert himself, it is rather naive to think that the duke would have launched an expedition for such trivial reasons. In the words of Anna Comnena: 'He [Guiscard] was always thinking out some more ambitious project. He seized on the pretext of his connection by marriage with the emperor [Michael VII] and dreamed of ascending the throne himself.'[25] The imperial crown is certainly considered one of Robert Guiscard's ambitions, and he was not alone in finding himself under the influence of Byzantine culture, language, state organisation and economic prosperity. Indeed, it is a fair assessment that Byzantium was omnipresent in the everyday life of an Italian, even in a province as distant as Longobardia. Could this have been, however, Guiscard's only motive?

Another reason has to do with the Byzantine involvement in the Apulian rebellions since the mid-1060s. Although the Byzantine military presence in Italy had been failing since the 1040s, Byzantine diplomacy seemed more omnipresent than ever, especially in relation to the role of the governor of Dyrrhachium, Perenus, in providing money for the 1067–8 Apulian revolt that for a time significantly

---

[20]   Sathas, *Bibliotheca Graeca*, V, p. 387.

[21]   McQueen, 'The Normans and Byzantium', p. 430.

[22]   H. Bibicou, 'Une page d'histoire diplomatique de Byzance au XIe siècle: Michael VII Ducas, Robert Guiscard et la pension des dignitaires', *Byzantion* 29 (1959), 43–75; V. von Falkenhausen, 'Olympias, eine normannische Prinzessin in Konstantinopel', in *Bisanzio e l'Italia. Raccolta di studi in memoria di Agostino Pertusi* (Milan, 1982), pp. 56–72.

[23]   Gregory's correspondence with William of Burgundy can be found in E. Emerton, ed., *The Correspondence of Pope Gregory VII* (New York, 1932), pp. 22–8.

[24]   For the use of an impostor to act as the deposed Michael VII, see *Alexiad*, I.12 (pp. 58–61); Sewter, pp. 58–61; *Gesta*, IV.260–72 (p. 218).

[25]   *Alexiad*, I.12 (p. 57); Sewter, p. 57.

undermined Guiscard's authority and brought the Sicilian and Apulian expansion to a standstill.[26] Two of the ringleaders of this rebellion, namely Joscelin of Molfetta and Roger Toutebove, sought refuge at the emperor's court, while Guiscard's nephew Abelard, himself a protagonist of almost every major Apulian insurrection in the 1060s to 1070s, also sought refuge at Constantinople after 1078 and was one of Alexius Comnenus' main negotiators between Constantinople and the papacy in 1081–2, as we sahll see later. Since the conquest of Bari in 1071, Apulia had seen two major rebellions that significantly diminished Robert Guiscard's resources in money and manpower and, most importantly, challenged his authority as duke of Apulia and Calabria.[27] Although the involvement of Byzantine agents in these insurrections cannot be certain, Robert Guiscard possibly held them responsible. The duke needed to act in order to avoid any other potentially threatening revolt in his core territories of Apulia, and the only way was to strike at the source of all the trouble, the Illyrian capital Dyrrhachium and possibly Constantinople itself.[28]

Another factor that would have contributed greatly to Guiscard's decision to launch his campaign is the nature of his rule in relation to his vassal lords. Even though Robert was invested by Pope Nicholas II as duke of Apulia and Calabria in 1059, this does not mean that his authority went unchallenged by his powerful counts. Those in particular who were related to him by blood, like Robert of Conversano, Geoffrey of Montescaglioso and members of the powerful Amicus kin, who belonged to the second generation of Normans in the peninsula, were unlikely to take orders from Robert Guiscard without any significant gains. Throughout the 1030s, 1040s and 1050s, a period when Byzantine resistance in Apulia and Calabria was collapsing rapidly, and more and more lands were lavishly given away to these counts, no revolt had taken place. When the Sicilian theatre of war, however, came to a standstill in the 1060s and the Byzantines locked themselves into their heavily fortified coastal cities in Apulia, then the situation became even more difficult for the Norman duke. In the 1070s, the enemies of the Normans in Italy had been defeated and there were no more lands to be given away to the increasingly demanding Apulian counts. The quest for more lands in the opposite side of the Adriatic can be seen as a major impetus for the Illyrian campaign.

A final point has to do with Robert Guiscard's son Bohemond and his position and standing in the Norman court. Although he was the eldest of the duke's sons, Guiscard had earlier repudiated his wife Alberada and had married Sigkelgaita in the early months of 1059, which made Bohemond, theoretically, a bastard. A twelfth-century historiographer stated that Guiscard had planned, if he was successful in his campaigns in the East, 'to make Bohemond emperor of the Byzantine Empire, and

---

[26]   Loud, *Robert Guiscard*, pp. 133–4; Chalandon, *Domination normande*, pp. 177–8 and 182.

[27]   Loud, *Robert Guiscard*, pp. 240–4; Chalandon, *Domination normande*, pp. 223–5 and 254–6.

[28]   A very good study of the level of contact between the successive Byzantine governments with Italy is Loud, 'Anna Komnena', pp. 41–6.

himself ruler of a great Mohammedan empire'.[29] Although surely a fantastic story and certainly far beyond the financial capabilities of the duke, if one looks beyond the exaggerated comments of the author of the *Chronica*, then one of the reasons – although certainly not the main one – may have been the establishment of a Norman principality for Bohemond at the opposite side of the Adriatic. The chronicler may have written on the basis of hindsight, since Bohemond's participation in the First Crusade sealed his fate as one of the key commanders of the expedition to the Holy Land, which opened the way for the establishment of his principality of Antioch; however, a similar ambition to channel Bohemond's insatiable appetite for lands and fame in the Balkans in the early 1080s should not be entirely written off.

The military operations in Illyria (spring to summer 1081)

From all quarters of Lombardy he gathered them, over age and under age, pitiable objects who had never seen armour even in their dreams.[30]

It is a challenging task to assess the size of the Norman force that set sail from Otranto in the spring of 1081. According to Anna Comnena the Norman expeditionary force consisted of some 30,000 men, with 150 ships of all types carrying them across the Adriatic with around 200 men and horses on each ship.[31] I believe that 30,000 men is an exaggerated figure given by Anna to enhance, in her readers' eyes, Alexius' victory over the Normans. Malaterra's figure of 1,300 knights, 'as those present have testified', is surely closer to the truth. Although this may seem relatively small, it represents the elite core of the Norman expeditionary force – the knights, most of whom, according to Malaterra's comments, formed a 'poorly armed mob'.[32] Other sources, like Orderic Vitalis, put the figure at no more than 10,000 men, Peter the Deacon notes 15,000 men, while Romuald of Salerno talks about 700 horsemen – a much more plausible figure as well.[33]

Anna also states the names of certain types of ships which the Normans used for the transportation of their army: 'Dromons, triremes, biremes and *sermones* and other transport vessels in great numbers were made ready'.[34] Since the princess was no expert in Byzantine ship-building and naval warfare, she has probably confused the dromons with the *khelandia*, which were more frequently seen in the waters of the Adriatic and the Tyrrhenian Seas. Thus, the ships of the Norman fleet must have been *khelandia* if the Normans were to 'meet the enemy in full armour and on the

---

[29] Richardus Pictaviensis, *Chronica*, MGH, SS, XXVI (p. 79).

[30] Anna Comnena on the Norman invading force, *Alexiad*, I.14 (pp. 68–9); Sewter, p. 65.

[31] *Alexiad*, I.16 (pp. 74–5); Sewter, p. 69.

[32] Malaterra, III.24.

[33] Orderic Vitalis, VII (p. 16); *Chronicon Casinensis*, III.49 (p. 429); Romuald of Salerno, *Chronicon*, s.a. 1081 (p. 194).

[34] *Alexiad*, III.9 (p. 170); Sewter, p. 124.

beaches', as this type of transport ship was equipped with ramps to unload horses on the beach.[35] Bennett, however, believes that the transport ships of the Normans at Dyrrhachium were Arabic *tarridas* that had a square stern with two stem-posts, which enabled the incorporation of a ramp that could be lowered to unload the horses.[36] Although possible, the Byzantine *khelandia* are more likely in this case. Also, triremes had not existed in Mediterranean waters since the early Roman times and, again, Anna is probably influenced by her readings of ancient Greek and Roman works.

The crews that manned the vessels of the Norman fleet were indigenous Italians that had served in the Norman navy since the Messina landing in 1061, namely Apulians and Calabrians of either Lombard or Greek origin, while it is likely that ships from Amalfi and Muslim crews would have been used as well.[37] William of Apulia also informs us of the existence of Ragusan elements in the Norman fleet, something which confirms an alliance between Robert and the semi-independent Slav principalities of the eastern Adriatic coast.[38] Perhaps Guiscard's relations with the Slav settlers in Italy, cordial since the 1050s, as we have seen, played a role in winning the alliance of these principalities.

Robert Guiscard gave orders for his fleet to sail from Otranto[39] in May 1081, after appointing his son Roger Borsa as heir to his dukedom, along with Robert of Loritello and Geoffrey of Conversano as his senior advisors.[40] Before that, however, he had already dispatched his son Bohemond, along with a small force ferried on fifteen ships, in a reconnaissance mission to capture Corfu and Aulon probably a few weeks before.[41] Aulon, because of its protected gulf that offers an excellent point of disembarkation, along with its strategic location on the Epirus coast, was crucial for the Norman operation. Bohemond managed to capture Aulon, Canina and Oricum, the three most important fortresses of the southern coastal approaches of the region of Dyrrhachium, but failed against the walls of the citadel of Corfu, and withdrew to the opposite fortified Epirus site of Buthrotum (Butrint), at a distance of about 16 kilometres, to await his father's arrival.[42]

After Robert Guiscard crossed the Adriatic with the main fleet of warships and transport ships, he headed towards Aulon to disembark his army and join his son. Before reaching Aulon, however, he launched an attack towards the citadel of Corfu,

---

[35] *Alexiad*, I.16 (pp. 74–5); Sewter, p. 69.

[36] Bennett, 'Amphibious Operations', pp. 54–5.

[37] *Alexiad*, IV.1 (p. 188); Sewter, p. 135.

[38] *Gesta*, IV.134–5 (p. 210). For these principalities, see Stephenson, *Byzantium's Balkan Frontier*, pp. 117–56; P. Stephenson, 'Balkan Borderlands', in *The Cambridge History of the Byzantine Empire c. 500–1492* (Cambridge, 2008), ed. J. Shepard, pp. 664–82.

[39] *Gesta*, IV.122–4 (p. 210); Malaterra, III.24; Orderic Vitalis, VII (p. 16); Anna erroneously mentions Brindisi as the port of embarkation: *Alexiad*, III.12 (p. 181); Sewter, p. 131.

[40] *Gesta*, IV.195–7 (p. 214).

[41] Malaterra, III.24.

[42] *Alexiad*, I.14 (pp. 69–70); Sewter, p. 66; Malaterra, III.24.

that had resisted his son's forces, probably intending to have it as a forward supply base. After landing troops at Cassiope, a favourable point for the disembarkation of the army in the north of the island, he proceeded south to commence the siege.[43] The citadel surrendered 'most willingly' on 21 May and paid tribute to Guiscard, who later resumed his operations, taking his army across the straits of Corfu. It is worth noting Chalandon's view that the Corfiots must have cooperated with Guiscard for the city to have surrendered so quickly. Perhaps the duke promised them lucrative trading privileges with the Italian ports.[44]

In another side-expedition, a part of the Norman fleet occupied the port of Vonitsa (Bundicia), further south into the Ambracian Gulf.[45] This side-expedition makes one wonder what the units of the Norman army were doing so far south from their main purported destination, Dyrrhachium. It is not likely that Robert wished to draw units of the Byzantine army away from Illyria, simply because the provincial units of the western Greek mainland were in complete disarray. Unless the town was mistaken for a wealthy merchant port, which as far as I am aware it was not,[46] its capture can be related to what Anna was writing about Guiscard's 'initial' plans of capturing Nicopolis, not far from Vonitsa on the Epirus coast, and Naupactus, further to the south-east, at the entrance of the Gulf of Patras.[47] The conquest of Naupactus would have opened the way for further naval raids against some of the wealthiest cities of the empire because of their silk industry, namely Corinth, Athens and Thebes, as happened during the 1147–9 Norman expedition in the Ionian and Aegean Seas.[48] Thebes had been a great trading centre of the empire since the eighth century because of its silk industry, with numerous Armenians, Jews, Venetians and other traders using it as a base. The city was almost completely destroyed by the Norman raids of 1147. Corinth shared the same fate as Thebes, enjoying an economic prosperity until 1147, when the Normans attacked and transferred all of its silk workers back to Palermo, instigating the city's demise.[49]

Having secured the area around Aulon, Guiscard and Bohemond proceeded north against Dyrrhachium, with the former assuming command of the fleet and the latter taking the land route with a part of the army. Bohemond marched northwards without

---

[43]   *Alexiad*, I.16 (p. 76); III.12 (p. 183); Sewter, pp. 69 and 131; *Gesta*, IV.201–5 (p. 214); Malaterra, III.24; Lupus Protospatharius, *Chronicon*, s.a. 1081.

[44]   Chalandon, *Alexis I*, p. 73.

[45]   This side-expedition is mentioned only by William of Apulia: *Gesta*, IV.207 (p. 214).

[46]   The town of Arta, a few kilometres from the north coast of the Gulf, which was later besieged by Bohemond in 1082, was a major trading port for the Venetians in the twelfth century, although we know nothing about the city before that. See *Oxford Dictionary of Byzantium*, I, p. 191.

[47]   *Alexiad*, I.16 (p. 75); Sewter, p. 69.

[48]   *O City of Byzantium: Annals of Niketas Choniatēs*, trans. H. J. Magoulias (Detroit, 1984), II.2 (pp. 43–5).

[49]   For further reading on the demise of these economic centres of the empire see Z. Tsirpanlis, Η μεσαιωνική δύση (5ος–15ος αιώνας) [*The Medieval West (5th–15th Centuries)*] (Thessaloniki, 2004), p. 242.

any severe interruptions, managing to take Levani at the Semeni River,[50] but the Norman fleet was much less fortunate. At Cape Glossa, in today's region of Cheimara at the tip of the Aulon Gulf, Robert Guiscard encountered a major storm that crippled his fleet and sank a large number of his ships. Although there is no information regarding the exact numbers of vessels destroyed or put out of action, it was a major setback for Guiscard's ambitious plans. Thus, he decided to remain at Glabinitza, to the south of Cape Glossa, for one week to allow his troops to recuperate.[51] Despite these significant losses, however, the Norman heavy cavalry and infantry had taken the overland route to live off the land, thus escaping unscathed from this disaster.

Alarmed by the events, and while waiting for his army to assemble, Alexius did not remain idle but rather took immediate steps to boost the morale of the Orthodox population of Corfu by upgrading the bishopric of Corfu and the Paxi islands to the status of a metropolis. He also improved the defences of the city of Dyrrhachium and set in motion the Byzantine diplomatic machinery in search of allies against the Norman duke.[52] Alexius' first action was to replace the governor of Dyrrhachium, George Monomachatus, with his faithful friend and brother-in-law George Palaeologus. This tactic of appointing members of the royal family in crucial administrative posts, both in the capital and in the provinces (typical examples being George Palaeologus, Alexius' brother Isaac and their mother Anna Dalassena, Constantine Ducas and Nicephorus Melissinus), was not out of the ordinary for the eleventh-century Byzantine administrative system. Michael VII Ducas had also relied on family members during his reign, but the practice had not been seen on such a scale before.[53] It is worth remembering that the emperor was a usurper and had been in power for only a few weeks; thus, he had not firmly established his authority over the provincial officials. He therefore had every right to be afraid of Monomachatus' loyalty, as he was placed in his position as governor of Dyrrhachium by Botaneiates and remained faithful to him. In addition, Anna repeatedly accuses Monomachatus of secret and treacherous dealings with Guiscard as well.[54] In fact, if William of Apulia's comments are true, Monomachatus did engage in talks with Guiscard when he learned that Botaneiates was dethroned before defecting to Bodin, the ruler of the

[50] *Anonymi Vaticani Historia Sicula*, RIS, VIII. col. 769.

[51] *Alexiad*, III.12 (pp. 184–5); Sewter, pp. 132–3; *Gesta*, IV.218–24 (p. 216).

[52] *Alexiad*, III.9 (pp. 172–3); Sewter, p. 126; G. Kharizanis, 'Ὁ μητροπολίτης Κέρκυρας Νικόλαος καὶ ἡ βυζαντινο-νορμανδικὴ σύγκρουση στο Ιόνιο (τέλη του 11ου αι.)' ['The Metropolitan of Corfu Nikolaos and the Byzantine–Norman Conflict in the Ionian (End of 11th Century)'], Βυζαντιακά [*Byzantiaka*] 24 (2004), 197–210.

[53] P. Frankopan, 'The Imperial Governors of Dyrrakhion in the Reign of Alexios I Komnenos', *Byzantine and Modern Greek Studies* 27 (2002), 65–103; P. Frankopan, 'Kinship and the Distribution of Power in Komnenian Byzantium', *English Historical Review* 495 (2007), 1–34; J.-C. Cheynet, *Pouvoir et contestations à Byzance, 963–1210* (Paris, 1990), pp. 359–78.

[54] *Alexiad*, I.16 (pp. 78–9); III.9 (pp. 171–2); Sewter, pp. 71 and 125–6; *Gesta*, IV.228–30 (p. 216).

semi-independent principality of Dioclea on the Adriatic coast.[55]

In order to disrupt Guiscard's communications with his Apulian dominions Alexius needed a combat fleet of his own. But the only certain thing is that the Byzantine naval units available were not up to the task. The squadrons that were to protect the coastal non-maritime *themata* such as Illyria, Cephalonia and Nicopolis consisted of light sailing ships, whose main duty was to patrol the coasts and major ports. Hence Alexius' immediate decision to call on his vassal and old ally, the maritime republic of Venice. In theory, Byzantium and Venice had enjoyed close ties since the fifth century, with Venice becoming a part of the Byzantine Empire during Justinian's expeditions against the Ostrogoths in the mid-sixth century. In 992 the first military-commercial agreement between Byzantium and Venice emerged, signed by Basil II and Peter II Orseolo (991–1009), by which Venice promised naval assistance whenever the Byzantine emperors planned to send an army to southern Italy in exchange for commercial privileges in Constantinople and Abydus. As proof of the validity of this agreement, it was Venice that relieved Bari from a long Arab siege in 1002.[56] Although much had changed since the death of Basil II in 1025, the Venetians still remained vassals of the Byzantine emperors, faithful to their alliance not because of the presence of imperial troops in their city but for a very different reason. Constantinople and the rest of the Byzantine ports were the treasure houses of Venetian trade, which was their gateway to Western European markets, while Venice also needed Byzantium as an ally against the growing ambition of the German emperors.

When Alexius appealed to his subjects in the summer of 1081 he knew that the Venetians would respond favourably for an additional reason. They had a common enemy who was trying to establish himself firmly on both sides of the Adriatic, thus being able to block the entrance to the sea if he so wished and severely cripple Venetian trade. It was not long since that Amicus II of Molfetta and Giovenazzo had attacked the Dalmatian coasts in 1074, resulting in a Venetian naval expedition being mobilised to oust them from Dalmatia. In addition, a significant percentage of Dyrrhachium's population was from Amalfi and Venice, traders who had settled many decades ago at the starting point of the ancient Via Egnatia that led to Constantinople, through Thessaloniki and Hadrianopolis.[57] The commercial privileges of Venice were officially ratified by the emperor the following May (1082) and these were undoubtedly the stimulus for the huge economic growth of Venice in the twelfth century.[58]

---

[55]   *Gesta*, IV.215–17 (p. 216); *Alexiad*, III.12 (p. 181); Sewter, p. 131.

[56]   D. M. Nicol, *Byzantium and Venice* (Cambridge, 1988), pp. 1–35; von Falkenhausen, 'Byzantine Italy', p. 144, especially n. 40.

[57]   *Alexiad*, V.1 (p. 223); Sewter, p. 155; A. Ducellier, *La façade maritime de l'Albanie au moyen âge: Durazzo et Valona du XIe au XVe siècle* (Thessaloniki, 1981), pp. 71 and 105.

[58]   *Alexiad*, VI.5 (pp. 285–7), Sewter, p. 191; E. Frances, 'Alexis Comnène et les privilèges octroyés à Venise', *Byzantinoslavica* 29 (1968), 17–23; M. E. Martin, 'The Chrysobull of Alexius I Comnenus to the Venetians and the Early Venetian Quarter in Constantinople', *Byzantinoslavica* 39 (1978), 19–23. On the debate regarding the dating of the chrysobull, see O. Tuma, 'The Dating of Alexius' Chrysobull to the

The most pressing danger for the empire, however, at this stage was the sultanate of Rum, and Alexius' top priority was to secure his flanks before embarking on a campaign so far from his home base. The sultanate of Rum, under Suleiman-ibn-Qutalmish I (1077/8–1086), had been established shortly before the accession of Alexius, previously being a vassal state to Nicephorus Botaneiates. It occupied most parts of Bithynia, large parts of Phrygia and Galatia, and the Aegean coasts as far south as Phocaea, and its capital was Nicaea, situated just 40 kilometres from Constantinople.[59] Alexius applied guerrilla tactics to repel the invading Seljuk detachments from the Asiatic suburbs of Constantinople, advised in the writings of Nicephorus Phocas and Leo VI centuries ago, and which Alexius, as a lifelong military officer, must have been aware of.[60] These repeated raids seem to have brought some results, with the Seljuks gradually retreating from the regions of Bithynia and Phrygia. Anna writes that after the Byzantine victories the Sultan sued for peace,[61] but Alexius, realising that his eastern borders were temporarily secured, probably pledged a truce while also promising to employ large numbers of Seljuk soldiers. Alexius did ask for troops from the sultan in the summer of 1081, but it is uncertain whether he received a favourable answer or not.[62] It was much later during the siege of Larissa in the winter of 1082/3 that Alexius again urgently requested reinforcements from Suleiman I and indeed received 7,000 men.[63]

Alexius was working in another direction as well, trying to stir up a rebellious mood in Guiscard's rear. William of Apulia mentions Abelard, Guiscard's rebellious nephew and one of the ringleaders of many of the previous insurrections in Apulia, including the one in 1078/9, who had taken refuge in Constantinople.[64] Alexius was able to use him as an emissary to send letters to Herman, Abelard's half-brother and lord of Cannae, to Archbishop Hervé of Capua and, of course, to Gregory VII.[65] Alexius also sent letters to Henry IV, whose relations with Rome had worsened severely, especially after the meeting at Canosa in June 1080 when he was excommunicated for the second time by Gregory and when Robert Guiscard became Rome's vassal, thus breaking a century-long tradition of Italian lords being appointed to their lordships by German emperors.

Venetians: 1082, 1084, or 1092?', *Byzantinoslavica* 62 (1981), 171–85; A. R. Gadolin, 'Alexius I Comnenus and the Venetian Trade Privileges. A New Interpretation', *Byzantion* 50 (1980), 439–46.

[59]   For more on Qutalmish' state, see Korobeinikov, 'The Turks', pp. 706–10. For a selected reading on the arrival of Turkish tribes in Asia Minor see T. T. Rice, *The Seljuks in Asia Minor* (London, 1961); A. Savvidis, Οι Τούρκοι και το Βυζάντιο [*The Turks and Byzantium*] (Athens, 1996).

[60]   *Alexiad*, III.11 (p. 179); Sewter, p. 129. All the *Taktika* underline the importance of ambushes in war with common stratagems found in many of our works: Maurice, *Strategikon*, X.2; *On Skirmishing*, IV, IX, XI and XXIII; Leo VI, *Taktika*, IX.25 and 27–8; XVII.37.

[61]   *Alexiad*, III.11 (p. 181); Sewter, p. 130.

[62]   *Alexiad*, IV.2 (p. 191); Sewter, p. 137.

[63]   *Alexiad*, V.5 (p. 244); Sewter, p. 167; Chalandon erroneously reports that the unit of 7,000 men was sent for the 1081 campaign, see Chalandon, *Alexis I*, p. 74.

[64]   *Gesta*, III.659–67 (p. 200).

[65]   *Alexiad*, III.10 (pp. 173 and 176–7); Sewter, pp. 126–7.

One would get a better idea of the empire's resources in able-bodied men and what the government in Constantinople could actually put in the field by examining the last major battle fought by the imperial forces, the civil conflict at Kalavrye (March 1078). The two parties that fought against each other on the outskirts of Hadrianopolis represented the two different worlds of the Byzantine Empire – the experienced governor of Dyrrhachium and one of the best officers the empire had in the West, Nicephorus Bryennius, against the aged emperor himself, a former governor of the *thema* of Anatolikon who was represented in the battlefield by Alexius Comnenus. Bryennius was able to collect troops from Macedonia, Thessaly and Thrace, probably around 8,000-strong, while as governor of Dyrrhachium he had managed to reinforce his army with Norman (the Maniacati) and Pecheneg mercenaries, again around 8,000-strong. Alexius, on the other hand, had a force of about 13,000 men consisting of 2,000 Turkish troops provided by Suleiman I, a few hundred mounted Franks, the cavalry *tagma* of the Immortals numbering around 1,000, and the indigenous troops from Choma, probably under 2,000-strong.

Since the establishment of the sultanate of Rum by Suleiman I, looking for indigenous troops in Asia Minor would have been fruitless. The decline of the empire in Asia Minor can be clearly seen by Anna's mentioning of the *toparkhes* (town governors) who were summoned by Alexius to send all the forces they could spare to the capital. Anna only writes about the governor of Pontic Heraclea and Paphlagonia, of 'Cappadocia and Choma' and 'of other officers', probably from the north-western regions of the old Opsician and Thracesian *themata*.[66] Anna adds to this: 'Turkish infiltration had scattered the eastern armies in all directions and the Turks were in almost complete control of all the districts between the Black Sea and Hellespont, the Syrian and Aegean waters'.[67] Further indication of the degree of Turkish infiltration in Asia Minor can be seen by the place names of Turkish-Oguz origin found predominantly in the transitional lands of Paphlagonia, Phrygia and Lycia.[68]

Around mid-August Alexius set out from the capital, heading for Dyrrhachium. He had with him 300 men from Choma and a contingent of the Varangian Guard under their leader Nampites, and although its numerical strength is unknown it has been estimated to be around 1,500–2,000 strong, bearing in mind that some units would have stayed in the capital and in other garrison towns in the Balkans (we find 300 Varangians at Castoria in 1082, for example).[69] With Alexius in the capital and his *domesticus* of the west, Gregory Pacurianus at Hadrianopolis, the armed units that the two of them managed to gather consisted of the *tagma* of the Excubitae, led by Constantine Opus, units from Macedonia and Thrace under Antiochus and Thessaly under Alexander Cabasilas. These Balkan units are unlikely to have been greatly

---

[66] *Alexiad*, III.9 (pp. 169–71); Sewter, p. 125.
[67] *Alexiad*, I.4 (p. 25); Sewter, p. 38.
[68] Roché, 'In the Wake of Manzikert', 142.
[69] Haldon, *The Byzantine Wars*, p. 134.

affected by the Pecheneg raids of the last decades, thus it is perhaps safe to assume that they would have been around 5,000-strong. These units consisted of veterans and large numbers of new recruits, judging by Anna Comnena's description of their march from Hadrianopolis to Thessaloniki.[70]

It is rather strange that we do not find units from the province of Hellas or the Peloponnese, which is probably because they may not have been summoned in time for the campaign. There were also units from the Vestiaritae, the emperor's household, and the 'Franks', mercenaries serving under the emperors' banner since the Maniacati of the early 1040s, led by Panoukomites and Humbertopulus. The emperor also had a corps of 2,000 Turkopoles under Taticius – converts to Christianity or the children of Christian–Turkish marriages. These were probably the Turks who had settled near Akhridos (Kardzhali), in the central Thracian region of Rhodope, which should not be confused with Achrida (Ohrid) in Macedonia. Their settlement took place at the beginning of the tenth century although the date is not known with certainty.[71] Other forces included the heretic Manichaeans from Philippopolis, some 2,800-strong, under Xantas and Culeon.[72] Finally, according to an Armenian source, there was a contingent of an unknown number of Armenians under a certain Prince Ochin.[73]

Alexius also called for his imperial ally and vassal the Serbian prince (zupan) Constantine-Bodin of Dioclea (Zeta).[74] The relations of this Slavic principality with Byzantium date back to the mid-1040s. At that time Michael, son of Vojislav, gradually emerged as the sole ruler of the principality of Dioclea (a term that would be replaced by 'Montenegro' in the fifteenth century) over his four brothers (1043–6). In order to secure his dominions from the Byzantine offensives he signed a treaty of peace and alliance. Michael ruled Dioclea from 1046 until 1081, when he is last mentioned in the primary sources, but his feelings towards the empire were not always cordial.

In the early winter of 1072, he sent an army under his son Bodin to support a Bulgarian rebellion in the vicinity of Skopje, which was timed to take advantage of the internal strifes in the empire after the defeat at Manzikert the year before.[75] In fact,

[70]   Lupus Protospatharius provides the exaggerated number of 70,000 men for the Byzantine army led by Alexius at Dyrrhachium: *Chronicon*, s.a. 1082.

[71]   A. Savvides, *Byzantino-Normannica. The Norman Capture of Italy and the First Two Norman Invasions in Byzantium* (Leuven, 2007), pp. 51–2; P. Charanis, 'The Transfer of Population as a Policy in the Byzantine Empire', *Comparative Studies in Society and History* 3 (1961), 148. For the introduction of Turkopoles in the imperial army, see P. Charanis, 'Late Byzantine and Western Historiographers on Turkish Mercenaries in Greek and Latin Armies: The Turcoples/Tourkopouloi', in *The Making of Byzantine History. Studies Dedicated to D. M. Nicol*, ed. R. Beaton, C. Roueché (Aldershot, 1993), pp. 122–36; J. Richard, 'Les Turcopoles au service des royaumes de Jérusalem et de Chypre: Musulmans convertis ou Chrétiens orientaux?', *Revue des études islamiques* 54 (1986), 259–70.

[72]   *Alexiad*, IV.4 (pp. 198–9); Sewter, p. 141.

[73]   Tchamtchiam, *Histoire d'Armenie* (Venice, 1784–6), III.10.

[74]   *Alexiad*, IV.5 (p. 204); Sewter, p. 144.

[75]   For this rebellion and its significance for the political status quo of the region, see J. Ferluga, 'Les insurrections des Slaves de la Macédoine au XIe siècle', in *Byzantium on the Balkans*, pp. 393–7.

Bodin was captured after his army was defeated and he spent the next five years as a prisoner of Michael VI Ducas in Constantinople. This Serbian involvement in the politics of the empire in the Balkans might seem insignificant at first glance, but it has much greater implications because it involved a third party as well – the Normans of southern Italy. As Fine has suggested, Michael of Dioclea sent his son Bodin to Skopje in 1072 in an attempt to move further away from the Byzantine sphere of influence, towards the pope of Rome, from whom Michael received his crown as papal vassal in 1077.[76] This diplomatic move suggests that Michael hoped that the pope would act in his favour and deter any expansionist attempts by the Normans against his principality, if we bear in mind Amicus II's campaign against Byzantine Dalmatia only three years before. Another point that further complicated the Byzantine–Serbian relations was Michael's wish to create his own church (archbishopric) that would have been independent from the Orthodox archbishops of Dyrrhachium and Ohrid. Again, all these facts might seem irrelevant to the Norman military operations in the Balkans, but I will return later to the Serbian role in the events of 1081.

To return to the main theme of this chapter, the Norman invasion of Illyria: after spending about a week at Glabinitza, resting his demoralised troops from the storm, Robert Guiscard appeared outside the fortifications of Dyrrhachium on 17 June,[77] setting up his camp in the 'ruins of the city formerly called Epidamnus',[78] probably the ruins of the city of Dyrrhachium that was devastated by the catastrophic earthquake of the second half of the fifth century. The city was very well defended, built on a long and narrow peninsula which ran parallel to the coast but with a marshy and swampy lagoon separating it from the mainland.[79] There were also two fortified outposts situated on the opposite mainland area and some 'four stadia' from it, both of them centred around two churches, the one dedicated to St Nicholas, from where Alexius would observe the enemy camp and the battlefield, and the other to the Archangel Michael, where the Varangians would seek refuge after their retreat from the battle.

Very little is known about the eleventh-century fortifications of the city, as little survives intact because of later use during the late Byzantine and Ottoman periods, and there is scant information from contemporary chroniclers. According to recent excavations, which have uncovered a part of the north-eastern fortifications, the city was surrounded by a rectangular curtain wall which was supported by semi-circular stone towers with irregular double brick bands and occasional vertical brickwork: a typical style of Byzantine military architecture of the late eleventh and early twelfth centuries. Three of these circular towers have been excavated so far, marking the

[76]   J. A. Fine, *The Early Medieval Balkans* (Ann Arbor, 2008), p. 214.
[77]   *Alexiad*, IV.1 (p. 187); Sewter, p. 135.
[78]   *Alexiad*, III.12 (p. 185); Sewter, p. 133; *Gesta*, IV.241–3 (p. 216).
[79]   On the topography of Dyrrhachium and its surrounding region: J. L. Davis, A. Hoti, I. Pojani, S. R. Stocker, A. D. Wolpert, P. E. Acheson and J. W. Haye, 'The Durrës Regional Archaeological Project: Archaeological Survey in the Territory of Epidamnus/Dyrrachium in Albania', *Hesperia: The Journal of the American School of Classical Studies at Athens* 72 (2003), 41–119.

eastern corner of the city's citadel, while other polygonal towers built on the north side represent the twelfth-century fortifications.[80] In addition to the archaeological evidence on Dyrrhachium's eleventh-century fortifications, historians also have Anna Comnena's brief mention of the city's walls. Thus, it is written in the thirteenth book of the *Alexiad*, which covers Bohemond's campaign in 1107, that 'its wall is interrupted by towers which all round the city rise to a height of eleven feet above it (the wall). A spiral staircase leads to the top of the towers and they are strengthened by battlements. So much for the city's defensive plan. The walls are of considerable thickness, hence wide indeed for more than four horsemen to ride abreast in safety.'[81]

The Normans pressed on with the siege from all accessible sides, meaning both from the north and east.[82] Siege machines were built, namely *helepoleis*, multi-storey wooden siege towers fitted with stone-throwing catapults and drawbridges and protected from fire by layers of hides.[83] According to Anna, however, these had little impact on the city's defences or on the morale of the soldiers, who made repeated sorties to burn down these machines.[84] And while the siege lingered on, a Venetian squadron of an unknown number of ships arrived in the Illyrian waters between late July and early August.[85]

The accounts of the ensuing naval battle between the Venetian and Norman fleets are rather contradictory. According to the *Alexiad*,[86] the Venetian fleet arrived at the promontory of Pallia, further to the north of the besieged city, at some 'eighteen stadia from Robert's camp', but they refused battle on the first day. And while they prepared the fleet during the night for the next day's naval confrontation, with wooden towers erected on the main mast and manned with experienced men, a fierce battle broke out between the two fleets. The Normans were unable to break the solid Venetian 'sea-harbour' (*pelagolimen*), meaning the defensive formation where the biggest and strongest vessels were tied tightly together forming a closing crescent, thus sheltering the smaller and more vulnerable vessels inside their formation. The Venetians eventually managed to rout the enemy fleet, which landed inshore and suffered a second major defeat by a sortie party led by Palaeologus. As a result of the Venetian naval victory, the doge was awarded the significant title of *protosebastos*, a title first

---

[80]   For the medieval fortifications of Dyrrhachium, see Stephenson, *Byzantium's Balkan Frontier*, p. 161. Stephenson's main source is G. Karaiskaj, 'Kalaja Durresit ne mesjete', *Monumentet* 13 (1977), 29–53. See also A. Ducellier, 'Dernières découvertes sur les sites albanais du Moyen Age', *Archeologia* 78 (1975), 35–45; reprinted in his *L'Albanie entre Byzance et Venise, Xᵉ–XVᵉ siècles* (London, 1987), p. 45.

[81]   *Alexiad*, XIII.3 (II, p. 190); Sewter, p. 403; cf. *On Strategy*, XII.1–56 (pp. 34–6).

[82]   *Gesta*, IV.213 (p. 216); Malaterra, III.25.

[83]   *Alexiad*, IV.1 (pp. 188–9); Sewter, p. 135; *Gesta*, IV.250–1 (p. 218).

[84]   A more detailed analysis of these siege-engines, along with their use in this period by the Normans and other crusader armies, can be found in the following chapter, which examines Bohemond's Illyrian campaign of 1107–8, based on the more detailed description provided by Anna Comnena.

[85]   Lupus Protospatharius, *Chronicon*, s.a. 1081; Anonymus Barensis, *Chronicon*, s.a. 1081.

[86]   *Alexiad*, IV.2 (pp. 192–4); Sewter, pp. 137–9.

invented by Alexius Comnenus and ranking fourth after the emperor himself, the *sebastokrator* Isaac Comnenus and the *Caesar* Nicephorus Melissenus. He was also awarded the title of *dux* of Dalmatia and Croatia; we have to note that these titles were awarded in addition to those of the May 1082 chrysobull.

Malaterra has a rather different story to tell, presenting the Venetians as a cunning and crafty enemy.[87] The Normans immediately attacked the Venetians once they perceived their arrival in Illyrian waters, and after a most violent naval battle, by sunset the Normans seemed to have won the day. The Venetians, promising to surrender the next day, asked for a truce, but during that night they erected wooden towers in the ships' main masts and made their vessels lighter and thus more manoeuvrable. By sunrise, the reorganised Venetian squadron attacked the unprepared Normans, forcing them to retreat while they were breaking the naval blockade imposed to the city. After consulting with the inhabitants of Dyrrhachium and making further preparations they attacked the Normans again early the next day, making effective use of Greek fire.

The main offensive weapons aboard a warship in the early period of the crusades were bows and javelins, though crossbows were already being used by the Muslim navies. It was only in the thirteenth century, however, that the crossbow became by far the most important naval weapon on board Italian ships; thus, small but elite units of crossbowmen could be seen dominating the ships of the period.[88] As a naval battle was limited most of the time to exchanging volleys of arrows, the rival fleets included certain superstructures in the form of wooden towers or 'castles' at the ship's stern and sometimes prow. From the tenth century, the use of forecastles on the ships had become the main characteristic of both the Byzantine and Muslim warships.[89] According to Malaterra, the Venetians busied themselves in erecting these wooden superstructures to provide better cover for their bowmen the following day. These wooden superstructures could also be used against coastal defences, but they rarely had any success.[90] Whether the Norman navy used any of these structures against Corfu in the spring of 1081 is unknown but since nothing is reported by our chroniclers we cautiously presume that this technique was still not used by the Norman navy.

This serious setback in Guiscard's siege of the city probably cost him the tribute paid by the people of Corfu (although the citadel remained in Norman hands until the Easter of 1084),[91] and his communications and supply routes with the Italian

---

[87]   Malaterra, III.26; Dandolus, *Chronicon*, s.a. 1081 (p. 216).

[88]   Nicolle, *Crusader Warfare*, I, pp. 142–8. The use of crossbowmen and javeliners, known as almugavars, dominated Aragonese naval tactics after the mid-thirteenth century: S. Rose, 'Islam versus Christendon: the Naval Dimension, 1000–1600', *Journal of Medieval History* 63 (1999), 570–1.

[89]   Leo VI, *Taktika*, XIX.7 (p. 504); Christides, *The Conquest of Crete*, pp. 44–5.

[90]   Bennett, 'Amphibious Operations', p. 57; Kaminiates mentions the use of wooden towers against fortifications by Leo of Tripoli (904) in the siege of Thessaloniki: I. Kaminiates,, 'Τια την αλωση της Θεσσαλονίκης', in Χρονικά των αλώσεων της Θεσσαλονίκης, ed. Kh. Messes, intr. Paolo Odorico (Athens, 2009), XXXIV (p. 113).

[91]   *Gesta*, IV.313–16 (p. 220).

mainland were completely cut off by the patrolling squadrons of the joint Venetian and Byzantine fleets. It has to be mentioned that some time in late summer a Byzantine squadron of an unknown size arrived to reinforce the Venetians, and although Anna leads us to think that the Byzantine squadron was not present in the area before August,[92] it seems more likely that the Byzantines were simply avoiding battle because of their small numbers. Finally, the Norman army was about to suffer another much more serious misfortune. Their naval defeat, the harassment by the Venetian-Byzantine naval squadrons and the Dyrrhachium garrison, the lack of supplies from Apulia, the humid environment of coastal Illyria along with the insalubrious conditions in a medieval camp had already spread starvation and disease, thus making the need to move the camp to another place pressing. Robert Guiscard took his forces further south to the estuary of the River Glycys (Acheron) and remained there for about two months.[93]

The battle of Dyrrhachium (18 October 1081)

We find Alexius in Thessaloniki some time in early September of 1081. Following the Via Egnatia, he arrived at Dyrrhachium on 15 October, pitching his camp on the banks of the River Charzanes.[94] He chose to camp on the opposite side of the lagoon, which separated the Dyrrhachium peninsula from the mainland, thus having a natural obstacle between his army and the Norman camp. Prior to his arrival the emperor had already sent Basil Mesardonites with 2,000 Turkopole mercenaries, elite cavalry archers, to reconnoitre Robert Guiscard's camp; however, this unit was involved in a skirmish and routed by the Normans.[95]

Anna Comnena gives us a vivid description of Alexius' war council before the battle. From this, we have two conflicting views of what tactics should be applied against the Norman siege of Dyrrhachium. The more experienced officers of the army, led by Palaeologus, who had been hastily summoned from the besieged city, insisted that no immediate action should be taken against the invaders, and urged a blockade of the Norman camp and continuous skirmishing that would reduce the enemy's numbers and morale.[96] This plan was a sensible response from an experienced and reliable officer, summarising everything that Leo VI, Nicephorus Phocas and Vegetius recommended about getting to know one's enemy, the terrain and avoidance of battle unless all opportunities were on one's side. It is doubtful, however, whether the Byzantines had any accurate intelligence of the enemy regarding its numbers,

---

[92] *Alexiad*, IV.3 (p. 195); Sewter, p. 139.
[93] *Alexiad*, IV.3 (pp. 196–7); Sewter, pp. 139–40.
[94] *Alexiad*, IV.5 (p. 203); Sewter, p. 143.
[95] *Gesta*, IV.324–43 (p. 222). Orderic Vitalis also gives an account of a small-scale military confrontation, which preceded the main battle on the outskirts of Dyrrhachium: Orderic Vitalis, VII (p. 18).
[96] *Alexiad*, IV.5 (p. 204); Sewter, pp. 143–4.

composition and morale or any detailed knowledge of the terrain of the region. This is
in striking contrast to Alexius' campaign against Bohemond at Larissa two years later,
when he specifically asked for information about the topography of the region from
a local. In addition, the defeat of an elite unit of the Turkopole cavalry even before
the arrival of the main imperial army in the area should have dictated caution and
prudence.

Alexius, however, followed the younger and hot-headed officers of his army, who
were calling for an immediate battle to be waged, probably raising issues of pride and
honour against a barbarian duke who dared to provoke the mighty Byzantine Empire,
thus leaving little room for the recently crowned emperor to manoeuvre. These officers
were Constantine Porphyrogenitus, the son of the former emperor, Constantine
X Ducas (1059–67), and brother of Michael VII (1071–8), Nampites, the leader of
the Varangian Guard, Nicephorus Synadenus and the sons of the former emperor
Romanus IV (1067–71), Leo and Nicephorus. It is possible that Constantine, who
is portrayed by Anna as the leader of the opposition against Palaeologus' plans for a
blockade, may have been hoping for a defeat of the Byzantine army, an event which
might have given him the chance to raise claims to the throne as a descendant of the
Ducades and a younger brother of the deposed Michael VII. After all, it was his elder
brother Andronicus Ducas who had betrayed Romanus IV at Manzikert ten years
earlier.

On 17 October, when it had become evident to the Normans that the Byzantine
army was preparing for an attack, Robert Guiscard ordered his ships to be burned.[97]
This was a desperate attempt to boost the morale of his soldiers and encourage them
to fight to the end, a tactic which was recommended by all the military treatises from
Onasander to Leo VI and Vegetius: 'trapped men draw extra courage from desperation,
and when there is no hope, fear takes up arms'.[98] Whether it was really his entire fleet
that Guiscard ordered to be burned or just the landing crafts that had transported the
Norman forces from the ships depends on how we interpret the chronicler's reports.

The emperor's initial plan was not to engage the Normans in a pitched battle but
rather to perform a surprise night-attack on the Norman camp from two sides. First
he would send his allies – the Serbs and the Turks – on the longer route through
the marshes towards Robert's rear, while he would then press for a frontal raid, most
likely with a coordinated sortie by the Dyrrhachium garrison as well.[99] During the

---

[97] *Alexiad*, IV.6 (p. 214); Sewter, p. 145; Malaterra, III.27.
[98] This quotation comes from: Vegetius, *Epitome*, III.21 (p. 107). Similar recommendations can be found
in Sextus Julius Frontinus, *The Stratagems and the Aqueducts of Rome*, trans. Charles E. Bennett (London,
1925), II.6. 10 (p. 169); Onasander, *Strategikos Logos: Aenean Tacticus, Asclepiodotus, Onasander*, trans.
by members of the Illinois Greek Club (New York, 1977), XXXII (pp. 475–81); Polyaenus, *Stratagems
of War Translated from the Original Greek, by Dr. Shepherd, F.R.S.* (London, 1796), I.30. 3, II.1. 6, III.9.
12/14, VIII.23. 29; *On Strategy*, XXXIX; Maurice, *Strategikon*, VIII.2, 92; IX.2; *On Skirmishing*, XXIV;
Leo VI, *Taktika*, XVII.19 (p. 400).
[99] *Alexiad*, IV.6 (pp. 208–9); Sewter, pp. 145–6.

night of 17–18 October, however, the Normans had already moved out of their camp opposite Dyrrhachium to the sanctuary of St Theodorus, a place much closer to the Byzantine camp on the opposite side of the Dyrrhachium lagoon. Whether it was simply a coincidence or the Byzantine plan had somehow reached Guiscard's ears we will never know for sure, but the next morning the Normans had placed themselves between the lagoon and Alexius' army, having the lagoon on their rear and the sea to the right.

After seeing the Normans in battle array on the morning of 18 October, Alexius had to adjust his plans to face them in pitched battle that same day. The Normans had arranged their battle lines as follows: Robert Guiscard, as the natural leader of the campaign, commanded the main force at the centre of the formation; his son Bohemond, the second-in-command, took charge of the left wing, while the right wing closer to the sea was entrusted to 'Amicetas' (probably Amicus II of Molfetta and Giovenazzo who had taken part in all three Apulian rebellions in 1067/8, 1072 and 1078/80). Unfortunately there is no information about the composition of each of the three battles of the Norman army. It is most likely though that Guiscard kept the bulk of his elite cavalry units in the centre of his formation, and probably behind the heavy infantry for better protection against enemy missiles, a tactic also used by William at Hastings. On the wings he probably put the conscript levies and the lighter or less experienced cavalry. Whether the Normans had brought any archers with them is not certain, but even if they did their presence was not felt during the battle that day.

Alexius arranged his battle lines accordingly, taking command of the centre division of the army, while Pacurianus was at the head of the left wing, closer to the sea, and Caesar Nicephorus Melissinus was in charge of the right wing. The Varangian Guard, fighting dismounted in the Anglo-Saxon custom, was put in the centre front line of the whole formation and projected a few yards forward. Alexius, by putting the Varangians in front of the central division, would probably have wanted to take advantage of their thick infantry formations against a possible charge of the Norman heavy cavalry, while he also would have been aware of the English hatred for the Normans over the conquest of their homeland.[100] In addition, units of lightly armed archers and peltasts were ordered to move through their lines and release volleys of arrows before retiring, in order to weaken the enemy advance units. Unfortunately, as with the Norman army, we have no information related to the composition of each of the three divisions of the imperial army. It is likely that Alexius kept the units of the Excubitae, the Vestiaritae and the Chomatiani with him, along with the elite cavalry troops of the Franks and, possibly, the Thessalians as well. The Macedonian and Thracian units may have been kept in the same division, as had happened in Kalavrye (1078) and Manzikert (1071), while the Armenians (if indeed there were any on that campaign) would have been placed under the command of Pacurianus, himself of Armenian origin.

---

[100]   Malaterra, III.27.

The first stage of the battle was opened by the Normans, with Robert Guiscard beginning his march towards the Byzantines. His first move was to send a body of his horsemen, most likely from his own division, to practise their feigned retreat tactics and entice the English to break their ranks and pursue them. The Byzantine reaction to this was immediate, with the archers and the peltasts that were put behind the ranks of the Varangians marching forward to repel the Norman charge by volleys of arrows. The peltasts engaged in moderate skirmishing with the Normans and while the Byzantine centre was occupied in repelling the first attack wave, Robert Guiscard was quickly covering the distance between the two armies.

While the first attackers must have been forced to retreat and the three Norman divisions were marching forward, Amicus' cavalry and infantry units charged forward and attacked Nampites' left flank, exactly at the point where it met with Pacurianus' division. This may be seen as an attempt to break the English ranks by attacking their exposed flanks which are every infantry unit's weak point. The Normans, however, were met with heavy resistance by the English while Pacurianus' units, along with certain elite units from Alexius' division, rushed forward to support them. The Normans broke into disorderly retreat, 'throwing themselves into the sea up to their necks and when they were near the Roman and Venetian ships begged for their lives – but nobody rescued them'.[101] It is at this point that Anna, by giving far the best account we have of the battle, adds the famous story of Robert's wife Sigkelgaita, who managed to bring the retreating Normans to their senses by grabbing a spear and charging at full gallop against them. If we are to believe Anna's account, the Norman right wing under Amicus must have consisted of conscript levies and light cavalry because of their poor morale and lack of discipline.

By the time the Norman right wing was forced to a panicky retreat by the Byzantine units, the rest of the army would have marched forward far enough to be involved in skirmishing with the Byzantine divisions of Alexius and Melissinus, but no unit made a decisive tactical move to tip the battle in its favour. The Varangians, however, who had just repelled a joint cavalry and infantry attack, could not resist joining their comrades in the pursuit of the fleeing Normans along the coast. This move was to prove disastrous for the Byzantine campaign, with their quick pace of marching forward resulting in their being separated from the main body of the imperial army and thus making them extremely vulnerable to flanking movements by the enemy.[102] Robert Guiscard was too experienced a tactician to let this opportunity pass by. He immediately ordered a unit of elite heavy infantry, probably spearmen, to fall upon them on their right flank and after a short time the exhausted, surprised and outnumbered Varangians suffered heavy casualties. Because they were not completely surrounded, a few of them managed to seek refuge in the nearby church of the Archangel Michael, where they were all burned to death by the Normans, who set the church alight.

---

[101] *Alexiad*, IV.6 (p. 210); Sewter, p. 147.
[102] Malaterra, III.27

With the Varangian Guard completely annihilated and his left wing in a disorderly pursuit of the retreating Normans, Alexius found his main division exposed to Norman cavalry attacks from the front and left flank. Robert Guiscard had not yet used his elite cavalry units, with the exception of the feigned retreat during the opening stages of the battle, and he saw that this was the right time to throw them against his enemy. This all-out attack by the Norman cavalry proved effective in shattering the Byzantine morale and discipline. Although Anna mentions that certain units did stand and fight courageously, many of their comrades abandoned the fight and ran away, with the entire front soon disintegrating rapidly. Only the emperor and his retinue resisted as long as they could, but they too realised that any further resistance would be pointless.

The losses for the Byzantine forces must have been heavy. It is possible that as much as a quarter of the total Byzantine forces engaged were killed or wounded,[103] if we include the entire Varangian contingent of some 2,000 men, units of the left wing that repelled Amicus' attack and units from the front ranks of the main and right divisions. The Manichaeans may have suffered some 300 casualties, since Anna gives us a number of 2,500 of them being discharged by Pacurianus some time after the battle,[104] while it is certain that the Dalmatians and Turkopole troops did not even engage the enemy. These units had just found the Norman camp abandoned and were marching towards the battlefield at the time when Guiscard was launching his feigned cavalry attack. They had every chance to attack the Normans from the rear but, as Anna writes, Bodin, the leader of the Diocleans, remained a spectator of the battle and awaited its outcome to see which side would prevail.[105]

The Norman casualties, on the other hand, must have been much lower since the only major unit that was dealt a severe blow was Amicus' division, which, after launching an attack on the Varangian left flank, was repelled and routed. Even though large numbers must have been killed or drowned in their desperate attempt to evade their pursuers, this would not have constituted a serious blow to Robert Guiscard's army since, as mentioned above, these men would probably have been inexperienced peasant levies and lightly armed cavalry.

The battle of Dyrrhachium – conclusions

Dyrrhachium can be seen as a typical example of a battle where the Norman battle tactics were used against an army which had developed a different mentality and concepts about warfare over at least the previous five centuries. Thus, what is really tempting is a comparison between the tactics used by Robert Guiscard against the Byzantines and those applied in the fields of southern Italy, Sicily, Normandy and England. If the battle is examined stage by stage, we first come across the feigned

---

[103]   Haldon, *The Byzantine Wars*, p. 137.
[104]   *Alexiad*, V.3 (p. 232); Sewter, p. 160.
[105]   *Alexiad*, IV.6 (p. 214); Sewter, p. 149.

retreat that was applied by Robert Guiscard in the opening stages of the battle. But before I relate this tactic to Sicily and what seems much more obvious, Hastings, we must consider how the eleventh-century Normans had learned about this battle tactic, especially since we know that they had used it at least three times before Dyrrhachium, at Arques (1053), Messina (1060) and Hastings (1066).[106]

The feigned retreat was a well-applied trick, which had been introduced to Europe by the mid-fifth century by the nomadic tribes of the Huns. Although contacts did exist between the Magyars, who as originally steppe nomads fought in a similar way,[107] and the eastern Franks, we cannot be sure whether there was any transmission of the experience gained in the region of Carinthia, Moravia and the middle Danube to mainland Francia. Bachrach has argued that the Alans, another steppe people, had been settled by the Romans in Armorica – the ancient name of the territory between the Seine and Loire rivers – and their influence on Armorican cavalry tactics dates from the fifth century.[108] Count Alan of Brittany was in command of the routed left wing of the Bretons and Angevins at Hastings, while Walter Giffard, a commander at Arques, was also present.[109] Since we have already established the steady flow of immigrants from 'beyond the Alps' to southern Italy after the second quarter of the eleventh century, the use of feigned retreat at Dyrrhachium in 1081 should come as no surprise.

Another theory suggests the feigned retreat has its roots in mock battles of Carolingian France and Flanders.[110] In fact, we read about a specific type of exercise taking place at Worms, on 14 February 842, between followers of Louis the German and Charles II the Bald. Saxon, Gascon, Austrasian and Breton cavalrymen would ride in teams against each other at full gallop but at the moment before impact one party would make a turn and pretend to escape while the other would play the role

[106]   Whether there was indeed a feigned retreat by William's cavalry in the second stage of the battle is a debate among scholars that has been fought almost as hard as by the two enemy armies at Hastings, and we need not engage with this issue further. I find the arguments of Oman, Brown, Verbruggen, Douglas and Bachrach, who suggest a 'cover-up' of a true retreat by the contemporary chroniclers, more convincing than those of Beeler, Lemmon and Delbrück: Oman, *The Art of War*, I, pp. 149–66; Verbruggen, *The Art of Warfare*, p. 96; R. A. Brown, 'The Battle of Hastings', *Anglo-Norman Studies* 3 (1980), 1–21; B. S. Bachrach, 'The Feigned Retreat at Hastings', *Medieval Studies* 33 (1971), 344–7; Douglas, *William the Conqueror*, pp. 203–4; C. H. Lemmon, *The Field of Hastings* (St-Leonards-on-Sea, 1956), pp. 24–31; Beeler, *Warfare in England*, pp. 21–2; H. Delbrück, *History of the Art of War*, 4 vols (London, 1990), III, pp. 158–9.

[107]   For the Magyar battle tactics and an analysis of the Battle of Lechfeld, see Oman, *The Art of War*, I, pp. 116–25; Delbrück, *History of the Art of War* III: *Medieval Warfare*, pp. 115–29; Contamine, *War in the Middle Ages*, p. 35.

[108]   Bachrach, 'The Feigned Retreat at Hastings', pp. 344–7; B. S. Bachrach, 'The Alans in Gaul', *Traditio* 23 (1967), 480–2 and 484–9; B. S. Bachrach, 'The Origin of Armorican Chivalry', *Technology and Culture* 10 (1969), 166–71.

[109]   William of Poitiers, p. 134.

[110]   Verbruggen, *The Art of Warfare*, p. 30. See also C. Gillmor, 'Practical Chivalry: the Training of Horses for Tournaments and Warfare', *Studies in Medieval and Renaissance History* 13 (1992), 7–29.

of the pursuer, and vice versa.[111] Einhard also refers to numerous military exercises undertaken by Charlemagne's sons 'as his ancestors had done, as no one matches the Franks in these arts'.[112] Could military training and the simulation of pitched battles in France have led to the development of this feigned retreat tactic? We cannot be certain but we can at least consider the possibility.

The battle of Dyrrhachium opened with Robert Guiscard sending a cavalry detachment, probably of the elite and experienced knights he kept in his division, to try to dislodge the defensive formation that dominated the centre of the enemy lines. Fortunately for the Varangians, however, Alexius had put archers and peltasts immediately behind them, in the space between the Varangians and Alexius' division, with orders to march through the Varangian lines and repel or slow down an enemy advance. As at Hastings, where the infantry and cavalry charges of William's army were met with a heavy shower of arrows, javelins, lances and other 'primitive casting weapons', this cavalry attack produced poor results, with the Varangians staying put and their defensive formation unshaken.

The second stage of the battle, however, proved to be the most crucial one. While the Norman cavalry detachment was engaged in a moderate skirmishing with the Varangians and the supporting peltasts, the Norman army had managed to cover most of the distance between them and the Byzantines and, at that important point of the battle, Amicus' division, probably composed of infantry levies and light cavalry, launched an attack which was directed at the Varangians' left flank. Although the latter must have still been supported by the peltasts, their flanks were exposed to the enemy attack since they were deployed at some distance at the front of the rest of the imperial army. The Varangians resisted stoutly without giving any ground to the Normans, receiving reinforcements from the Byzantine left wing and centre, which resulted in the attackers being routed. And it was at this point that disaster struck for Alexius' army.

With their right wing in a disorderly retreat that had left the main division exposed to flanking enemy movements, this would have seemed like a perfect opportunity for Alexius to strike a serious blow on Robert Guiscard's army and perhaps even win the field. But as had happened at Hastings, where after the first charge Harold's men from his right wing broke ranks to pursue their enemies downhill and were cut to pieces, the same fate followed Nampites' men in Dyrrhachium. Because of 'their inexperience and hot temper' they broke their dense defensive formation in a foot pursuit of the retreating Norman right wing. Why this division should abandon their phalanx formation, which gave them such a great advantage over the Norman heavy cavalry, is a frustrating problem. Being separated from the main body of the imperial

---

[111]   Nithard, *Histoire des fils de Louis le Pieux*, ed. and trans. P. Lauer and H. Champion (Paris, 1926), III.6 (pp. 110–12).

[112]   Einhard, *Vita et Gesta Karoli Magni [Vie de Charlemagne]*, ed. and trans. L. Halphen, 4th edn (Paris, 1967), XIX (p. 58) and XXII (p. 68).

army and out of breath, they presented an easy target for Guiscard, who immediately ordered his elite infantry to fall upon them. The result was a massacre; not only was an elite unit of the imperial army completely annihilated, but its main body was also left exposed to the Norman cavalry attack.

If we countenance dismissing the idea of the Varangian hot-headed pursuit, then another version of events should be considered. It is possible that the emperor, seeing his enemy's right wing in disorderly retreat and thus realising Guiscard's vulnerability on his right flank, signalled a general advance. But with the centre and right divisions of the Byzantines already involved in a moderate skirmish and the Varangians advancing well beyond the Byzantine line, the cardinal sin would have been Alexius' failure to catch up and support their advance. It is unlikely that this version would have been presented to us by Anna, but although it is not even mentioned by Malaterra or William of Apulia, at least we have to consider it as a possibility.

The retreat and subsequent annihilation of the Varangians brings out an issue that has been mentioned while studying the battle at Civitate:[113] that heavy cavalry units could make no impression upon well-equipped and disciplined foot soldiers who kept their formation unbroken. The basic logic behind this is that no horse would attempt to throw itself against a wall of shields, which the dense infantry formations would ressemble from a distance. The cavalry charge was mainly a psychological weapon aimed at frightening the enemy soldiers enough to create gaps in their formation that the heavily armed knights could then penetrate; or they had to wait for the archers – if there were any – to shoot volleys of arrows to thin down the front ranks of the enemy. If a charge failed to break the line of infantry, the cavalry could then either retreat and renew its charge, or slow down in the last few yards and engage in single combat. That brought desirable results for Edward I at Falkirk in 1298, given that the Scots had lost the support of their mounted men.

A unit of well-equipped and disciplined foot soldiers, on the other hand, was clearly a defensive formation which, like the Varangian Guard or the Scottish schiltron (shield wall), had to be sufficiently deep and dense and needed the support of units of cavalry and archers because, although it could repel the cavalry charges, its speed and ability for manoeuvres made any counter-attack almost unthinkable. And in the cases when the foot soldiers did break ranks and charged against their enemies, as at Hastings and Dyrrhachium, they got slaughtered. At Civitate, however, the Swabian infantry took full advantage of their only weapon in the battlefield, their disciplined and tight formations, and resisted stoutly against the repeated charges of the Norman cavalry. Being surrounded and heavily outnumbered, however, they stood no chance. Throughout history, the armies that effectively combined both armed forces, infantry and cavalry, were the most successful.

[113]   Gillingham, 'An Age of Expansion', pp. 64 and 76–8; Bennett, 'Military Supremacy', pp. 304–16, especially pp. 310–16; Morillo, 'The "Age of Cavalry" Revisited', pp. 45–58; Verbruggen, *The Art of Warfare*, pp. 46–9.

With regard to the battle of Dyrrhachium, the reasons behind the retreat of the main units of the imperial army, many of them war veterans, are not given by Anna and speculations around this subject can be tricky. One possible reason may be the fact that the 'heavy' cavalry of the late-eleventh-century Byzantine army was no match for the cavalry charge of the Norman chivalry, because of the latter's equipment and training. Combining this with the fact that Alexius had to call up recruits with no previous military experience, we understand why the Byzantine army's numerical superiority over the invading Normans did not bring victory on the battlefield. Alexius could have been counting on the dense phalanx formations of his Varangians to repel any Norman cavalry charge, while he launched an all-out cavalry attack on the weaker Norman flanks. But when his protective shield was annihilated, the Normans had all the room to take full advantage of their tactic that had practically given them the victory in so many battlefields thus far – a heavy cavalry attack.

Since the battle of Dyrrhachium is a perfect example of the clash of two different military cultures in one operational theatre of war, a question that immediately comes to mind is what knowledge did the Byzantine officers, and Alexius Comnenus in particular, have of their enemies? Were they studying the military treatises compiled in the previous decades or centuries that analysed the strategy and tactics of their neighbouring people, or had these works become archaic, valued as literary pieces rather than as real handbooks? Undoubtedly, the greatest difference between the Byzantines and other neighbouring cultures lies in the fact that it was the former, like the Romans before them, who were writing down the useful knowledge and experience their generals had gained on the battlefields, thus giving the false impression that others like the Muslims were more inexperienced or even inferior in their strategies compared to the Byzantines. As the author of *On Skirmishing* writes, 'In order that time, which leads us to forget what we once knew, might not completely blot out this useful knowledge, we think we ought to commit this [knowledge] to writing'.[114] A number of manuals would have been available to the young nobles of the Constantinopolitan court or the officers of the provincial armies, whose fundamental occupation would have been the study of classical Greek, Roman and contemporary books that referred to war.

Research on a number of Byzantine chronicle accounts of battles and military campaigns and the comparison of their accounts with the military manuals of the period has led me to conclude that the military leaders were, indeed, aware of the existing military manuals and frequently consulted them.[115] The late-tenth-century anonymous author of the Byzantine treatise *On Tactics* writes that:

> the ancients have passed on to us the necessity of training and organising the army, which is obviously useful and quite fundamental. They would train not only the army as a unit, but they

---

[114]   *On Skirmishing*, p. 146–8.

[115]   A very important study on this topic is T. G. Kolias, 'Η πολεμική τακτική των Βυζαντινών: θεωρία και πράξη' ['The Military Tactics of the Byzantines: Theory and Practice'], in *Byzantium at War (9th–12th Century)*, ed. N. Oikonomides (Athens, 1997), pp. 153–64.

would also teach each individual soldier and have him practise how to use his weapons skilfully [. . .] Many of the Romans and Greeks of old with small armies of trained and experienced men put to flight armies of tens of thousands of troops.[116]

But the most famous reference to the use of military manuals comes from the reign of Constantine Porphyrogenitus (913–59) when among the books that the emperor had were those which examined the art of war (*biblia strategika*) and siege engineering (*biblia mekhanika*).[117] Cecaumenus notes in his late-eleventh-century *Strategikon* that 'when you [the officer] finish with your daily business and go home to rest, do read the military manuals and the histories and all the ecclesiastical books; and do not ask, how does that benefit you [to read] these dogmas and ecclesiastical books; they are overwhelmingly beneficial'.[118] In the same period, Bryennius writes that a prince's training included 'how to put in order a phalanx, set a camp, put a pole into the ground and all the rest that the manuals (*taktika*) teach us'.[119] Similarly, the author of the *On Skirmishing*, when examining the defensive measures during the siege of a town, notes that 'matters such as these and other devices used in sieges [. . .] have been carefully and precisely explained before us by the authors of books on tactics and strategy'.[120] Finally, we read in Psellus' *Chronographia* that Basil II 'knew the various formations suited to his men. Some he had read in books, others he devised himself during the operations of war, the result of his own intuition'.[121] It is hard, however, to imagine a Byzantine officer directing his battlefield units with a military manual in his hands; it seems only reasonable that the influence of classical works on Byzantine officers had been mainly academic and reflected only a small – but undoubtedly very important – part of their training as commanders. Whatever the case, Alexius, instead of imposing a blockade as he did against Bohemond twenty-six years later, gave to the Normans exactly what they wanted, a pitched battle and ample opportunity to use their heavy cavalry.

A final matter is the passive role of Bodin, the leader of the Dioclean Serbs, and his reluctance to support the emperor during the crucial moments that preceded the annihilation of the Varangian Guard. The relations between the Serbian *zupan* and the Byzantines were hostile, even though the Diocleans had been imperial allies since the mid-1040s. But what would Bodin hope to get from a Norman victory at Dyrrhachium in 1081? I have already highlighted the Byzantine aggressiveness in the region of the principality of Dioclea throughout the century, along with Michael's (Bodin's father) wish for an independent archbishopric, while we should also bear in mind the danger that the Normans posed to the Serbs. Was Bodin hoping for a future alliance with a

---

[116]   *On Tactics*, XXVIII (p. 318).
[117]   Constantine Porphyrogenitus, *Three Treatises on Imperial Military Expeditions*, Corpus Fontium Historiae Byzantinae, XXVIII, ed. J. F. Haldon (Vienna, 1990), p. 106.
[118]   Cecaumenus, p. 19.
[119]   Bryennius, p. 75.
[120]   *On Skirmishing*, XXI.12–15 (p. 224).
[121]   Psellus, I.33 (p. 46).

Norman principality in the western Balkans, as both he and the Normans were papal vassals; an arrangement that would not only have diminished the danger posed by the Byzantine emperors but might also have brought the archbishopric of Dyrrhachium under Serbian control?

A letter to Michael by Gregory VII on 9 January 1078 implies some sort of correspondence between the two coasts of the Adriatic regarding the bishopric of Antibari on the Adriatic coast and a request for its upgrade into an archbishopric under Rome's jurisdiction.[122] But even though this is nothing more than speculation we can, at least, consider it as a possibility. Bodin would have been aware that, in the case of a Norman victory, the Normans would not attempt to proceed north towards Dalmatia – perhaps to establish an Adriatic principality – but rather would continue east to Thessaloniki, and he was perfectly aware that the best route would take them along the Via Egnatia, which was further south. Thus, he may have chosen to keep his army intact in case the Byzantines won the battle in order to defend his country from any punitive attack, which indeed was to take place some time between 1089 and 1091.[123]

---

[122]   *The Register of Pope Gregory VII*, V.12 (p. 258).
[123]   Fine, *Early Medieval Balkans*, p. 224.

7

The Norman Advances in the Balkans and the End of the Dream

From Dyrrhachium to Larissa (1082–3)

It was not just the Varangian regiment that was annihilated at Dyrrhachium; the Byzantine nobility also suffered a severe blow, with 'several fine soldiers killed' during the battle, such as the *porphyrogenitos* Constantine Ducas, Nicephorus Palaeologus, General Aspietes, and Nicephorus Synadenus.[1] Alexius and his personal guard avoided arrest by seeking sanctuary at a place called Kake Pleura (Ndroq), just north of Dyrrhachium, and then at the castle of Lake Achrida (Ohrid). After probably spending the months of November and December there, winter months accompanied by severe snowfalls in the mountainous areas of Epirus and western Macedonia, Alexius entrusted the defence of Dyrrhachium's citadel to the Venetians, thus acknowledging their important role in the defence of the city. He also appointed a native Illyrian-Albanian as *komeskortes*, meaning commander of the forces of the lower city.[2] As for the rest of the castles in the Dyrrhachium region, the Italian sources confirm that most of them capitulated.[3]

We have two different accounts for the surrender of the city of Dyrrhachium. The first version of events provided by Anna shows the citizens of the city – with the role of the Amalfitans and the Venetians in the making of the decisions being highlighted – contemplating the surrender of Dyrrhachium to avoid any possible retaliation, after hearing of Robert Guiscard's intention to resume the siege the following spring.[4] Both Malaterra and William of Apulia give us another version of the events: after four

---

[1] *Alexiad*, IV.4 (pp. 211–13); Sewter, p. 148.

[2] *Alexiad*, IV.8 (p. 221); Sewter, p. 153; *Gesta*, IV.436–48 (p. 228). *Korte* meant the emperor's tent. The main duty of the *komes tes kortes* was to escort the drungarie of the Watch around the camp for the night inspection. See Bury, *The Imperial Administrative System*, p. 43

[3] Malaterra, III.27; *Gesta*, IV.440 (p. 228).

[4] *Alexiad*, V.1 (p. 223); Sewter, p. 155.

months of negotiations the siege of the city was at a standstill because of the winter period when a certain Domenico, a nobleman of Venetian origin to whom the defence of a principal tower was delegated, reached an agreement with Robert Guiscard to betray the city to them in exchange for the hand of the latter's niece, the daughter of William I of Principate.[5] Domenico was probably the son of the former doge of Venice, Otto Orseolo (1008–26, 1030–2), who had been banished from Venice, accused of nepotism, and received in Constantinople with great honours.[6] Anna Comnena may well have been less informed about the precise circumstances of the surrender, as she was writing some six decades after the events, and the two versions may in fact amount to the same thing. Whatever the case, the city opened its gates on 21 February 1082.[7]

The harsh winters in the mountainous regions of Illyria and western Macedonia were the main cause for Robert Guiscard's inability to take advantage of his success over Alexius' army. While the Norman campaign was proceeding slowly in the surrounding areas of the River Diabolis, the emperor had already established Thessaloniki as a rallying point for the remnants of his troops returning from Illyria. But the imperial treasury was empty and the collapsed Byzantine economy could not afford the hiring of extra mercenary troops.[8] Thus, the emperor resorted to the unpopular measure of confiscating precious ecclesiastical objects from various churches in the capital.[9] According to old ecclesiastical canons the emperor had the right to confiscate ecclesiastical objects in order to pay the ransom for prisoners of war. In this case, the entire Christian population of Asia Minor was held to ransom by the Seljuks, according to the emperor. The government had the support of the residential synod and of the patriarch Eustathius Garidas (1081–4), and so the measure went ahead with no serious protests.

With the coming of the spring, Robert Guiscard left Illyria and marched further east. He would have been expected to follow the Via Egnatia that ran from Achrida to Thessaloniki. The Via Egnatia was one of the two most strategically important military roads that linked Constantinople with Europe and Italy. It followed a course from the capital through Thrace (Hadrianopolis), Macedonia, Thessaloniki and Edessa (Vodena), proceeding north of Castoria to Achrida and then directly west to the Illyrian port of Dyrrhachium that linked the Balkans with Italy.[10] Instead of

---

[5]   Malaterra, III.28; *Gesta*, IV.449–60 (p. 228).

[6]   Nicol, *Byzantium and Venice*, pp. 45–9.

[7]   Our only source for the exact date is Anonymus Barensis, *Chronicon*, s.a. 1082.

[8]   *Alexiad*, V.1 (pp. 225–6); Sewter, p. 156.

[9]   *Alexiad*, V.2 (pp. 226–7); Sewter, pp. 157–8; A. Glavinas, Η επί Αλεξίου Κομνηνού (1081–1118) περί ιερῶν σκευῶν, κειμηλίων και αγίων εικόνων ἔρις (1081–1095) [*The Controversy (1081–1095) regarding the Holy Relics and Saintly Images during the Reign of Alexius Comnenus (1081–1118)*] (Thessaloniki, 1972), ch. 2, pp. 51–72.

[10]   F. O' Sullivan, *The Egnatian Way* (Newton Abbot, 1972); G. L. F. Tafel, *De Via Militari Romanorum Egnatia, qua Illyricum, Macedonia et Thracia iungebantur*, 2nd edn (London, 1972).

marching his army to Thessaloniki, however, Robert Guiscard turned south towards the western Macedonian city of Castoria. Since the emperor was in the capital until May, our main primary source for the events that unfolded is Malaterra.

We are not sure about Guiscard's motives in turning south, but I suspect that he might have wanted to have his flanks covered from enemy attacks. Castoria was also one of the major cities of the Greek mainland and a great mercantile centre in the Ottoman period.[11] Guiscard may also have been aware that 300 Varangians – probably a regiment detached by Alexius while on his way to Dyrrhachium the previous October – were defending the city, since this is one of the few numbers that Malaterra provides in his entire narrative of the campaign.[12] Whatever the case, the siege of the city did not last long since the Varangians decided to come to terms before the Normans had even brought their siege machines before the city's defences, another sign of the declining morale in the imperial army's units. The city probably fell in March or early April 1082.[13]

For the military preparations of the Byzantines, the primary sources do not provide any information about the units employed apart from the hiring of an unknown number of Seljuk troops.[14] These soldiers must have been individuals from the sultanate of Rum, flocking to the empire in search of pay, and must not be confused with the 7,000 Seljuks officially sent by Suleiman I in the following year. In addition, Alexius once more set in motion the mechanisms of Byzantine diplomacy that had worked so well for him some eight months before. In early April 1082, the emperor sent another embassy to the German emperor Henry IV, promising lavish gifts and a royal marriage.[15] But while these negotiations were under way, Henry was already marching south to Italy in full force against Gregory VII, and a fresh Apulian revolt had broken out, probably stirred up by Byzantine agents – most likely by Abelard, since he was already acting as an imperial agent in Apulia the previous year.[16] A messenger arrived in April 1082 to notify Guiscard about the events back home and preparations for his departure immediately got under way.

This was a significant turning point for the Norman campaign in the Balkans, and although no Norman troops were taken back to Italy, the leader and mastermind of the entire expedition leaving his army in enemy territory and in the middle of a military expedition overseas was to prove a fatal decision. Not only was the capture of Thessaloniki postponed indefinitely (it was finally captured 103 years later) but

[11]   *Oxford Dictionary of Byzantium*, II, pp. 1110–11.

[12]   Malaterra, III.29.

[13]   A. Glavinas, 'Οι Νορμανδοί στην Καστοριά (1082–1083)' ['The Normans in Castoria (1082–1083)'], Βυζαντινά [*Byzantina*] 13ii (1985), 1255–65, at p. 1256, n. 2.

[14]   *Alexiad*, V.3 (p. 231); Sewter, p. 160.

[15]   See *Alexiad*, V.3 (pp. 231–3); Sewter, pp. 160–1. Compare with the previous round of negotiations: *Alexiad*, III.10 (pp. 173–5); Sewter, pp. 126–8.

[16]   Taviani-Carozzi, *La terreur du monde*, pp. 452–68; McQueen, 'The Normans and Byzantium', pp. 443–4.

Bohemond was left to face an opponent of about the same age but with much greater experience in warfare, who also had the advantage of fighting on home ground.

Bohemond, who was chosen to lead the campaign after his father's departure for Italy, was, no doubt, a brave and ambitious officer not yet at the peak of his military career. Robert Guiscard's forty years of combat experience in the battlefields of southern Italy and Sicily would have been more suitable in times of crisis, such as during the stalemate on the outskirts of Larissa in the winter of 1082/3. The Norman duke, however, thought it best to attend to his affairs in Italy in person, while he appointed his son Bohemond as commander-in-chief of his forces in Greece, with the count of Brienne (constable of Apulia and lord of San Mango sul Calore) as his deputy. He hastily embarked in a monoreme for Italy, probably around the end of April 1082.[17]

Bohemond resumed the operations in north-western Macedonia and immediately marched south-west towards Ioannina, the capital of the region of Epirus in north-western Greece.[18] The first question that comes to mind is why the Norman army deviated from its main target, Thessaloniki, and why Bohemond decided to occupy Ioannina, so much further south from the Via Egnatia. The answer to the first part of the question is not difficult to imagine, since with Robert Guiscard back in Italy it would seem almost inconceivable for the small, inexperienced and not properly equipped Norman army to undertake such a task, especially with young Bohemond in command. We cannot be sure about Bohemond's motives on his turn south towards Epirus, but it is highly likely that his decision was greatly influenced by his father's advice before his departure. He may have thought that his affairs in Italy would not keep him there for long and that he would soon be back in Greece to resume hostilities. Thus, Guiscard may have wanted his son to secure what had already been conquered, meaning the areas of Illyria, coastal Epirus and western Macedonia. As we saw before, it is possible that Guiscard was aware of the presence of the 300 Varangians at Castoria and, fearful for his army's flanks and for the presence of any other strong contingents of enemy troops in his rear, he would have wanted to sweep Epirus and western Macedonia of any enemy elements.

Another factor that may have influenced the Norman advance south to Castoria and then east to Larissa is the role of the Vlach populations of these regions and their cooperation with the Normans. This was only superficially mentioned by Chalandon and has not been picked up by any scholar since. The first use of the term Vlach in Byzantine primary sources is by Scylitzes, in vague reference to the Latinised populations of the predominately Greek-speaking areas of the Balkans during the imperial Roman period. The origin of the designation is Germanic (*walhs*) meaning

---

[17]   *Alexiad*, V.3 (pp. 232–3); Sewter, pp. 161–2; *Gesta*, IV.524–7 (p. 232).
[18]   For a comparison with Bohemond's march through the Greek mainland fifteen years later: J. H. Pryor, 'Modelling Bohemond's March to Thessalonike', in *Logistics of Warfare in the Age of the Crusades*, ed. Pryor (Aldershot, 2006), pp. 1–25.

'foreigner' or 'neighbour'.[19] These pockets of Latin-speaking populations on the Greek mainland took the name Aromanians (from 'Romani', meaning citizens of the Roman state), and they could be found mainly in Thessaly (Larissa being its capital) and western Macedonia in the ninth and tenth centuries.[20]

The great dissatisfaction of these populations of Thessaly caused by high taxation and corrupt state officials stirred up a great revolt around the end of 1065 or the beginning of 1066, which was led by a powerful magnate of the region of Larissa called Niculitsa Delphin – clearly of Bulgarian origin, judging by his name. This revolt, however, proved short-lived, and an agreement was eventually reached between its leader and the emperor's officials. Hence, I wish to raise the following question in connection with Chalandon's argument about possible alliance talks between Robert Guiscard and Vlach leaders in 1066:[21] do we consider Bohemond's turn southwards a coincidence? Bearing in mind the almost certain hatred of these mainly nomadic populations for the Byzantine government, along with the view of the Vlachs as liars, thieves and beggars by contemporary Byzantine authors,[22] the answer would be negative. I have not come across any evidence in the primary sources that could support beyond any doubt my previous assumption regarding possible talks held in 1066 or later; but I believe that we do have to be suspicious of Bohemond's movements in the Greek mainland in the following years.

In late April 1082, Bohemond marched from western Macedonia to Epirus and towards Ioannina, following roughly the course Korçë – Konitsa – Kalpakion – Bella – Kalama.[23] Throughout his journey, his army was reinforced by elements of the Byzantine army who deserted to the Normans. Bohemond could have taken advantage of these men's knowledge of the local terrain, meaning the routes leading southwards through the rough and inhospitable Pindus mountains, while they could have also betrayed to him the numbers of Ioannina's garrison. The inhabitants of Ioannina, however, quickly capitulated in order to avoid any retribution and pillaging by the Normans if they resisted.

Bohemond's contribution to the reinforcement of the city's defences during his short stay in the region is significant, although it has been pointed out that he has been credited with more than he could conceivably have achieved. This is due to the usual problem that archaeologists face when a site has been used for many periods in

---

[19] Scylitzes, II (p. 329).

[20] V. A. Friedman, 'The Vlah Minority in Macedonia: Language, Identity, Dialectology, and Standardization', *Selected Papers in Slavic, Balkan, and Balkan Studies* 21 (2001), 26–50; D. Dvoichenko-Markov, 'The Vlachs', *Byzantion* 54 (1984), 508–26.

[21] Chalandon, *Alexis I*, pp. 60–1 and 85–6.

[22] 'The Vlachs are a nation of wicked liars who are completely untrustworthy, and do not believe in God or in any king, relative or friend': Cecaumenus, pp. 74–5. Cecaumenus was probably a high-ranking military official of the eastern aristocracy writing in the 1070s.

[23] *Alexiad*, V.4 (p. 236); Sewter, p. 163; Savvides, *Byzantino-Normannica*, p. 57.

history, in our case the Byzantine and the Ottoman periods.[24] From what scattered evidence we get from archaeology, we know that the city's citadel was built some time in the tenth century. The fact, however, that the Normans reinforced Ioannina's fortifications with a second 'most strong' acropolis, a typical strategy employed by them in Italy and Sicily, as indicated in a previous chapter, is supported by Anna: 'After making an inspection of the ramparts and recognising that the citadel was in a dangerous condition, he [Bohemond] not only did his best to restore it, but built another of great strength at a different section of the walls where it seemed to him that it would be most useful'.[25]

Alexius left Constantinople with the troops he had managed to gather over the previous three to four months to face the Normans at Ioannina. Trying to assess the numbers and consistency of the emperor's army is difficult because even Anna, our only detailed source for this period, gives us little information to work with. It is most likely, however, that a large part of the conscripts recruited for the Dyrrhachium campaign returned home instead of reporting to Thessaloniki. We can be all but certain that the Byzantine army was outnumbered by the Norman host. From Anna's narrative it emerges that Alexius had learned a valuable lesson from his previous experience against the Normans – hence his decision to send skirmishing detachments to harass the Norman camp and gather intelligence regarding their numbers and the commanding skills and fighting capabilities of their leader, Bohemond.[26] The emperor, 'fearing the first charge of the Latins', also adopted a new and innovative battle tactic. He had a number of small and light chariots, with spears fixed on top of them, put behind the first lines of his division in the centre with infantry men hiding underneath and ready to emerge and manoeuvre them when the Norman cavalry charge was at a striking distance from the Byzantine lines. Surprisingly, 'as though he had foreknowledge of the Roman [i.e. Byzantine] plan he [Bohemond] had adapted himself to the changed circumstances': Bohemond's answer was to divide his forces into two major units and attack the flanks of the imperial army, thus engaging in a mêlée that quickly led the terrified Byzantines to flee the battlefield. The disorderly Byzantine retreat suggests that either there was no heavy cavalry at all, or that that unit was simply swept away by the Norman knights, who then immediately turned and attacked the infantry.

The next confrontation is poorly placed chronologically and geographically, but the *Alexiad* gives the impression that it took place a couple of days after the first battle of Ioannina. In fact, it must have taken several weeks for Alexius to get to Thessaloniki, to ready his troops and then to march back west to Epirus. From Anna's brief statement that 'the armies were assembled once more and when the mercenaries were ready he [Alexius] marched against Bohemond', it seems obvious that these units were

[24]   L. Vranousses, Ιστορικά και τοπογραφικά του μεσαιωνικού κάστρου των Ιωαννίνων [*History and Geography of the Medieval Castrum of Ioannina*] (Athens, 1968).

[25]   *Alexiad*, V.4 (pp. 236–7); Sewter, p. 163.

[26]   *Alexiad*, V.4 (pp. 237–9); Sewter, pp. 163–4.

summoned to Thessaloniki for the previous campaign, but probably failed to arrive on time and simply stayed there and waited for new orders.[27] Meanwhile, Bohemond probably left Ioannina and headed south-east towards the southern Epirus coast and the city of Arta, just a few kilometres north of Vonitsa, taken by his father at the end of May 1081.[28]

Alexius devised a similar plan to that at Ioannina, with his primary aim being to disrupt the Norman heavy cavalry charge that had proved irresistible so far. According to Anna, who once again is our only detailed source for the events, on the previous day of the battle the emperor had his men set up iron caltrops (*triboloi*) in front of the centre of his formation, where he expected the Norman cavalry attack to take place, in order 'to frustrate the first (and decisive) charge when the caltrops pierced the horses' hooves'.[29] In addition, this time the Byzantine front lines would have had the support of peltasts, who were deployed behind the infantry front lines of the centre.

The plan included an advance by the wings (for which we do not know the composition, but it was probably light cavalry units) against the frustrated knights immediately after the first Norman cavalry charge had been neutralised: an encircling manoeuvre that could well have won the battlefield for Alexius. The course of the battle, however, was a repetition of what had taken place at Ioannina, with Bohemond finding out about the Byzantine plans, either by treason or simply by sending scouts close to the enemy lines. The result was another cavalry attack on the Byzantines' flanks which quickly melted away once again, probably because of low morale: 'They were frightened before the battle started because of their previous disaster and did not dare to look their opponents in the face'.[30]

What we need to emphasise at this point is the knowledge of this specific tactic of using obstacles, in our case chariots and caltrops, to obstruct the advance of a heavy cavalry unit. According to the military treatise called *Strategikon*, probably compiled around the second decade of the seventh century by the 'master of the soldiers in the east', obstacles such as caltrops were used on the perimeter of a camp to protect it from surprise cavalry attacks.[31] The caltrops were apparently tied together with strings so that they could be recovered even when hidden in grass. The author of the early-tenth-century treatise *On Strategy* also refers to caltrops as a measure to defend a camp from enemy attack, while he specifically writes about iron plates put on the horses' hooves so that they will not be injured during an attack.[32]

Some three centuries later other military treatises like the *Taktika* of Nicephorus Uranus (written between 999 and 1007) and the *On Tactics* – probably compiled by

[27] *Alexiad*, V.4 (p. 239); Sewter, p. 164.
[28] Malaterra, III.29.
[29] *Alexiad*, V.4 (pp. 239–40); Sewter, pp. 164–5.
[30] *Alexiad*, V.4 (p. 241); Sewter, p. 165.
[31] Maurice, *Strategikon*, IV.2 (p. 54).
[32] *On Strategy*, VI.12 (p. 22); XVII.17–18 (pp. 56–8); XXXVIII.25–7 (p. 114). Repeated in Leo VI, *Taktika*, VI.23 (p. 94).

the same general between 991 and 995 – also mention caltrops, as well as other devices, to be placed in the ditches surrounding a camp.[33] I am not aware of any cases where Alexius had actually used this specific battle tactic before in any operational theatre, but this proves the continuity of long-established battle tactics and reinforces the argument that sees the officers of the Byzantine army as studying military manuals dating back as far as ancient Greek and Roman times.[34]

With the emperor retiring to Thessaloniki and then to the capital, Bohemond was free to expand his dominions on the Greek mainland and march further north and east.[35] From Arta he turned north-east towards Skopje and the surrounding regions of the two Polovoi, south of Skopje, and Achrida to the west. We learn from Anna the names of his two senior officers that were sent to occupy these towns: Peter of Aulps, who took the two Polovoi, and Raoul, count of Pontoise, who subdued Skopje. The castle of Achrida was defended by a certain Ariebes who managed to repel the repeated attacks made by Bohemond's troops, forcing him to quit the siege and move towards Ostrobus, east of modern day Florina in western Macedonia, where he was again forced to withdraw. From there he plundered Beroea (Veria), Servia (a town south of Verroia), Edessa (Vodena) and Almopia (Moglena, east of Edessa), although Anna's narrative is not entirely clear whether these areas were indeed occupied or not, reaching through the Vardar valley to Aspres Ekklesies, just to the north-west of Thessaloniki. He captured the town and stayed there for about three months until the autumn of 1082, before marching to Castoria.

The course that Bohemond followed was carefully planned, and if we trace his route on a map we can understand why. Once more it seems that the primary target of the Norman campaign was the capital of Macedonia, Thessaloniki, and the main route that connected it with Dyrrhachium, the Via Egnatia. The cities of Achrida, Florina and Edessa were situated exactly on the Egnatia, while Verroia, Servia and Almopia controlled its southern approaches. Attempting to besiege Thessaloniki, however, was not on the agenda for the small Norman army and, because of Castoria's cold and damp winter climate, the Norman leader decided to transfer his winter camp further south to the fields of Thessaly, one of the warmest and most fertile places in the Balkans. His march southwards took him through Pelagonia and Trikala (between Ioannina and Larissa), while another detachment subdued Tziviskos, clearly intending to spend the winter in the Thessalian fertile plains.[36]

For the date of the start of the siege of Larissa, Anna Comnena writes the following: 'He [Bohemond] then moved on to Larissa, arriving in full force on St George the

[33] J.-A. De Foucault, 'Douze chapitres inédits de la tactique de Nicéphore Ouranos', *Traveaux et memoires* 5 (1973), 298–300; *On Tactics*, II.17–20 (p. 262).

[34] G. Theotokis, 'From Ancient Greece to Byzantium: Strategic Innovation or Continuity of Military Thinking?', in *Antiquitas Viva 4: Studia Classica*, ed. I. Rūmniece, O. Lāms, B. Kukjalko (Riga, 2014), pp. 106–18.

[35] *Alexiad*, V.5 (pp. 242–4); Sewter, pp. 166–7.

[36] *Alexiad*, V.5 (p. 244); Sewter, p. 167.

Martyr's Day'.[37] All the non-Greek scholars who have dealt with this event have accepted 23 April, St George's day, as the day when Bohemond came to Larissa, assuming that until then he had pitched his camp at Trikala and had sent a detachment to enforce a blockade of the city.[38] It is most likely, however, that Anna Comnena meant 3 November, which commemorates the consecration of a cathedral dedicated to St George in Lydda, south-east of today's Tel Aviv in Israel, during the reign of Constantine the Great (305–37).[39] This does not seem to have any major implications for the turn of events that winter, although we have to note that the defenders of Larissa would certainly have been more reluctant to try to break the blockade if that was enforced by the main Norman force under Bohemond himself. As for the city of Larissa, for which we know next to nothing of its medieval fortifications, its defence was entrusted to the experienced officer Leo Cephalas, who managed to resist the besiegers for around six months before the blockade began to take its toll on the morale of the population.[40]

Alexius once again resorted to diplomacy to deal with the Normans and spread discord and discontent among Bohemond's senior officials. Unfortunately, the *Alexiad* does not give us any details about this conspiracy, but we do know that three senior figures in the Norman army, Peter of Aulps, a certain Renaldus and another called William were accused of plotting to desert to the emperor. Also, the emperor asked for a large mercenary force from Suleiman I in the early winter of 1082, thus receiving a force of 7,000 men under a certain Camyres.[41] The Byzantine preparations went on throughout the winter with the intention of marching towards Thessaly early in the spring of 1083. While Alexius was raising troops in the capital, the patriarch of Jerusalem, Euthemius, along with Pacurianus, were sent to Thessaloniki in late 1082 or early 1083 to gather additional troops and see if they could broker some sort of deal with Bohemond.[42]

Probably in March (1083) the emperor left Constantinople to raise the siege of the Thessalian capital. Nothing is related in regard to the numbers and consistency of his army, with his march towards Larissa taking him through a series of strategically important locations in Thessaly; passing through the very narrow valley of Tempe (the only route southwards coming from Thessaloniki), he reached Plabitza, north-east of Larissa and close to a river which is not named by Anna because of a deliberate *lacuna*,

---

[37]   *Alexiad*, V.5 (p. 244); Sewter, p. 167.
[38]   Chalandon, *Alexis I*, p. 88; R. B. Yewdale, *Bohemond I, Prince of Antioch* (Amsterdam, 1970), p. 20; Loud, *Robert Guiscard*, p. 219; Taviani-Carozzi, *La terreur du monde*, p. 471.
[39]   A. Glavinas, 'Οι Νορμανδοί στην Θεσσαλία και η πολιορκία της Λάρισας (1082–1083)' ['The Normans in Thessaly and the Siege of Larisa (1082–1083)'], Βυζαντιακά 4 (1984), 39–40.
[40]   *Alexiad*, V.5 (pp. 245–7); Sewter, p. 168.
[41]   *Alexiad*, V.5 (p. 244); Sewter, p. 167.
[42]   *Typicon Gregorii Pacuriani interpretatus est Michael Tarchnisvili*, Corpus Scriptorum Christianorum Orientalium, CXLIV (Louvain, 1954), p. 49. Anna only mentions Pacurianus at Moglena, east of Edessa, where he put to the sword the small Norman garrison. See *Alexiad*, V.5 (p. 244); Sewter, p. 167.

but probably the Peneius.[43] Alexius obviously wished to avoid direct contact with the Norman troops for now, and so he marched through the southern approaches of the city of Larissa and headed west, through the gardens of Delphina towards Trikala, where he arrived in late March or early April without encountering any resistance.[44]

Aware of the poor morale and fighting experience of his troops, the emperor wisely decided to avoid a fourth battle with the Normans and to set a series of ambushes instead. But before that, he followed the necessary steps dictated by Nicephorus Phocas' *Praecepta Militaria* and Vegetius' *De Re Militari* regarding the precautions taken before an encounter with an enemy force.[45] Anna does not tell us whether he sent any scouts to reconnoitre the enemy camp, although it seems likely that he did, but Alexius got hold of a local man and asked numerous questions about the topography of Larissa and the surrounding areas, for 'he wished to lay an ambush there and so defeat the Latins by guile, for he had given up any idea of open hand-to-hand conflict; after many clashes of this kind – and defeats – he had acquired experience of the Frankish tactics in battle'.[46]

The ambush that was planned against the Normans was primarily based on the use of the feigned retreat tactics. Anna Comnena describes in detail Alexius' war-council that took place on the day before the battle, where he explained his strategy to his senior officers, including the Caesar Nicephorus Melissinus and Basil Curticius.[47] Alexius' plan was simple but brilliant: he intended to hand over the command of his forces and his personal standards to these officers, and instruct them to form their battle lines 'in their usual manner followed in former engagements', somewhere to the east of the city. The orders that the officers in command were given were to attack the Norman front lines and engage in moderate skirmish before turning their backs to them in a disorderly retreat towards a location named Lycostomium ('Wolf's mouth'), probably somewhere to the west of Larissa. In the meantime, Alexius would have taken a unit of elite cavalry to the area close to Lykostomion the night before,[48] to pillage the Norman camp and ambush the unsuspecting Norman knights.

The Byzantine strategy worked as planned. The Normans immediately fell into Alexius' trap by opening the battle themselves with a full-frontal cavalry charge that was directed against the division where the imperial standards could be seen. While the main Byzantine forces were being pursued by the two cavalry divisions led by Bohemond and the count of Brienne, Alexius' next move was to send a small force of

[43]   *Alexiad*, V.5 (p. 245); Sewter, pp. 167–8; Savvides, *Byzantino-Normannica*, pp. 60–1.

[44]   I could not identify the location of the 'Gardens of Delphis', but they should be somewhere west of Larissa. See *Alexiad*, V.5 (p. 245); Sewter, p. 168.

[45]   *Praecepta Militaria*, IV.192–208 (p. 50); Vegetius, *Epitome*, III.9 (p. 84–5).

[46]   *Alexiad*, V.5 (pp. 246–7); Sewter, p. 168–9.

[47]   *Alexiad*, V.5 (pp. 247–8); Sewter, p. 169.

[48]   Anna mentions the defile of Livotanion, Rebenikon and Allage that mark his course from the east to the west of the city, but I was unable to trace these places on a map. See *Alexiad*, V.5 (p. 249); Sewter, pp. 169–70.

mounted archers and peltasts to harass the pursuing Normans and tempt them to turn around and engage them. Alexius had advised these soldiers to 'shoot great numbers of arrows from a distance and at the horses rather than the riders. For all Celts whenever they dismount become very easy prey'.[49] This was clever advice given by Alexius, as he must have been aware that the short bows of his mounted archers were unlikely to penetrate a Norman knight's shield or hauberk,[50] but their horses were much more vulnerable, and when dismounted the Normans were, indeed, much more vulnerable too.

For a second time in a few hours the Normans under Brienne took the bait. The Byzantine archers did what they were ordered to do and soon 'Bryennius' men, as their chargers fell, began to circle round and round in a great mass'.[51] The count, however, managed to send for reinforcements and, if Anna is right in her account, the messengers found Bohemond having pitched a temporary camp on a small river-island called Salabria, and himself eating grapes.[52] From this small detail we understand that, even though Anna and William of Apulia do not give us any date for these events, this may have taken place in late July, since Bohemond would not have been able to eat grapes in May or June. Since this inference means skipping a period of around three months, however, we have to be very cautious of Anna's accuracy, even more so since William of Apulia does not mention this detail. Is Anna trying to conceal any negotiations between Alexius and Bohemond? We cannot be sure, but it is at least possible, especially if we bear in mind that Pacurianus and the patriarch of Jerusalem were sent early that year to Thessaloniki to do just that.

The final defeat of the Norman contingents took place the next morning in a narrow and marshy area on the outskirts of Larissa, where they had pitched their camp. A few elite 'Turkish and Sarmatian' mounted archers were sent by Alexius to lure the Normans out of their camp. Bohemond did not take the bait this time and, instead, he ordered his men to dismount (if they had even managed to mount their horses) and 'stand firm in serried ranks, protecting themselves shield to shield', clearly deployed in a phalanx formation, probably after Bryennius' bitter experience the previous day. Panic, however, spread in the Norman ranks when Bohemond's standard-bearer was killed, and they eventually fled to Trikala.[53]

After Bohemond's retreat, Alexius went back to Thessaloniki, from where he once again set the mechanisms of Byzantine diplomacy against his enemies. His aim was to spread discord and disaffection amongst the senior officers of Bohemond's army against their leader, with the officers' demanding their payment for two and a half years of campaigning in a hostile country. The emperor promised lavish gifts, high

---

[49] *Alexiad*, V.6 (p. 251); Sewter, p. 171.
[50] Kaegi, 'The Contribution of Archery', pp. 237–49
[51] *Alexiad*, V.6 (p. 251); Sewter, p. 171; *Gesta*, V.32–42 (p. 238).
[52] *Alexiad*, V.6 (p. 252); Sewter, p. 171.
[53] *Alexiad*, V.7 (pp. 253–5); Sewter, pp. 172–3; *Gesta*, V.71–4 (p. 240).

court titles and a welcome for any deserters to the imperial army.[54] With Bohemond being unable to meet the demands of his nobles, he was forced by the deteriorating atmosphere in his camp to withdraw with an unknown number of men, first to Castoria, where he installed the count of Brienne as governor and also Peter of Aulps as governor of the two Polovoi, and then to Aulon in early August 1083.[55]

With the main Norman army ready to embark for Italy, the most significant outpost left in Norman hands was Castoria. We do not know whether Bohemond had left garrison troops in the town since the spring of 1082, but it seems to me highly unlikely that he would have had sufficient manpower with him to afford a strong garrison in the city. A similar tactic to the one applied during the conquest of Calabria and Sicily two decades earlier, meaning the extraction of tribute or a simple oath by the local population, may have been enough. So what made Castoria so important to the Normans as to install a garrison when everything seemed to be so desperate? The answer probably lies in the city's location, as it was the only major city on the Via Egnatia between Achrida and Thessaloniki that they thought they could hold. Even that last Norman outpost in the Greek mainland, however, was about to fall to Byzantine hands.

The *Alexiad* once again is our only source for the siege of Castoria by the imperial troops.[56] With siege machines, namely *helepoleis*, making little impact on the city's defences and enemy morale, Alexius came up with a brilliant plan which reminds us of the conquest of Palermo (1072) and Jerusalem (1099). In brief, he was to send a number of elite troops under George Palaeologus in small vessels to launch an attack on the city from the lake. At the same time the emperor would attack from the land and attempt to draw the attention of the defenders towards him while Palaeologus' party would be climbing the walls almost undetected. Because everything worked as planned Bryennius' followers decided to draw matters to a conclusion, with the majority of them actually deserting to the emperor, while the count of Brienne was made to swear never to take up arms against the empire again. Thus ended the siege of the last outpost still in Norman hands, probably around the end of October or early November 1083. None of the primary sources mention the departure of Bohemond to Italy, but it seems likely that he decided to spend the winter in Illyria, not risking a passage to Italy in November, especially if one considers the fact that he joined his father at Salerno soon after Henry IV had left Italy, in May 1084.[57]

In the aftermath of the lifting of the siege of the city of Larissa, within the next few months almost all the Norman conquests in the Illyrian and Greek mainland had been recovered by Alexius. From the summer of 1083 a Venetian naval expeditionary force

[54]   *Alexiad*, V.7 (pp. 255–6); Sewter, p. 173.
[55]   *Alexiad*, V.8 (p. 256); Sewter, p. 173; William of Apulia only mentions Bohemond's retreat to Aulon and Bryennius' placement at Castoria: *Gesta*, V.75–6 (p. 240).
[56]   *Alexiad*, VI.1 (pp. 269–72); Sewter, pp. 181–2.
[57]   *Alexiad*, V.3 (p. 234); Sewter, p. 162.

of unknown size recaptured the city of Dyrrhachium, with the exception of the citadel, which resisted stoutly.[58] The Venetians spent the winter in the city, but recognising the danger the proximity of the citadel posed to them they chose to remain in their ships and in a small wooden *castrum* they hastily erected close to the city's port. Also, Aulon was captured shortly after Bohemond's departure while the local population of Corfu, apparently after finding out about the failed Norman expedition, rebelled against the duke, with only the citadel remaining firmly in Norman hands.[59]

The causes of the Norman failure are numerous, but all of them have their roots in one important factor – the Norman army was operating far from its home base and on hostile ground. The adversities were manifold. The terrain of the Illyrian, Epirotic and western Macedonian regions, with their cold and humid winters, were inhospitable. Diseases that could have depleted any medieval army in a very short time, especially in the marshy area of Dyrrhachium, as we saw earlier, were rife. The task of transporting provisions and reinforcements from the home bases, something imperative when the land was incapable of sustaining an army, as the areas around Dyrrhachium proved to the Normans, was immensely difficult. In addition, there were the eventual casualties in battle and siege operations, and even if Bohemond had 1,300 knights when his father left him in charge of the army in 1082, he certainly would have been unable to spare a single unnecessary loss. But he had to man a number of castles that would secure his route back to Dyrrhachium, and although we are unaware of the numbers involved in this task, it must have been a heavy burden for the small army Bohemond commanded. Finally, there is the absence of the campaign's natural leader, Robert Guiscard; although he had left a capable commander in his place, his absence would have been felt throughout the ranks of his army, and especially among his knights, many of whom were veterans of the Italian and Sicilian campaigns, and thus used to serving under him in almost every battle or siege.

Robert Guiscard's second expedition to the Balkans (1084–5)

Robert Guiscard's preparations for his second invasion of Byzantine Illyria in the autumn of 1084 began immediately after he was freed from his engagements in Rome, whither he had marched in May that year to rescue Gregory VII from Henry IV's imperial troops. By the time he arrived in the city with his army, in late May, the German emperor had already retired to Germany, and the Normans engaged in a fierce urban conflict with the citizens of Rome, who wanted Gregory expelled from the throne of St Peter.[60] Examining the size of the Norman army that was mobilised against Henry IV, William of Apulia reports that the Norman duke led some 6,000 cavalry and 30,000 foot-soldiers

---

[58]   *Gesta*, V.80–93 (p. 240).
[59]   *Alexiad*, VI.5 (p. 286); Sewter, p. 189.
[60]   *Gesta*, IV.546–64 (p. 234); Malaterra, III.37.

to Rome.[61] These numbers may seem an exaggerated figure, but if we reduce the cavalry to about one half of what the *Gesta* gives us we may approach closer to the truth, bearing in mind that troops from Sicily under Guiscard's brother Roger had arrived as reinforcements.[62] The crucial question is how many of these troops mobilised in May 1084 took part in the Illyrian campaign four months later.

Sadly, the primary sources are even more silent about the numbers and consistency of the Norman army in 1084 than they were for the 1081 campaign. The only names of high-ranking officers that are mentioned as following Guiscard across the Adriatic were his four sons, namely Bohemond, Roger Borsa, Robert and Guy, while Geoffrey of Conversano was also made to join the duke after his earlier rebellion in 1082–3.[63] Judging by the size of the expeditionary force and the danger posed by a German army marching against the Norman capital, Salerno, many of Robert Guiscard's vassals would have been summoned to bring their quotas to Salerno in preparation for the march northwards. Would the duke have been able to force them for a second time within less than six months to mobilise their troops, this time for a campaign overseas? The answer would be affirmative only if we consider that they would have been promised large sums of money and a share of the spoils of war because, as we shall see, this time Robert was aiming at the financial centres of the southern Greek mainland, namely Athens, Corinth and Thebes.

For this campaign, William of Apulia gives us the figure of some 120 ships mobilised to carry the Norman army across the Adriatic in the autumn.[64] We do not know with certainty the ratio between transport ships and warships, but probably less than a quarter of this fleet would have been warships, bearing in mind that Guiscard had twenty-five warships at his disposal in the following naval engagements between the Norman and the Venetian fleets, all of them being 'inferior to their [Byzantine and Venetian] ships'.[65] This leaves us with around eighty to ninety transport vessels that would have carried the bulk of Guiscard's army to Aulon. Even if all of them were specially modified horse-transport ships, something highly unlikely in my view considering that the average capacity of each ship was fifteen horses, this would give us a number of 1,275 horses carried from Italy.

This number, although reasonable if we recall the numbers of the 1081 campaign, must be an exaggeration, since Anna Comnena mentions that Robert Guiscard had dispatched all of his cavalry force, under Roger and Guy, to capture Aulon some time prior to the departure of the main fleet.[66] The figure should thus probably be reduced

---

[61]   *Gesta*, IV.565–6 (p. 234).

[62]   Malaterra, III.36.

[63]   *Alexiad*, VI.5 (p. 282); Sewter, pp. 188–9; *Gesta*, V.154–8 (p. 244); Orderic Vitalis, IV (p. 32); VII (p. 32).

[64]   *Gesta*, V.143 (p. 244). Not 150 ships as Chalandon erroneously notes: Chalandon, *Alexis I*, p. 91.

[65]   *Gesta*, V.155–8 (p. 244).

[66]   *Alexiad*, VI.5 (p. 282); Sewter, p. 189. Malaterra reports that Bohemond was sent as well: Malaterra, III.40.

by about a half. As for the foot-soldiers, bearing in mind the maximum capacity of 108 men in a tenth-century Byzantine dromon, which would not have been the case for the Norman transport ships, this would give us a maximum of 9,180 men. Again this number is surely exaggerated and we should narrow it down to at least a third.

Even after these contentious calculations, it can be argued that the numbers mobilised for the 1084 campaign were almost certainly much lower than those of three years before (both Anna and William of Apulia overestimate, in their usual manner, the size of the Norman host).[67] If Robert Guiscard's army was indeed huge in size, then why did he not choose to march against Thessaloniki, the second largest and wealthiest city-port of the empire, as had been done three years earlier? Instead, he turned south-east towards Corinth, Athens and Thebes, cities that belonged to the poorly defended *themata* of Hellas and the Peloponnese.

Meanwhile, Alexius went on to ensure that the last enclaves of Norman military presence in the Balkans were wiped out. Aulon, as already noted, was captured soon after Bohemond's departure in the spring of 1084, while in the same period, a combined Venetian and Byzantine fleet attacked the citadel of Corfu, since the lower city and the rest of the island had rebelled against the Normans.[68] But this expedition failed to dislodge the Normans from the well-fortified citadel. Alexius seems to have been aware of Robert's preparations, and some time during the summer he asked Venice for naval assistance to defend the Illyrian coastline, since a Venetian squadron was already active there by the time the Normans crossed to Aulon.[69]

At the end of September or in early October, Robert Guiscard departed from Brindisi, after sending his two sons, Roger and Guy, with a reconnaissance force of knights to capture Aulon.[70] The Normans occupied the town and joined up with the main expeditionary force somewhere between Aulon and Buthrotum, probably close to the *castra* of Oricum and Canina, as they had done three years ago. William of Apulia, who was much better informed about this part of the Norman campaign, wrote about a weather system that forced the Normans to remain in their base near Buthrotum for the next two months, unable to sail to Corfu to raise the siege of the city's citadel.[71] Around late November or early December, Robert Guiscard took his army across to the island of Corfu, landing at the northern port of Cassiope just as he had done in 1081.[72] The only difference was that this time he found a joint Venetian-Byzantine fleet waiting to attack him.

We do not know the number of ships that were sent by the doge, but we should not expect a large expeditionary force since it only took the Venetians a few weeks to

---

[67] *Alexiad*, VI.5 (pp. 281–2); Sewter, p. 188; *Gesta*, V.127–56 (pp. 242–4).

[68] *Gesta*, V.96–105 (pp. 240–2).

[69] *Alexiad*, VI.5 (p. 283); Sewter, p. 189.

[70] Malaterra, III.40; *Gesta*, V.143–53 (p. 244). Anna erroneously reports Otranto as the port of departure: *Alexiad*, VI.5 (p. 283); Sewter, pp. 188–9.

[71] *Gesta*, V.147–9 (p. 244).

[72] *Alexiad*, VI.5 (pp. 282–3); Sewter, p. 189; *Gesta*, V.156–9 (p. 244).

prepare and sail south.[73] Both William of Apulia and Anna Comnena use vague terms like *triremes* and *naves* to describe the consistency of the Venetian fleet, although by reading the *Alexiad* we understand that both large vessels, like *khelandia* or types of dromons, and lighter and faster ships, like the *galeai*, would have been deployed.[74] For the Byzantine navy's numbers and types of ships, the presence of the same admiral, Mauricas, makes it more likely that it would have been the same squadron of ships that had faced them three years earlier.[75]

What is most interesting about William's narrative is that, for the first time, he uses the term *khelandia* to describe the types of ships of the Byzantine fleet, as opposed to the term *naves* for the Venetian ships of the 1081 naval battles. Since we know that Mauricas' fleet is highly unlikely to have been reinforced by newly built ships during the years 1082–4, it can be surmised that the Normans faced *khelandia* in 1081 as well. His identification, however, of the Norman ships as triremes is completely wrong, because he writes that 'Robert Guiscard's *naves* were seen as inferior by the Venetians, who attacked them'.[76]

According to the *Alexiad*,[77] before the Norman crossing to Corfu, the Venetians had established their headquarters in the harbour of Passaron, close to Cassiope in the north-eastern side of the island. During their first encounter, the Venetians managed to rout the Norman squadron, but Anna gives us few if any details about the course of the battle. Three days later the allied fleet attacked the Normans once more, trying to inflict a significant blow upon the relatively small Norman squadron of warships, but again their victory was not decisive enough to force Robert Guiscard to retreat to Aulon. This time, however, the Venetians made the serious mistake of overestimating the enemy's losses and, almost certain of their crushing victory, they sent envoys to their doge in Venice to announce the news. With the small and fast Venetian ships sent back home, the Normans attacked their enemies in earnest.[78] Their assault was not expected by the Venetians, who barely had the time to tie their ships together and form the sea-harbour, the defensive formation also used three years earlier at Dyrrhachium.[79] The Norman ships, having been made much lighter the day before, took full advantage of their speed and mobility and overwhelmingly defeated the Venetians.

[73] 'They [Venetians] had not been long in the harbour of Passaron before they heard of his [Guiscard's] move'. *Alexiad*, VI.5 (p. 283); Sewter, p. 189.
[74] *Alexiad*, VI.5 (pp. 283–4); Sewter, pp. 189–90.
[75] *Gesta*, V.99 (p. 240).
[76] 'Roberti naves dum conspicit inferiores esse suis': *Gesta*, V.163–4 (p. 244); *inferiores* means inferior in quality, as opposed to numbers.
[77] *Alexiad*, VI.5–6 (pp. 283–7); Sewter, pp. 189–91; *Gesta*, V.147–98 (pp. 244–6); Dandolus, *Chronicon*, s.a. 1084 (p. 218); Lupus Protospatharius, *Chronicon*, s.a. 1084; Anonymus Barensis, *Chronicon*, s.a. 1085; Romuald of Salerno, *Chronicon*, s.a. 1085.
[78] Anna tells us that Guiscard was given this information by a certain Venetian called Pietro Contarini, probably a member of the powerful Contarini family: *Alexiad*, VI.5 (p. 284); Sewter, p. 190.
[79] William of Apulia tells us that the Byzantine squadron had left the scene of the naval battle: *Gesta*, V.186–7 (p. 246).

Both Anna Comnena and William of Apulia report large numbers of fatalities and prisoners. Anna mentions around 13,000 Venetian casualties, surely an exaggerated figure, which reflects, however, the serious blow to Venice's prestige, and 2,500 prisoners, who were probably sent back to Aulon.[80] Lupus Protospatharius writes of more than a thousand men killed in action, five ships captured by the Normans and two sunk with their entire crew, a much more realistic estimate for the Venetian casualties.[81] It is only in the *Alexiad*, however, where we get an idea of the way in which the Venetian prisoners were treated by Robert Guiscard: 'Unfortunately Robert behaved in cruel fashion after his famous victory. Many of the prisoners were treated with hideous savagery: some were blinded, others had their noses cut off, and others lost hands or feet or both.'[82]

There was no precedent in Robert Guiscard's behaviour against prisoners of war, either at Dyrrhachium three years before or against the Bariots, the Palermitans or the people of Naples in the 1070s. Probably the duke wished to send a powerful message to the Venetians never to launch another naval campaign against his army. A similar approach was followed by Roger after the battle of Misilmeri (1068), where hardly any Muslim survived to bring the news to the inhabitants of the Sicilian capital. Instead, the Normans used carrier-pigeons, supposedly writing the notes with the blood of the dead Muslim soldiers. This gruesome method of psychological warfare proved very effective, with Malaterra reporting: 'When the people of Palermo heard the news, the whole city was shaken: the tearful voices of the children and women rose up through the air to the heavens'.[83]

By mid-December 1084, Robert Guiscard was free to sail southwards and relieve the besieged Norman garrison of the Corfu citadel. Later, he returned to his winter quarters on the banks of the river Glycys (Acheron) on the Epirus coastline to spend the winter, with himself and his elite cavalry pitching camp further south at Vonitsa, the town they had captured in a side expedition three years ago.[84] Meanwhile, famine and an outbreak of malaria had swept through his army and claimed, according to both Anna and William of Apulia, some 10,000 men, of whom 500 were knights – another exaggerated figure.[85] This disease must have had a demoralising effect on the soldiers and officers of the army, especially if we consider the fact that even Bohemond requested to return to Italy for treatment.[86]

While examining Robert Guiscard's conquests in the Illyrian and Greek mainland and the islands of the Ionian Sea, it is crucial to keep a careful eye on a detailed map in

---

[80]   *Alexiad*, VI.5 (p. 285); Sewter, p. 190; *Gesta*, V.193–7 (p. 246).

[81]   Lupus Protospatharius, *Chronicon*, s.a. 1084.

[82]   *Alexiad*, VI.5 (p. 285); Sewter, p. 190.

[83]   Malaterra, II.41 and 42.

[84]   *Gesta*, V.202–9 (p. 246).

[85]   *Gesta*, V.210–20 (pp. 246–8); Anna erroneously dates the outbreak of the disease in the first campaign of 1081: *Alexiad*, IV.3 (p. 196); Sewter, pp. 139–40.

[86]   *Gesta*, V.223–5 (p. 248).

order to note down these initial conquests. This facilitates the cross-referencing and tracking down of Guiscard's next moves, bearing in mind his long-term goal to reach the cities of Athens, Corinth and Thebes. In sailing from the straits of Otranto the main trunk routes that a medieval fleet could take lay inshore of the islands of Corfu, Cephalonia and Zante, and then heading southwards towards the island of Crete through the west coast of the Peloponnese, because of the prevailing north-westerly winds.[87] If a fleet targeted the areas of Attica, Corinth and Boeotia, it was better to sail east, passing Patras and Naupactus, and through the Gulf of Corinth, and land a raiding party off the coasts of Corinth, than sail all the way around the Peloponnese. Thus far, Robert Guiscard had managed to subjugate the port of Aulon and the island of Corfu as his main supply bases, and having established himself at Vonitsa, at the entrance of the Ambracian Gulf, he had under his control the sea routes half-way to the entrance of the Gulf of Corinth. His next step would have been to subdue the island of Cephalonia, which was the capital of the coastal *thema* of Cephalonia that included the seven islands of the Ionian Sea.

In the early summer of 1085 Robert Guiscard sent his son Roger Borsa, along with a small force of elite troops, to Cephalonia in an attempt to capture the island's capital Hagius Georgius.[88] The Byzantine castle of the island's capital was probably built in the eleventh century and formed the most important settlement nucleus on the island and was the seat of the governor.[89] At first, Roger proved unsuccessful in his siege of the town and it was Robert Guiscard who arrived to take command of the operations, landing at the promontory of Atheras in the north-west of the island. William of Apulia and Anna Comnena give slightly different versions of what happened next. According to the *Alexiad*, Robert Guiscard arrived in a single *galea* at the promontory of Atheras, while the rest of his army remained on the opposite Epirus coast in battle positions, ready to sail and bring reinforcements if necessary. He had not sent for the rest of his army to embark for Cephalonia, and before he even managed to reach his son, Robert Guiscard was stricken 'by a violent fever'.[90] William of Apulia tells us that the duke, after sending his son to besiege the town of Hagius Georgius, returned to Vonitsa to take his entire army across the sea and march against the island's capital. He embarked from the Norman base-camp, heading for Cephalonia, but 'before he managed to see the castle fortifications [of Hagius Georgius] he went down with fever'.[91]

Robert Guiscard died on 17 July 1085, after suffering from intense fever for six days, in an area which still recalls the Norman duke's name in the form of 'Fiskardo' (former Panormus). Although a historian of medicine might give a better explanation as to

[87]   Pryor, *Geography, Technology and War*, pp. 12–24 and 87–101, see especially the map in p. 14.
[88]   *Alexiad*, VI.6 (p. 287); Sewter, pp. 191–2; *Gesta*, V.228–32 (p. 248).
[89]   *Castrorum Circumnavigatio*, ed. I. Georgopoulou-d'Amico (Athens, 2008), pp. 58–61.
[90]   *Alexiad*, VI.6 (pp. 287–8); Sewter, pp. 191–2.
[91]   *Gesta*, V.288–9 (p. 252).

the duke's cause of death, the most likely illness to have brought his life to an end so rapidly and, indeed, unexpectedly must have been malaria. As we have already seen, the Norman camp was struck by a violent disease that cost the lives of thousands of men, both foot-soldiers and knights, and although the figures provided by our chroniclers may seem to be exaggerated, they certainly reveal the severity of the situation. Malaria[92] is a vector-borne infectious disease caused by parasites, which is transmitted by an already infected individual to another through a mosquito bite. Typical symptoms include fever, chills, nausea and other flu-like effects, which match what was described by Anna Comnena and William of Apulia of the violent fever that killed Robert Guiscard. Since mosquitoes reproduce in large numbers in damp places, Vonitsa's location in the extremely humid Ambracian Gulf must have been the worst place Robert Guiscard could have picked to pitch his winter camp.

The consequences of Guiscard's death for the Norman campaign were disastrous. For the men following the duke in his expedition against the empire, the effect on their morale was immediate, as we read in the rather ostentatious comments by William of Apulia: 'If all the Greeks, Persians and Arabs ['gens Agarena'] had attacked them, and all the peoples of the world flocked together, armed themselves, and come upon them while they were themselves unarmed, they could not have been more afraid than they were now'.[93] For his inexperienced son Roger (Borsa), this had now turned into a struggle for survival and recognition of his legitimacy as the leader amongst the great magnates following the expedition. Despite the fact that he had already been recognised as heir by Robert Guiscard's vassals since the spring of 1073, Roger managed to take advantage of the absence in Italy of his older half-brother Bohemond to arrange for his succession and win over the allegiance of his father's high-ranking vassals.[94] He immediately called for a meeting of all the counts that were camped at Vonitsa and demanded an oath of fealty to him in person, before sailing to Apulia to assume the command of his dukedom.

But the most significant consequence of Robert Guiscard's death was the Byzantine capture of Dyrrhachium, the last remaining outpost of Norman military presence on the east side of the Adriatic Sea since the spring of 1082. Alexius once again set in motion the mechanisms of Byzantine diplomacy and, as Anna writes:

> to sow dissension among them [Normans] by letters and every other method. He also persuaded the Venetians who resided in Constantinople to write to their fellow-countrymen in Epidamnus, and to the Amalfitans and all other foreigners there, advising them to yield to his [Alexius'] wishes and surrender the place. Unceasingly, with bribes and promises, he works to this end.[95]

As for the Venetians of the lower city, the fact that Alexius used their countrymen

---

[92] For more information on malaria, see the World Health Organization's website: http://www.who. int/mediacentre/factsheets/fs094/en/.

[93] *Gesta*, V.290–2 (p. 254).

[94] *Gesta*, IV.195–7 (p. 214); Amatus, VII.20.

[95] *Alexiad*, VI.6 (p. 289); Sewter, pp. 192–3.

at Constantinople as intermediaries makes it likely that even more privileges and future trading agreements were promised to them in addition to the 1082 and 1084 chrysobulls. The Normans were eventually persuaded by the inhabitants of the lower city, the Venetians, to surrender the city to Alexius' officers.[96] The surrender of the city must have taken place in late autumn 1085.[97]

[96]   *Alexiad*, VI.6 (pp. 289–90); Sewter, pp. 289–90; *Gesta*, V.377–90 (p. 256).
[97]   *Alexiad*, VI.8 (p. 295); Sewter, p. 196; see also: Buckler, *Anna Comnena*, p. 39. Savvides' erroneous dating is striking: Savvides, *Byzantino-Normannica*, pp. 68–9.

8

Bohemond of Taranto and the First Crusade

For in that same year, on the instructions of Pope Urban, an expedition to Jerusalem was recruited on a massive scale from every land. Bohemond had previously, along with his father Guiscard, invaded Romania [Byzantium], and had always wanted to conquer it for himself. Seeing a great multitude of people travelling through Apulia but lacking a leader, he hastened there, and wishing to be the army's leader and to make them his followers, he placed the badge of this expedition, namely the cross, on his garments.[1]

The preaching of the First Crusade certainly presented Bohemond with a unique opportunity to escape the relentless pressure put on him by his half-brother Roger, who was acting in his own interests as the legitimate heir of Robert Guiscard and had the protection of his uncle Roger of Sicily, who intervened several times in favour of his namesake nephew. Ever since the death of their father in Cephalonia in 1085, the two half-brothers had been locked in an almost continuous civil strife for five years, which saw the emergence of Bohemond as a significant landowner in Apulia and Calabria.

Whether or not Bohemond had possessions of his own before 1085 from which he could draw troops is impossible to say. A rebellion, however, mounted against Roger immediately after receiving news of his father's death, with the aid of Jordan of Capua and other magnates, was a complete success for Bohemond; Roger had to cede to him the important cities of Oria, Taranto, Otranto, Gallipoli and the lands of his cousin Geoffrey of Conversano, which included Conversano, Montepeloso, Polignano, Monopoli and Brindisi.[2] Peace was made in March 1086, but not before Bohemond was made one of the most powerful lords in southern Italy. In September or October 1087, Bohemond began a second war against Roger, mainly taking place in Calabria and, more specifically, around Cosenza, which dragged on for almost two years.[3] Through the exchange of cities that sealed the peace between the two half-brothers in August 1089, however, Bohemond acquired Bari, the richest and most important city

[1] Malaterra, IV.24.
[2] Malaterra, IV.4.
[3] Malaterra, IV.10.

in Apulia and a commercial hub for the Adriatic and Ionian Seas. The gain of Bari and of possessions in Calabria now assured Bohemond of almost as much power as Duke Roger himself possessed.[4]

We cannot be sure when exactly the preaching of the First Crusade began in southern Italy and Sicily, but if we believe Lupus Protospatharius' version of events it is most likely that soon after the council of Piacenza in March 1095, religious fever spread throughout Italy. A particular shower of falling stars which was seen throughout Apulia and Calabria on a Tuesday night in April 1095 acted as a revelation for the launch of the First Crusade, because 'from that time on, the people of Gaul, and, indeed, of all of Italy too, began to proceed with their arms to the Holy Sepulchre of the Lord, bearing on their right shoulders the sign of the cross'.[5]

Whether Bohemond was planning to follow the crusade long before the summer of 1096, and simply grabbed his chance when the crusaders were passing by from Apulia, we cannot be sure. Malaterra and Anna Comnena, two of our main chronicle accounts for this period, suggest that his motives for taking the cross were not the result of any religious zeal or deep desire for pilgrimage to the Holy Land.[6] In fact, so opportune for him was this unique expedition that William of Malmesbury alleges that the whole idea of the crusade had been conceived by Bohemond:

> His [Urban's] more secret intention was not so well known; this was, by Bohemond's advice, to excite almost the whole of Europe to undertake an expedition into Asia, that in such a general commotion of all countries, auxiliaries might easily be engaged, by whose means both Urban might obtain Rome, and Bohemond, Illyria and Macedonia.[7]

It must be emphasised, however, that these views are in contrast with the writings of Ralph of Caen, a chronicler who, as a nephew, had close personal ties with Bohemond, and whose work provides a striking Norman point of view, and Lupus Protospatharius, whose (rather idealistic) view follows:

> While they [Roger of Sicily and Bohemond] were continuing with this [siege of Amalfi], then suddenly and through the inspiration of God, Bohemond, with other counts and more than five hundred knights, fixing the sign of the cross on the right shoulder of their garments, abandoned the siege, took ship and journeyed to the royal city, that with the help of Emperor Alexius they might fight against the pagans and travel to Jerusalem to the Holy Sepulchre of our Lord Jesus Christ, our Redeemer.[8]

Modern historians find it very difficult to assess the exact number of Bohemond's followers for the First Crusade. Albert of Aachen, a contemporary of the First

---

[4]   Yewdale, *Bohemond I*, pp. 27–8.
[5]   Lupus Protospatharius, *Chronicon*, s.a. 1095.
[6]   Malaterra, IV.24; *Alexiad*, X.6 (II, pp. 34–5); Sewter, pp. 311 and 313. Anna's comments should be viewed with some caution.
[7]   William of Malmesbury, I, pp. 592–4.
[8]   Lupus Protospatharius, *Chronicon*, s.a. 1096. See also Ralph of Caen, *The Gesta Tancredi of Ralph of Caen: A History of the Normans on the First Crusade*, trans. B. S. Bachrach and D. S. Bachrach (Aldershot, 2005), II (p. 23).

Crusade living in Germany, who wrote his narrative on the basis of eye-witness accounts, recounts about 10,000 cavalry and 'very many troops of infantry', which is surely a greatly exaggerated figure.[9] Lupus Protospatharius' 500 knights sound more realistic, and a number which confirms that the Italian Norman contingent was, indeed, one of the smallest in the crusading army.[10] If we assume that the infantry was between five and seven times the size of the cavalry, then a number of between 2,500 and 3,500 would have been reasonable, if we include Tancred's contingent of about 2,000 men.[11] Additionally, we have a list of the counts that followed Bohemond on his expedition, namely his nephew Tancred, Richard of Principate and his brother Rainulf, Humphrey of Montescaglioso, and nine others.[12] What is very important in this case is the presence of Richard and Humphrey, the two most powerful and influential Apulian magnates after Roger Borsa himself, even if it is almost impossible to estimate the size of their contingents.

Some of the facts about Bohemond's army can explain why he eventually became the leading figure of the First Crusade. The crusading army was a hybrid force that had in its ranks several knights who had served as mercenaries in the East: Peter of Aulps, to whom the crusade leaders gave custody of a city they took in Asia Minor, and others further afield, like Hugh Bunel, who turned up to help Robert of Normandy during the siege of Jerusalem after twenty years in Islamic territory, whither he had fled after murdering Mabel of Bellême in 1077.[13] The Norman army, however, was the most experienced and the most suited for what lay ahead. A significant number of their knights had faced the Byzantines in battle several times in the past decades in Italy and Sicily. During the Sicilian expansion they had faced local Muslim armies and Bohemond had fought against Turkopoles during his first campaign in Dyrrhachium fifteen years earlier. Also, if we are to believe the author of the *Historia Belli Sacri*, a monk at Monte Cassino writing in the 1130s who seems to be well informed on south Italian affairs of the period, both Tancred and Richard of Principate, along with a large number of their followers, could speak Arabic, something very rare for the armies of the First Crusade.[14] Finally, it is highly likely that Bohemond himself spoke Greek, something which can explain his advantage over the other Latin leaders in their dealings with the Byzantine emperor, his representatives and the Greek merchants that they had to conduct business with on their way to the Holy Land.

Bohemond entered Constantinople on 17 April 1097, taking the oath of homage which the emperor had demanded from him and from all the other Latin leaders before

[9]   Albert of Aachen, II.18 (p. 88).
[10]   Lupus Protospatharius, *Chronicon*, s.a. 1096; *Alexiad*, X.11 (II, p. 60); Sewter, p. 326.
[11]   *Gesta Francorum et Aliorum Hierosolimitanorum, The Deeds of the Franks and the Other Pilgrims to Jerusalem*, ed. R. Hill (London, 1962), IV (p. 9).
[12]   *Gesta Francorum*, III (p. 8).
[13]   J. Riley-Smith, *The First Crusade and the Idea of Crusading* (London, 1986), p. 43.
[14]   *Historia Belli Sacri*, Recueil des historiens des croisades, Historiens Occidentaux, vol. 67 (p. 198).

him.[15] Before proceeding further inland in Asia Minor, the crusaders had first to take Nicaea, a city that effectively controlled all the roads leading to the Anatolian plateau and was situated only 40 kilometres from Constantinople. Nicaea was the capital of the Seljuk sultanate of Rum, which had been established in Asia Minor as a result of the Turkish invasions of Anatolia and their victory at Manzikert some two and a half decades earlier.[16] The crusading armies needed provisions in order to besiege the city effectively and it was at this stage of the crusade that we can see for the first time the significant role played by Bohemond in the campaign, since he was the leader who managed to negotiate sufficient supplies to be sent to Nicomedia, just 20 kilometres north-east of Nicaea.[17]

The siege of Nicaea began on 14 May and lasted for about five weeks, mostly because of the crusaders' difficulty in organising an efficient blockade of the city.[18] Although the Seljuk sultan, Kilij Arslan, was pre-occupied with his war against the Danishmenids of central Asia Minor, he hurried to relieve his capital with a force of around 10,000. A key role in the ensuing battle was played by Bohemond's troops and the Germans, who supported the contingent of Provençals on the south side of the city. In the end, it was a combination of the sheer size of the crusader force and the confined space that did not allow the Turks to fully exploit their encircling tactics, thus forcing Kilij Arslan to retreat from the vicinity of the city. Once the defenders realised that they had no hope of being rescued, they decided to surrender to the imperial unit that was besieging them from the direction of the lake. We are informed by the sources that Batumites, the general with a force of 2,000 men acting under Alexius' orders, had secretly negotiated the surrender with the Seljuks.[19]

The huge crusader army that had gathered at Nicaea marched south towards Dorylaeum in two groups, obviously in order to keep up with the supply and baggage trains and for better defence against possible enemy attacks. Unsurprisingly, Bohemond was at the head of the first group of armies.[20] After leaving the Bithynian

[15] *Alexiad*, X.11 (II, pp. 63–6); Sewter, pp. 328–9. J. Shepard, 'When Greek meets Greek: Alexius Comnenus and Bohemond in 1097–98', *Byzantine and Modern Greek Studies* 12 (1988), 185–277. Regarding the date of Bohemond's arrival in Constantinople, see H. Hagenmeyer, *Die Kreuzzugbriefe aus den Jahren 1088–1100* (Innsbruck, 1901), pp. 64–5; J. W. Nesbitt, 'The Rate of March of Crusading Armies in Europe: A Study and Computation', *Traditio* 19 (1963), 167–81.

[16] For an introduction to the settlement of Turks in Asia Minor in the eleventh century: Korobeinikov, 'The Turks', pp. 692–710; C. Cahen, *Pre-Ottoman Turkey* (London, 1968). Cahen's work is still a classic study in the field.

[17] *Gesta Francorum*, VII (p. 14).

[18] *Alexiad*, XI.1 (II, pp. 69–82); Sewter, pp. 333–40; Le "Liber" de Raymond d'Aguilers, ed. J. Hugh and L. L. Hill (Paris, 1969), pp. 39–47; Raymond D'Aguilers, *Historia Francorum qui ceperunt Iherusalem*, trans. J. H. Hill and L. Hill (Philadelphia, 1968), pp. 25–9.

[19] *Alexiad*, XI.2 (II, p. 77); Sewter, pp. 337–8; *Gesta Francorum*, VIII (pp. 16–17); William of Tyre, *A History of the Deeds Done beyond the Sea*, ed. and trans. E. Atwater Babcock and A. C. Krey (New York, 1976), I 3. 11 (pp. 165–6); Albert of Aachen, II.37 (p. 126).

[20] *Gesta Francorum*, IX (p. 18); Albert of Aachen, II.38 (p. 128); *Alexiad*, XI.3 (II, p. 84); Sewter, pp. 341–2.

Mountains behind and coming into central Anatolia, the crusaders found themselves in a broken country with no easily defensible positions and one very well suited to the tactics characteristic of the Seljuks. Thus, on the morning of 31 June, Bohemond deployed his forces in front of a marsh, which may have provided some safety from the Turkish encircling manoeuvres. He left the infantry to guard the baggage train and ordered the cavalry to stand in a dense mass and hold the line.

We have no credible account of the numbers involved in this first clash between the crusaders and the Seljuks and an attempt to propose an estimate would be futile. Fulcher of Chartres and the *Gesta* report some 360,000 Seljuk troops, while William of Tyre reduces it to 200,000, both of which are surely exaggerated figures.[21] France has suggested, based on Cahen's conclusions about the Turkish settlement in Anatolia in the previous decades, that the Seljuk army was many times smaller than the crusader force, or roughly equal to the total mounted host of the Latins. Hence, a battle of movement on the part of the Turks could have nullified the numeric advantage of the Westerners simply by attacking their vanguard.[22] This time Kilij Arslan chose to approach from a high plateau to ambush the Latin vanguard, a less confined space in comparison to his attack against the Provençals at Nicaea.[23]

Before the crusaders had the chance to be fully deployed in their battle formations, the Seljuks arrived en masse and attacked the Westerners from all directions in an attempt to encircle them. They applied their usual steppe tactics of releasing constant showers of arrows from a distance and falling back when their enemies charged forward to neutralise them. Then, pretending to retreat, they would make a sudden turn and come back to harass them. Their horses were quicker, more agile and more manoeuvrable than the Frankish cavalry, mostly because their equipment was significantly lighter, although the horses themselves did not differ much.[24] Their principal weapon was the bow, but they also carryied a small round wooden shield, a lance and a sword. It is very difficult to know what kind of armour they wore in the later decades of the eleventh century as defensive equipment. The influence from the Byzantines was becoming strong and from the time of the crusade the chroniclers mention heavily armed knights with hauberks.[25] There is significant evidence to show

[21]   Fulcherius Carnotensis, *Historia Hierosolymitana*, ed. H. Hagenmeyer (Heidelberg, 1913), I 11.3; *Gesta Francorum*, IX (p. 20); William of Tyre, I III.13 (p. 170).
[22]   France, *Victory in the East*, pp. 157 and 174–5; C. Cahen, 'The Turkish Invasion: The Selchukids', in *A History of the Crusades*, 6 vols, ed. K. Setton (Madison, 1969–89), I, pp. 135–76.
[23]   Ibn-al-Qalanisi, *The Damascus Chronicle of the Crusades*, ed. and trans. H. A. R. Gibb (London, 1932), pp. 41–2.
[24]   J. France, 'Technology and the Success of the First Crusade', in *War and Society in the Eastern Mediterranean*, p. 165; A. Hyland, *The Medieval Warhorse from Byzantium to the Crusades* (Stroud, 1994), pp. 140–68.
[25]   The influence of the Romans in the armour and battle formations of the Arabs is emphasised in the early tenth-century *Taktika*: 'They [Saracens] make use of armament, and their cavalry uses bows, swords, lances, shields, and axes. They wear full armour, including body armour, cuirasses, helmets, shin guards, gauntlets, and all the rest in the Roman manner'. Leo VI, *Taktika*, XVIII.110 (pp. 476–8).

that all these were much lighter than the Western European ones.[26] Their aim was to confuse and demoralise the enemy, and isolate and break up their formations before charging in with their swords and lances.[27]

As most of our Latin sources agree, these steppe tactics were, with the exception of Bohemond and the several Latin mercenaries serving the Byzantine emperors since the mid-eleventh century, completely unknown to the crusaders, who could not have fought against any large Seljuk force before.[28] We are informed by Anna Comnena, however, that the emperor not only sent a Turk named Taticius to accompany the crusaders with a force of about 2,000 light cavalry, but that he had also instructed the crusader leaders during their stay in the capital in the spring of 1097 'in the methods normally used by the Turks in battle; told how they should draw up their battle-line, how to lay ambushes; advised not to pursue too far when the enemy ran away in flight'.[29]

The first stage of the battle found the crusaders completely enveloped by the Seljuk cavalry. This would have been exactly Kilij Arslan's main tactical objective, as he had ambushed the Latins in a relatively narrow point where two valleys met.[30] Although there was no main body which Bohemond could order to advance, an attempt was made by the Frankish cavalry to counter-attack, which was probably a spontaneous reaction to the shower of arrows: 'but the Turks [. . .] purposely opened their ranks to avoid the clash, and the Christians, finding no one to oppose them, had to fall back deceived'.[31] They soon realised that any sallies forward would accomplish nothing and the crusaders resorted to closing in their ranks and holding the line. Smail insisted that this was the best action they could take, because this mass 'represented a formidable defensive power', while Oman argued that 'this passive policy only made them more helpless prey to the Turks'.[32] I would have to agree with the latter opinion because, since we know that the Latin foot did not have the equipment or training and discipline of the Roman *testudo* to hold back enemy volleys of arrows, staying idle would not have been the best choice. It was only when they had gained greater experience on the battlefield after Antioch that they became a cohesive and effective fighting force.

---

[26]	France, *Victory in the East*, pp. 148–9 and 204–5; J. France, 'Technology and the Success of the First Crusade', in *War and Society in the Eastern Mediterranean*, ed. Y. Lev (Leiden, 1997), pp. 163–76, at p. 169; D. Nicolle, 'The Impact of the European Couched Lance on Muslim Military Tradition', *Journal of the Arms and Armour Society* 10 (1980), 13.

[27]	The most expert works on Seljuk warfare are R. Amitai-Preiss, *Mongols and Mamluks: The Mamluk-Ilkhanid War, 1260–1281* (Cambridge, 2005), especially pp. 214–35; J. Waterson, *The Knights of Islam, the Wars of the Mamluks* (London, 2007), especially pp. 37–44; Smail, *Crusading Warfare*, pp. 75–83; Nicolle, *Crusader Warfare*, II, pp. 107–69.

[28]	*Gesta Francorum*, IX (p. 19); Fulcherius Carnotensis, pp. 194–5; William of Tyre, I 3. 14 (pp. 170–1); Albert of Aachen, II.39 (p. 130).

[29]	*Alexiad*, X.11 (II, pp. 67–8); Sewter, pp. 329–31.

[30]	For the topography of the region see France, *Victory in the East*, pp. 173–5.

[31]	William of Tyre, I 3. 14 (p. 171).

[32]	Smail, *Crusading Warfare*, p. 169; Oman, *The Art of War*, I, p. 274.

At this crucial stage of the battle, when Bohemond's battle group was in danger of being completely cut off, he sent an urgent message to Godfrey and the mounted armies of the second group arrived just in time to save the day, forming their lines to the right of Bohemond's battle-group. Once the crusaders had crossed the mountain ridge that led to the battlefield they did not waste any time forming a front but immediately charged upon the surprised and frustrated Seljuks, mainly focusing on their left flank and centre, forcing them to flee.[33] Contrary to the advice Alexius had given them, the crusaders pursued the defeated foe for many hours, thus preventing them from regrouping and taking large amounts of booty from their camp.

The first encounter of the crusaders with a relatively unknown enemy resulted in a complete victory. But this was a victory of chance and, although it was one of the rare cases where the Westerners enjoyed numerical superiority over their enemies, it was in no way due to the superior battle-tactics applied by the crusaders or to the mistakes made by the Seljuks. If the messengers sent by Bohemond to Godfrey had not made it through the Turkish lines, or if the Latin reinforcements had not arrived on time, things would have been very different. Most likely the armies of Bohemond and Robert of Normandy would have been cut to pieces or forced into a disorderly retreat, something which Kilij Arslan was hoping for. But in the moment of crisis, when the crusaders' front was ready to collapse, religious fervour kicked in: 'Stand fast all together, trusting in Christ and in the victory of the Holy Cross. Today, please God, you will all gain much booty.'[34]

Without any doubt, this first battle experience proved useful to the crusaders because of the valuable lessons it taught them on steppe warfare. They witnessed first-hand the thick formations of mounted archers attacking them from all sides, using the mobility of their horses to attack both the front and rear of their units, constantly employing the tactic of feigned retreat, not just in large divisions but in smaller units as well. The enemy was able to combine all the above with their archery which, according to many contemporary chroniclers, was deadly accurate, aiming not just at the men but at their horses as well. The heavy Frankish cavalry's battle formations and its cooperation with the still inexperienced masses of infantry proved a tactical failure against the mounted troops of the Seljuks.

The crusaders might have been lucky outside the walls of Nicaea, but Antioch was one of the most heavily defended cities of the empire, with a strong natural position, while on its most exposed sides it was surrounded by double walls which, allegedly, were wide enough for a chariot to ride on the battlements.[35] As they were to find out soon enough, there were three ways to subdue the city – by starvation, by treachery or by trickery.[36] The two major problems for the crusaders during the winter months

---

[33]   *Gesta Francorum*, IX (p. 20); William of Tyre, I 3. 15 (pp. 171–3); Albert of Aachen, II.41 (pp. 132–4).

[34]   *Gesta Francorum*, IX (pp. 19–20).

[35]   Rogers, *Latin Siege Warfare*, pp. 26–30.

[36]   In 969, a daring party of Byzantine soldiers scaled the walls of Antioch using ladders while the

were the provision of food and other supplies for the army and the prevention of desertion among its ranks. Logistics were crucial at this point in the campaign, and the task of bringing supplies to the crusader army was taken over by Bohemond, who held foraging expeditions in the region of Antioch during the winter (1097/8) and attempted to neutralise several smaller garrisons in the area that were harassing the crusaders.

Supplies for the Latins were supposed to be provided by the Byzantines operating from the bases in Cilicia and Cyprus. As such, the role of the Byzantine navy in supplying the crusaders was paramount for the success of the operation.[37] But in a hostile area like Syria and so far from the rest of the Byzantine centres it was apparent that an alternative supply source had to be found. Even though the crusaders officially chose Stephen of Blois as their leader, the task was in practice carried out by Bohemond, who did everything within his power to look like the leader of this operation.[38] His strategic thinking, his high morale and his resourcefulness certainly helped him greatly. He led numerous foraging expeditions further inland and towards the port of St Symeon, and he was involved in numerous skirmishes with the Turks, one of them developing into a small-scale battle with a Seljuk force from the castle of Harem (a constant source of harassment some three hours to the east of Antioch) in the middle of November 1097.[39]

By the end of the winter, Bohemond would have the chance to lead a cavalry force against a relief party sent by the Seljuks and ambush it, thus demonstrating his resourcefulness and strategic thinking. The Seljuks under Ridwan of Aleppo, Malik Shah's (1072–92) son, had managed to gather a large force of about 12,000 to 28,000 men to inflict a blow on the besiegers of Antioch. A smaller expedition had already been launched by Duqaq of Damascus, another of Malik Shah's sons, in late December but had brought poor results and was dealt with by Bohemond and Robert of Flanders. It needs to be emphasised here that there is a difference between these Moslem troops and the Turks that had engaged the crusaders at Dorylaeum. The forces that Duqaq, Ridwan and later the governor of Mosul, Kerbogha, put in the field were composite armies of Arabs, Seljuks and probably other nationalities like the Iranian Daylami, Kurds and other Bedouin tribes, and in which the Seljuks were the dominant party. In contrast, Kilij Arslan's army was almost entirely Turkish.[40]

Muslim guards were asleep: *The History of Leo the Deacon*, pp. 132–4.

[37]   B. S. Bachrach, 'Some Observations on the Role of the Byzantine Navy in the Success of the First Crusade', *Journal of Medieval Military History* 1 (2002), 83–100.

[38]   Yewdale, *Bohemond I*, pp. 57–62.

[39]   Latin sources report this harassment by the Turkish garrisons: Raymond d'Aguilers, *Liber*, pp. 48–9, Hill and Hill, pp. 31–2; Fulcherius Carnotensis, pp. 215–24; *Gesta Francorum*, XII (p. 29); Albert of Aachen, III.59 (p. 230).

[40]   Some of the Latin chroniclers could understand this difference and use different terms, like Turks and Saracens. See Albert of Aachen, III.62 (p. 236) and V.29 (p. 374); *Gesta Francorum*, IX (p. 20); XVII (pp. 35–7).

The news of their mobilisation quickly alerted the crusader chiefs, especially Bohemond, who was effectively the leader, and a force of every available knight was dispatched to face the Turks. By that time the horses that had survived the march though Anatolia would not have been more than 1,000 strong and hence this would also have been the number of the mobilised Frankish knights.[41] Bohemond decided to pursue an aggressive strategy and ambush the Seljuks on a narrow neck of land, which passes between Lake Bengras and the River Orontes, some 11 kilometres east of Antioch. His other option would have been to wait for the Seljuks on the iron bridge that led to Antioch, where Bohemond could have made better use of his infantry units. But the size of Ridwan's army quickly led the crusaders to take the initiative.

The outcome of this battle is significant because it is the first time that we see Bohemond pursuing an aggressive strategy and setting an ambush against a large Seljuk force. He had seen first-hand at Dorylaeum how difficult it was for the Frankish cavalry to resist the encircling manoeuvres and the showers of arrows of the Turkish cavalry and so he decided to take the initiative himself. He used the topography of the region to his advantage, probably influenced by the outcome of the battle at Nicaea into choosing narrow ground where his enemies did not have the space to perform their usual encircling tactics; thus, he was able to trap them more easily with the few hundred horsemen he had brought with him. Once he managed to get his cavalry into close quarters with their enemies, the Turks were no match for their superior Frankish counterparts.

In this battle, we also see Bohemond keeping a division in reserve, in case the main body of the army was to be encircled by the Turks. This tactic reminds us of the third line of cavalry added by Nicephorus Phocas to combat the encircling tactics of the Bedouin units of the Hamdanids of Aleppo in the middle of the tenth century.[42] I have argued elsewhere that the Latins of the First Crusade probably owed their adoption of a third line of cavalry and their characteristic square fighting march, seen in Ascalon in 1099, to Byzantine influence communicated by the thousands of mercenaries who had been employed by the Byzantine emperors since the 1030s.[43] Finally, the battle against Ridwan was the first time during this crusade that the Latins fought under a single count who had the overall command of the dispatched force, since at Dorylaeum there was no leader and they had been under no unified command hitherto. This remarkable adaptability of Bohemond to battle tactics, and his pursuit of an aggressive battle-seeking strategy to make optimum use of limited forces, highlights why he was viewed by his allies and his enemies as the true military leader of the First Crusade.

---

[41]   Oman, *The Art of War*, I, p. 280; J. Riley-Smith, *The Crusades* (London, 1987), p. 28; Riley-Smith, *The First Crusade*, pp. 64–5; Verbruggen, *The Art of Warfare*, pp. 225–7; Nicolle puts the figure down to 200, see Nicolle, *Crusader Warfare*, I, p. 137.

[42]   *Praecepta Militaria*, IV.180–4 (p. 48).

[43]   G. Theotokis, 'The Square "Fighting March" of the Crusaders at the Battle of Ascalon (1099)', *Journal of Medieval Military History* 11 (2013), 57–71.

According to our chroniclers, after the capitulation of the lower city of Antioch (3 June 1098), the count of Taranto was one of the protagonists of the siege of the city's citadel.[44] But Bohemond's role as a Latin leader was to be highlighted once more in the second major battle against the Seljuks, this time when a large relief force arrived outside Antioch to find the Westerners locked inside their newly acquired trophy. What is important to emphasise here is not only Bohemond's place amongst the rest of the leaders, with Raymond of Aguilers crediting him as the general who proposed the battle plan, but also the battle plan itself, which was, in essence, similar to the one applied against the Turks from Aleppo in February. He used the topography of the region in his favour and kept a number of units in reserve in case the army was surrounded.

The governor of Mosul, Kerbogha, had pitched his camp on the north side of the Orontes along with the main body of his army. Thus, the only way for the Latins to reach the camp was to exit the city through the Bridge Gate, which was the only one that connected the two banks of the river.[45] On 28 June, the crusaders sallied out of the city in battle order in four major divisions: Hugh of Vermandois, Robert of Flanders and Robert of Normandy were deployed in the right wing; the Lorrainers, Burgundians and other French troops, under the command of Godfrey of Bouillon, formed the centre, and Provençal and Aquitanian troops were posted in the left wing under Bishop Adhemar. Tancred and Bohemond's units formed the reserve divisions of the crusaders' army. The infantry and the archers were placed in front to hold back the enemy's attacks, while the cavalry was kept behind in order to break out and win the battle with its heavy charge.[46]

This tactic of deploying the cavalry behind the foot soldiers of the infantry and the archers had been seen before, both at Hastings (1066) and Dyrrhachium (1081), and indeed resembles the whole idea of the infantry serving as a shield for the cavalry. This was a principle which the Byzantines had employed for many centuries since its appearance in the early-seventh-century *Strategikon* as a battle formation for fighting against the 'Scythians', a nation who preferred battles 'fought at long range, ambushes, encircling their adversaries, simulated retreats and sudden returns, and wedge-shaped formations, that is, in scattered groups'.[47] As the Byzantines adapted to the tactics of a new enemy at the time in the Balkans, so were the Latins in the Middle East some four

[44]   *Gesta Francorum*, XXIV (pp. 57–9); William of Tyre, XI.5 (pp. 266–8); *Alexiad*, XI.4 (II, pp. 86–91); Sewter, pp. 342–5.

[45]   *The Chronicle of Ibn al-Athīr for the Crusading Period from al-Kāmil fī'l-ta'rīkh*, trans. D. S. Richards (Aldershot, 2006–7), part 1, 276, p. 16. The main primary sources for the battle are *Gesta Francorum*, XXIX (pp. 67–71); William of Tyre, VI.16–21 (pp. 284–94); Albert of Aachen, IV.47–56 (pp. 320–36); Raymond d'Aguilers, *Liber*, pp. 77–83, Hill and Hill, pp. 59–64; Ralph of Caen, *Gesta Tancredi*, 83–90, pp. 105–10.

[46]   Albert of Aachen, IV.49 (p. 324); Raymond d'Aguilers, *Liber*, p. 79, Hill and Hill, p. 61; *Gesta Francorum*, XXIX (p. 68).

[47]   Maurice, *Strategikon*, XI.2 (pp. 117–18).

centuries later. Precautions were also taken by Bohemond to prevent the encirclement of the army by the Seljuks, thus keeping a division in reserve while the flanks of the crusaders were covered by the Orontes on the right and the high mountains on the left.[48]

The crucial stage of the deployment of the crusader army would have been their crossing of the Orontes bridge. Bohemond was afraid that the Seljuks would allow one or two divisions across the river and then fall upon them while the rest of the army was crossing the bridge. But despite Bohemond's fear, the Latins were left free to be deployed as they wished, probably because Kerbogha wanted to use his encircling tactics and outflank the entire army. There is a debate, however, on the deployment of the crusader forces on the battlefield right after they had marched over the Orontes River and whether the divisions changed their formation from column into line.[49] Kerbogha would have seen that the left wing of the Latins, under Adhemar, was the last to have crossed the Orontes bridge to be deployed alongside the rest of the divisions and he ordered his right-wing units to attack them before they were ready for action.

These mounted troops – 15,000 horsemen from the sultanate of Rum –[50] managed to bypass Adhemar's divisions and arrive at the rear of the crusaders' left wing, thus becoming completely cut off from the main Seljuk army. Bohemond's precaution of keeping his Norman troops in reserve proved a wise decision since, if the detached right wing of the Seljuks was left unchecked to attack the Latin centre from the rear, it would have been a disaster. After the rest of the army was overpowered by Godfrey and Hugh, the Anatolian Turks kept up an immense pressure on the Normans and dropping their usual encircling tactics charged against them with their swords and lances, before they were eventually beaten off by the Norman infantry units, who formed a perimeter ring around the cavalry.

A rather different approach on how the events unfolded that day is given by France.[51] He believes that since the plain between the Orontes and the mountains opposite the Bridge Gate was too wide – about 4–5 kilometres – for the small crusader force to cover its full extent, the argument of the crusading army taking advantage of the topography of the battlefield to avoid any encircling is invalid. The Latins rather took full advantage of the dispersal of the Turkish forces on the perimeter of Antioch's fortifications, something that they had been at pains to avoid throughout their siege of the city. Since Kerbogha had pitched his camp up the valley of the Orontes at a distance of some 5 kilometres to the north of the city and had sent infantry and irregular mounted Turkoman detachments to blockade the main gates of Antioch, the Latins wisely decided to exit the city through the Bridge Gate and face the Turkish besieging detachments before the main army had time to organise and march against

[48] Raymond d'Aguilers, *Liber*, p. 78, Hill and Hill, p. 60.
[49] Smail, *Crusading Warfare*, p. 173; France, *Victory in the East*, pp. 284–5.
[50] Albert of Aachen, IV.49 (p. 326); William of Tyre, VI.20 (p. 291).
[51] France, *Victory in the East*, pp. 287–93.

them. Thus, Hugh of Vermandois's division would have opened the way out through the forces that were blocking the Bridge Gate and each division would have been deployed next to the one preceding it and on its left flank, following the order I have already mentioned, although it is unlikely that they would have had time to deploy into tidy formations before attacking their enemies.

The short fight and retreat that developed following the crusaders' fighting exit from the city must have been a result of their being attacked piecemeal and in no order by Turkish infantry detachments that were gradually leaving their besieging posts and pressing forward with the attack without waiting for orders from Kerbogha's headquarters. And perhaps the force that arrived at their rear was a force that was besieging St George's Gate to the south of the city. What France suggests is that the crusaders' first and second divisions were engaged in a fight with the Turks from the Bridge Gate while Adhemar's long march westwards towards the plain would have served to cover the flanks of the army and eventually received the piecemeal attacks of several Turkish detachments. Bohemond's division was, indeed, placed as a reserve to prevent the encirclement of the army while an improvised unit was detached from the armies of Godfrey of Bouillon and Robert of Normandy to deal with a unit of 15,000 men, as reported by Albert of Aix, that had managed to bypass Adhemar's division.

The lessons learned by the crusaders on the aftermath of this battle were simple enough. In order to diminish their numerical disadvantage and to check the attacks of the mounted Seljuk archers, they put their infantry in front of their formations and kept the cavalry at the back, waiting for the perfect chance to break out and fight them at close quarters. Thus, the Latin East experienced for the first time the mixed units of infantry and cavalry where the foot-soldiers acquired a fundamental role in Middle Eastern warfare. We should underline the fact, however, that by this stage of the crusade the infantry would have evolved into a formidable fighting unit – with better armour protection as well – which was most needed in the East. This comment is not to suggest that the foot-soldiers of the First Crusade were a mere rabble of untrained men when they crossed into Asia Minor in 1097, but that it took several months of intense interaction with the Turks to develop into a cohesive and disciplined unit. And even if the Latins did not actually use natural obstacles to cover their flanks, we have to admire the keeping of a reserve division under Bohemond that seemed to offer great protection for the Latins' flanks. The victories at Antioch and Harem depended on their command, with the Latin leaders – and Bohemond in particular – adapting to Middle Eastern warfare quickly and effectively.

Bohemond's establishment at Antioch

In March 1099 Bohemond was officially proclaimed prince of Antioch. His dominions extended from the vicinity of Antioch to northern Syria and southern Cilicia, including the strategic passes of the Taurus and the Armenian principalities of the region. To the north-east his flanks were covered by Baldwin's principality of Edessa, while from the east and south his domains were exposed to the Turkish principality of Aleppo, which was under the rule of Ridwan and thus posed no immediate danger. To the south, Bohemond had to face the Byzantine outposts of Laodicea, Balanea (Baniyas), Tortosa (Tartus) and Maraclea, Syrian coastal cities handed over to the Byzantine legates in April 1099. A number of Norman troops under Tancred departed for Jerusalem, but the bulk of Bohemond's men would have stayed with him (certainly not numbering more than a few hundred).[52] Apart from a border dispute with imperial troops and the loss of two Cilician coastal towns – Seleucia and Curicus,[53] Bohemond's major target in 1099 was Laodicea, one of the most strategic ports of the Eastern Mediterranean. The Norman count even enlisted the help of Daimbert of Pisa, the new papal legate in the east who was also supported by a large fleet, but because of the arrival of Raymond of St-Gilles from Jerusalem in September and the flaring up of the old rivalry between the two leaders, the siege reached a halt.[54]

In 1100, Bohemond managed to get involved in the internal politics of the Seljuk dynasty of the Danishmenids, who controlled a large area of Asia Minor, from Caesarea to Ankara and Sinope. He marched with an army towards Melitene and, according to Albert of Aachen he took with him 500 knights, a reasonable number if we compare it with Ibn-al-Athir's implausible figure of 5,000. They were ambushed by the Turks and in the ensuing fight Richard of Principate and Bohemond were taken prisoner, probably in July or early August 1100.[55] There is no detailed description of the battle, but from the chroniclers' accounts we can see that the Norman knights were completely surprised by the Turks, probably because of Bohemond's neglect of sending scouts to reconnoitre the area, and the Turks were then able to apply their usual encircling tactics until 'the whole company was overcome: killed or put to flight and scattered'.[56]

Nearly a year after his release from captivity, there is one last battle where Bohemond took part before his return to Italy, a disaster in terms of the battle tactics applied. The battle of Harran (1104) was the result of an expedition carried out by the combined forces of Bohemond of Antioch and Baldwin of Edessa to neutralise a threat to Baldwin's principality coming from the Seljuk stronghold of the town of Harran, some 40 kilometres east of Edessa.[57] While the siege of the town was under way, a Seljuk relief army of about 10,000 men arrived with a plan to attack the Latin camp while attempting to supply the garrison of Harran. As Sir Charles Oman put it, the battle of Harran may be taken as an example of the manner in which even the most practised veterans of the First Crusade could fail when they neglected obvious

[52] *Gesta Francorum*, XXXVII (p. 87).
[53] *Alexiad*, XI.9 (II, p. 112); Sewter, pp. 358–9; XI.10 (II, p. 120); Sewter, pp. 363–4.
[54] Albert of Aachen, VI.57 and 60 (pp. 480 and 484).
[55] Ibn-al-Athir, I.300 (p. 32); Albert of Aachen, VII.27 (p. 524).
[56] *The Chronicle of Matthew of Edessa*, II.134 (pp. 176–7); Ralph of Caen, *Gesta Tancredi*, 141 (p. 157).
[57] The main primary sources for this battle are William of Tyre, I 10. 29 (pp. 456–8); Ralph of Caen, *Gesta Tancredi*, pp. 164–5.

precautions and fought on unfavourable ground. But what were, exactly, the tactical blunders of Bohemond and Baldwin in this case and why did they prove so disastrous at Harran in particular?

The crusaders deployed their forces in three battles, once again throwing the infantry in front of the cavalry, while the Seljuks applied their usual tactics of encirclement and feigned retreat. Despite their great experience in Middle Eastern warfare, Bohemond and Baldwin followed the Seljuk retreat into the sandy and hilly terrain east of Harran, a serious tactical error. By the afternoon hours, with the infantry and cavalry unable to carry on with the chase, the Latins halted the march and for the first time experienced an attack by their enemies when least expected: during the night. Night attacks were not uncommon in the Middle East, with the Fatimids using them several times since the late tenth century, while the Byzantine treatise *On Skirmishing* sets out in detail how a night attack should be organised.[58] Thus, the disaster at Harran was due to the failure of Bohemond and Baldwin to follow a series of simple precautions against an enemy that they had faced numerous times in the last seven years and had grown tactically accustomed to. Bohemond's decision to follow the Turks far from Harran and his failure to place any guards in the camp during the night are wholly inexcusable.

*

Bohemond's leading role in the crusade was obvious even before the first major operation of the Latin armies in the East – the siege of Nicaea. He was certainly the most experienced of the officers for what lay ahead, as he had fought against Byzantine and Turkish forces in the previous decades, both in Italy and in the Balkans. It is very likely that his forces would have consisted of veterans of the Apulian and Sicilian expansion and soldiers who would have taken part in Robert Guiscard's Illyrian expedition, not to mention the unknown number of Western mercenaries serving in the Byzantine army since the 1030s, with a large number of them returning to their countries with huge experience in fighting against the Seljuks. Thus, it should not come as a surprise to see Bohemond negotiating the amount of supplies shipped to Nicomedia while the rest of the Latin army was besieging Nicaea, or his leading role in conducting foraging expeditions and neutralising enemy garrisons during the siege of Antioch.

Bohemond's resourcefulness and great strategic thinking, however, have to be viewed through the study of the three major battles of the period. At Dorylaeum, Bohemond was the commander of the group of armies including an unknown number of cavalry and infantry, as well as a large number of civilians, that was attacked by Kilij Arslan on 31 June 1097. The tactical mistake that Bohemond made that day was that he left his infantry to guard the baggage train, while the cavalry was ordered to hold the line against the Turkish attacks in a single mass of horsemen. In a clearly defensive formation, this mass of Latin knights was hopeless against the encircling manoeuvres

---

[58]   *On Skirmishing*, XXIV (pp. 234–7). For the use of night-attacks by the Muslim armies see Nicolle, *Crusader Warfare*, II, pp. 124–35.

of the Turkish mounted archers. Their attempts to counter-attack were to no avail and it was only the timely arrival of the second group of armies under Godfrey that saved the day for the crusaders. If the Latins had formed a mixed unit of infantry and cavalry as in Antioch or Ascalon, they would have found themselves in a less desperate situation and would have suffered fewer losses. Kilij Arslan set an ambush on the vanguard of the Latins, being able to choose a battleground that would suit both the relatively small size of his army and the encircling tactics of his mounted archers. At Dorylaeum it was the Seljuks who held the initiative, something that the Latins – and especially Bohemond – would never let happen again.

Bohemond was the undisputed leader who proposed the battle plan for the clash with Kerbogha's army outside Antioch. He took advantage of the dispersal of Kerbogha's forces and decided to sally out of the city suddenly in order to bring the enemy forces into close combat and neutralise them as soon as possible before the arrival of the main army. He had divided the Latin army into five divisions, keeping one in reserve, thus having both his flanks covered from any encircling movement by the enemy. And it was at Antioch that we see for the first time in the history of the Latin armies in the Middle East units of infantry being put in front of the cavalry for better protection of the knights from the Turkish mounted archers. This, however, does not imply that this tactic was unknown to Western armies, as the examples of Hastings and Dyrrhachium prove. Bohemond's strategic thinking demonstrates his adaptability to the Middle Eastern way of fighting and to the worsening conditions in his army – the crusaders would have had probably fewer than 300 horses by that time.

Compared to the battle of Harem a few months earlier, the basic strategic principles applied against the Seljuks were the same. The strategic initiative belonged to Bohemond, who ambushed a large relief army heading for Antioch. He used the topography of the region in his favour, trapping the Turks in a narrow defile between Lake Bengras and the River Orontes, where it would have been impossible for them to apply their usual tactics. Also, having divided his 700 horsemen into five divisions, he kept one in reserve in case the main body of his army was encircled. He knew that the crucial strategic move was to bring his knights in contact with the enemy as quickly as possible, and that was exactly what gave him the field eventually.

Bohemond was, indeed, a soldier with great experience in fighting overseas. He had fought against Greek, Anglo-Saxon and Turkish troops during his father's Illyrian campaign some fifteen years ago, having defeated the emperor's army in pitched battle three times before he was forced to pull back to Dyrrhachium after his failure at Larissa. In 1083, it was a series of ambushes and feigned retreats conducted by units of the Byzantines that defeated Bohemond's army, with the Normans easily falling into the trap that was planned in every detail by Alexius Comnenus. Thus, his experience in the East should have made him more cautious and innovative on the battlefield, because for years he was facing a cunning enemy – as the Turkish night attack at Harran in 1104 proves – whose battle tactics were very different from what the Normans were used to.

9

The Count's Campaign of 1107
and the Treaty of Devol

I want you [Alexius] to know that, although I was 'dead', I have escaped your clutches [...] I have
handed over the city of Antioch to my nephew Tancred, leaving him as a worthy adversary for
your generals [...] If I reach the mainland of Italy and cast eyes on the Lombards and all the Latins
and the Germans and our own Franks, men full of martial valour, then with many a murder I will
make your cities and your provinces run with blood, until I set up my spear in Byzantium itself.[1]

Bohemond returned to Italy in the early months of 1105, after having to fake his
own death and be transported from Syria to Italy through Corfu.[2] By 1104, he had
left his territories in Syria under serious pressure from the imperial forces, with the
Byzantine army firmly in control of Cilicia and the lower city of Laodicea, while the
imperial navy was moving offensive operations from Cyprus and the Cilician ports.[3]
Hence, if Bohemond had taken his newly recruited army back to Antioch he would
not have achieved much, with the Byzantine resources in manpower and money far
outnumbering what the Normans could put on the field.[4] Since Bohemond must
have been perfectly aware of this, he thought that he had to strike at the root of all
his troubles in Syria, the Byzantine emperor himself, and attempt to replace him with
someone more sympathetic to him – a plan that brings to mind the Fourth Crusade
some hundred years later.[5]

We know little of Bohemond's whereabouts in Italy during the second half of 1105,
but his intentions were to raise an army of volunteers and mobilise powerful allies
for his planned invasion. Pope Paschal II (1099–1118) seemed like an obvious ally,

---

[1] *Alexiad*, XI.12 (II, pp. 128–30); Sewter, pp. 367–8.
[2] In January, according to Anonymus Barensis, *Chronicon*, s.a. 1105.
[3] Yewdale, *Bohemond I*, pp. 85–105.
[4] R.-J. Lilie, *Byzantium and the Crusader States* (Oxford, 1994), p. 74; J. Flori, *Bohémond d'Antioch, chevalier d'aventure* (Paris, 2007), p. 278.
[5] Ostrogorsky, *Byzantine State*, pp. 401–15, especially pp. 413–15; Treadgold, *Byzantine State and Society*, pp. 656–66.

along with Philip of France and Henry of England, but exactly how fruitful did his journey through Italy and France prove to be? Bohemond remained in southern Italy, probably at Taranto or Bari, preparing his fleet from the early months of 1105 until September of the same year, whereupon he departed for Rome.[6]

Paschal was a crusading enthusiast and he, like others, held the Byzantine emperor accountable for the misfortunes of the 1101 crusade, as testified by the famous denunciation of Alexius by Bishop Manasses of Barcelona at the papal court in 1102.[7] Paschal gave Bohemond the banner of St Peter, if we are to believe Bartolf of Nangis, the continuator of Fulcher of Chartres, writing in Syria around 1108–9 and our only source for this event.[8] Paschal also appointed as papal legate Bruno, bishop of Segni, a Cluniac and the bishop who had escorted Urban II on his visit to France in 1095–6 to preach against Byzantium for the upcoming campaign.[9] As for what may have encouraged Paschal to give his blessing to the Norman count, we have to turn to Orderic Vitalis, who informs us about the presence of a supposed son of the deposed Byzantine emperor Romanus IV Diogenes (1068–71) and a number of Byzantine nobles at his papal court.[10] This is significant in the sense that we see Bohemond using the same approach to win over the pope as his father had done twenty-five years before.

Bohemond stayed in Rome until mid-November 1105,[11] and then departed for France to recruit the bulk of his followers by launching his anti-Byzantine propaganda campaign. He sent envoys to Henry I of England (1100–35) before he even left Italy, but since Henry's preoccupations at the time lay across the Channel and against Robert Curthose, that meeting never took place.[12] In March 1106, Bohemond was in the Limousin fulfilling a vow he had made to St Leonard, the patron saint of prisoners, and some time later he requested an audience from Philip of France concerning a possible marriage between him and Philip's daughter.[13] The marriage took place at

[6]   Anonymus Barensis, *Chronicon*, s.a. 1105.

[7]   This sentiment can be clearly seen in Ekkehard, *Hierosolymita*, ed. H. Hagenmeyer (Tubingen, 1877), pp. 29–32 and 37–8; Fulcherius Carnotensis, p. 521; Orderic Vitalis, X, p. 18; William of Tyre, XI, pp. 79–80, 460–2 and 470–1; Albert of Aachen, VIII.45–6 (pp. 634–6). There are two different views of the 'Manasses incident': S. Runciman, *A History of the Crusades*, 3 vols. (Cambridge, 1951–4), II, p. 35; J. G. Rowe, 'Paschal II, Bohemund of Antioch and the Byzantine Empire', *Bulletin of the John Rylands Library* 49 (1966–7), 170–6. For the crusade of 1101 see Riley-Smith, *The First Crusade*, pp. 120–34.

[8]   Bartolf of Nangis, *Gesta Francorum Iherusalem Expugnatium*, Recueil des historiens des croisades, Historiens Occidentaux, vol. 65.3 (p. 538). For the reliability of this source see Rowe, 'Paschal II', p. 180; Yewdale, *Bohemond I*, p. 108.

[9]   *Chronicon Casinensis*, IV (p. 493); Suger, Abbot of St Denis, *Vie de Louis VI le gros*, ed. H. Waquet (Paris, 1929), p. 48.

[10]   Orderic Vitalis, XI (p. 70).

[11]   On 18 November we find Paschal issuing a privilege in favour of a church in Bari requested by Bohemond: Patrologia Cursus Completus, Series Latina, vol. 163, col. 178.

[12]   Orderic Vitalis, XI (p. 68).

[13]   Orderic Vitalis, XI (p. 70); *Alexiad*, XII.1 (II, p. 132); Sewter, p. 369; Romuald of Salerno, *Chronicon*, s.a. 1106.

Chartres right after Easter, while during Lent Bohemond travelled around France, spreading his anti-Byzantine propaganda. Some Latin chroniclers attest that he went far into the south-west of France and even to Spain, both of which areas were important centres of recruitment for a crusade.[14] He was accompanied by bishop Bruno of Segni in an effort to add a more religious tone to his appeal, before finally returning to Apulia in August 1106.

Both Anna Comnena and Orderic Vitalis write that in his tour of France he incited hatred among the French population, not only by accusing Alexius Comnenus of being 'a pagan who was helping pagans wholeheartedly', but also through the parade of the supposed son of Emperor Romanus and a number of Byzantine nobles.[15] Modern historians have also proved that Bohemond distributed copies of the *Gesta Francorum* in which he had inserted a passage suggesting that the emperor had promised him the lordship of Antioch. This was undoubtedly an attempt to advertise his crusading achievements, attract more followers, and display the wickedness of Emperor Alexius to his French audience.[16]

But even though Bohemond's real objective was Constantinople, he would have presented the expedition to his listeners as a pilgrimage to Jerusalem, a *via Sancti Sepulchri*, after the Byzantine Empire had been pacified.[17] According to Orderic Vitalis, Bohemond 'urged all who bore arms to attack the emperor with him, and promised his chosen followers wealthy towns and castles. Many taking the Lord's cross left all their belongings and set out on the road for Jerusalem'.[18] We cannot be certain whether the statement about attacking the empire was made with the advantage of hindsight, but Orderic Vitalis' reliability is difficult to question. Adding to these accounts, a number of Latin sources, namely Ekkehard, Albert of Aachen, the author of the *Historia Belli Sacri* and the Anonymous of Bari, note that Bohemond's purpose in coming to Italy and France was to raise troops for an invasion of Byzantium.[19]

From the evidence that we have mentioned so far, we can conclude that Bohemond's expedition was preached as a *via Sancti Sepulchri*, that the banner of St Peter was provided and that a papal legate was sent to preach and inspire the masses. Whether or not Pope Paschal had given his full support for this campaign is a matter of debate and all depends on whether we think that the primary sources are credible enough or

---

[14]   Ekkehard, *Hierosolymita*, p. 293.

[15]   *Alexiad*, XII.1 (II, pp. 132–3); Sewter. p. 371; Orderic Vitalis, XI (p. 70).

[16]   A. C. Krey, 'A Neglected Passage in the Gesta and its Bearing on the Literature of the First Crusade', in *The Crusades and Other Historical Essays Presented to D. C. Munro*, ed. J. L. Peatow (New York, 1927), pp. 57–78.

[17]   Suger, pp. 44–50; Orderic Vitalis, XI (pp. 68–70).

[18]   Orderic Vitalis, XI (p. 70).

[19]   Ekkehard, *Hierosolymita*, p. 293; Albert of Aachen, IX.47 (p. 702); Anonymus Barensis, *Chronicon*, s.a. 1105; *Historia Belli Sacri*, III (pp. 228–9). Rowe argues about how reliable Ekkehard's and Albert's accounts are: Rowe, 'Paschal II', 176–7. His views have come under scrutiny by McQueen, 'The Normans and Byzantium', pp. 458–62.

whether they should be dismissed for providing information based on hindsight.

Christopher Tyerman and Ralph-Johannes Lilie are two of the so-called moderates, who consider the possibility that Paschal may not have approved of Bohemond's plans, even though they believe that Bohemond's official strategy for the period 1105–6 was, indeed, a campaign targeting Alexius Comnenus. Many historians believe that this crusade was an expedition against the Byzantine Empire from the outset, and that Paschal did favour Bohemond's ambitions, which aimed to break the power of the eastern empire and replace Alexius with a more sympathetic emperor.[20] In opposition, we find J. B. Rowe, who argues that the pope had given his apostolic blessing to a crusade against the Muslims, and was ignorant about Bohemond's ambitions for a deviation of the campaign, while Bruno of Segni was powerless to restrain the count of Taranto from launching his anti-Byzantine propaganda during his tour of France. In building his arguments, Rowe dismisses a large number of mainly Latin sources.[21]

In his effort to counter the Norman propaganda launched in France, Alexius decided to mediate for the release of 300 Western knights of the kingdom of Jerusalem who had been captured by the Fatimids at Ramlah in May 1102.[22] This can be viewed as Comnenus' answer to the rapidly diminishing popularity of the empire in the West after the 1101 crusade and the Manasses incident. He also took immediate steps to recall several senior officers of his army and navy from distant posts to Dyrrhachium. Generals (like Cantacuzenus and Monastras) with experienced troops who were serving in Coele-Syria and Cilicia, a very important and strategic post neighbouring the newly established Latin principalities and the Seljuks, were sent for duty at Dyrrhachium.[23]

Alexius also sought to win over any Italian naval power that might provide assistance or reinforcements to Bohemond's army. Anna Comnena talks about a number of letters sent to the great Italian naval powers like Pisa, Genoa and Venice, seeking to persuade them not to join forces with the Normans.[24] Alexius' actions in this direction were reasonable if one considers that all three cities had actively taken part in the crusade; Genoa had helped the Latins to take Antioch (1098), Jerusalem (1099), Caesarea (1101) and Acre (1104), while Venice, although reluctantly, had helped Baldwin of Edessa take Haifa and Tripoli in 1100.[25]

[20]   Tyerman, *God's War*, pp. 261–2; Riley-Smith, *The Crusades*, p. 90; R.-J. Lilie, *Byzantium and the Crusader States* (Oxford, 1994), p. 74; Rowe, 'Paschal II', 165–202; J. Harris, *Byzantium and the Crusades* (London, 2006), pp. 88–92; Runciman, *History*, II, p. 48; Yewdale, *Bohemond I*, pp. 106–14; Flori, *Bohemond d'Antioch*, pp. 266–72, especially pp. 275–7; Angold, *The Byzantine Empire*, p. 164; J. France, *The Crusades and the Expansion of Catholic Christendom, 1000–1714* (London, 2005), p. 102; McQueen, 'The Normans and Byzantium', pp. 458–62.

[21]   Rowe, 'Paschal II', pp. 165–202.

[22]   *Alexiad*, XII.1 (II, p. 133); Sewter, pp. 370–1.

[23]   *Alexiad*, XII.2 (II, p. 136); Sewter, p. 371.

[24]   *Alexiad*, XII.1 (II, p. 132); Sewter, p. 369.

[25]   Nicol, *Byzantium and Venice*, pp. 68–78.

The emperor was deeply concerned at Bohemond's possible flirting with Pisa, since it was Pisa's navy that had devastated Corfu, Cephalonia, Leucas and Zante, had clashed with a Byzantine naval squadron off Rhodes and had later joined Bohemond in the siege of Laodicea in the summer of 1099. But why would the relations of the Pisans with Byzantium amount to dislike, if not hatred? In theory, at least, Venice was still a vassal state of the empire and after the chrysobull of 1082 it had become by far the most important player in Byzantium's commercial life. Alexius was perfectly aware of the antagonism between the Italian naval states, and it is, indeed, unfortunate that we do not have the details of any diplomatic correspondence between the two sides to see what kind of language the emperor used to address the Pisan municipality.

Alexius left the capital for Thessaloniki in September 1105, where he spent the following winter and spring calling for recruits.[26] There would certainly have been a large number of veterans from past conflicts in the Balkans responding to his call, but new recruits also formed a significant part of Alexius' army. The emperor replaced John Comnenus, the former governor of Dyrrhachium, with Alexius, the second son of the *sebastokrator* Isaac Comnenus. He also gave the latter strict instructions concerning the strengthening of the city's defences.[27]

Alexius' affairs in Thessaloniki became more complicated when a rebellion broke out, instigated by the Serbs, and John Comnenus was defeated in Dalmatia, an event that forced the emperor to stay in the city for fourteen more months before dismissing his troops and retiring to Constantinople. Since during that time Bohemond was busy spreading his anti-Byzantine propaganda in France, any cooperation between the Normans and the Serbs of Raska, the dominant Serb principality in the region since 1091, can be ruled out.[28]

During this time Alexius appointed Isaac Contostephanus as grand duke of the fleet. Orders were also issued for a naval squadron to be assembled from several maritime and coastal areas of the empire such as the Cyclades and 'the cities on the coast of Asia and from Europe itself'.[29] His fleet would probably have consisted of relatively small and fast ships, purpose-built for patrolling the coastline, rather than large dromons or *khelandia*, which were expensive to build and difficult to keep at sea for long periods. Once again, we cannot be certain of the consistency of the navy, as Anna's terminology is not precise enough. Isaac Contostephanus, however, being ignorant of naval affairs and of the coastal topography of Epirus and Illyria, took the decision to attack and besiege Otranto on the opposite Adriatic coast (early in 1107), an undertaking that proved an utter failure for the Byzantine commander.[30]

[26]   *Alexiad*, XII.4 (II, pp. 141 and 147–8); Sewter, pp. 374 and 378–9.
[27]   *Alexiad*, XII.4 (II, p. 148); Sewter, p. 379.
[28]   Fine, *Early Medieval Balkans*, pp. 230–2.
[29]   *Alexiad*, XII.4 (II, p. 148); Sewter, p. 379; XII.8 (II, p. 165); Sewter, p. 389.
[30]   *Alexiad*, XII.8 (II, pp. 165–9); Sewter, p. 389.

Bohemond's invasion of Illyria

Bohemond was in Apulia from August 1106 until September 1107, making his fleet ready.[31] In late summer 1107 his army was ordered to gather at Bari and from there they marched to Brindisi, where the fleet had already assembled. The Norman forces set sail from Brindisi on 9 October and landed on the opposite coast of Aulon.[32] Trying to assess the size of the army or of the naval force gathered by Bohemond for his expedition is a challenge since the Latin sources and Anna Comnena provide vague and rather confusing assessments. We do know, however, that the Norman navy had evolved since the times of the Sicilian invasion or Robert Guiscard's Illyrian campaign and, as Pryor has argued, by the end of the eleventh century the south Italian ports seem to have developed a technological and technical capacity to carry more horses per ship than the fifteen or so of the Byzantine navy at the time.[33]

According to the *Alexiad*, Bohemond had deployed a core of twelve warships, described as biremes, but Anna does not give a precise number for his transport vessels, thus making it impossible to assess accurately how many men and horses were carried across the Adriatic.[34] The Anonymous of Bari writes about a nucleus of thirty warships, again probably biremes, and some two hundred large and small ships for the transportation of his army and supplies. This appears an excessive number, which has to be reduced by a half for it to be credible. The Anonymous also estimates the total of men, both infantry and cavalry, at around 34,000, which is once more an exaggerated number.[35] Other Latin sources like Fulcher of Chartres give a number of 5,000 cavalry and 60,000 infantry; William of Tyre writes about the same number of cavalry but notes a figure of 40,000 foot, while Albert of Aachen pulls the figures up to 12,000 cavalry and 60,000 infantry.[36] The figure provided by the Anonymous of Bari seems to be closer to the truth concerning the foot soldiers, but even 5,000 men is an excessive number for the cavalry and has to be reduced by around a half (probably to somewhere between 2,500 and 3,000), although any such speculations remain insecure.

Anna Comnena tells us that Bohemond had with him 'a countless host of Franks and Celts, together with the entire contingent of men from the Isle of Thule who normally serve in the Roman army but had through force of circumstances then

---

[31]   Anonymus Barensis, *Chronicon*, s.a.1106–7.
[32]   Fulcherius Carnotensis, pp. 519–20. The Anonymous of Bari mentions 10 October, which probably was the day of landing at Aulon: Anonymus Barensis, *Chronicon*, s.a. 1107. Anna Comnena does mention 9 October but erroneously gives the port of Bari as the point of embarkation: *Alexiad*, XII.9 (II, p. 172); Sewter, p. 392.
[33]   Pryor, 'Transportation of Horses by Sea', p. 14.
[34]   *Alexiad*, XII.9 (II, p. 170); Sewter, p. 392.
[35]   Anonymus Barensis, *Chronicon*, s.a. 1107.
[36]   Fulcherius Carnotensis, p. 521; William of Tyre, XI.6 (p. 471); Albert of Aachen, X.40 (p. 754).

joined him; not to mention an even stronger force of Germans and Celtiberians'.[37] It was French, Italians, Germans, Spaniards and Anglo-Norman soldiers who answered Bohemond's and Bruno's crusading call against the 'pagan supporters', with the Anglo-Normans, however, probably joining Bohemond's contingent from Normandy and not England.[38]

Isaac Contostephanus had been informed about Bohemond's gathering of troops on the opposite coast and, based on his little experience of naval affairs, concluded that the landing would take place at Aulon rather than Dyrrhachium. Surprisingly, after posting the bulk of his units off the coast of Aulon, Isaac Contostephanus pretended to fall ill and retired to the local baths. The officer who took effective command of the Byzantine naval units was a certain Landulph, who had 'vast experience of surprise attacks in naval warfare over a long period'.[39] Landulph was an officer born in Italy and the first time he is mentioned by Anna Comnena he was a grand duke of the fleet that intercepted the Pisan naval squadron heading for the Holy Land in 1099, while he was also in command of a fleet that attacked a Genoese squadron off the Cilician coast in 1104.[40]

After disembarking his army at Aulon and securing and plundering the surrounding region, Bohemond must have taken over the smaller castles of Canina and Orikon to secure his flanks, as his father had done in 1081.[41] After a failed attempt to take the city by surprise, Bohemond pitched his camp to the east of the city, probably close to the ruins of the ancient city of Epidamnus where Robert Guiscard had pitched his own camp twenty-six years ago. Thus, by late October 1107, Bohemond began laying down his plans and preparing different types of siege machines to breach the city's defences, with his troops occupying the castles of Mylus and Petrula on the banks of the River Diabolis.[42]

The emperor, having been alerted a few weeks before, set out from the capital towards Thessaloniki on 6 November 1107, crossing the River Hebrus (Maritsa) a few days later and arriving probably at the end of the month at the Macedonian capital to spend the winter.[43] Anna Comnena describes how, while Alexius was on his way to Thessaloniki, he was eagerly drilling his army to march properly as a coherent unit and perform certain basic battle formations.[44] Also, some time in early December, a naval squadron of unknown size arrived from Venice under the doge, Ordelafo Falier,

---

[37] *Alexiad*, XII.9 (II, p. 172); Sewter, p. 392.
[38] Orderic Vitalis, XI (p. 68).
[39] *Alexiad*, XII.8 (II, p. 170); Sewter, p. 391.
[40] *Alexiad*, XI.10–11 (II, pp. 115–26); Sewter, pp. 360–4.
[41] Anonymus Barensis, *Chronicon*, s.a. 1107; William of Tyre, XI.6 (p. 471); *Alexiad*, XII.9 (II, p. 172); Sewter, pp. 392–3.
[42] Fulcherius Carnotensis, p. 521; *Alexiad*, XIII.2 (II, p. 183); Sewter, p. 399.
[43] *Alexiad*, XIII.1 (II, p. 177); Sewter, p. 395.
[44] *Alexiad*, XIII.2 (II, pp. 182–3); Sewter, pp. 398–9.

in accordance with the treaty that was drawn up in 1082.[45] But most importantly, the local levies refused access further inland to the foraging parties of the Norman army, strongly defending the mountain and coastal passes. 'Hence came famine which continually affected horses and men alike. Bohemond's army also suffered from dysentery; it was apparently caused by some unsuitable diet, but the truth is that this countless, invincible multitude was visited by the wrath of God, and they died like flies.'[46]

Bohemond made no further serious attempts to take the city before the coming of the spring. When the spring of 1108 finally arrived, the Norman leader burned his ships[47] as his father had done and vigorously pressed on with the siege, bringing every siege machine his engineers could build before the city's defences. Anna Comnena provides us with a brief account of the siege machines used by Robert Guiscard in 1081, namely belfries (described below), but in this second siege of Dyrrhachium she devotes a relatively large part of her thirteenth book to describe in much detail the construction, use, and destruction or failure of each of these machines that were used against the city of Dyrrhachium in the spring of 1108. But what is the history of these machines?[48]

Perhaps the biggest and most dangerous of them was the *belfry*, a multi-storey wooden siege tower moving on wheels or rollers, protected from the enemy by thick hides. It had to be made at least a storey taller than the walls so that the besiegers could lower the drawbridges or jump onto the ramparts of the wall. It was used in Western Europe at least since the tenth century, with the Normans also using it in southern Italy in the mid-eleventh century. It was undoubtedly of Roman origin and there are several authors like Vegetius, the author of the *On Strategy*, Leo VI and Cecaumenus who give a description of a tower in their works, along with ways to set it on fire.[49]

Undermining the city's walls was a very common way of trying to break through the city's defences. It usually involved two methods. First, there were the miners who were called to undermine the foundations of the walls by digging with picks and chisels. Armoured sheds or wooden roofs protected these vulnerable workers. These

---

[45] Dandolus, *Chronicon*, s.a. 1107 (pp. 223–4).

[46] *Alexiad*, XIII.2 (II, pp. 185–6); Sewter, p. 400.

[47] Anna specifically talks about the cargo and horse-transport ships: *Alexiad*, XIII.2 (II, p. 184); Sewter, p. 399.

[48] A selected bibliography on the topic: C. Foss and D. Winfield, *Byzantine Fortifications: An Introduction* (Pretoria, 1986); E. McGeer, 'Byzantine Siege Warfare in Theory and Practice', in *The Medieval City under Siege*, ed. I. A. Corfis and M. Wolfe (Woodbridge, 1995), pp. 123–9; D. Sullivan, 'Tenth Century Byzantine Offensive Siege Warfare: Instructional Prescriptions and Historical Practice', in *Byzantium at War (9th–12th Century)*, ed. N. Oikonomides (Athens, 1997), pp. 179–200; Nicolle, *Crusader Warfare*, I, pp. 117–18 and 213–18.

[49] Vegetius, *Epitome*, IV.17, 18 (pp. 130–1); *On Strategy*, XIII (pp. 36–42); Leo VI, *Taktika*, XV.45 (p. 370); Cecaumenus, pp. 30–1.

were constructed by light wood and protected from enemy shots and fire by hides. A second impressive siege machine was the battering ram or the so-called 'tortoise'. This was a wooden construction, usually of a parallelogram shape (although it could have been triangular as well), moving on wheels with an iron-tipped head that was slung from a framework of beams and projected against the city walls. Both Vegetius and Leo describe the methods of undermining the curtain walls in much detail, along with the appropriate counter-measures taken by the defenders.[50]

The *Alexiad* narrates vividly the three attempts made by the Normans to capture Dyrrhachium using several siege methods.[51] First, Bohemond brought a battering ram before the city's walls, on the east side facing the lagoon. From the description of the attack it seems obvious that the city of Dyrrhachium lacked a moat, which is probably the reason why the defenders were able to approach the walls so easily. Despite advice given in contemporary Byzantine military manuals, moats – with or without water – are rarely found in either the early or the later Byzantine period while other outer defence works are even rarer.[52] It would have been futile for the Normans to force a crack on the walls of Dyrrhachium, especially considering Anna's exaggerated comments about walls 'of considerable thickness, so wide indeed that more than four horsemen can ride abreast in safety'.

The Normans also attempted to undermine the city's walls by digging a tunnel on the northern side of the city. Immediately, however, the defenders dug out an excavation from which to shoot Greek fire to repel the Normans.

Finally, Bohemond resolved upon building an enormous wooden siege tower. Once the defenders realised that they could not burn the tower down by shooting Greek fire directly at it, they came up with the idea of filling in the space between the walls and the tower with any flammable material they could find and then proceeding to set it on fire.

In the meantime, Alexius had left Thessaloniki for Dyrrhachium in the early spring and pitched his camp at the River Diabolis just a couple of weeks later.[53] Sadly, Anna Comnena does not give any figures for Alexius' army or any other specific information about its consistency. It is only from Latin sources that we get some information on the Byzantine numbers: the *Narrative of Fleuri* provides us with a figure of 60,000 men, while Albert of Aachen writes of 10,000 men.[54]

Throughout Anna's narrative, however, we get an idea of the different nationalities that had gathered under the imperial banner of the Comneni. These included Greeks (probably from Macedonia and Thrace), Alans, Seljuk Turks, Turkopoles, Pechenegs

[50]   Vegetius, *Epitome*, IV.13–15 and 21–2, pp. 127–8 and 132–4; Leo VI, *Taktika*, XV.44–5 (p. 370).
[51]   *Alexiad*, XIII.3 (II, pp. 186–93); Sewter, pp. 400–4.
[52]   McGeer, 'Byzantine Siege Warfare', pp. 123–9; *Castrorum Circumnavigatio*, p. 28.
[53]   *Alexiad*, XIII.4 (II, p. 193); Sewter, p. 404.
[54]   *Narratio Floriacensis de Captis Antiochia et Hierosolyma*, Recueil des historiens des Croisades, Historiens occidentaux (Paris, 1844–95), vol. 5 (p. 361); Albert of Aachen, X.42 (p. 756).

and Cumans.[55] The Cumans were nomads from southern Russia, probably from the same Turkic ethnic background as the Pechenegs. They had been employed by Constantinople ever since they were defeated in battle in 1094.[56] The Pechenegs were well-known mercenaries serving under the Byzantines, and it is not surprising that they took part in the 1107–8 campaign. After their defeat at Mount Levounion in 1091, a number of them settled in areas of eastern and central Macedonia guarding the approaches to Thessaloniki.[57] In addition, similar to what had happened in the summer of 1081, Alexius asked for troops from Malik Shah of Iconium, with whom he renewed the old treaties that had been signed by his predecessors Suleiman I (1077–86), Abul-Kasim (1086–92) and Kilij Arslan I (1092–1107).[58] What is most striking, however, is the absence of the Varangian Guard from Anna's account. Why would Alexius have left his personal guard in Constantinople? Perhaps, since he had finalised his plans for a land blockade he knew that his Varangian heavy infantry units would have been of limited use against the Norman knights in the Dyrrachian terrain. But this is just speculation.

Having learnt a valuable lesson at Dyrrhachium twenty-six years earlier and perhaps because he did not have any opposition to his plans as he had in 1081, Alexius' plan this time was not to risk a pitched battle. He had already instructed his local troops to control the passes that led beyond the vicinity of Dyrrhachium, denying the Normans the chance to conduct any foraging further inland. Now that the main army had arrived to deal with Bohemond's invasion, it was time to tighten the blockade to a point where the Normans would seek for peace.[59] It seems remarkable how Byzantine generalship had adapted itself against the same enemy it had faced in battle a quarter of a century ago, and it seems that the First Crusade had provided some useful lessons on how to deal with Western European knights. Anna attempts to explain to her readers the deeper reasons behind her father's decision to adopt a Vegetian strategy against the Normans:

> For reasons already mentioned, despite the fact that he [Alexius] was most impatient for war, he acknowledged the rule of reason in everything and his desire was to conquer Bohemond by another method. The general (I think) should not invariably seek victory by drawing the sword; there are times when he should be prepared to use finesse and so achieve a complete triumph. So far as we know, a general's supreme task is to win, not merely by force of arms; sometimes, when the chance offers itself, an enemy can be beaten by fraud.[60]

Alexius also had the most suitable troops for the strategy he wished to follow, namely expert lightly armed horse archers like the Seljuks, the Turkopoles, the

---

[55] *Alexiad*, XIII.5–8 (II, pp. 199–217); Sewter, pp. 408–13; Albert of Aachen, X.42 (p. 756).
[56] Vasiliev, *Byzantine Empire*, II, pp. 24–5.
[57] Angold, *The Byzantine Empire*, pp. 132–4.
[58] C. Cahen and P. M. Holt, *The Formation of Turkey: The Seljukid Sultanate of Rūm* (Harlow, 2001), pp. 7–15.
[59] *Alexiad*, XIII.4 (II, p. 194); Sewter, pp. 404–5.
[60] *Alexiad*, XIII.4 (II, pp. 194–5); Sewter, p. 405.

Pechenegs and the Cumans. Unaccustomed as these troops were to the Norman way of fighting on horseback, they were unlikely to be able to resist the impetus of a heavy Norman cavalry charge. Instead, they were much more suited to a war of attrition, and this was exactly the strategy chosen by the Byzantines.

Local knowledge of the terrain of operations was paramount for a general, especially one like Alexius Comnenus, who had already been defeated three times in pitched battle by the Normans. Keeping in line with all the necessary precautions before a battle, as recommended by the *Praecepta Militaria* and the *De Re Militari*,[61] another point that brings out Alexius' tactical adaptation was his summoning of three Westerners who had defected to the Byzantine army in previous years; one of them was a veteran of the 1081 Norman invasion of Illyria and Greece, the senior commander Peter of Aulps, who joined the imperial army while at Antioch in June 1098. The two others were Marinus Sebastus, a noble from Naples, and a certain Roger, himself a Frankish noble.[62] It is difficult to track any possible links between Marinus, Roger and Bohemond and, indeed, whether they had ever met the Norman count in person. But, along with Peter of Aulps, they were certainly familiar with Frankish battle tactics and the methods that could spread discord among a Western army.

The crucial move was to win over Bohemond's senior commanders by sending a number of trusted servants to Bohemond's officers – his younger brother, Guy of Conversano, who was in imperial service during the First Crusade, Richard of Salerno, Richard of Principate and a certain Coprisianus – carrying treacherous letters as though in response to ones supposedly sent to the emperor, in the hope of their falling into Bohemond's hands and spreading dissent in his army.[63] This stratagem was recommended by Emperor Leo VI in his *Taktika* and the influence from this early-tenth-century work is more than obvious at this point.[64] Bohemond, however, took no actions against his officers even if a number of Western sources, and especially Orderic Vitalis, were keen to accuse Guy and Robert de Montford of having collaborated with the emperor.[65] But why were these allegations not made by Anna herself, who was always willing to write about Frankish duplicity and avarice? Perhaps for the Latin chroniclers this was the most convenient explanation for the failure of the campaign and the humiliating Treaty of Devol that followed.

In the meantime, Anna Comnena notes her father's next moves in tightening the blockade around the Norman camp at Dyrrhachium. She tells us that he sent four of his most able and trusted officers, Michael Cecaumenus, Alexander Cabasilas, Leo Niceritas and Eustathius Camytzes, to occupy Aulon, Canina and Oricum, Petrula, Deura and Arbanum.[66] The first three of these castles must have been occupied by

---

[61] *Praecepta Militaria*, IV.192–208 (p. 50); Vegetius, *Epitome*, III.9 (pp. 84–5).
[62] *Alexiad*, XIII.4 (II, p. 195); Sewter, pp. 405–6.
[63] *Alexiad*, XIII.4 (II, p. 195); Sewter, p. 406.
[64] Leo VI, *Taktika*, XX.29 (p. 546).
[65] Orderic Vitalis, XI (p. 102); Albert of Aachen, X.44 (p. 758).
[66] *Alexiad*, XIII.5 (II, p. 199); Sewter, p. 408.

the Normans since their landing at Aulon in October 1107, even though this was not mentioned by Anna. It is possible that the princess was not aware of this and that these officers were actually sent to control the mountain passes leading to the castles and not the castles themselves, a possibility heightened by her mention of the *xyloklasiai*, the road-blocks made from felled timber that were used to block the passes.

Bohemond's reaction to the tightening of the land blockade was to send his younger brother Guy, a certain count called Saracenus (of Arab origin?) and another count called Paganus with a significant force to attack Alexius' commanders. Anna Comnena reports that Camytzes' men were caught in the middle of two Norman units and were overwhelmingly defeated on 5 April 1108, although we have no exact figures of the casualties on both sides. Alyates was also engaged in the *mêlée*, either because he had heard of the encirclement of Camytzes' troops or while conducting a reconnaissance of the area. With two of his senior officers, along with their units, out of action, Alexius summoned Cantacuzenus and dispatched him to Glabinitza with a significant number of reinforcements.

Having re-established his position on the right of the River Charzanes, Cantacuzenus now had to fight Guy's forces after the latter had sent a number of his men to Oricum and Canina and inflicted a defeat on Cecaumenus, the commander of the castles mentioned above. Cantacuzenus commanded the centre of the formation in the battle, having given the right wing to the Alans and the left to the Seljuks, while the Pechenegs were ordered to advance and harass the Normans with volleys and arrows, using their feigned retreat tactics in an attempt to confuse them and break their tight formation. With the Pecheneg attacks bringing no result, however, the Normans were then attacked, initially by the Turks on the left flank and later by the Alans from the right. Both of the attacks were checked, and the centre of the Byzantine army under Cantacuzenus made a final frontal attack on the Norman centre, managing to break their formation and forcing them to retreat back to the castle at Mylus. We have very little information about the number of Norman troops engaged in this battle. Albert of Aachen writes of 300 mounted troops and 500 foot soldiers, a reasonable number for a small-scale battle like this.[67] No figures of the Byzantine casualties are given.

The victory of Cantacuzenus certainly boosted the morale of his men and made the situation even more desperate for Bohemond, who was seeing his supplies running lower day by day. His only choice was to order a plundering expedition in the area of Aulon, Canina and Oricum where he hoped that he would catch the Byzantines off guard. Cantacuzenus, who had replaced Cecaumenus as commander of the Aulon, Canina and Oricum area, was not surprised by this Norman expedition and dispatched a strong force under a certain Beroetes, who managed to route them.[68] A second expeditionary force was sent by Bohemond (this time 6,000-strong) including both infantry and cavalry, again hoping to catch the Byzantines unprepared for battle and

---

[67] Albert of Aachen, X.43 (pp. 756–8); *Alexiad*, XIII.6 (II, p. 205); Sewter, p. 411.
[68] *Alexiad*, XIII.6 (II, p. 206); Sewter, p. 412.

overrun them. In this battle, Cantacuzenus waited for the Norman army to reach a halt at the River Bouses and for all the necessary preparations to be made for the crossing of the river. The general decided to make his move at the time when the Normans would have been at their most vulnerable.[69] No details are given for this battle, but its result must have been disastrous for the Normans as the Byzantine general was able to apply for the second time the tactic of attacking an enemy when crossing a river, which indicates his vast experience in laying ambushes as a commander of small units of cavalry.

The conditions in Bohemond's camp were gradually becoming intolerable after the emperor made several attempts to strengthen the land blockade. A crucial move was to place Marianus Maurocatacalon at the head of the naval forces patrolling the Illyrian waters, after the failure of the Contostephani to prevent reinforcements from Apulia reaching the Normans.[70] At this stage of the blockade, the Byzantine units deployed in the passes leading to the Norman camp were given orders not just to prevent the Normans from foraging and gathering supplies but to harass them by applying guerrilla tactics. Alexius also passed on the exact same piece of advice to his troops that he had twenty-six years ago, namely that they were to shoot their arrows not at the Norman knights but rather at their horses, which were much more vulnerable, because 'the Celts, when they are dismounted, would be easily dealt with.'[71]

Alexius had serious doubts about the loyalty of some of his men and officers, and staying faithful to his strategy, which had brought him ample results so far, he did not risk a pitched battle with the Normans, but rather 'sat back like a spectator, watching what was happening on the plains of Illyria'. In addition, much useful information about the conditions in the Norman camp and the prevailing degree of desperation was brought to the emperor by Norman deserters who were leaving their camp, either alone or in small bands, and were received by Alexius with gifts and titles and then sent on their way.[72]

Bohemond was eventually persuaded by his senior officers to seek a way out of this deadlock and open negotiations with the emperor.[73] A number of Byzantine dignitaries were demanded as hostages by the Norman count and the negotiations eventually took place some short distance away from the camp, so that the Byzantines would not see first-hand the miserable condition that Bohemond's men had descended into.[74] After receiving permission from the Byzantine dignitaries to move his camp to a more salubrious spot in the immediate vicinity of the city of Dyrrhachium and

[69] *Alexiad*, XIII.6 (II, p. 207); Sewter, p. 412. Vegetius recognises the danger of an ambush on a river-crossing and urges a commander to place armed guards and even construct temporary timber fortifications: Vegetius, *Epitome*, III.7 (p. 79).
[70] *Alexiad*, XIII.7 (II, p. 210–12); Sewter, pp. 414–15.
[71] *Alexiad*, XIII.8 (II, p. 214); Sewter, p. 416.
[72] *Alexiad*, XIII.8 (II, p. 215); Sewter, p. 417; Albert of Aachen, X.44 (p. 758).
[73] *Narratio Floriacensis*, p. 362.
[74] *Alexiad*, XIII.9 (II, p. 216); Sewter, p. 418.

allowing for some brief communication between the Byzantines and the governor of the city, Bohemond was allowed to visit the emperor in his imperial tent, where they agreed a treaty that was to seal the end of Bohemond's designs and ambitions against the Byzantine Empire.

The Treaty of Devol (September 1108)

The Treaty of Devol was drawn up in September 1108, eleven years after Bohemond had become *homo ligius* of the emperor in Constantinople on the eve of the First Crusade. The *Alexiad* is once more our most detailed and reliable source. Two documents were drawn up. The first, signed by Bohemond and given to Alexius, included a statement of Bohemond's obligations towards the emperor and was preserved in the imperial archives, from where it was copied by Anna. The second document, a *chrysobull* that was written by Alexius for Bohemond and included the grants given to the latter, has been lost. Some parts of it, however, were reconstructed in the *Alexiad*.

Much has been written about the Treaty of Devol and there is no need to repeat past analyses of its clauses and the obligations of each party.[75] The most fundamental part is what follows the annulment of the 1097 pact: 'By the terms of this second pact I shall become the *liege-man* (*lizios anthropos*) of Your Highnesses'. This time in writing, Bohemond would become the vassal of the Byzantine emperor Alexius and of his son and successor John, and by the terms of this feudal contract he was to provide military support to all the enemies of the Byzantine Empire.[76] Another significant clause of the treaty had to do with the future of the patriarchate of Antioch, which was to return to the jurisdiction of Constantinople, with John the Oxite restored as the Orthodox patriarch. Finally, there is a huge list of cities and surrounding areas, which were either given to Bohemond as a fief or were introduced into the empire. In brief, Bohemond received Antioch and many of its surrounding areas, while several other territories that surrounded this newly formed principality were incorporated into the empire, namely almost all of Cilicia and the coastal cities of Laodicea, Jabala, Valania, Maraclea and Tortosa in northern Lebanon.[77]

---

[75] *Alexiad*, XIII.12 (II, pp. 228–46); Sewter, pp. 424–33. For further reading on the Treaty of Devol see Yewdale, *Bohemond I*, pp. 127–30; Lilie, *Byzantium and the Crusader States*, pp. 75–82; Chalandon, *Alexis I*, pp. 246–9.

[76] John was twenty-one years old and he is constantly mentioned in the treaty as *basileus*. This was a title which Heraclius (610–41) received for himself and also gave to his son and co-emperor, and was held by all co-emperors ever since. The designation was certainly an attempt by Alexius to secure his newly founded imperial house: I. Shahid, 'The Iranian Factor in Byzantium during the Reign of Heraclius', *Dumbarton Oaks Papers* 26 (1972), 293–320; L. Bréhier, 'L'origine des titres impériaux à Byzance', *Byzantinische Zeitschrift* 15 (1906), 161–78.

[77] An appendix was included at the end of the treaty at the request of Bohemond, who asked for a number of cities and territories as compensation for those that had been taken away from his principality of Antioch: *Alexiad*, XIII.12 (II, pp. 242–3); Sewter, p. 432.

By examining the exact areas of Syria that were given to Bohemond, it becomes perfectly clear that for someone who appeared to have been defeated and humiliated, Bohemond did receive plenty. But why was he given these specific areas and for what purpose? What Alexius would have expected was the establishment of a new principality, which would have worked as a buffer state against the surrounding Muslim states of Mesopotamia and the Fatimids of Egypt and which could have significantly disrupted the Seljuk communications between Iconium and Mesopotamia. He must have been aware that the kingdom of Jerusalem would not hold out for long and possibly he could have taken a further step and expanded the vassal state of Antioch further to the south. Again, these are only speculations but it is difficult to accept that Alexius would have made so many concessions to Bohemond without expecting something in return in the long run.

What the Treaty of Devol had earned Alexius, however, was a vassal, and a well-paid one indeed, since Bohemond would earn 200 gold pounds as an annual income and the accompanying title of *sebastos* ('revered'). He would also establish his base at a most strategic region for the empire, which was a much-valued source of renowned warriors; he would direct the expansion of his lands further to the east against Aleppo and Edessa; and act as a buffer zone for imperial Cilicia and the Taurus. This task would have overstretched the military mechanism of the Byzantine Empire, if one bears in mind the serious danger that the Seljuks of Iconium posed to the safety of its communications and supplies. As long as the empire was fully recognised as the suzerain of Syria and especially of Antioch, and all the Orthodox clergy were restored, Alexius' task was a success.

Alexius, however, was destined to be let down by Bohemond once more. His promises became a dead letter once he left Illyria, not for Antioch, but for Apulia, where he died, probably in March 1111. Tancred, the count of Taranto's nephew and successor in the principality of Antioch, proved a match for his uncle and a very stubborn and persistent thorn in the empire's expansion to the East until his death in 1112. He never realised his uncle's promises and demonstrated great arrogance and defiance towards Alexius' envoys in Antioch.[78] The fact remains, however, that one of the most prominent enemies of the empire for almost three decades had now died. It would take another century for a crusader army to finally reach and conquer the City of Cities and the bulwark of Eastern Christendom.

[78] *Alexiad*, XIV.2 (II, pp. 253–7); Sewter, pp. 438–40.

Conclusions

Norman infiltration in the Italian peninsula can be viewed as the story of a few hundred men who descended upon Italy to make a career for themselves as mercenaries, as soldiers of fortune. These people were predominantly Norman, as most of our sources agree, but perhaps as many as a third of them were immigrants from regions neighbouring Normandy, such as Maine, Anjou and Brittany. In this light, one should expect them to have attempted to introduce into Italy an administrative system based on their own experience at home, influenced no doubt by the forms of lord–vassal relations, and the customs of tenure, military service and inheritance established in Normandy and other parts of France in the previous decades.

The political and social backdrop of southern Italy was ideal for them, as the politically fragmented Lombard principalities, the Byzantine catepans, the great ecclesiastical institutions of the time and even the German emperors were more than willing to hire these fine cavalrymen into their service. A sharp distinction, however, should be drawn between the pre-Civitate period and that which followed the battle at the River Fortone in 1053. Civitate should be viewed as a pivotal moment in Italian medieval history for the simple reason that it established the Normans as a major player in the political arena of Italy. For the first four decades leading up to Civitate, the Normans served in Lombard rebel armies as elite cavalry units in a conspicuously auxiliary role. Their low numbers (just a few hundred) rendered them unable to influence Italian politics to any great measure. It was only after the late 1050s that the major Norman expansion in mainland Apulia, Calabria and Sicily began to take shape.

As mentioned, the Normans would probably have attempted to apply to Italy the basic principles of the administrative system they had experienced in pre-conquest Normandy. There is no firm evidence, however, in any charter or other primary material that confirms this assumption. Thus, it would probably have been stipendiary troops – both household and mercenary – that would have played a protagonistic role in the territorial expansion of the Norman principalities in mainland Apulia, Calabria and Sicily from the 1050s to the 1070s. In addition, military service from vassals and *fideles* would have been requested by the duke of Apulia for large-scale operations, which included, of course, the Illyrian expedition of 1081. Well-established feudal quotas, however, did not exist in that early period of Norman infiltration into the south and it is clear from the number of serious rebellions that took place between 1067 and 1082 that this demand would not have been accepted without protests from senior Apulian magnates, who did not consider themselves to be holding their lands as ducal grants. Also, institutions like the *arrière-ban* and the *service d'host* had significant geographical and time limitations. This is why Robert Guiscard would almost certainly have negotiated the terms of overseas service with his senior vassals when he called for the *arrière-ban* in 1081, following a similar course of action to William II in 1066.

The period following the death of Basil II in 1025 was characterised by the serious decline of the Byzantine army. The rising power of the landed aristocracy in Asia Minor and its struggle for power against the senior civil servants in the capital had caused the military lands of the provinces to disappear and the thematic levies (the *stratiotai*) to be turned into dependants or to be given the right to buy off their military service, thus eroding the foundations of the oldest military institution of the imperial army, dating from the seventh century. This, along with budget cuts in the middle of the century, led the central government to gradually replace the indigenous troops with foreign mercenaries from the West, such as German Nemitzi, Anglo-Saxon Varangians, Frankish knights and Venetian seamen, as well as from neighbouring countries, like Seljuk Turks, Pechenegs, Rus and Armenians.

The inadequacy of this system was proved at Manzikert in 1071, when the numerically superior but heterogeneous and undisciplined army of Diogenes IV was defeated by Alp Arslan. Thus by 1081, the old thematic system was dead and the tagmatic armies had been significantly reduced in numbers because of the civil strife and economic decline of the period. In 1081, Alexius Comnenus resorted to hiring even more mercenaries to deal with Robert Guiscard's invasion, a decision that triggered a crisis in the imperial treasury in the same year. Later in his reign he made bold steps to introduce strong and centralised land and naval armies and reunite the civilian and military authorities of the provinces under an army officer (duke-catepan). In addition, small-holders were settled in rural areas of the empire with the obligation to provide military service. In this way, the army that the emperor led against Bohemond in 1108 was significantly different in structure and composition from twenty-seven years earlier. Foreign mercenaries were, indeed, the core of the army but one can also find many units of indigenous troops organised in battalions that resembled the old tagmatic structure and bore the name of their place of origin.

In view of the wider debate among modern scholars such as Rogers, Gillingham and Morillo about Vegetian strategy, what follows is an attempt to elucidate the degree to which one can characterise the Norman and Byzantine strategies in Italy, Sicily and the Balkans as Vegetian.[1] Under the term 'Vegetian Strategy' scholars have

---

[1]   J. Gillingham, 'Richard I and the Science of War in the Middle Ages', in *War and Government in the Middle Ages*, ed. J. Gillingham and J. C. Holt (Woodbridge, 1984), pp. 78–91; Gillingham, '"Up with

identified a particular type of warfare in which the commander sought to avoid battle at all costs unless the chances were overwhelmingly in his favour. Instead, he would seek to defeat his enemy by other means, such as the use of fortifications, harassment and blockades.[2] I would first like to focus on Italy in the post-Civitate period, which was characterised by the territorial expansion of the Norman principalities and a marked absence of any major battles. A basic principle that one has to keep in mind is that the party who wanted to expand and conquer – the aggressor – would often be more willing to seek a decisive battle, while the party already controlling territories – the defender – would wish to deny his enemy this advantage. In post-Civitate Italy it is easy to identify who was the aggressor and who the defender of the territories of Apulia and Calabria. But why did no major battles take place?

One would expect the Normans, operating close to their bases, conscious of their numerical inferiority and certainly short of cash, to avoid pitched battles and focus on the piecemeal conquest of towns in mainland Apulia. This is exactly what they did, partly because of the paucity of their numbers, as well as the challenges of reinforcement provision but also because of the realisation that a major battle would probably not have achieved anything, given the high number of fortified sites in Apulia. By the late 1050s, the Byzantines had to rely on local levies and elite troops furnished from the mainland. Expensive expeditions like the 1025 and 1038 Sicilian campaigns were nothing but distant memories by now. Asia Minor was a far more important operational theatre for the central government and the catepans of Longobardia had to go on the defensive, shutting themselves in their fortified cities. That Guiscard knew about this situation from the Frankish mercenaries serving in the imperial army in Asia Minor is possible, but not certain.

Numerous similarities can be identified with two other operational theatres, Sicily and Illyria, where the Normans also appeared as the aggressors. In both cases they operated far from their home bases, with no substantial reinforcements, and had to rely on plundering expeditions in order to supply their armies but also to undermine the political authority of their enemies. The Normans were aware of the political fragmentation of Sicily into three contesting emirates, while the civil conflicts on the opposite side of the Adriatic would also have been known to Guiscard. Further, they had clear strategic objectives in subduing Palermo and the second largest city of the empire, Thessaloniki. Considering the above, it becomes obvious why the Normans wished to engage their enemies in battle. Although numerically inferior to both their enemies, their aim was to achieve a victory in the field that would have significant consequences for their enemy's morale. Even victories in the field, however, could not necessarily bring progress in an operational theatre, as Castrogiovanni (1061) and Cerami (1063) demonstrate. After the conquest of Palermo in 1072, the Muslims

---

Orthodoxy!"', pp. 149–58; Morillo, 'The Context and Limits of Vegetian Strategy', pp. 21–41; Rogers, 'The Vegetian "Science of Warfare"', pp. 1–19.
[2]   Vegetius, *Epitome* III.9, 22 and 26, pp. 83–6, 108–10 and 116–17.

successfully defended themselves in their numerous fortified sites for a number of years. In fact, it was not until 1091 that the Normans finally expelled the last Muslim garrison in the Val di Noto.

If one focuses specifically on the Balkan operations, then Dyrrhachium is a characteristic example of a victory for morale. Robert Guiscard was well aware of the numerical inferiority of his army, and with the city of Dyrrhachium putting up a stout resistance and the Norman navy unable to keep the communication and supply lines open with Italy, he desperately needed a victory in a pitched battle against a senior general or the emperor himself. The battle on 18 October 1081 led to the surrender of the city of Dyrrhachium. In the following months the towns of Castoria, Ioannina and Arta also capitulated to the Normans in order to escape devastation. This had clearly become a war of attrition, in which the party that had greater determination and resources would prevail. Alexius had to confiscate ecclesiastical objects in order to fund the raising of a mercenary army, while Guiscard had underestimated the stability of his domestic affairs in Italy.

In the two years that followed Guiscard's departure for Italy in April 1082, Bohemond actively pursued battle by marching up and down the north-western Greek mainland, covering a great geographical area and targeting strategic cities that controlled the approaches to the Via Egnatia, reaching as far east as the outskirts of Thessaloniki. However, even though Bohemond accepted the surrender of Byzantine towns, thus significantly undermining the emperor's authority, no massacre of population or any serious devastation was reported by any of the contemporary chroniclers. Perhaps his plan was to secure the areas already under his control while waiting for his father to return from Italy with the necessary reinforcements. The suppression of the Apulian rebellion and Guiscard's affairs in Rome, however, delayed him for more than two years, and it was this lack of money and provisions from Italy that proved fatal for the continuation of Norman operations in Greece.

Alexius Comnenus experienced first-hand the main weapon of the Norman army at Dyrrhachium: the heavy cavalry charge and the effects of the Norman attack on Byzantine units after the Varangian Guard – the protective shield of the army – had been annihilated. Even though he further pursued a confrontation with the Normans at Ioannina, one can see the first signs of Alexius' resourcefulness from the early summer of 1082 on. As the emperor did not have any units of heavy infantry to place at the forefront of his army in order to repel the Norman cavalry attack, he instead posted a number of light chariots and caltrops. His Vegetian strategy became even more apparent during the siege of Larissa in 1083, for 'he wished to lay an ambush there and so defeat the Latins by guile, for he had given up any idea of open hand-to-hand conflict'.[3] Although his victory left the Norman army largely intact, Bohemond was forced to pull back to Dyrrhachium as exhaustion and desertion were becoming endemic among his men. It is likely that Alexius had become aware of this from the

---

[3] *Alexiad* V.5 (pp. 246–7); Sewter, pp. 168–9.

deserters that had joined his army in the past months.

The same protagonists were to meet again on the outskirts of Dyrrhachium twenty-four years later under very different circumstances. Bohemond had taken part in the First Crusade, having fought numerous times against the Seljuk forces of the sultanate of Rum and the emirates of Aleppo and Mosul and having learnt valuable lessons on steppe battle tactics and warfare. He was the undisputed leader of the Latins during the battles of Antioch and Harem and the commander of the vanguard that was ambushed by Kilij Arslan at Dorylaeum a year earlier. He had experienced first-hand the charge of the Turkish horse-archers in great numbers and their deadly accurate showers of arrows. He knew that any attempt to counter-attack was doomed to fail because of the mobility and manoeuvrability of the Seljuk units. Thus, a combination of infantry units at the forefront of the cavalry would guarantee better protection for the vulnerable knights. Dismissing the infantry and putting the cavalry in a single dense mass at Dorylaeum was a tactical error. The fact that this battle tactic was not repeated at Antioch proves Bohemond's strategic adaptability in Middle Eastern warfare. Furthermore, the Norman count learned to take advantage of the topography of the battlefield to offset his enemy's numerical superiority and likely use of any encircling tactics or, in the case of Harem, to place an ambush.

In spite of the invaluable experience that Bohemond had acquired in the Middle East, he made the error of leaving the strategic initiative to the Byzantine emperor when he invaded Illyria in 1107. The Norman count allowed his army to be drawn into a prolonged siege of the city of Dyrrhachium that put a strain on his supplies and had a serious impact on the morale of his army. His timing for the invasion was also ill-conceived. When he landed at Illyria in October, he only had a few weeks to intensify his operations before having to halt for the winter, obviously not considering the great logistical task of getting supplies for the army in enemy territory. Alexius had also learnt much from his previous experiences with the Normans and this time he carefully implemented the advice of Leo VI by imposing a blockade on Bohemond's army and using tricks to raise suspicions amongst senior Norman officers. He denied battle to the Normans and by controlling access in and out of Dyrrhachium with the placement of reliable and disciplined units in the mountain passes in the vicinity, he simply left hunger and discord to force the Norman army into surrender.

Historians cannot be sure if the writings of Vegetius were known in Byzantium or if, indeed, they were read by Byzantine nobles in the capital. A cardinal distinction, however, between the Byzantines and other cultures lies in the fact that they were intent on recording the useful knowledge gained on the battlefield over centuries of fighting against countless enemies. All military handbooks of the period, from Maurice's *Strategikon* to Leo's *Taktika* and the writings of Cecaumenus argue repeatedly for resorting to battle only as a last option, and even then only when the odds were overwhelmingly in favour of the commanding general. While it may still be a matter of debate whether or not officers of the eleventh century had access to these manuals, judging from the quotations taken from contemporary primary sources like the *Alexiad*, Cecaumenus' *Strategikon* and the *On Skirmishing* it seems highly likely. If that is the case, then why did Alexius Comnenus choose to offer the Normans battle in 1081 – exactly what they wanted – instead of imposing a blockade as he did in 1108? Probably he succumbed to the pressing demands of his younger and more impetuous officers, who would have raised the matter of prestige and its importance for a usurper who had been on the throne for less than six months.

This brings out a relatively neglected but crucial issue about Byzantine warfare throughout the history of the empire, from Theodosius I to the era of the Palaeologi. This has to do with a specific doctrine that was passed on to the Byzantine officers by the ancient Greeks and the Roman tacticians through the writings of a number of military thinkers of the first and second centuries like Aeneas Tacticus, Asclepiodotus, Onasander, Arrian and Aelian.[4] This was the doctrine of avoiding pitched battle at any cost, engaging in warfare of attrition, exhibiting an initial passive resistance to an invading force which had to be followed by continuous harassment, the cutting off of supply lines and the attack on the enemy when at their most vulnerable, such as on their way back loaded with booty and prisoners. Scholars such as Ralph-Johannes Lilie, John Haldon and Warren Treadgold have highlighted the continuity of this doctrine by the Byzantines when defending Asia Minor against the Arabs in the seventh and eighth centuries,[5] but these ideas and general mentality become even more relevant when the Byzantines fought against the Turkish nomads three centuries later. It is pertinent, I believe, to conclude this section with a remark by Kaegi: 'It is probable that the longevity of the Byzantine Empire owes very much to its adoption of a cautious military strategy that avoided bloody and risky pitched battles. Such battles did occur, but the tendency and prevailing policy was to try to avoid them.'[6]

Another crucial question that arises from my analysis is why Robert Guiscard's invasion of Illyria failed to establish a Norman principality in the Balkans, especially when compared to William's successful invasion of England fifteen years before. First, William transported 7,000 men and 3,000 horses across the Channel in 1066,[7]

---

[4]   Onasander, *Strategikos Logos: Aeneas Tacticus, Asclepiodotus, Onasander*, trans. by members of the Illinois Greek Club (New York, 1977). Kaegi compares an abstract from the first-century AD Greek strategist Onasander with Maurice's *Strategikon*. The similarities are indeed remarkable: Kaegi, *Byzantine Military Strategy*, pp. 11–16. On the issue of the historical value of the a number of Ancient Greek and Roman *Strategika* of the first and second centuries AD, and how these works influenced the transmission of military knowledge from Ancient Greece to Byzantium and early Modern Europe: Theotokis, 'From Ancient Greece to Byzantium'.

[5]   R.-J. Lilie, *Die byzantinische Reaktion auf die Ausbreitung der Araber* (Munich, 1976); J. Haldon, H. Kennedy, 'The Arab-Byzantine Frontier in the Eighth and Ninth Centuries', *Zbornik radova, Srpska akademija nauka i umetnosti, Vizantoloski institut* 19 (1980), 79–116; Haldon, *Warfare, State and Society*, pp. 34–46; W. Treadgold, 'Byzantium, the Reluctant Warrior', in *Noble Ideas and Bloody Realities*, ed. N. Christie and M. Yazigi (Leiden, 2006), pp. 209–33, pp. 209–33.

[6]   Kaegi, *Byzantine Military Strategy*, p. 14.

[7]   These numbers are, of course, just estimates: Brown, *The Normans*, pp. 149–51; Oman, *The Art of War*, I, p. 158; Beeler, *Warfare in England*, p. 12; Delbrück, *Medieval Warfare*, III, p. 152.

while Robert Guiscard would have had maybe less than half of that. His cavalrymen numbered between 700 and 1,300 and their number was wholly inadequate for such an undertaking. Second, Harold Godwineson was one of the victims of the battle of Hastings; a fatality of tremendous importance for the future of the Anglo-Saxon kingdom. At Dyrrhachium, even though Alexius was hotly pursued and surrounded by the Normans, he managed to escape and establish a rallying point at Thessaloniki. His death would definitely have brought the empire to the brink of a renewed civil war.

Third, even though England was as heavily fortified as Illyria or Macedonia, the key point is that the decisive nature of the victory at Hastings and the rapid capitulation of the Anglo-Saxons saved William from having to besiege a number of burghs in a war of attrition that could have seriously crippled his forces.[8] That was not the case for Robert Guiscard, and even though Dyrrhachium, Castoria and Ioannina did capitulate to avoid any destruction by the vengeful Normans, there were plenty of fortified places on the Greek mainland that would have resisted the invaders. Finally, the fate of William the Conqueror and the new Norman aristocracy were closely entwined; thus, a great number of Norman lords eagerly supported the duke in his invasion. Robert Guiscard, on the other hand, was nowhere near having the same level of support from his own vassal lords. In fact, the ringleaders of all the Apulian rebellions were senior Apulian lords – some of them related to Guiscard by blood – and it was a rebellion in April 1082 that forced the duke to return to Italy, a significant turning point in the Illyrian expedition of 1081–3.

A final point involves Norman battle tactics and the Normans' perceived invincibility on the battlefield, with victory so often portrayed by the contemporary chroniclers as being promised to them by God. In line with the argument first presented by Bates nearly three decades ago,[9] I would contend that the Normans do not exhibit any innovation on the battlefields of Normandy, England, Italy, Sicily or the Balkans. In all cases they relied on the charge of their heavy cavalry units and the shock impact this would have on their enemies, especially if the latter's army consisted of infantry levies, as in the cases of Civitate and Dyrrhachium from the Mediterranean theatre.[10] Heavy cavalry attacks, however, were common in Frankish warfare and the Normans simply implemented what they had experienced in France for decades. There is also evidence that the Byzantines were well aware of the charge of the Frankish chivalry, judging by the writings of Leo VI.[11] The same applies to the feigned retreat tactic, as the examples of Hastings and Messina demonstrate. Before one completely dismisses the Norman reputation for distinctive martial prowess, one has to ask whether it was simply by good fortune and strong leadership that a band of Norman bandits conquered half

---

[8] Strickland, 'Military Technology and Conquest', pp. 372–3.
[9] Bates, *Normandy before 1066*, pp. 245–6.
[10] Cf. Nicolle, 'The Impact of the European Couched Lance', 6–40.
[11] Leo VI, *Taktika*, XVIII.80–98, pp. 467–9.

of the Italian peninsula and Sicily in just half a century, and seriously threatened the Byzantine Empire more than once. In the south, bands of Normans were employed by every rival camp precisely because they were the best. Their reputation for excellence was cultivated by such staples as strong leadership and unified command, along with a combination of elite mounted warriors, acting in co-ordination with recruited foot-soldiers, all of which were supported, when necessary, by fleets.

List of Byzantine Emperors (years of reign)

Basil II 'the Bulgar-slayer' (976–1025)
Constantine VIII (1025–1028)
Romanus III Argyrus (1028–1034)
Michael IV 'the Paphlagonian' (1034–1041)
Michael V 'the Caulker' (1041–1042)
Zoe Porphyrogennita 1042
Constantine IX 'Monomachos' (1042–1055)
Theodora Porphyrogennita 1055–1056
Michael VI 'Bringas' (1056–1057)
Isaac I Comnenus (1057–1059)
Constantine X Ducas (1059–1067)
Michael VII Ducas (1067–1078)
Romanus IV 'Diogenes' (co-emperor, 1068–1071)
Nicephorus III 'Botaneiates' (1078–1081)
Alexius I Comnenus (1081–1118)

The Hauteville family

William Iron Arm (born before 1010 – died 1046), count of Apulia (1042–1046)

Drogo (c. 1010 – 1051), count of Apulia (1046–1051)

Humphrey (c. 1010 – 1057), count of Apulia (1051–1057)

> **Abelard** (d.1081)

> **Herman** (c. 1045 – 1097), count of Cannae (1081–1097)

Geoffrey, count of the Capitanate (d.1071)

> **Robert I**, count of Loritello (1061–1107)

Robert II, count of Loritello (1107–1137)

William, count of Loritello (born 1137)

Serlo (born before 1010), a son of Tancred of Hauteville by his first wife, Muriella, and heir to estates in Normandy after 1041

> **Serlo II** (d.1072) married the daughter of Roger de Moulins, count of Boiano.

Robert Guiscard (c. 1015 – 17th July 1085), count (1057–1059) and duke of Apulia (1059–1085)

> **Bohemond I** (c. 1058 – 1111), prince of Taranto (1088–1111) and Antioch (1098–1111)

>> **Bohemond II** (1108 – 1131), prince of Taranto (1111–1128) and Antioch (1111–1131)

> **Roger Borsa** (1061 – 1111), duke of Apulia (1085–1111)

> **William II** (1095 – July 1127), duke of Apulia (1111–1127)

Roger I (1031 – 1101), count of Sicily (1071–1101)

> **Jordan** (after 1055 – 1092), count of Syracuse (1091–1092)

> **Geoffrey**, count of Ragusa

> **Mauger** (d. after 1098), count of Troina

> **Simon** (1093–1105), count of Sicily (1101–1105)

> **Roger II** (22 December 1095 – 26 February 1154), count (1105–1130) and king of Sicily (1130–1154)

Glossary

allelengyon The law that made the powerful responsible for the paying of the outstanding taxes of small-holders

anthypatos A provincial governor – it is used as a title of honour after the ninth century

aposobetai The flanks of a cavalry army consisting of two fify-man banda of both mounted archers and lancers

arkhon A governor; in a general sense it can also designate the powerful

arkhon-abydikos A middle-ranking official in command of an important naval base or a major thematic port

arkhontopouloi Elite tagmatic unit of the eleventh century consisting of the sons of fallen soldiers in the field of battle

castellia Smaller *castra* that were situated either in a strategic area or usually in the surroundings of a major fortified city

castle service An element of the tenurial obligations of a vassal to his lord, combined with service in the lord's host

castrum Fortified settlement which formed the administrative centre and the seat of the bishop

catepan The commander of a military unit and – after the tenth century – the governor of a major province

catepanate The Byzantine provinces in Apulia under the command of a catepan

climax The ramp used to disembark horses and supplies from a ship

dromon A two-masted fully decked bireme with two banks of oars

drungaraton A regularly imposed military tax raised, probably, in support of the local naval forces

drungarius A military officer commanding a unit of 1,000 soldiers

ducates Larger administrative units commanded by a duke-katepan, comprised of several smaller themes

dynatoi The powerful; the wealthy landowners

ek prosopou A temporary representative of a *strategos*, a catepan or a *kleisourarches*

eparchiai The late Roman provinces where the administration was dominated by a *praetorian prefect*; an important civil functionary of the late Roman period responsible for a praetorian prefecture (Gaul, Italy, Illyricum and the Orient) with administrative and judicial responsibilities

epi ton kriseon Judicial office created between 1043 and 1047 under the office of the judge-praetor

galea A light and rapid ship, similar in design to the *dromon* but with one bank or rows

gastald A Lombard official with administrative and judicial authority

gynekonete The women's quarters

haplekton A fortified camp

helepoleis A wooden siege tower

hesperioi arithmoi A tagmatic unit established during the period of the Epigonoi, probably 2,000-men strong and stationed in the capital

hetaireia A unit of the emperor's bodyguard consisting solely of foreign mercenaries

homoethneis A tagmatic unit established during the period of the Epigonoi, probably 2,000-men strong and stationed in the capital

hoplitai Infantry soldiers

hyperkerastai The outflankers of a cavalry army consisting of two fify-man banda of both mounted archers and lancers

incastellamento The creation by local lords of small fortified villages

judge-praetor The head of the ministry of *epi ton kriseon*

kapnikon A tax on household property

kataphraktos The heavily armed Byzantine cavalry man mounted on an armoured horse

khelandion A type of warship that had the same features as the *dromon* but used primarily as a horse-transport

kleisoura A territorial unit of a theme which preserved some sort of independence

klibanion A cavalry-man's short-sleeved, waist-length lamellar cuirass, supplemented by extra cuirass sleeves

komeskortes An official of the *strategos*'s staff with judicial and police duties

kontaratoi Lance-bearers

kremasmata A cavalry-man's skirt-like coverings of the area from the waist to the knees

logothesion A bureau of the imperial government

manganon A machine used in siege and naval warfare; it may refer to a machine employing a windlass

manikelion Thick gauntlets protecting a cavalry-man's arms and forearms

megathymoi A tagmatic unit established during the period of the Epigonoi, probably 2,000-men strong and stationed in the capital

menaulatoi A type of infantry soldier armed with a *menaulion*, a heavy javelin or spear, designed for thrusting and not for casting

misthophoros A mercenary; a person who receives pay

mitaton An obligation of private individuals to provide shelter to military and state officials

nearai Byzantine legislative documents

ousia The standard complement of a war galley – its crew excluding the marines and the officers

pamphylos A type of round-hull transport vessel

paramerion A type of single-edged curved sword of Avar influence

paroikoi Dependants; the men who either sold or willingly gave their land to a patron-aristocrat in exchange for their freedom in order to avoid military service and paying taxes to the state

pelagolimen See *sea-harbour*

ploimoi A sailor; *loipoi ploimoi* were the rest of the coastal themes of the Byzantine Empire besides the three maritime themes of the Cibbyrrhaeots, the Aegean Sea and Samos

porphyrogenitos 'Purple-born', an epithet designating the Byzantine emperors and their sons and daughters

primikerios A senior member of a group of functionaries

procursatores The lightly armed reconnaissance and skirmishing unit that galloped ahead of the main army

pronoia The piece of land handed over from the imperial demesne to imperial favourites to administer; a conditional grant that sometimes implied military service

protosebastos A high title of the Byzantine court granted to members of the imperial family

protospatharios A high title granted to commanders of themes

saqat The third line of a Byzantine cavalry formation (of Arabic origin)

sarakontarios stratos 'The army of forty coins', named after each soldier's pay for the naval expedition against Crete in 845

schiltron A compact circular formation of pikemen used by the Scots in the thirteenth and fourteenth centuries

sea-harbour The defensive naval formation where the biggest and strongest vessels were tied tightly together, forming a closing crescent, sheltering the smaller and more vulnerable vessels inside their formation

sebastokrator One of the highest Byzantine court titles, created by Alexius I Comnenus for his closest relatives

sebastos An honorific epithet meaning 'venerable'

siphones Bronze pumps used to project Greek fire

stenitai The crews of the imperial fleet who were recruited from the areas surrounding the capital (after the narrow pass of the Bosphorus)

strategos A general, the head of the civil and military authority of a theme

strateia Military service; the obligation to maintain a soldier

stratelatai A tagmatic unit established during the period of the Epigonoi, probably 2,000-men strong and stationed in the capital

stratiotai Soldiers; the holders of a *strateia* (military service)

synone A land-tax

tarida A Byzantine merchant ship; originally, a Muslim reed canoe used on the Red Sea

tarrada See *tarida*

tasinarioi See *trapezitai*

taxiarchy An infantry unit of a thousand men, introduced in the mid-tenth century, comprising 400 heavy infantry, 300 archers, 200 skirmishers and 100 pikemen

toparkhes A local independent ruler

topoteretes The second-in-command of a tagmatic unit, a unit of the imperial fleet and the head of a thematic subdivision

tourmarkhes A military commander in charge of a unit of a thousand men (*tourma*) and the head of the fiscal and judicial authority in his thematic region

toxotai Archers

trapezitai Light cavalry-men organised in small units and used for reconnaissance

triboloi Caltrops, an anti-horse and anti-personnel weapon made of sharp nails, one of which projects upwards, to obstruct the charge of the enemy cavalry

Vestiaritae An imperial bodyguard; a courtier close to the emperor

xyloklasiai Road-blocks made from felled timber

zabai Sections of chain-mail, or plates of leather that complemented the armour of a *kataphraktos*

zupan the leader of an administrative division of the south and west Slavs

Bibliography

Primary sources

Actes de Lavra, ed. G. Rouillard and P. Collomp (Paris, 1937).

Albert of Aachen, *Historia Ierosolimitana, History of the Journey to Jerusalem*, ed. and trans. S. B. Edgington (Oxford, 2007).

Alexandrini Telesini Abbatis Ystoria Rogerii Regis Sicilie, Calabrie atque Apulie, ed. L. De Nava (Rome, 1991).

Amatus of Monte Cassino, *L'Ystoire de li Normant et la Chronique de Robert Viscart par Aimé, moine du Mont-Cassin*, ed. M. Champollion-Figeac (Paris, 1835).

Amatus of Monte Cassino, *The History of the Normans*, trans. P. Dunbar and ed. with notes by G. A. Loud (Woodbridge, 2004).

Annae Comnenae Alexiadis libri XV, with annotations by Ludovicus Schopenus, CSHB, 2 vols. (Bonn, 1839–78).

Annales Casinenses, MGH, SS, vol. 19.

Annales Pisani, RIS, vol. 6. ii, ed. B. Maragone and N. Zanichelli (Bologna, 1930).

Anonymi Vaticani Historia Sicula, RIS, vol. 8.

Anonymus Barensis, *Chronicon*, RIS, vol. 5.

The Anonymous Byzantine Treatise On Skirmishing by the Emperor Lord Nicephoros, in *Three Byzantine Military Treatises*, trans. G. T. Dennis (Washington, DC, 2008).

The Anonymous Byzantine Treatise On Strategy, in *Three Byzantine Military Treatises*, trans. G. T. Dennis (Washington, DC, 2008).

The Anonymous Book on Tactics, in *Three Byzantine Military Treatises*, trans. G. T. Dennis (Washington, DC, 2008).

Ansari, Umar Ibn Ibrahim al-Awsi al-, *A Muslim Manual of War: Being Tafrij al Kurub fi Tadbir al Hurub*, ed. and trans. G. T. Scanlon (Cairo, 1961).

Asochik, *Histoire universelle*, trans. E. Dulaurier and F. Macler (Paris, 1883–1917).

Attaliotae, Michaelis, *Historia*, CSHB, vol. 47, ed. I. Bekker and E. Weber (Bonn, 1853).

Attaleiates, Michael, *History*, ed. and trans. D. Krallis and A. Kaldellis (Cambridge MA, 2012).

Bartolf of Nangis, *Gesta Francorum Iherusalem Expugnantium*, Recueil des historiens des croisades, Historiens Occidentaux, vol. 65.

Basileios Patrikios, Ναυμαχικά που συντάχθηκαν με εντολή του πατρίκιου και παρακοιμώμενου Βασιλείου' ['Naumachika compiled under the order of the patrikios and parakoimomenos Basileios'], in Ναυμαχικά Λέοντος ς´ Μαυρικίου, Συριανού

Μαγίστρου, Βασιλείου Πατρίκιου, Νικηφόρου Ουρανού [*The Naumaukhika of Leo VI, Maurice, Syrianos Magister, Basileios Patrikios, Nikephoros Ouranos*], introduction, translation and commentary by I. X. Dimitroukas (Athens, 2005), pp. 152–73.

Bryennius, Nicephorus, *Commentarii*, CSHB, vol. 25, ed. A. Meineke and E. Weber (Bonn, 1835).

Cecaumenus, *Strategikon*, ed. B. Wassiliewsky and V. Jernstedt (Amsterdam, 1965).

Chanson d'Antioche, ed. P. Paris, 2 vols (Paris, 1848)

Choniates, Nicetas, *O City of Byzantium: Annals of Niketas Choniatēs*, trans. H. J. Magoulias (Detroit, 1984).

Chronica Monasterii Casinensis, MGH, SS, vol. 34, ed. H. Hoffmann (Hanover, 1980).

The Chronicle of John of Worcester, 3 vols., ed. R. R. Darlington and P. McGurk (Oxford, 1995).

Codex diplomaticus Cavensis, ed. S. Leone and G. Vitolo (Badia di Cava, 1984–90)

Codice diplomatico barese, vol. III: *Le pergamene della Cattedrale di Terlizzi (971–1300)*, ed. F. Carabellese (Bari, 1899)

Codice diplomatico barese, vol. V: *La leggenda della traslazione di S. Nicola di Bari. I Marinai*, ed. F. Nitti de Vito (Bari, 1902)

Codice diplomatico barese, vol. VIII: *Le pergamene di Barletta, Archivio Capitolare (897–1285)*, ed. F. Nitti de Vito (Bari, 1914)

Codice diplomatico barese, vol. IX: *I documenti storici di Corato (1046–1327)*, ed. G. Beltrani (Bari, 1923)

Comnena, Anna, *The Alexiad*, trans. E. R. A. Sewter (London, 2003).

Constantine Porphyrogenitus, *Three Treatises on Imperial Military Expeditions*, *Corpus Fontium Historiae Byzantinae*, vol. 28, ed. J. F. Haldon (Vienna, 1990).

—— *De Administrando Imperio*, Greek text edited Gy. Moravcsik; English translation R. J. H. Jenkins (Budapest, 1949).

—— *De Cerimoniis Aulae Byzantinae*, CSHB, vols. 5–6, ed. I. Reiski and E. Weber (Bonn, 1829–30).

—— *De Thematibus et de Administrando Imperio*, CSHB, vol. 7, ed. I. Bekker and E. Weber (Bonn, 1840).

Dandolus, Andrea, *Chronicon*, RIS, vol. 7.i.

De Foucault, J.-A., 'Douze chapitres inedits de la tactique de Nicephore Ouranos', *Traveaux et mémoires* 5 (1973), 281–312.

Eadmer, *The Life of St Anselm*, ed. R. W. Southern (Oxford, 1962).

Ekkehard, abbot of Aura, *Chronicon*, ed. F. J. Aschmale and I. Schmale-Ott (Darmstadt, 1972).

—— *Hierosolymita*, ed. H. Hagenmeyer (Tubingen, 1877).

Frontinus, Sextus Julius, *The Stratagems and the Aqueducts of Rome*, trans. Charles E. Bennett (London, 1925).

Fulcherius Carnotensis, *Historia Hierosolymitana*, ed. H. Hagenmeyer (Heidelberg, 1913).

Gesta Francorum et Aliorum Hierosolimitanorum. The Deeds of the Franks and the Other Pilgrims to Jerusalem, ed. R. Hill (London, 1962).

Guy, *The Carmen de Hastingae Proelio of Guy, Bishop of Amiens*, ed. and trans. F. Barlow (Oxford, 1999).

Historia Belli Sacri, Recueil des historiens des Croisades, Historiens occidentaux (Paris, 1844–95), vol. 67.

Ibn al-Athīr, *Chronicle for the Crusading Period from al-Kāmil fī'l-ta'rīkh*, trans. D. S. Richards (Aldershot, 2006–7).

—— *Kamil fit-ta ta'rih*, trans. M. Canard, in *Byzance et les Arabes, 867–959*, ed. A. A. Vasiliev (Brussels, 1950).

Ibn al-Qalanisi, *The Damascus Chronicle of the Crusades*, trans. H. A. R. Gibb (London, 1932).

Kaminiates, Ioannes, Ἰα την Ἅλωση της Θεσσαλονίκης' ['For the Fall of Thessaloniki'], in Χρονικά των αλώσεων της Θεσσαλονίκης [*Chronicles for the Falls of Thessaloniki*], trans. Ch. Messis, preface P. Odorico (Athens, 2009)

Leo VI, *The Taktika of Leo VI*, text, translation and commentary G. T. Dennis (Washington, DC, 2010).

Leo the Deacon, *The History of Leo the Deacon: Byzantine Military Expansion in the Tenth Century*, trans. A. M. Talbot (Washington, DC, 2005).

Leonis Diaconi Caloënsis Historia libri decem et liber de Velitatione Bellica Nicephori Augusti, CSHB, vol. 4, ed. C. B. Hass, E. Weber (Bonn, 1828).

Lupus Protospatharius, *Annales*, MGH, SS, vol. 60.

Lupus Protospatharius, *Chronicon Rerum in Regno Neapolitano Gestarum*, MGH, SS, LX

Malaterra, Goffredus, *De Rebus Gestis Rogerii Calabriae et Siciliae Comitis et Roberti Guiscardi Ducis Fratris Eius*, ed. E. Pontieri, RIS, vol. 5.i (Bologna, 1925–8)

Malaterra, Geoffrey, *The Deeds of Count Roger of Calabria and Sicily and of his Brother Duke Robert Guiscard*, ed. and trans. K. B. Wolf (Ann Arbor, 2005).

Matthew of Edessa, *Armenia and the Crusades: Tenth to Twelfth Centuries: The Chronicle of Matthew of Edessa*, trans. A. E. Dostourian (London, 1993).

Matthew of Edessa, *Chronique*, trans. E. Dulaurier (Paris, 1858).

Maurice, *Maurice's Strategikon: Handbook of Byzantine Military Strategy*, trans. G. T. Dennis (Philadelphia, 2010 [1984]).

Narratio Floriacensis de Captis Antiochia et Hierosolyma, Recueil des historiens des Croisades, Historiens occidentaux (Paris, 1844–95), vol. 5.

Nicephoros, *Presentation and Composition on Warfare of the Emperor Nicephoros*, in *Sowing the Dragon's Teeth: Byzantine Warfare in the Tenth Century*, ed. and trans. E. McGeer (Washington, DC, 1995).

Nitti, F., *Le pergamene di S. Nicola di Bari, periodo normanno (1075–1194)* (Rome, 1968).

Onasander, *Strategikos Logos: Aenean Tacticus, Asclepiodotus, Onasander*, trans. by members of the Illinois Greek Club (New York, 1977).

Orderic Vitalis, *The Ecclesiastical History of Orderic Vitalis*, 6 vols, ed. M. Chibnall (Oxford, 1969–80).

Polyaenus, *Stratagems of War Translated from the Original Greek, by Dr. Shepherd, F.R.S.* (London, 1796).

Procopius, *Historiae*, ex recensione Guilielmi Dindorfii, ed. E. Weber, CSHB, 3 vols. (Bonn, 1833–8).

Psellus, Michael, *Fourteen Byzantine Rulers: The 'Chronographia' of Michael Psellus*, trans. E. R. A. Sewter (London, 1966).

Ralph of Caen, *The Gesta Tancredi of Ralph of Caen: A History of the Normans on the First Crusade*, trans. B. S. Bachrach and D. S. Bachrach (Aldershot, 2005).

Raymond d'Aguilers, *Historia Francorum qui ceperunt Iherusalem*, trans. J. H. Hill and L. L. Hill (Philadelphia, 1968).

Raymond d'Aguilers, *Le 'Liber' de Raymond d'Aguilers*, ed. J. Hugh and L. L. Hill (Paris, 1969).

Recueil des actes des ducs de Normandie de 911 à 1066, ed. M. Fauroux (Caen, 1961).

Recueil des historiens des Croisades, Historiens occidentaux, par les soins de l'Académie royale des inscriptions et belles-lettres (Paris, 1844–95).

The Register of Pope Gregory VII, 1073–85, trans. H. E. J. Cowdrey (Oxford, 2002).

Rerum Italicarum Scriptores: Raccolta degli storici Italiani dal cinquecento al mille-cinquecento, L. A. Muratori (Città di Castello, 1900–).

Rodulphus Glaber, *Historiarum libri quinque*, ed. and trans. J. France (Oxford, 1989).

Romualdus Salernitatis, *Chronicon*, RIS, vol. 7.

Sathas, C. N., *Bibliotheca Graeca Medii Aevi*, 6 vols. (Venice and Paris, 1872–94).

Skylitzes, John, *A Synopsis of Byzantine History, 811–1057*, trans. J. Wortley with notes by B. Flusin and J.-C. Cheynet (Cambridge, 2010).

Skylitzes, Ioannes, and Georgius Cedrenus, *Synopsis Historiarum*, CSHB, vols. 34 and 35, ed. I. Bekker and E. Weber (Bonn, 1838–9).

Snorri Sturluson, *Heimskringla*, ed. Bjarni Aðalbjarnarson (Reykjavík, 1941–51).

Suger, Abbot of St-Denis, *Vie de Louis VI le Gros*, ed. H. Waquet and H. Champion (Paris, 1929).

Sun Tzu, *The Art of War*, trans. into Greek by K. Georgantas (Thessaloniki, 1998)

Syrianus Magister, 'Οι ναυμαχίες' ['Naval Battles'], in Ναυμαχικὰ Λέοντος ϛ,' Μαυρικίου, Συριανού Μαγίστρου, Βασιλείου Πατρίκιου, Νικηφόρου Ουρανού [*The Naumakhika of Leo VI, Maurice, Syrianus Magister, Basileios Patrikios, Nikephoros Ouranos*], pp. 112–43.

Theophanes Continuates, Ioannes Cameniata, Symeon Magister, Georgius monachus, Οι μετὰ Θεοφάνην [*The continuators of Theophanes*], CSHB, vol. 33, ed. I. Bekker and E. Weber (Bonn, 1838).

Three Byzantine Military Treatises, ed. and trans. G. T. Dennis (Washington, DC, 2008).

Tou sophotatou basileos Leontos ta eupiskomena panta; Leonis, romanorum imperatoris Augusti, cognomine sapientis, Opera quae reperiri potuerunt omnia, nunc primum in unum corpus collecta, Patrologia Graeca, ed. J. P. Migne, vol. 107 (Paris, 1863).

Vegetius, *Epitome of Military Science*, trans. N. P. Milner (Liverpool, 2001).

Vita St Nili Iunioris, Patrologiae Cursus Completus. Series Graeca, ed. J.-P. Migné, 161 vols (Paris, 1855–67), vol. 70.

Walter the Chancellor, *The Antiochene Wars*, trans. T. S. Ashbridge and S. B. Edgington (Aldershot, 1999).

Wace, *The History of the Norman People: Wace's Roman de Rou*, trans. G. S. Burgess with notes by G. S. Burgess and E. van Houts (Woodbridge, 2004)

William of Apulia (Guillaume de Pouille), *La Geste de Robert Guiscard*, ed. and trans. M. Mathieu (Palermo, 1961).

William of Jumièges, *The Gesta Normannorum Ducum of William of Jumièges, Orderic Vitalis, and Robert of Torigni*, 2 vols., ed. E. van Houts (Oxford, 1992–5).

William of Malmesbury, *Gesta Regum Anglorum*, ed. and trans. R. A. B. Mynors (Oxford, 1998).

William of Poitiers, *Gesta Guillelmi of William of Poitiers*, ed. and trans. R. H. C. Davis and M. Chibnall (Oxford, 1998).

William of Tyre, *A History of the Deeds Done beyond the Sea*, ed. and trans. E. Atwater Babcock and A. C. Krey (New York, 1976).

Yahia-ibn-Said, *Histoire*, ed. and trans. I. Krachkovskii and A. A. Vasiliev, *Patrologia Orientalis*, 18.5 and 23.3 (Paris, 1925–32).

Zachariae a Lingenthal, *Jus Graeco-Romanum* (Lipsiae, 1867).

Zonaras, Ioannes, *Annales*, ed. E. Weber, CSHB, vols. 41, 42.1, 42.2 (Bonn, 1841–97).

Secondary works

Abels, R., 'Household Men, Mercenaries and Vikings in Anglo-Saxon England', in *Mercenaries and Paid Men: The Mercenary Identity in the Middle Ages*, ed. J. France (Boston, 2008), pp. 143–65.

—— and Morillo, S., 'A Lying Legacy? A Preliminary Discussion of Images of Antiquity and Altered Reality in Medieval Military History', *Journal of Medieval Military History* 3 (2005), 1–13.

Agius, D., *Classic Ships of Islam, From Mesopotamia to the Indian Ocean* (Leiden, 2008).

Ahmad, A., *A History of Islamic Sicily* (Edinburgh, 1975).

Ahrweiler, H., *Byzance et la mer* (Paris, 1966).

—— 'Rechérches sur l'administration de l'empire Byzantin aux IXᵉ–XIᵉ siècles', *Bulletin de correspondance hellénique* 84 (1969), 1–109; reprinted in *Études sur les structures administratives et sociales de Byzance* (London, 1971).

Albu, E., *The Normans in their Histories: Propaganda, Myth and Subversion* (Woodbridge, 2001).

Alexandris, K., Η θαλάσσια δύναμις εἰς τὴν ἱστορία τῆς Βυζαντινῆς αὐτοκρατορίας [*Naval Power in the History of the Byzantine Empire*], (Athens, 1956)

Amari, M., *Storia dei Musulmani di Sicilia*, 3 vols. (Catania, 1935).

Angold, M., 'The Byzantine State on the Eve of the Battle of Manzikert', in *Manzikert to Lepanto: The Byzantine World and the Turks 1071–1571*, ed. A. Bryer (Amsterdam, 1991), pp. 9–34.

—— *The Byzantine Empire, 1025–1204* (London, 1997).

—— *Church and Society in Byzantium under the Comneni, 1081–1261* (Cambridge, 2000).

—— 'Belle Époque or Crisis? (1025–1118)', in *The Cambridge History of the Byzantine Empire c. 500–1492* (Cambridge, 2008), ed. J. Shepard, pp. 598–601.

Arnold, J. C., 'Arcadia becomes Jerusalem: Angelic Caverns and Shrine Conversion at Monte Gargano', *Speculum* 75 (2000), 567–88.

Ayton, A., 'Arms, Armour, and Horses', in *Medieval Warfare*, ed. M. Keen (Oxford, 1999), pp. 186–209.

Bachrach, B. S., 'The Alans in Gaul', *Traditio* 23 (1967), 480–9.

—— 'The Origin of Armorican Chivalry', *Technology and Culture* 10 (1969), 166–71.

—— 'The Feigned Retreat at Hastings', *Medieval Studies* 33 (1971), 344–7.

—— 'Fortifications and Military Tactics: Fulk Nerra's Strongholds circa 1000', *Technology and Culture* 20 (1979), 531–49.

—— 'The Angevin Strategy of Castle Building in the Reign of Fulk Nerra, 987–1040', *American Historical Review* 88 (1983), 171–207.

—— 'On the Origins of William the Conqueror's Horse Transports', *Technology and Culture* 26 (1985), 505–31.

—— 'Some Observations on the Military Administration of the Norman Conquest', *Anglo-Norman Studies* 8 (1985), 1–27.

—— 'Early Medieval Military Demography: Some Observations on the Methods of Hans Delbrück', in *The Circle of War in the Middle Ages*, ed. D. Kagay and L. J. Andrew Villalon (Woodbridge, 1999), pp. 3–20.

—— *Early Carolingian Warfare: Prelude to Empire* (Philadelphia, 2001).

—— 'Some Observations on the Role of the Byzantine Navy in the Success of the First Crusade', *Journal of Medieval Military History* 1 (2002), 83–100.

Bachrach, B., and R. Aris, 'Military Technology and Garrison Organization: Some Observations on Anglo-Saxon Military Thinking in Light of the Burghal Heritage', *Technology and Culture* 31 (1990), 1–17.

Barlow, F., *The Feudal Kingdom of England, 1042–1216* (Harlow, 1999).

Bartlett, R., *The Making of Europe, Conquest, Colonization and Cultural Change, 950–1350* (London, 1994).

Bates, D., *Normandy before 1066* (London, 1982).

—— *William the Conqueror* (Stroud, 2001).

Beeler, J., *Warfare in England, 1066–1189* (New York, 1996).

Belke, K., 'Communications, Roads and Bridges', in *The Oxford Handbook of Byzantine studies*, ed. E. Jeffreys, J. Haldon, R. Cormack (Oxford, 2008), pp. 295–308.

Bennett, M., 'Norman Naval Activity in the Mediterranean, 1060–1108', *Anglo-Norman Studies* 15 (1992), 41–58.

—— 'The Myth of the Military Supremacy of Knightly Cavalry', in *Armies, Chivalry and Warfare in Medieval Britain and France, Proceedings of the 1995 Harlaxton Symposium*, ed. M. Strickland (Stamford, 1998), pp. 304–16.

—— 'The Crusaders' "Fighting March" Revisited', *War in History* 8 (2001), 1–18.

—— 'Amphibious Operations from the Norman Conquest to the Crusades of St. Louis, *c*.1050–*c*.1250', in *Amphibious Warfare 1000–1700*, ed. D. J. B. Trim and M. C. Fissel (Leiden 2006), pp. 51–68.

Beshir, B. J., 'Fatimid Military Organization', *Der Islam* 55 (1978), 37–56.

Bibicou, H., 'Une page d'histoire diplomatique de Byzance au XIe siecle: Michael VII Doukas, Robert Guiscard et la pension des dignitaires', *Byzantion* 29 (1959), 43–75.

Birkenmeier, J. W., *The Development of the Komnenian Army* (Leiden, 2002).

Blondal, S., 'Nabites the Varangian', *Classica et Mediaevalia* 2 (1939), 145–67.

—— *The Varangians of Byzantium*, ed. and trans. B. Benedikz (Cambridge, 2007).

Bon, A., 'Fortresses mediévales de la Grèce Centrale', *Bulletin de correspondance hellénique* 61 (1937), 136–208.

—— *La morée franque* (Paris, 1969).

Bouard, M., 'Quelques donées Francaises et Normand concernant le probleme de l'origine des mottes', *Chateau Gaillard* 2 (1964), 19–26.

Bradbury, J., *The Medieval Siege* (Woodbridge, 1992).

Bresc, H., 'Terre e castelli: le fortificazioni nella Sicilia araba e normanna', in *Castelli. Storia e archaeologia*, ed. R. Comba and A. A. Settia (Turin, 1984), pp. 73–87.

—— 'Les normands constructeurs de chateaux', in *Les Normandes en Mediterranée aux XIe–XIIe siècles*, ed. P. Bouet and F. Neveux (Caen, 2001), pp. 63–77.

Brown, R. A., *English Medieval Castles* (London, 1956).

—— *The Normans and the Norman Conquest* (London, 1969).

—— 'The Battle of Hastings', *Anglo-Norman Studies* 3 (1980), 1–21.

Bruschi, A., and C. Miarelli-Mariani, *Architettura sveva nell'Italia meridionale* (Prato, 1975).

Buckler, G., *Anna Comnena, A Study* (Oxford, 1968).

Bury, J. B., *The Imperial Administrative System in the Ninth Century* (London, 1911).

Cahen, C., 'La campagne de Manzikert d'après les sources musulmanes', *Byzantion* 9 (1934), 613–42.

—— *Le régime féodal de l'Italie normande* (Paris, 1940).

—— *La Syrie du Nord a l'époque des croisades* (Paris, 1940).

—— 'La première pénétration turque en Asie Mineure', *Byzantion* 18 (1948), 5–67.

Cahen, C., and P. M. Holt, *The Formation of Turkey: The Seljukid Sultanate of Rūm* (Harlow, 2001)

Capitani, O., 'Specific Motivations and Continuing Themes in the Norman Chronicles of Southern Italy in the Eleventh and Twelfth Centuries', in *The Normans in Sicily and Southern Italy*, ed. O. Capitani, G. Galasso and R. Salvini. Lincey Lectures 1974 (Oxford, 1977).

Castrorum Circumnavigatio, ed. I. Georgopoulou-d' Amico (Athens, 2008).

Chalandon, F., *Essai sur le règne d'Alexis Ier Comnène, 1081–1118* (Paris, 1900).

—— *Histoire de la domination normande en Italie et en Sicile*, 2 vols. (Paris, 1907).

Charanis, P., 'The Byzantine Empire in the Eleventh Century', in *A History of the Crusades*, ed. K. Setton, 6 vols (Madison, 1969–89), vol. I, pp. 177–219.

Charizanis, G., 'Ὁ μητροπολίτης Κέρκυρας Νικόλαος και η βυζαντινο-νορμανδική σύγκρουση στο Ιόνιο (τέλη του 11ου αι.)' ['The Metropolitan of Corfu Nikolaos and the Byzantino-Norman Clash in the Ionian Sea (End of 11th Century)'], Βυζαντιακά [*Byzantiaka*] 24 (2004), 197–210.

Cheynet, J.-C., 'Manzikert: un desastre militaire?', *Byzantion* 60 (1980), 410–38.

—— *Pouvoir et contestations à Byzance, 963–1210* (Paris, 1990).

—— 'Basil II and Asia Minor', in *Byzantium in the Year 1000*, ed. P. Magdalino (Leiden, 2003), pp. 71–108.

Chibnall, M., 'Military Service in Normandy before 1066', *Anglo-Norman Studies* 5 (1982), 65–77.

—— *Anglo-Norman England, 1066–1166* (Oxford, 1987).

—— 'Mercenaries and the Familia Regis under Henry I', in *Anglo-Norman Warfare*, ed. M. Strickland (Woodbridge, 1992), pp. 84–92.

Christides, V., *The Conquest of Crete by the Arabs (ca. 824): A Turning Point in the Struggle between Byzantium and Islam* (Athens, 1984)

—— 'The Naval Battle of Dhat as-Sawari AH 34/AD 655–656. A Classical Example of Naval Warfare Incompetence', Βυζαντινά [*Byzantina*]13 (1985), 1331–45.

—— 'Naval History and Naval Technology in Medieval Times, the Need for Interdisciplinary Studies', *Byzantion* 58 (1988), 321–2.

—— 'Byzantine *Dromon* and Arab *Shini*: The Development of the Average Byzantine and Arab Warship and the Problem of the Number and Function of the Oarsmen', in *Tropis III. Proceedings of the Third International Symposium on Ship Construction in Antiquity*, ed. H. Tzalas (Athens, 1995), pp. 111–22.

—— 'Arab-Byzantine Struggle in the Sea: Naval Tactics (7th–11th Centuries AD): Theory and Practice', in *Aspects of Arab Seafaring*, ed. Y. Y. Al-Hijji and V. Christides (Athens, 2002), pp. 87–106.

Christophilopoulou, A., Βυζαντινή ιστορία [*Byzantine History*] (Thessaloniki, 1997)

Chrysostomides, J., 'A Byzantine Historian: Anna Comnena', in *Medieval Historical Writing in the Christian and Islamic Worlds*, ed. D. O. Morgan (London, 1982).

Church, S. D., *The Household Knights of King John* (Cambridge, 1999).

Coniglio, G., *Le pergamene di Conversano (901–1265)* (Bari, 1975).

Contamine, P., *War in the Middle Ages*, trans. M. Jones (Oxford, 2005).

Cowdrey, H. E. J., 'Pope Gregory VII's "Crusading" Plans of 1074', in *Outremer, Studies in the History of the Crusading Kingdom of Jerusalem*, ed. B. Z. Kedar and R. C. Smail (Jerusalem, 1982), pp. 27–40.

—— *Pope Gregory VII* (Oxford, 1998).

Cuozzo, E., *'Quei maledetti Normanni'. Cavalieri e organizazzione militare nel Mezzogiorno normanno* (Naples, 1989).

—— and Martin J. M., *Cavalieri alla conqueta del Sud. Studi sull'Italia normanna in memoria di Leon-Robert Menager* (Rome and Bari, 1998).

—— *La cavalleria nel regno normanno di Sicilia* (Atripalda, 2002).

Davidson, H. R. E., *The Viking Road to Byzantium* (London, 1976).

Davis, J. L., A. Hoti, I. Pojani, S. R. Stocker, A. D. Wolpert, P. E. Acheson and J. W. Haye, 'The Durrës Regional Archaeological Project: Archaeological Survey in the Territory of Epidamnus/Dyrrachium in Albania', *Hesperia: The Journal of the American School of Classical Studies at Athens* 72 (2003), 41–119.

Davis, R. H. C., *The Normans and their Myth* (London, 1997).

Dawson, T., 'Kremasmata, Kabadion, Klibanion: Some Aspects of Middle Byzantine Military Equipment Reconsidered', *Byzantine and Modern Greek Studies* 22 (1998), 38–50.

—— 'Syntagma Hoplon: The Equipment of Regular Byzantine Troops, *c.*950 to *c.*1204', in *A Companion to Medieval Arms and Armour*, ed. D. Nicolle (Woodbridge, 2002), pp. 81–90.

Debord, A., 'Les fortifications de terre en Europe occidentale du Xe au XIIe siècles', *Archaeologie médiévale* 11 (1981), 83–105.

Decaens, J., 'Le patrimoine des Grentemesnil en Normandie, en Italie et en Angleterre aux XIe et XIIe siècles', in *Les Normands en Mediterranée dans le sillage des Tancrèdes*, ed. P. Bouet and F. Neveux (Caen, 1994), pp. 123–40.

Delbrück, H., *Numbers in History* (London, 1913).

—— *History of the Art of War*, 4 vols (London, 1990).

Dennis, G. T., 'The Byzantines in Battle', in *Byzantium at War (9th–12th Century)*, ed. N. Oikonomides (Athens, 1997), pp. 165–78.

DeVries, K., *Medieval Military Technology* (North York, Ontario, 1992).

—— 'Medieval Mercenaries', in *Mercenaries and Paid Men: The Mercenary Identity in the Middle Ages*, ed. J. France (Boston, 2008), pp. 43–60.

—— 'The Use of Chroniclers in Recreating Medieval Military History', *Journal of Medieval Military History* 2 (2004), 1–17.

Douglas, D. C., *The Norman Achievement 1050–1100* (London, 1969).

—— *William the Conqueror, The Norman Impact upon England* (London, 1999).

Drell, J. H., 'Cultural Syncretism and Ethnic Identity: The Norman "Conquest" of Southern Italy and Sicily', *Journal of Medieval History* 25 (1999), 187–202.

Duby, G., 'Les "Jeunes" dans la société aristocratique dans la France du nord-ouest au XIIe siècle', in *Hommes et structures du Moyen Age* (Paris, 1973), pp. 213–25.

Ducellier, A., *La façade maritime de l'Albanie au moyen âge: Durazzo et Valona du XIe au XVe siècle* (Thessaloniki, 1981).

—— 'Dernières decouvertes sur les sites albanais du Moyen Age', *Archeologia* 78 (1975), 35–45; reprinted in his *L'Albanie entre Byzance et Venice, X^e–XVe siècles* (London, 1987).

Dvoichenko-Markov, D., 'The Vlachs', *Byzantion* 54 (1984), 508–26.

Eales, R., 'Royal Power and Castles in Norman England', in *The Ideals and Practice of Medieval Knighthood III*, ed. C. Harper-Bill and R. Harvey (Woodbridge, 1990), pp. 54–63.

Ellis-Davidson, H. R., 'The Secret Weapon of Byzantium', *Byzantinische Zeitschrift* 66 (1973), 61–74.

Emerton, E., *The Correspondence of Pope Gregory VII* (New York, 1932).

English, B., 'Towns, Mottes and Ring-works of the Conquest', in *The Medieval Military Revolution*, ed. A. Ayton and J. L. Price (London, 1995), pp. 45–62.

Ferluga, J., 'Sur la date de la création du thème de Dyrrachium', in his *Byzantium on the Balkans, Studies on the Byzantine Administration and the Southern Slavs from the VIIth to the XIIth Centuries* (Amsterdam, 1976), pp. 215–24.

—— 'Les insurrections des Slaves de la Macedoine au XIᵉ siècle', in *Byzantium on the Balkans*, pp. 379–97.

Fine, J. A., *The Early Medieval Balkans* (Ann Arbor, 2008).

Flambard-Hericher, A.-M., 'Un instrument de la conquête et du pouvoir: les châteux normands de Calabre. L'exemple de Scribla', in *Les Normandes en Mediterranée aux XIᵉ–XIIᵉ siècles*, ed. P. Bouet and F. Neveux (Caen, 2001), pp. 89–111.

Flori, J., 'Un probléme de méthodologie. La valeur des nombres chez les chroniquers du Moyen Age. À propos des effectifs de la première croisade', *Le Moyen Age* 119 (1993), 399–422.

—— *Bohémond d'Antioch, chevalier d'aventure* (Paris, 2007).

Foss, C., and D. Winfield, *Byzantine Fortifications: An Introduction* (Pretoria, 1986).

Fournier, G., *Le Château dans la France Médiévale* (Paris, 1978).

France, J., 'The Occasion of the coming of the Normans to Southern Italy', *Journal of Medieval History* 17 (1991), 185–205.

—— 'Technology and the Success of the First Crusade', in *War and Society in the Eastern Mediterranean*, ed. Y. Lev (Leiden, 1997), pp. 163–76.

—— *Victory in the East, A Military History of the First Crusade* (Cambridge, 1999).

—— *The Crusades and the Expansion of Catholic Christendom, 1000–1714* (London, 2005).

Frances, E., 'Alexis Comnène et les privileges octroyés à Venice', *Byzantinoslavica* 29 (1968), 17–23.

Frankopan, P., 'The Imperial Governors of Dyrrakhion in the Reign of Alexios I Komnenos', *Byzantine and Modern Greek Studies* 27 (2002), 65–103.

—— 'Challenges to Imperial Authority in Byzantium: Revolts on Crete and Cyprus at the End of the 11th Century', *Byzantion* 74 (2004), 382–402.

—— 'Kinship and the distribution of power in Komnenian Byzantium', *English Historical Review* 495 (2007), 1–34.

Friedman, V. A., 'The Vlah Minority in Macedonia: Language, Identity, Dialectology, and Standardization', *Selected Papers in Slavic, Balkan, and Balkan Studies* 21 (2001), 26–50.

Friendly, A., *The Dreadful Day: The Battle of Manzikert, 1071* (London, 1981).

Gadolin, A. R., 'Alexius I Comnenus and the Venetian Trade Privileges. A New Interpretation', *Byzantion* 50 (1980), 439–46.

Gardiner, R., *The Earliest Ships: The Evolution of Boats into Ships* (London, 1996).

Gautier, P., 'Defection et soumission de la Crete sous Alexis Ier Comnène', *Revue des études byzantines* 35 (1977), 215–27.

Gay, J., *L'Italie méridionale et l'empire Byzantin depuis l'avènement de Basile Ier jusqu'à la prise de Bari par les Normands (867–1071)* (Paris, 1904).

Gillingham, J., 'Richard I and the Science of War in the Middle Ages', in *War and Government in the Middle Ages*, ed. J. Gillingham and J. C. Holt (Woodbridge, 1984), pp. 78–91.

—— 'An Age of Expansion, c.1020–1204', in *Medieval Warfare*, ed. M. Keen (Oxford, 1999), pp. 59–89.

—— '"Up with Orthodoxy!" In Defence of Vegetian Warfare', *Journal of Medieval Military History* 2 (2004), 149–58.

Gillmor, C. M., 'Naval Logistics of the Cross-Channel Operation, 1066', *Anglo-Norman Studies* 7 (1984), 105–31.

Glavinas, A., Η επί Αλεξίου Κομνηνού (1081–1118) περί ιερών σκευών, κειμηλίων και αγίων εικόνων έρις (1081–1095) [*The Controversy (1081–1095) regarding the Holy Relics and Saintly Images during the Reign of Alexius Comnenus (1081–1118)*] (Thessaloniki, 1972).

—— 'Οι Νορμανδοί στην Θεσσαλία και η πολιορκία της Λάρισας (1082–1083)' ['The Normans in Thessaly and the Siege of Larisa (1082–1083)'], Βυζαντιακά [*Byzantiaka*] 4 (1984), 35–45.

—— 'Οι Νορμανδοί στην Καστοριά (1082–1083)' ['The Normans in Castoria (1082–1083)'], Βυζαντινά [*Byzantina*] 13ii (1985), 1255–65.

Godfrey, J., 'The Defeated Anglo-Saxons Take Service with the Eastern Emperor', *Anglo-Norman Studies* 1 (1978), 63–74.

Gorecki, D., 'The Strateia of Constantine VII: The Legal Status, Administration, and Historical Background', *Byzantinische Zeitschrift* 82 (1989), 157–76.

Gregory, T. E., *A History of Byzantium* (Oxford, 2005).

Guilhiermoz, P., *Essai sur l'origine de la noblesse en France au moyen âge* (Paris, 1902).

Guillard, R., 'Le drongaire de la flotte, le grand drongaire de la flotte, le duc de la flotte, le megaduc', in *Recherches sur les institutions* (Amsterdam, 1967), vol. I, pp. 535–62.

Guillou, A., 'La Lucanie byzantine: étude de géographie historique', *Byzantion* 35 (1965), 119–49.

Haldane, D., 'The Fire-Ship of Al-Salih Ayyub and Muslim Use of "Greek Fire"', in *The Circle of War in the Middle Ages*, ed. D. J. Kagay and L. J. A. Villalon (Woodbridge, 1999), 137–44.

Haldon, J., 'The Feudalism Debate Once More: The Case of Byzantium', *Journal of Peasant Studies* 17/1 (1989), 5–40; reprinted in his *State, Army and Society in Byzantium* (London, 1995).

Haldon, J., 'Military Service, Military Lands, and the Status of the Soldiers: Current Problems and Interpretations', *Dumbarton Oaks Papers* 47 (1993), 1–67; reprinted in his *State, Army and Society in Byzantium* (London, 1995).

—— 'The Organisation and Support of an Expeditionary Force: Manpower and Logistics in the Middle Byzantine Period', in *Byzantium at War (9th–12th Century)*, ed. N. Oikonomides (Athens, 1997), pp. 111–51.

—— *Byzantium in the Seventh Century: The Transformation of a Culture*, 2nd edn (Cambridge, 1997)

—— *Warfare, State and Society in the Byzantine World, 565–1204* (London, 1999).

—— *The Byzantine Wars: Battles and Campaigns of the Byzantine Era* (Stroud, 2000).

—— 'Greek Fire Revisited: Recent and Current Research', in *Byzantine Style, Religion, and Civilization: In Honour of Sir Steven Runciman*, ed. E. Jeffreys (Cambridge, 2006), pp. 290–325.

—— and H. Kennedy, 'The Arab-Byzantine Frontier in the Eighth and Ninth Centuries', *Zbornik radova vizantološkog institut* 19 (1980), 79–116.

—— and M. Byrne, 'A Possible Solution to the Problem of Greek Fire', *Byzantinische Zeitschrift* 70 (1977), 91–9.

Hamblin, W. J., 'The Fatimid Army during the Early Crusades' (unpublished Ph.D. thesis, University of Michigan, 1985).

Harris, J., *Byzantium and the Crusades* (London, 2006).

Harvey, A., *Economic Expansion in the Byzantine Empire, 900–1200* (Cambridge, 1989).

Harvey, S., 'The Knights and the Knight's Fee in England', *Past and Present* 49 (1970), 1–43.

Haskins, C. H., *The Norman Institutions* (Cambridge, MA, 1918).

Hendy, M., *Studies in the Byzantine Monetary Economy, 300–1450* (Cambridge, 1985).

Herve-Commereuc, C., 'Les Normands en Calabre', in *Les Normandes en Mediterranée aux XIᵉ–XIIᵉ siècles*, ed. P. Bouet and F. Neveux (Caen, 2001), pp. 77–89.

Higham, R., and P. Barker, *Timber Castles* (London, 1992).

The History of the King's Works, ed. H. M. Colvin, 6 vols., HMSO (London, 1963–82)

Hollister, C. W., 'The Annual Term of Military Service in Medieval England', *Medievalia et Humanistica* 13 (1960), 40–7.

—— *Anglo-Saxon Military Institutions* (Oxford, 1962).

—— *The Military Organization of Norman England* (Oxford, 1965).

Holt, J. C., *The Northerners* (Oxford, 1992).

Holmes, C., 'Political Elites in the Reign of Basil II', in *Byzantium in the Year 1000*, ed. P. Magdalino (Leiden, 2003), pp. 35–69.

Howard-Johnston, J., 'Studies in the Organization of the Byzantine Army in the Tenth and Eleventh Centuries' (unpublished D.Phil. thesis, Oxford, 1971).

Hyland, A., *The Medieval Warhorse from Byzantium to the Crusades* (Stroud, 1994).

Joranson, E., 'The Inception of the Career of the Normans in Italy – Legend and History', *Speculum* 23 (1948), 353–96.

Kaegi Jr, W. E., 'The Contribution of Archery to the Turkish Conquest of Anatolia', *Speculum* 39 (1964), 96–108.

—— *Some Thoughts on Byzantine Military Strategy* (Brookline, MA, 1983).

—— 'Changes in Military Organization and Daily Life on the Eastern Frontier', in Η καθημερίνη ζωή στο Βυζάντιο [*Everyday life in Byzantium*] (Athens, 1989), pp. 507–21.

Keegan, J., *The Face of Battle, A Study of Agincourt, Waterloo and the Somme* (London, 2004 [1976]).

Keen, M., *Chivalry* (London, 2005).

Kenyon, J. R., *Medieval Fortifications* (London, 2005).

Kolias, T. G., 'Ζάβα, ζαβάρετον, ζαβαρειώτης' ['Zaba, zabareton, zabareiotes'], *Jahrbuch der österreichischen byzantinistik* 29 (1980), 27–35.

—— *Byzantinische Waffen. Ein Beitrag zur byzantinischen Waffenkunde von den Anfangen bis zur lateinischen Eroberung* (Vienna, 1988).

—— 'Η πολεμική τεχνολογία των βυζαντινών' ['The Military Technology of the Byzantines'], Επιστημονική επετηρίδα του Τμήματος Ιστορίας και Αρχαιολογίας του Πανεπιστημίου Ιωαννίνων [*Scientific Journal of the Department of History and Archaeology of the University of Ioannina*] 18 (1989), 17–41.

—— 'Η πολεμική τακτική των βυζαντινών: θεωρία και πράξη' ['The Military Tactics of the Byzantines: Theory and Practice'], in *Byzantium at War (9th–12th Century)*, ed. N. Oikonomides (Athens, 1997), pp. 153–64.

Korobeinikov, D. A., 'Raiders and Neighbours: The Turks (1040–1304)', in *The Cambridge History of the Byzantine Empire c. 500–1492* (Cambridge, 2008), ed. J. Shepard, pp. 692–731.

Korres, Th., «Υγρόν πύρ», ένα όπλο της βυζαντινής ναυτικής τακτικής ['*Holy Fire', A Byzantine Naval Tactical Weapon*] (Thessaloniki, 1995).

Kreutz, B. M., 'Ships, Shipping, and the Implications of Change in the Early Mediterranean', *Viator* 7 (1976), 79–109.

—— *Before the Normans: Southern Italy in the Ninth and Tenth Centuries* (Philadelphia, 1991).

Le Patourel, J., *The Norman Empire* (Oxford, 1976).

Lemerle, P., *The Agrarian History of Byzantium from the Origins to the Twelfth Century. The Sources and the Problems* (Galway, 1979).

Lemmon, C. H., *The Field of Hastings* (St-Leonards-on-Sea, 1956).

Lev, Y., *State and Society in Fatimid Egypt* (Leiden, 1991).

—— *War and Society in the Eastern Mediterranean, 7th–15th Centuries* (Leiden, 1997).

—— 'Infantry in Muslim Armies during the Crusades', in *Logistics of Warfare in the Age of the Crusades*, ed. J. H. Pryor (Aldershot, 2006), pp. 185–206.

Lewis, A., and T. Runyan, *European Naval and Maritime History, 300–1500* (Bloomington, 1985).

Lilie, R.-J., *Die byzantinische Reaktion auf die Ausbreitung der Araber* (Munich, 1976).

—— *Byzantium and the Crusader States* (Oxford, 1994).

Loud, G. A, 'Abbot Desiderius of Montecassino and the Gregorian Papacy', *Journal of Ecclesiastical History* 30 (1979), 305–26.

—— 'How Norman was the Norman Conquest of Southern Italy?', *Nottingham Medieval Studies* 25 (1981), 13–34.

—— 'The "Gens Normannorum" – Myth or Reality?', *Anglo-Norman Studies* 4 (1981), 104–16.

—— 'The Church, Warfare and Military Obligation in Norman Italy', *Studies in Church History* 20 (1983), 31–45.

—— 'Byzantine Italy and the Normans', in *Proceedings of the XVIII Spring Symposium of Byzantine Studies*, ed. J. D. Howard-Johnston (Amsterdam, 1988), pp. 215–33.

—— 'Anna Komnena and her Sources for the Normans of Southern Italy', in *Church and Chronicle in the Middle Ages, Essays Presented to John Taylor*, ed. I. Wood and G. A. Loud (London, 1991), pp. 41–57.

—— 'Coinage, Wealth and Plunder in the Age of Robert Guiscard', *English Historical Review* 114 (1999), 815–43.

—— *The Age of Robert Guiscard: Southern Italy and the Norman Conquest* (London, 2000).

—— 'The Kingdom of Sicily and the Kingdom of England, 1066–1266', *History* 88 (2003), 540–67.

Magdalino, P., 'The Byzantine Army and the Land: from Stratiotikon Ktema to Military Pronoia', in *Byzantium at War (9th–12th Century)*, ed. N. Oikonomides (Athens, 1997), pp. 15–36.

Mallett, M., *Mercenaries and their Masters, Warfare in Renaissance Italy* (London, 1974).

—— 'Mercenaries', in *Medieval Warfare*, ed. M. Keen (Oxford, 1999), pp. 209–29.

Maniati-Kokkini, T., 'Μία πρώτη προσέγγιση στη μελέτη του βυζαντινού θεσμού της πρόνοιας: οι προνοιάριοι' ['A First Approach to the Study of the Institution of the *Pronoia*: the *Pronoiarioi*'], *Hellenic Historical Company. 9th National Historical Conference, May 1988* (Thessaloniki, 1988), pp. 49–60.

Martin, J.-M., 'Modalités de l' "incastellamento" et typologie castrale en Italie méridionale (Xe–XIIe siècles)', in *Castelli. Storia e archeologia. Relazioni e comunicazioni al Convegno di Cuneo (1981)*, ed. R. Comba, A. A. Settia (Turin, 1984), pp. 89–104.

—— *La Pouille du VIᵉ au XIIᵉ siècle* (Rome, 1993).

—— 'L'attitude et le role des Normandes dans l'Italie meriodale byzantine', in *Les Normandes en Mediterranée aux XIᵉ–XIIᵉ siècles*, ed. P. Bouet and F. Neveux (Caen, 2001), pp. 111–23.

Martin, M. E., 'The Chrysobull of Alexius I Comnenus to the Venetians and the Early Venetian Quarter in Constantinople', *Byzantinoslavica* 39 (1978), 19–23.

Matthew, D. J. A., 'The Chronicle of Romuald of Salerno', in *The Writing of History in the Middle Ages: Essays Presented to Richard William Southern*, ed. R. H. C. Davis, J. M. Wallace-Hadrill (Oxford, 1981), pp. 239–74.

—— *The Norman Kingdom of Sicily* (Cambridge, 2001).

McGeer, E., 'Byzantine Siege Warfare in Theory and Practice', in *The Medieval City under Siege*, ed. I. A. Corfis and M. Wolfe (Woodbridge, 1995), pp. 123–9.

—— 'The Legal Decree of Nicephoros II Phocas concerning Armenian Stratiotai', in *Peace and War in Byzantium*, ed. T. Miller and J. Nesbitt (Washington, DC, 1995), pp. 123–37.

—— *Sowing the Dragon's Teeth: Byzantine Warfare in the Tenth Century* (Washington, DC, 1995).

McQueen, W. B., 'Relations between the Normans and Byzantium, 1071–1112', *Byzantion* 56 (1986), 427–69.

Ménager, L. R., 'Pesanteur et étiologie de la colonisation normande de l'Italie', in *Roberto il Guiscardo e il suo tempo. Relazzioni e communicationi nelle prime giornate normanno-sueve (Bari, Maggio 1973)* (Rome, 1975), pp. 189–214.

—— 'Inventaires des familles normandes et franques émigrées en Italie Meridionale et en Sicile (XIᵉ–XIIᵉ siècles)', in *Roberto il Guiscardo e il suo tempo. Relazzioni e communicationi nelle prime giornate normanno-sueve (Bari, Maggio 1973)* (Rome, 1975), pp. 260–390.

Metcalfe, A., 'The Muslims of Sicily under Christian Rule', in *The Society of Norman Italy*, ed. G. A. Loud and A. Metcalfe (Leiden, 2002), pp. 289–317.

—— *The Muslims of Medieval Italy* (Edinburgh, 2009).

Morillo, S., *Warfare under the Anglo-Norman Kings, 1066–1135* (Woodbridge, 1994).

—— 'Mercenaries, Mamluks and Militia, towards a Cross-Cultural Typology of Military Service', in *Mercenaries and Paid Men: The Mercenary Identity in the Middle Ages*, ed. J. France (Boston, 2008), pp. 243–59.

—— 'The "Age of Cavalry" Revisited', in *The Circle of War in the Middle Ages*, pp. 45–58.

—— 'Battle Seeking: The Context and Limits of Vegetian Strategy', *Journal of Medieval Military History* 1 (2003), 21–41.

Morris, R., 'The Powerful and the Poor in Tenth-Century Byzantium: Law and Reality', *Past & Present* 73 (1976), 3–27.

Musset, L., 'Les circonstances de la pénétration normande en Italie du sud et dans le monde méditerrannéen', in *Les Normands en Méditerranée aux XIᵉ–XIIᵉ siècles* ed. P. Bouet and F. Neveux (Caen, 2001), pp. 41–51.

Nicol, D. M., *Byzantium and Venice* (Cambridge, 1988).

Nicolle, D., 'The Impact of European Couched Lance on Muslim Military Tradition', *Journal of the Arms and Armour Society* 10 (1980), 6–40.

—— *Crusader Warfare*, 2 vols. (London, 2007).

Nitti, F., *Le pergamene di S. Nicola di Bari, periodo normanno (1075–1194)* (Bari, 1968)

Norwich, J. J., *The Normans in the South, 1016–1130* (London, 1967).

Noye, G., 'Problemes posés par l'identification et l'étude des fosses-silos sur un cite d'Italie méridionale', *Archaelogia Medievale* 8 (1981), 421–38.

—— 'Quelque données sur les techniques de construction en Italie centro-meridionale, X^e–XIIe siècles', in *Artistes, artisans et production artistique au Moyen Age*, ed. X. Barral (Rennes, 1983), pp. 275–306.

Obolensky, D., *The Byzantine Commonwealth* (London, 1971).

Oikonomides, N., 'L'évolution de l'organisation administrative de l'empire byzantin au XIe siècle (1025–1118)', *Travaux et mémoires* 6 (1976), 125–52.

—— 'Middle-Byzantine Provincial Recruits: Salary and Armament', in *Byzantine Warfare*, ed. J. Haldon (Aldershot, 2007), pp. 151–66.

Oman, C. W. C., *A History of the Art of War in the Middle Ages AD 378–1485*, 2 vols. (London, 1991).

Ostrogorsky, G., *Quelques problèmes d'histoire de la paysannerie byzantine* (Brussels, 1956).

—— 'Pour l'histoire de l'immunité à Byzance', *Byzantion* 28 (1958), 165–254.

—— *History of the Byzantine State* (Oxford, 1989).

The Oxford Dictionary of Byzantium, ed. A. Kazhdan et al., 3 vols. (New York, 1991).

Painter, S., *French Chivalry, Chivalric Ideas and Practices in Mediaeval France* (London, 1940).

Painter, S., *The Reign of King John* (Baltimore, 1949).

Papasotiriou, K., Βυζαντινή Υψηλή Στρατηγική, 6ος–11ος αιώνας [*Byzantine High Strategy, 6th–11th Centuries*] (Athens, 2001).

Partington, J. R., *A History of Greek Fire and Gunpowder* (London, 1999).

Pattenden, P., 'The Byzantine Early Warning System', *Byzantion* 53 (1983), 258–99.

Pesez, J.-M., and Jean-Michel Poisson, 'Le château du castrum sicilien de Calathamet (XIIe siecle)', in *Castelli. Storia e archaeologia*, ed. R. Comba and A. A. Settia (Turin, 1984), pp. 63–72.

Pounds, N., *The Medieval Castle in England and Wales: A Social and Political History* (Cambridge, 1990).

Powicke, F. M., *The Loss of Normandy*, 2nd ed. (Manchester, 1961).

Prestwich, J. O., 'The Military Household of the Norman Kings', *English Historical Review* 96 (1981), 1–35.

Prestwich, M., *Armies and Warfare in the Middle Ages* (London, 2006).

Pryor, J. H., 'Transportation of Horses by Sea during the Era of the Crusades: Eighth Century to 1285 A.D.', *Mariner's Mirror* 68 (1982), 9–27, 103–25.

—— *Geography, Technology, and War, Studies in the Maritime History of the Mediterranean, 649–1571* (Cambridge, 2000).

—— 'Byzantium and the Sea: Byzantine Fleets and the History of the Empire in the Age of the Macedonian Emperors, c.900–1025', in *War at Sea in the Middle Ages and the Renaissance*, ed. John B. Hattendorf and Richard W. Unger (Cambridge, 2003), pp. 83–105.

—— 'Modelling Bohemond's March to Thessalonike', in *Logistics of Warfare in the Age of the Crusades*, ed. J. H. Pryor (Aldershot, 2006), pp. 1–25.

Pryor, J. H., and E. Jeffreys, *The Age of the Δρόμων, The Byzantine Navy ca 500–1204* (Leiden, 2006).

Renn, D. F., *Norman Castles in Britain* (London, 1968).

Rice, T. T., *The Seljuks in Asia Minor* (London, 1961).

Richard, J., 'Les Turcopoles: Musulmans convertés ou chrétiens orientaux?', *Revue des études islamiques* 54 (1986), 259–70.

Riley-Smith, J., *The First Crusade and the Idea of Crusading* (London, 1986).

—— *The Crusades* (London, 1987).

—— *What were the Crusades?* (Basingstoke, 4th edn, 2009).

Robinson, I. S., 'Gregory VII and the Soldiers of Christ', *History* 58 (1973), 169–92.

—— *The Papacy, 1073–1198* (Cambridge, 1990).

Roché, J. T., 'In the Wake of Manzikert: The First Crusade and the Alexian Reconquest of Western Anatolia', *History* 94 (2009), 135–53.

Rodger, N. A. M., *The Safeguard of the Sea*, vol. I (660–1649) (London, 1997).

Rogers, C. J., 'The Vegetian "Science of Warfare" in the Middle Ages', *Journal of Medieval Military History* 1 (2003), 1–19.

Rogers, R., *Latin Siege Warfare in the Twelfth Century* (Oxford, 1992).

Roland, A., 'Secrecy, Technology, and War: Greek Fire and the Defence of Byzantium, 678–1204', in *Warfare in the Dark Ages*, ed. J. France and K. DeVries (Aldershot, 2008), pp. 655–79.

Rose, S., 'Islam versus Christendon: The Naval Dimension, 1000–1600', *Journal of Medieval History* 63 (1999), 561–78.

Round, J. H., *Feudal England* (London, 1895).

Rowe, J. G., 'Paschal II, Bohemund of Antioch and the Byzantine Empire', *Bulletin of the John Rylands Library* 49 (1966–7), 165–202.

Runciman, S., *A History of the Crusades*, 3 vols. (Cambridge, 1951–4).

Sanders, J., *Feudal Military Service in England* (London, 1956).

Savvides, A., Τα βυζαντινά επτάνησα, 11ος-αρχές 13ου αι. Το ναυτικό θέμα Κεφαλληνίας στην υστεροβυζαντινή περίοδο [*The Byzantine Eptanisa, 11th to early 13th Century. The Naval Theme of Cephalenia in the Late Byzantine Period* (Athens, 1986).

—— Οι Τούρκοι και το Βυζάντιο [*The Turks and Byzantium*] (Athens, 1996)

—— Γεώργιος Μανιάκης. Κατακτήσεις και υπονόμευση στο Βυζάντιο του 11ου αιώνα, 1030–1043 μ.Χ. [*Georgios Maniaces. Conquests and Subversion in 11th Century Byzantium, 1030–1043*] (Athens, 2004)

—— 'Notes on the Armenian-Byzantine Family of Aspietes, Late 11th – Early 13th Centuries', *Byzantinoslavica* 52 (1991), 70–9.

—— 'Taticius the Turcopole', *Journal of Oriental and African Studies* 3–4 (1991–2), 235–8.

—— *Byzantino-Normannica. The Norman Capture of Italy and the First Two Norman Invasions in Byzantium* (Leuven, 2007).

Schlumberger, G. L., *Un empereur byzantin au dixième siècle, Nicéphore Phocas* (Paris, 1890).

Schlumberger, G. L., *L'épopée byzantine à la fin du dixième siècle: guerres contre les Russes, les Arabes, les Allemands, les Bulgares: luttes civiles contre les deux Bardas*, 3 vols. (Paris, 1896–1905).

Shahid, I., 'The Iranian Factor in Byzantium during the Reign of Heraclius', *Dumbarton Oaks Papers* 26 (1972), 293–320.

Shepard, J., 'The English and Byzantium: A Sudy of their Role in the Byzantine Army in the Later Eleventh Century', *Traditio* 29 (1973), 53–92.

—— 'When Greek Meets Greek: Alexius Comnenus and Bohemond in 1097–98', *Byzantine and Modern Greek Studies* 12 (1988), 185–277.

—— 'The Uses of the Franks in Eleventh-Century Byzantium', *Anglo-Norman Studies* 15 (1993), 275–305.

—— (ed.), *The Cambridge History of the Byzantine Empire c. 500–1492* (Cambridge, 2008).

Simpson, A., 'Three Sources of Military Unrest in Eleventh Century Asia Minor: The Norman Chieftains Hervé Frankopoulos, Robert Crispin and Roussel of Bailleul', *Mesogeios/Méditerranée* 9–10 (2000), 181–207.

Sitwell, N. H. H., *Roman Roads of Europe* (London, 1981).

Skinner, P., 'Room for Tension: Urban Life in Apulia in the Eleventh and Twelfth Centuries', *Papers of the British School at Rome* 65 (1998), 159–77.

Smail, R. C., *Crusading Warfare (1097–1193)* (Cambridge, 1956).

Stanton, C. D., 'Naval Power in the Norman Conquest of Southern Italy and Sicily', *Haskins Society Journal* 19 (2008), 120–36.

—— *Norman Naval Operations in the Mediterranean* (Woodbridge, 2011)

Stenton, F. M., *The First Century of English Feudalism: 1066–1166, Being the Ford Lectures Delivered in the University of Oxford in Hilary Term 1929* (Oxford, 1950).

Stephenson, P., *Byzantium's Balkan frontier: A Political Study of the Northern Balkans, 900–1204* (Cambridge, 2000).

—— *The Legend of Basil the Bulgar-Slayer* (Cambridge, 2003).

—— 'Balkan Borderlands', in *The Cambridge History of the Byzantine Empire c. 500–1492* (Cambridge, 2008), ed. J. Shepard, pp. 664–82.

Strickland, M., 'Military Technology and Conquest: The Anomaly of Anglo-Saxon England', *Anglo-Norman Studies* 9 (1996), 353–82.

—— *War and Chivalry: The Conduct and Perception of War in England and Normandy, 1066–1217* (Cambridge, 1996).

Sullivan, D., 'Tenth Century Byzantine Offensive Siege Warfare: Instructional Prescriptions and Historical Practice', in *Byzantium at War (9th–12th Century)*, ed. N. Oikonomides (Athens, 1997), pp. 179–200.

Tabuteau, E., *Transfers of Property in Eleventh-Century Norman Law* (London, 1988).

Takayama, H., The *Administration of the Norman Kingdom of Sicily* (Leiden, 1993).

Tavianni-Carozzi, H., *La terreur du monde, Robert Guiscard et la conquête normande en Italie* (Paris, 1996).

Theotokis, G., 'The Norman Invasion of Sicily (1061–1072): Numbers and Military Tactics', *War in History* 17 (2010), 381–402.

—— 'Rus, Varangian and Frankish Mercenaries in the Service of the Byzantine Emperors (9th–11th Century) – Numbers, Organisation and Battle Tactics in the Operational Theatres of Asia Minor and the Balkans', *Byzantina Symmeikta* 22 (2012), 126–56.

—— 'Geoffrey Malaterra as a Military Historian for the Norman Expansion in Italy and Sicily – Strengths and Weaknesses in his Narrative', *Mediterranean Chronicle* 2 (2012), 105–15.

—— 'The Square Fighting March of the Crusaders at the Battle of Ascalon (1099)', *Journal of Medieval Military History* 11 (2013), 57–72.

—— 'From Ancient Greece to Byzantium: Strategic Innovation or Continuity of Military Thinking?', in *Antiquitas Viva 4: Studia Classica*, ed. I. Rūmniece, O. Lāms and B. Kukjalko (Riga, 2014), pp. 106–18.

Tobias, N., 'The Tactics and Strategy of Alexius Comnenus at Calavrytae, 1078', *Byzantine and Modern Greek Studies* 6 (1979), 193–211.

Tramontana, S., *I normanni in Italia. Linee di recerca sui primi insediamenti i aspetti politici e militari* (Messina, 1970).

Treadgold, W., 'The Military Lands and the Imperial Estates in the Middle Byzantine Empire', *Harvard Ukrainian Studies* 7 (1983), 619–31.

—— *The Byzantine Revival: 780–842* (Stanford, 1988).

—— 'The Army in the Works of Constantine Porphyrogenitus', *Rivista di studi bizantini e neoellinici* 29 (1992), 77–162.

—— *Byzantium and its Army, 284–1081* (Stanford, 1995).

—— *A History of the Byzantine State and Society* (Stanford, CA, 1997)

—— 'Standardized Numbers in the Byzantine Army', *War in History* 12 (2005), 1–14.

—— 'Byzantium, the Reluctant Warrior', in *Noble Ideas and Bloody Realities*, ed. N. Christie and M. Yazigi (Leiden, 2006), pp. 209–33.

Trinchera, F., *Syllabus Graecarum Membranarum* (Naples, 1865).

Tsamakda, V., *The Illustrated Chronicle of Ioannes Skylitzes in Madrid* (Leiden, 2002).

Tsirpanles, Z., Η μεσαιωνική δύση (5ος-15ος αιώνας) [*The Medieval West (5th–15th Centuries)*] (Thessaloniki, 2004).

Tuma, O., 'The Dating of Alexius' Chrysobull to the Venetians: 1082, 1084, or 1092?', *Byzantinoslavica* 62 (1981), 171–85.

Tyerman, C., *God's War, A New History of the Crusades* (London, 2006).

van Houts, E., 'Normandy and Byzantium', *Byzantion* 55 (1985), 544–59.

—— 'The Ship List of William the Conqueror', *Anglo-Norman Studies* 10 (1987), 159–74.

—— 'L'exil dans l'espace anglo-normand', in *La Normandie et l'Angleterre au Moyen Age*, ed. P. Bouet and V. Gazeau (Caen, 2003), pp. 117–27.

Vasiliev, A. A., *History of the Byzantine Empire*, 2 vols. (Madison, 1928–9).

—— 'The Opening Stages of the Anglo-Saxon Immigration to Byzantium in the Eleventh Century', *Annales de l'Institute Kondakov* 9 (1937), 39–70.

Vasiliev, A. A., *Byzance et les Arabes, 867–959* (Brussels, 1950).

Vernadsky, G., *The Origins of Russia* (Oxford, 1959).

Verbruggen, J. F., *The Art of Warfare in Western Europe During the Middle Ages, From the Eighth Century to 1340*, trans. S. Willard and R. W. Southern (new edn, Woodbridge, 1997).

—— *L'armée et la stratégie de Charlemagne* (Dusseldorf, 1965).

von Falkenhausen, V., *La dominazione bizantina nell'Italia meridionale dal IX all'XI secolo* (Bari, 1978).

—— 'The Greek Presence in Norman Sicily: The Contribution of Archival Material in Greek', in *The Society of Norman Italy*, ed. G. A. Loud and A. Metcalfe (Leiden, 2002), pp. 253–88.

—— 'Between Two Empires: Byzantine Italy in the Reign of Basil II', in *Byzantium in the Year 1000*, ed. P. Magdalino (Leiden, 2003), pp. 135–59.

Waley, D. P., 'Combined Operations in Sicily, AD 1060–78', *Papers of the British School at Rome* 22 (1954), 118–25.

Walker, D. S., *A Geography of Italy* (London, 1967).

Waterson, J., *The Knights of Islam, the Wars of the Mamluks* (London, 2007).

Webber, N., *The Evolution of Norman Identity, 911–1154* (Woodbridge, 2005).

Whitton, D., 'Papal Policy in Rome, 1012–1124' (unpublished D.Phil. thesis, Oxford University, 1979).

Whittow, M., 'The Middle Byzantine Economy (600–1200)', in *The Cambridge History of the Byzantine Empire c. 500–1492* (Cambridge, 2008), ed. J. Shepard, pp. 465–93.

—— 'The Political Geography of the Byzantine World – Geographical Survey', in *The Oxford Handbook of Byzantine Studies*, ed. E. Jeffreys, J. Haldon, R. Cormack (Oxford, 2008), pp. 219–31.

Yewdale, R. B., *Bohemond I, Prince of Antioch* (Amsterdam, 1970).

Yver, J.-M., 'Les châteaux forts en Normandie jusqu'au milieu du XIIᵉ siècle', *Bulletin de la Société des antiquaires de Normandie* 53 (1955), 28–115.

—— 'Les premières institutions du duché de Normandie', in *I normanni e la loro espansione in Europa nell'alto medioevo, Settimane di studio del Centro italiano di studi sull'alto medioevo* 16 (Spoleto, 1969).

Index

Warfare in History

www.ingramcontent.com/pod-product-compliance
Ingram Content Group UK Ltd.
Pitfield, Milton Keynes, MK11 3LW, UK
UKHW021927100325
456014UK00009B/180